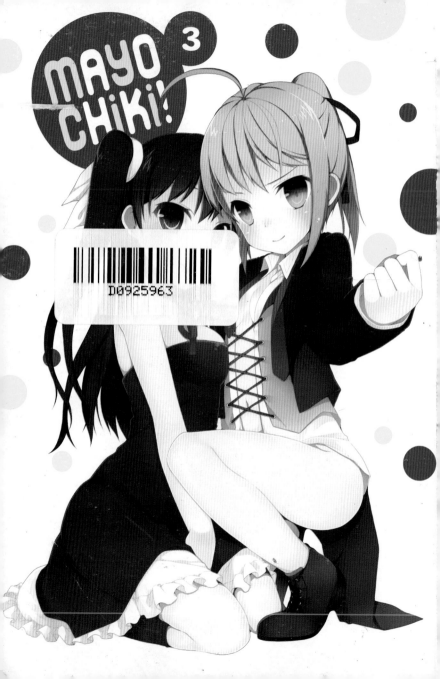

MAYO CHIKI! ³

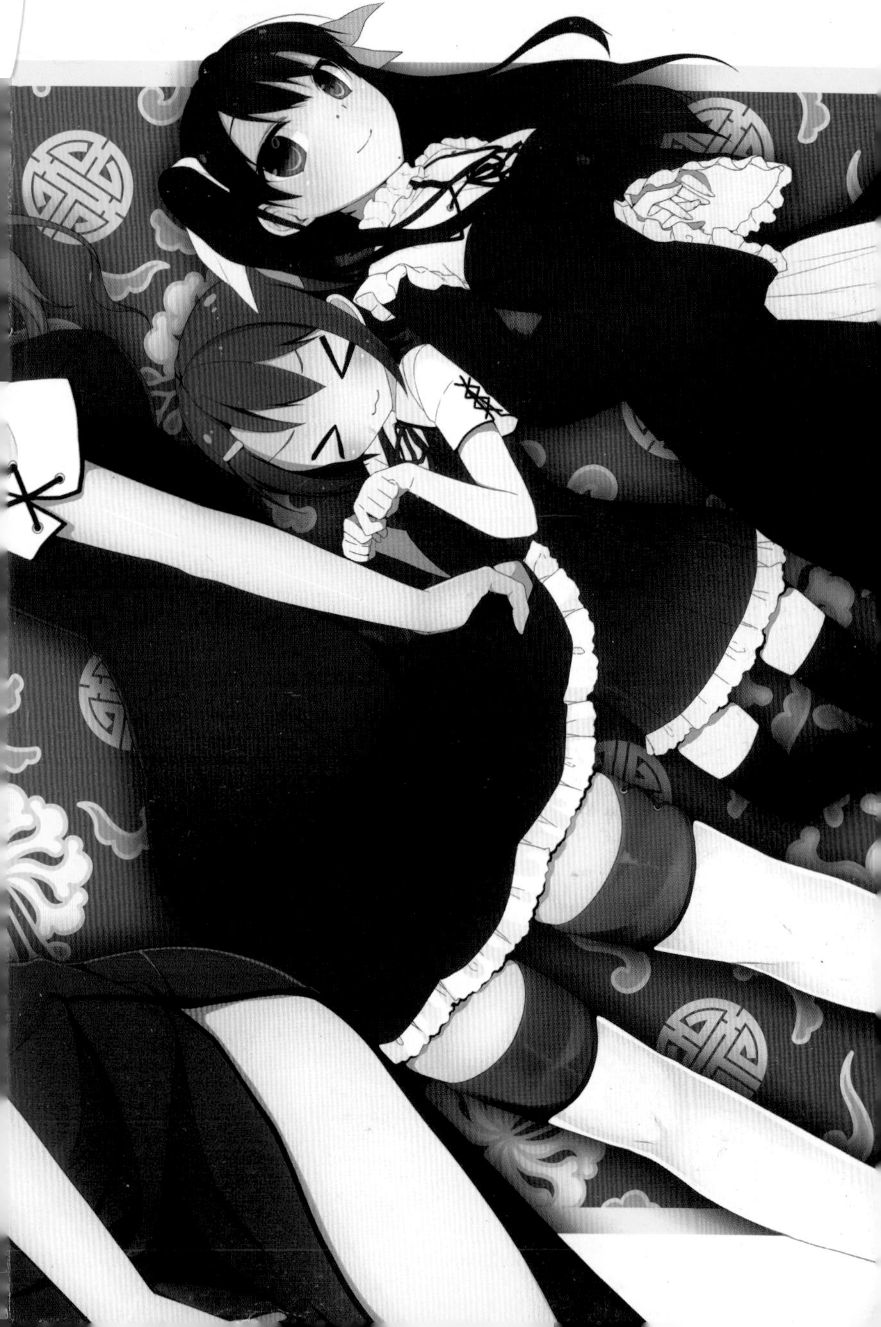

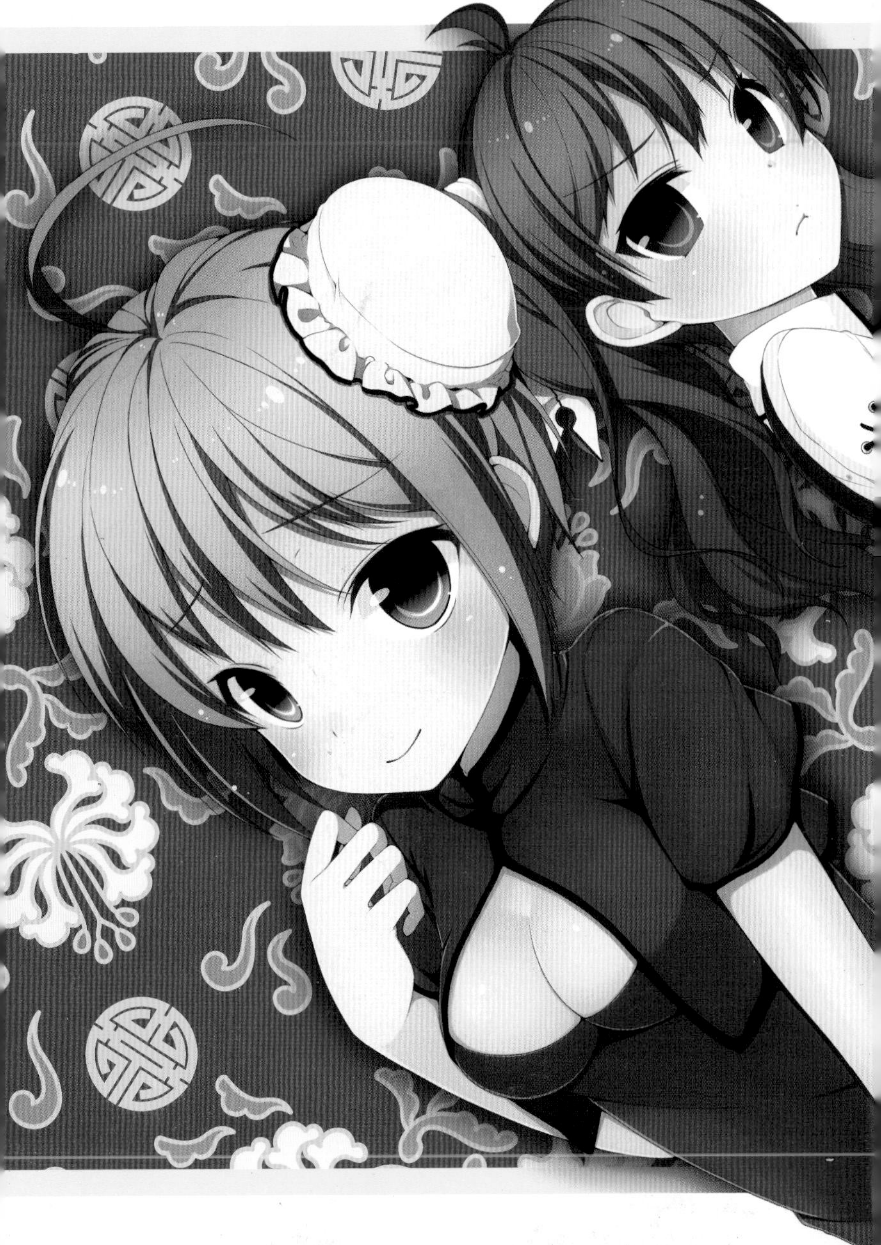

MAYO CHIKI!

Art by
NEET

Story by
HAJIME ASANO

Character Design
SEIJI KIKUCHI

VOLUME 3

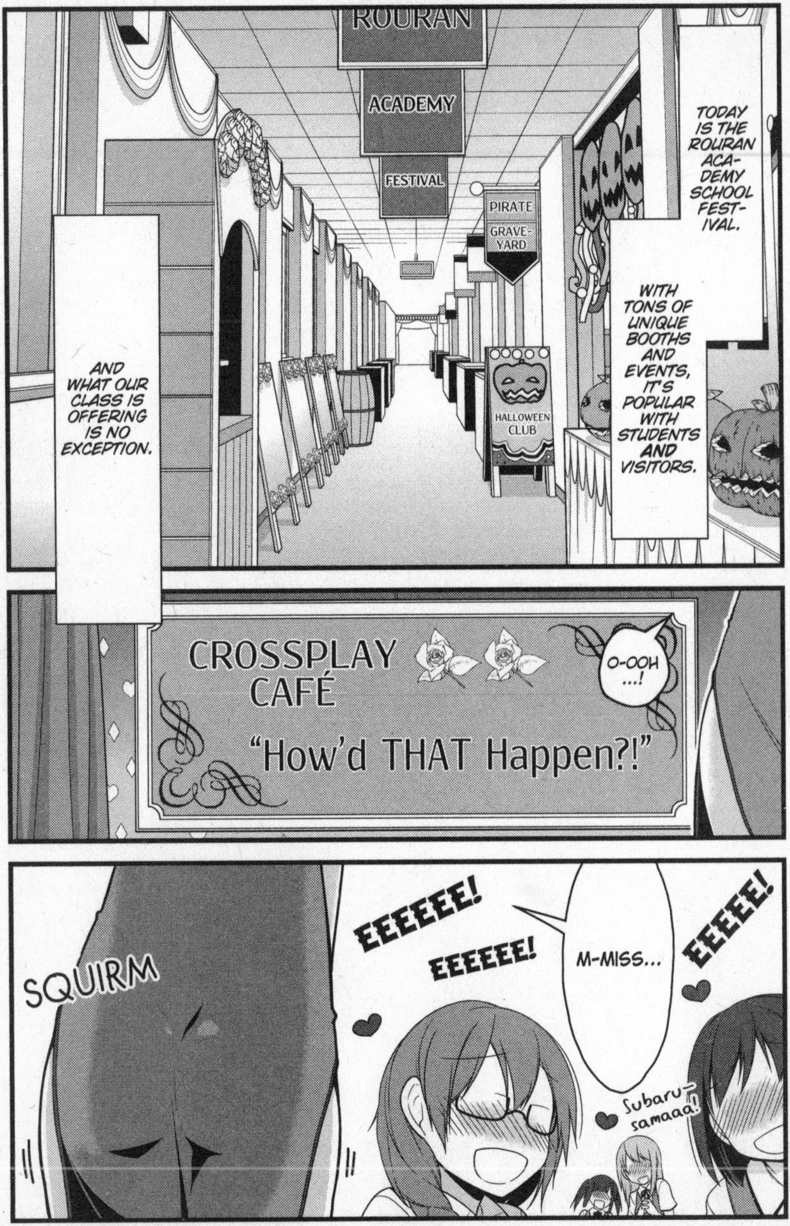
ROURAN
ACADEMY
FESTIVAL
TODAY IS THE ROURAN ACADEMY SCHOOL FESTIVAL.
WITH TONS OF UNIQUE BOOTHS AND EVENTS, IT'S POPULAR WITH STUDENTS AND VISITORS.
PIRATE GRAVE-YARD
HALLOWEEN CLUB
AND WHAT OUR CLASS IS OFFERING IS NO EXCEPTION.
O-OOH ...!
CROSSPLAY CAFÉ
"How'd THAT Happen?!"
EEEEEE!
M-MISS...
EEEEEE!
EEEEEE!
Subaru-samaaa!
SQUIRM

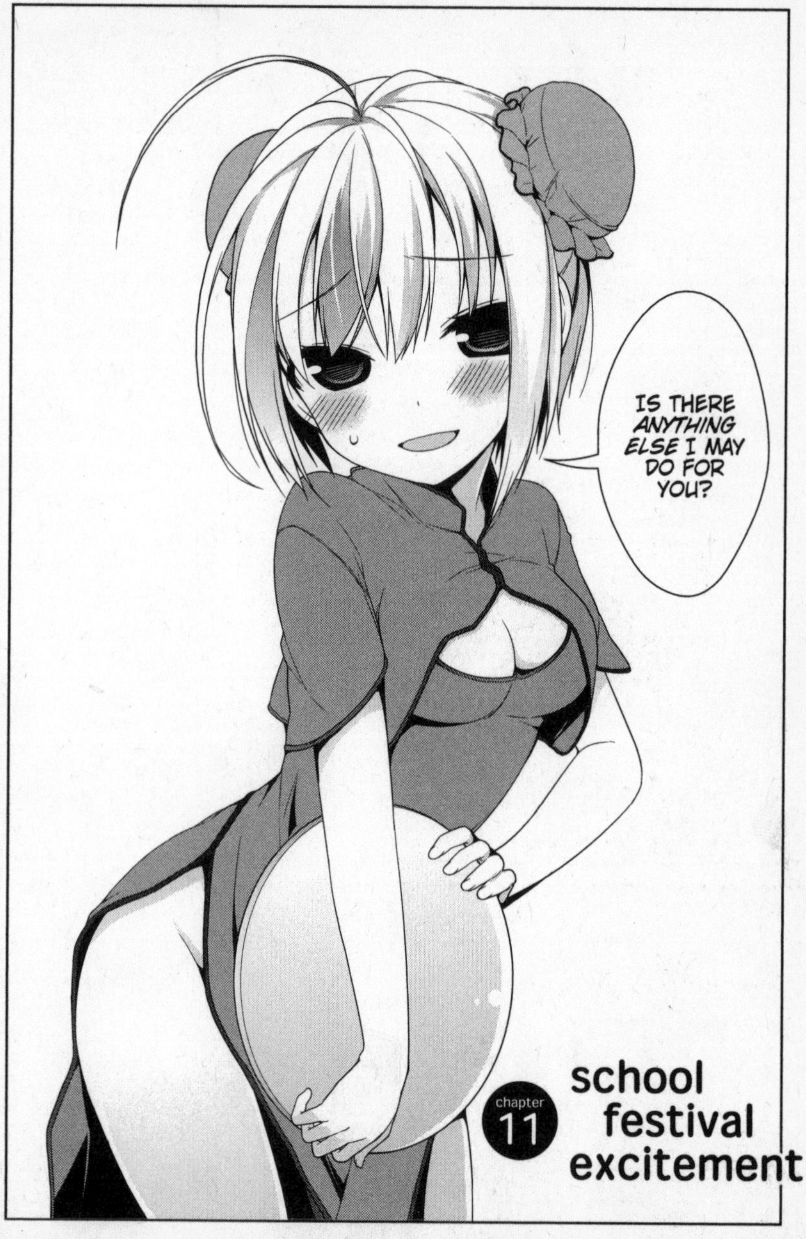
IS THERE ANYTHING ELSE I MAY DO FOR YOU?

chapter 11 school festival excitement

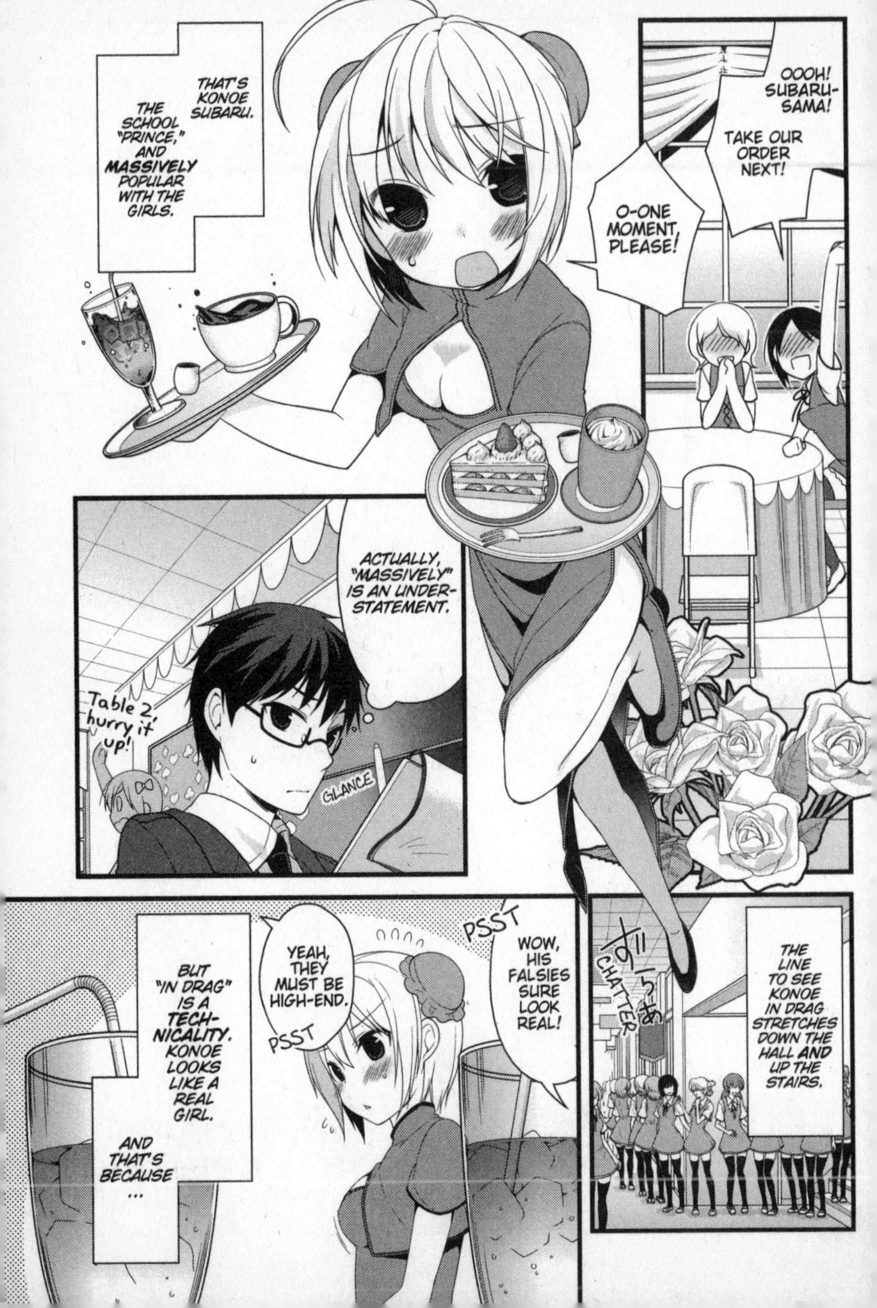
OOOH! SUBARU-SAMA!
TAKE OUR ORDER NEXT!
O-ONE MOMENT, PLEASE!
THAT'S KONOE SUBARU.
THE SCHOOL "PRINCE," AND MASSIVELY POPULAR WITH THE GIRLS.
ACTUALLY, "MASSIVELY" IS AN UNDER-STATEMENT.
Table 2, hurry it up!
GLANCE
THE LINE TO SEE KONOE IN DRAG STRETCHES DOWN THE HALL AND UP THE STAIRS.
CHATTER
WOW, HIS FALSIES SURE LOOK REAL!
PSST
YEAH, THEY MUST BE HIGH-END.
PSST
BUT "IN DRAG" IS A TECH-NICALITY. KONOE LOOKS LIKE A REAL GIRL.
AND THAT'S BECAUSE ...

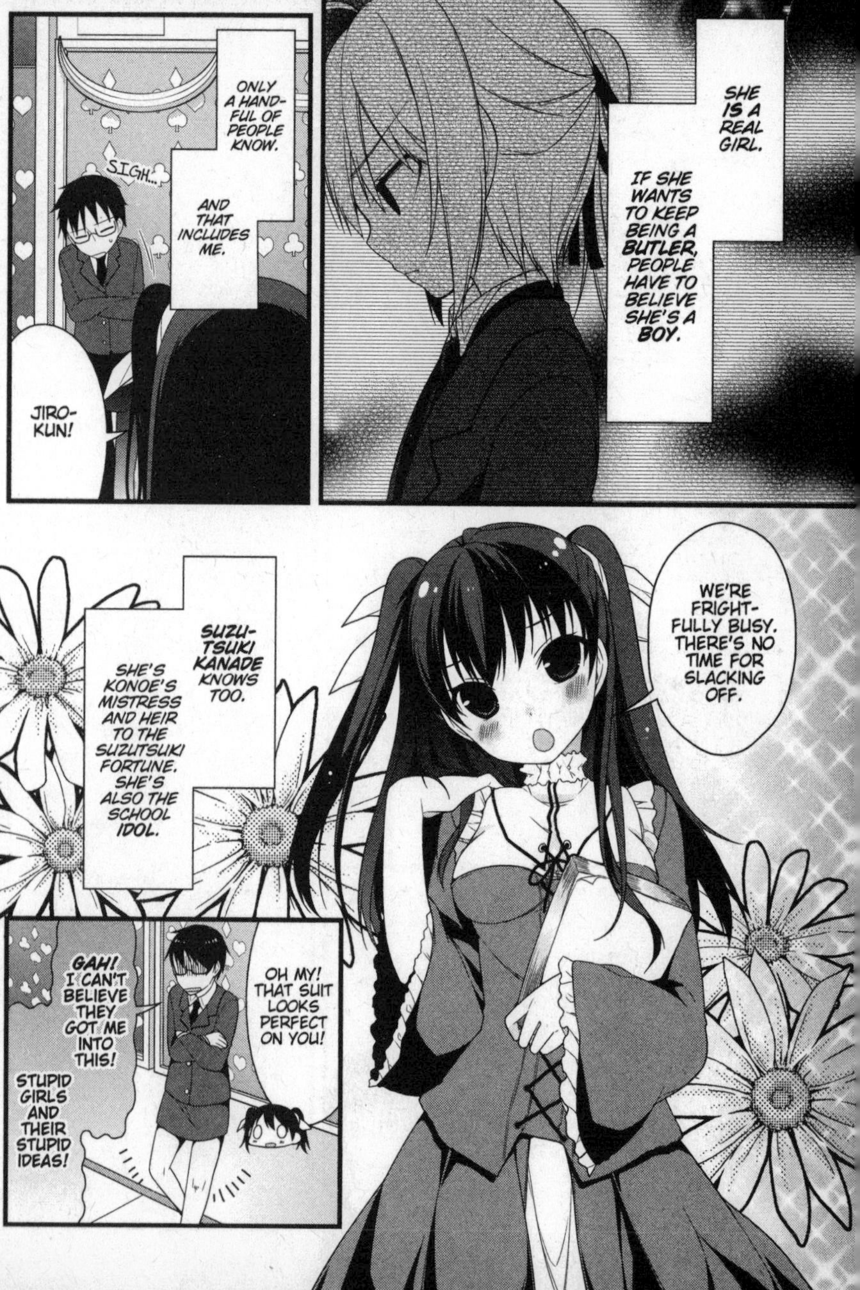

SHE IS A REAL GIRL.
IF SHE WANTS TO KEEP BEING A BUTLER, PEOPLE HAVE TO BELIEVE SHE'S A BOY.
ONLY A HAND-FUL OF PEOPLE KNOW.
AND THAT INCLUDES ME.
SIGH...
JIRO-KUN!
WE'RE FRIGHT-FULLY BUSY. THERE'S NO TIME FOR SLACKING OFF.
SUZU-TSUKI KANADE KNOWS TOO.
SHE'S KONOE'S MISTRESS AND HEIR TO THE SUZUTSUKI FORTUNE. SHE'S ALSO THE SCHOOL IDOL.
OH MY! THAT SUIT LOOKS PERFECT ON YOU!
GAH! I CAN'T BELIEVE THEY GOT ME INTO THIS!
STUPID GIRLS AND THEIR STUPID IDEAS!

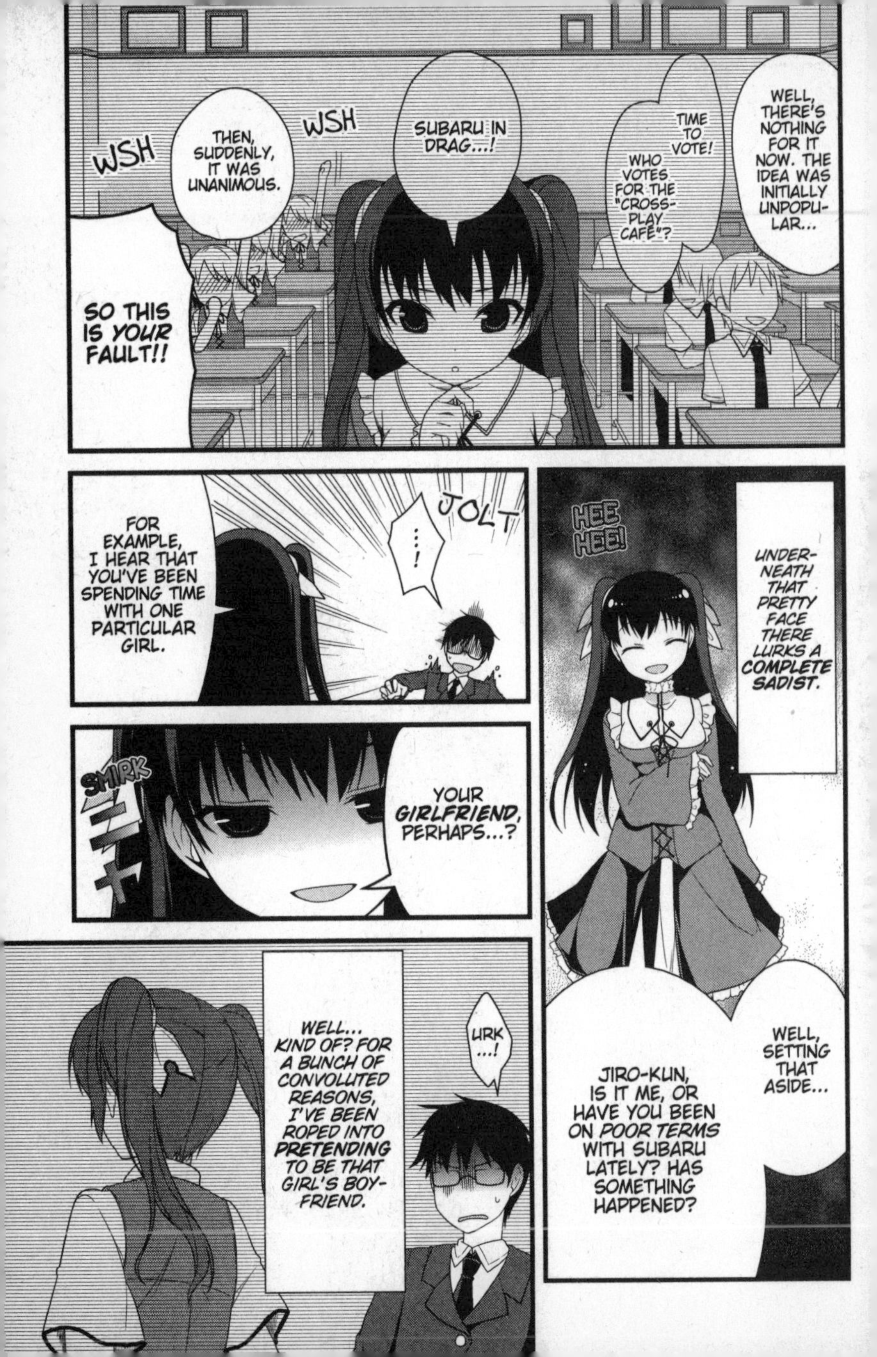
WELL, THERE'S NOTHING FOR IT NOW. THE IDEA WAS INITIALLY UNPOPULAR...
TIME TO VOTE!
WHO VOTES FOR THE "CROSS-PLAY CAFÉ"?
SUBARU IN DRAG...!
WSH
THEN, SUDDENLY, IT WAS UNANIMOUS.
WSH
SO THIS IS *YOUR* FAULT!!
HEE HEE!
UNDERNEATH THAT PRETTY FACE THERE LURKS A ***COMPLETE SADIST.***
WELL, SETTING THAT ASIDE...
JIRO-KUN, IS IT ME, OR HAVE YOU BEEN ON *POOR TERMS* WITH SUBARU LATELY? HAS SOMETHING HAPPENED?
JOLT
...!
FOR EXAMPLE, I HEAR THAT YOU'VE BEEN SPENDING TIME WITH ONE PARTICULAR GIRL.
YOUR ***GIRLFRIEND,*** PERHAPS...?
SMIRK
URK ...!
WELL... KIND OF? FOR A BUNCH OF CONVOLUTED REASONS, I'VE BEEN ROPED INTO ***PRETENDING*** *TO BE THAT GIRL'S BOY-FRIEND.*

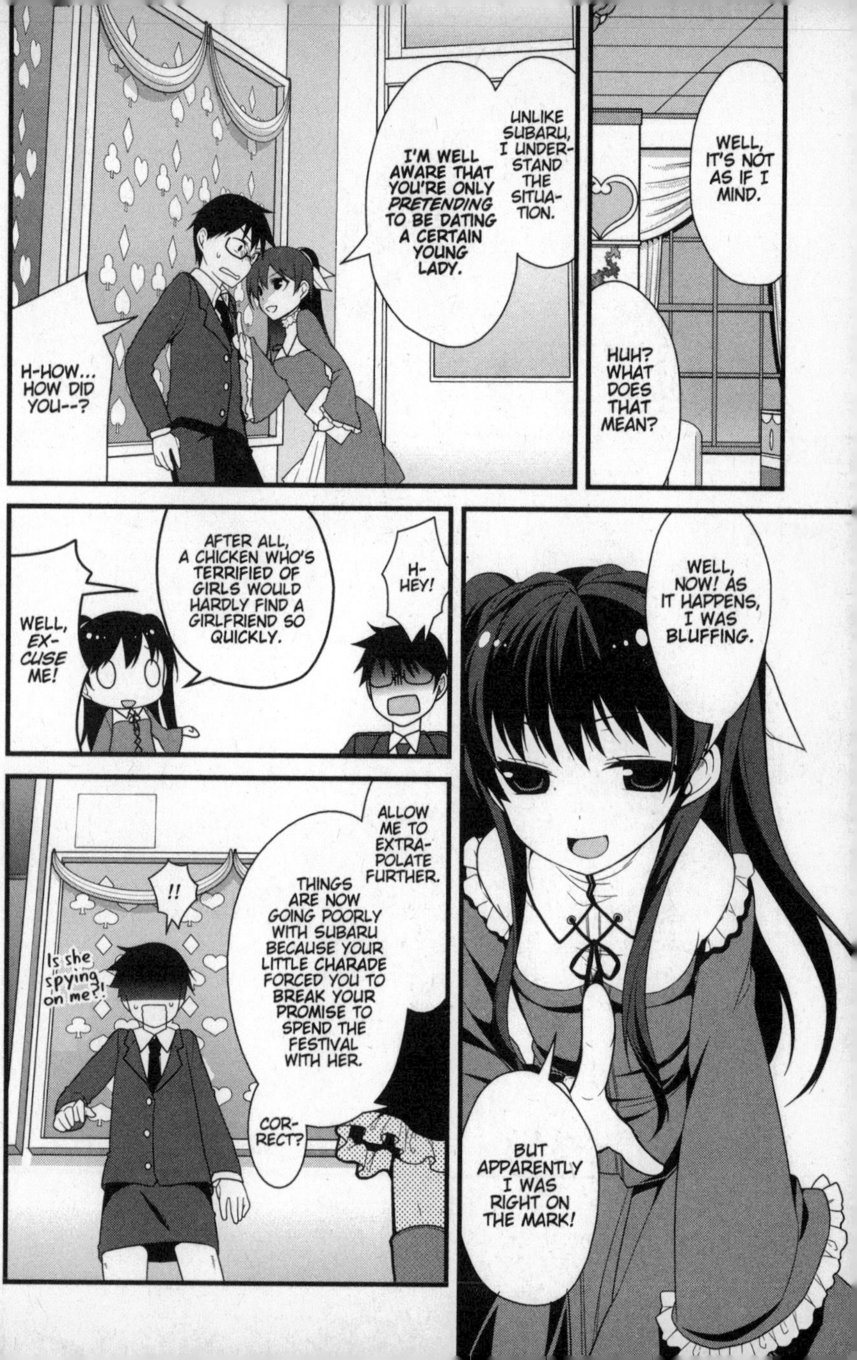
WELL, IT'S NOT AS IF I MIND.
HUH? WHAT DOES THAT MEAN?
UNLIKE SUBARU, I UNDERSTAND THE SITUATION.
I'M WELL AWARE THAT YOU'RE ONLY *PRETENDING* TO BE DATING A CERTAIN YOUNG LADY.
H-HOW... HOW DID YOU--?
WELL, NOW! AS IT HAPPENS, I WAS BLUFFING.
BUT APPARENTLY I WAS RIGHT ON THE MARK!
AFTER ALL, A CHICKEN WHO'S TERRIFIED OF GIRLS WOULD HARDLY FIND A GIRLFRIEND SO QUICKLY.
H-HEY!
WELL, EXCUSE ME!
ALLOW ME TO EXTRAPOLATE FURTHER.
THINGS ARE NOW GOING POORLY WITH SUBARU BECAUSE YOUR LITTLE CHARADE FORCED YOU TO BREAK YOUR PROMISE TO SPEND THE FESTIVAL WITH HER.
!!
CORRECT?
Is she spying on me?!

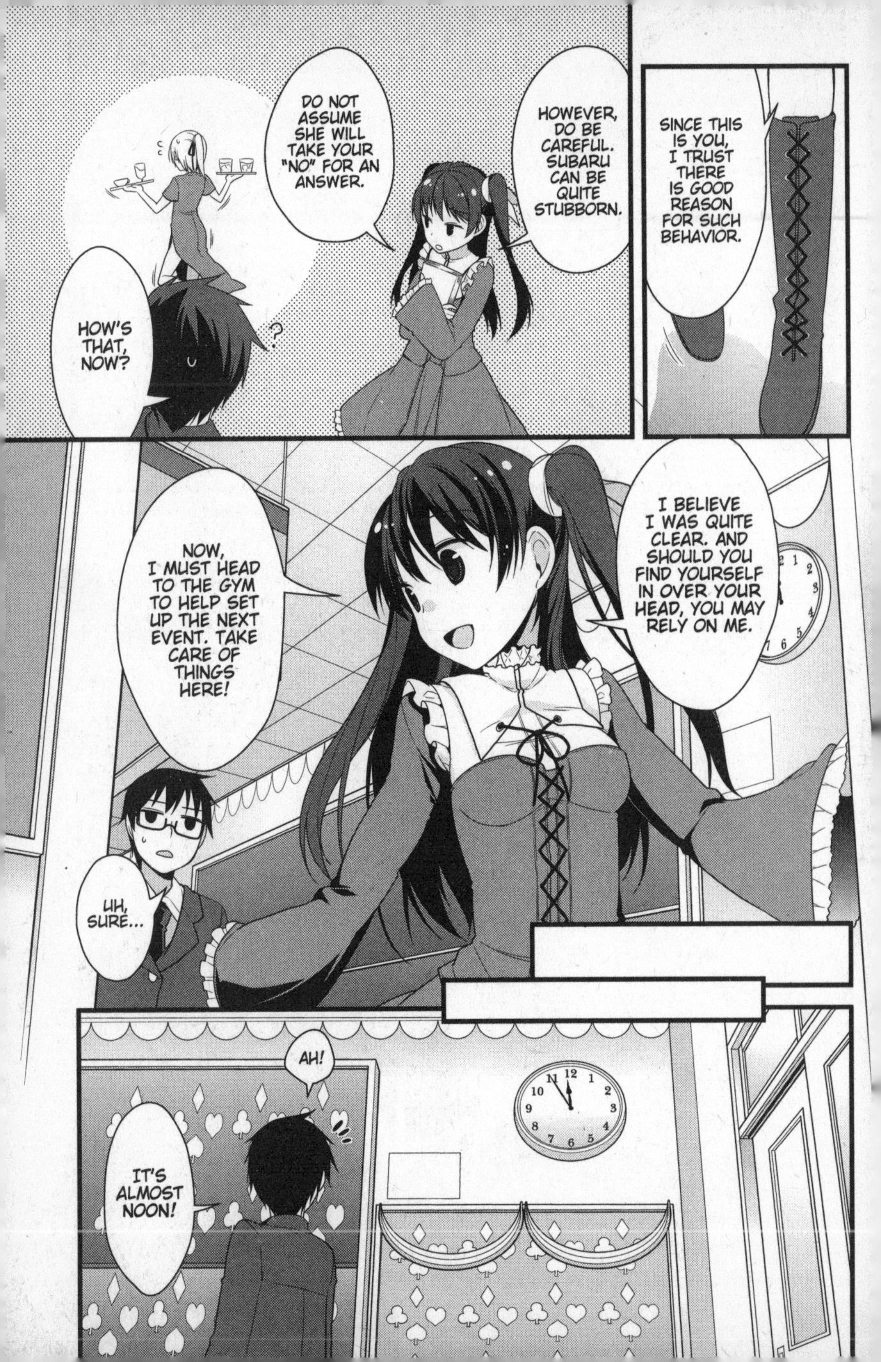
SINCE THIS IS YOU, I TRUST THERE IS GOOD REASON FOR SUCH BEHAVIOR.
HOWEVER, DO BE CAREFUL. SUBARU CAN BE QUITE STUBBORN.
DO NOT ASSUME SHE WILL TAKE YOUR "NO" FOR AN ANSWER.
HOW'S THAT, NOW?
I BELIEVE I WAS QUITE CLEAR. AND SHOULD YOU FIND YOURSELF IN OVER YOUR HEAD, YOU MAY RELY ON ME.
NOW, I MUST HEAD TO THE GYM TO HELP SET UP THE NEXT EVENT. TAKE CARE OF THINGS HERE!
UH, SURE...
AH!
IT'S ALMOST NOON!

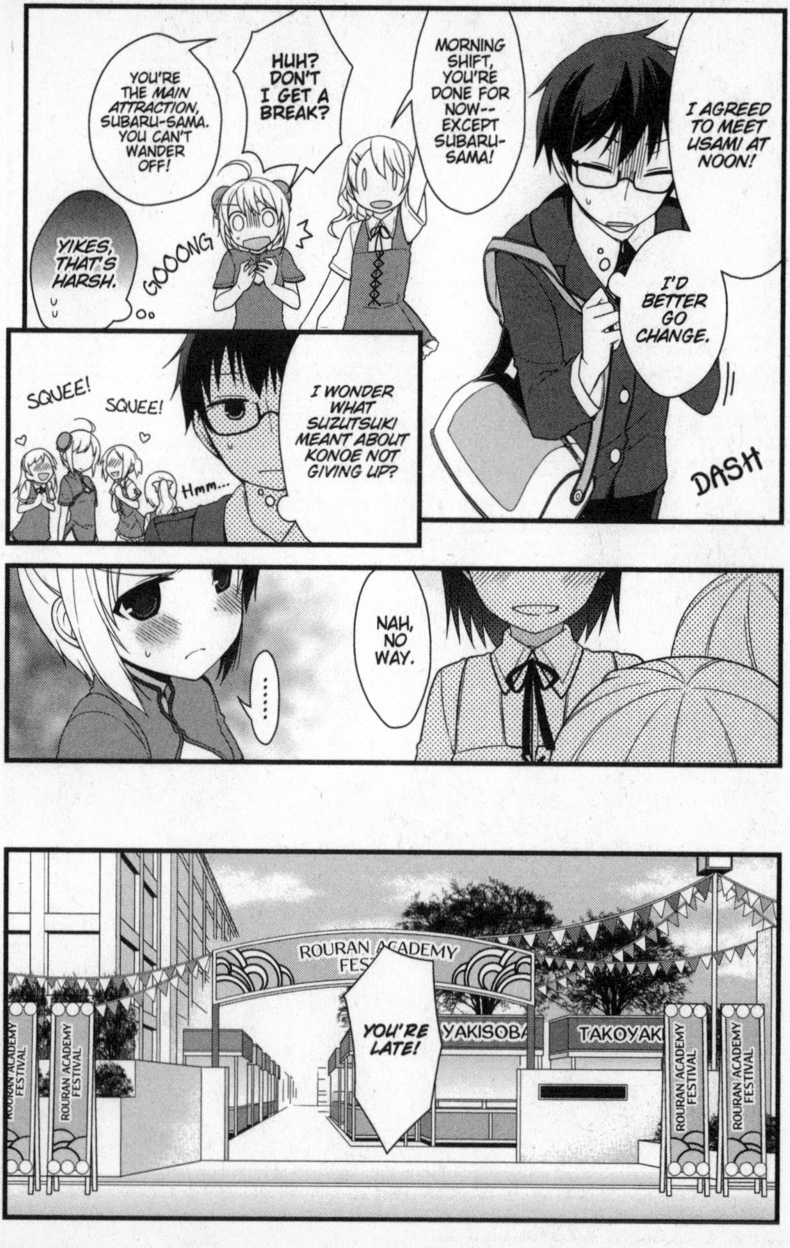
I AGREED TO MEET USAMI AT NOON!
I'D BETTER GO CHANGE.
DASH
MORNING SHIFT, YOU'RE DONE FOR NOW-- EXCEPT SUBARU-SAMA!
HUH? DON'T I GET A BREAK?
YOU'RE THE *MAIN ATTRACTION,* SUBARU-SAMA. YOU CAN'T WANDER OFF!
YIKES, THAT'S HARSH.
GOOONG
I WONDER WHAT SUZUTSUKI MEANT ABOUT KONOE NOT GIVING UP?
SQUEE!
SQUEE!
Hmm...
NAH, NO WAY.
......
ROURAN ACADEMY FEST
YAKISOBA
TAKOYAK
ROURAN ACADEMY FESTIVAL
ROURAN ACADEMY FESTIVAL
ROURAN ACADEMY FESTIVAL
ROURAN ACADEMY FESTIVAL
YOU'RE LATE!

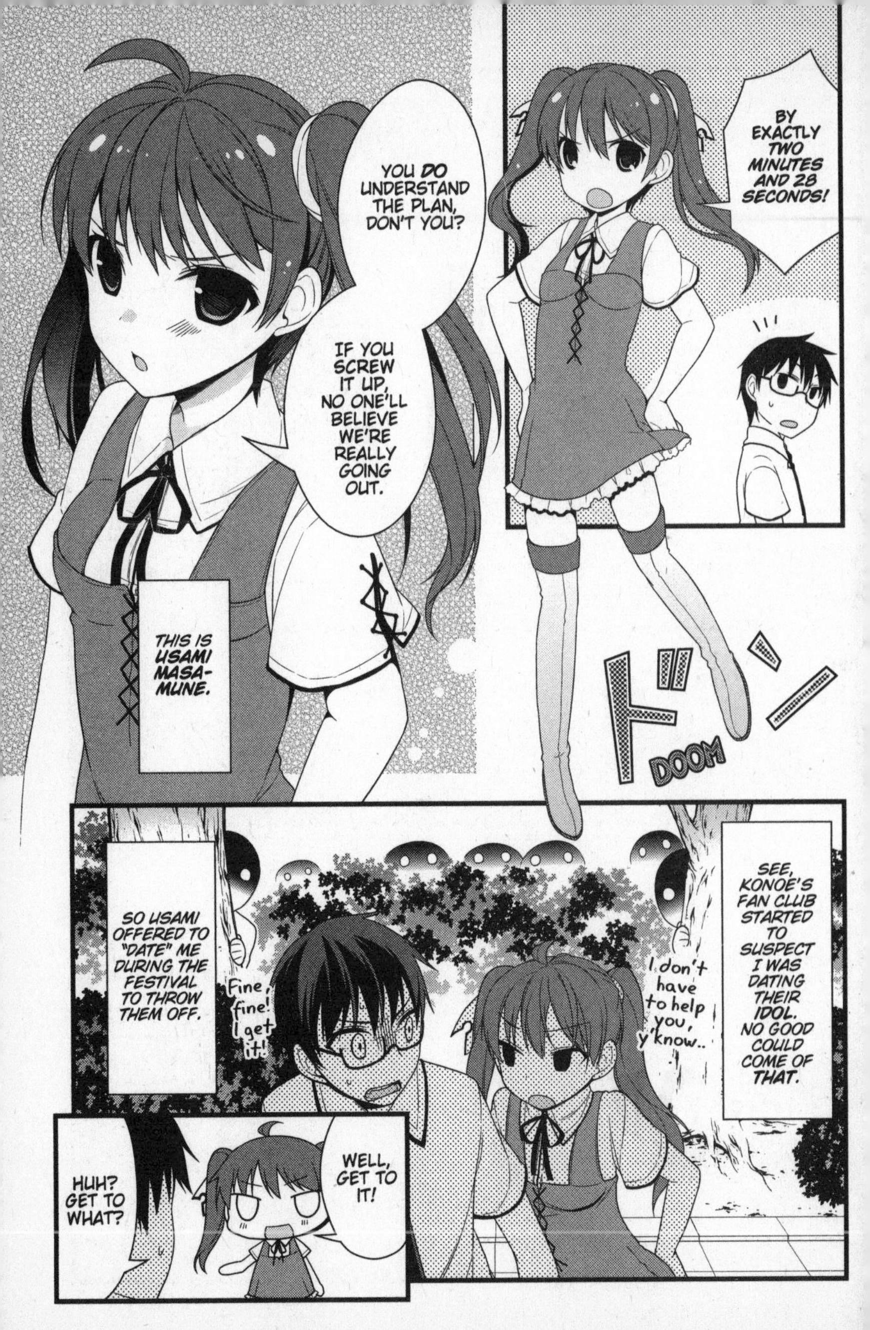
BY EXACTLY TWO MINUTES AND 28 SECONDS!
DOOM
YOU DO UNDERSTAND THE PLAN, DON'T YOU?
IF YOU SCREW IT UP, NO ONE'LL BELIEVE WE'RE REALLY GOING OUT.
THIS IS USAMI MASAMUNE.
SEE, KONOE'S FAN CLUB STARTED TO SUSPECT I WAS DATING THEIR IDOL. NO GOOD COULD COME OF THAT.
I don't have to help you, y'know..
Fine, fine! I get it!
SO USAMI OFFERED TO "DATE" ME DURING THE FESTIVAL TO THROW THEM OFF.
WELL, GET TO IT!
HUH? GET TO WHAT?

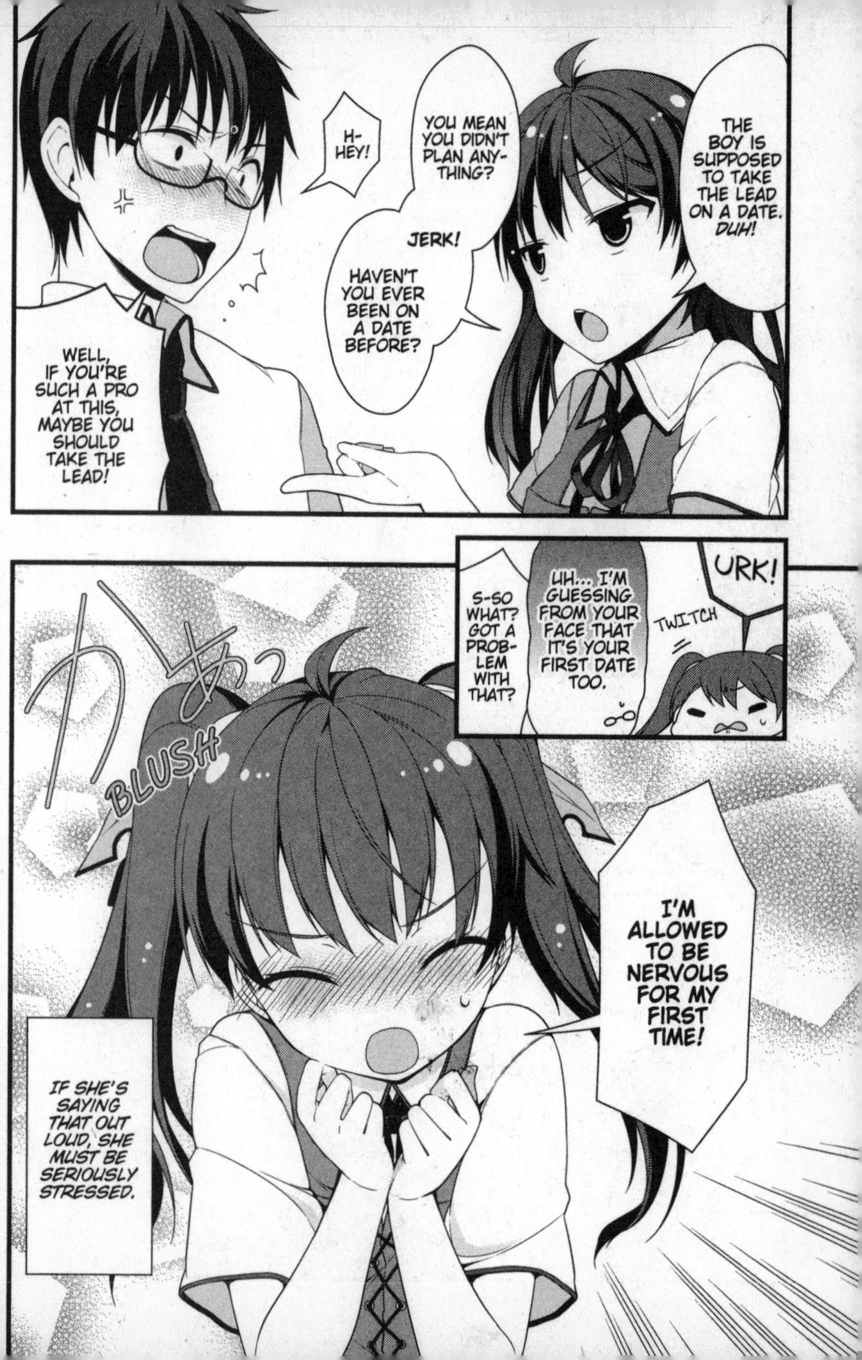
THE BOY IS SUPPOSED TO TAKE THE LEAD ON A DATE. DUH!
YOU MEAN YOU DIDN'T PLAN ANYTHING?
H-HEY!
JERK!
HAVEN'T YOU EVER BEEN ON A DATE BEFORE?
WELL, IF YOU'RE SUCH A PRO AT THIS, MAYBE YOU SHOULD TAKE THE LEAD!
URK!
TWITCH
UH... I'M GUESSING FROM YOUR FACE THAT IT'S YOUR FIRST DATE TOO.
S-SO WHAT? GOT A PROBLEM WITH THAT?
BLUSH
I'M ALLOWED TO BE NERVOUS FOR MY FIRST TIME!
IF SHE'S SAYING THAT OUT LOUD, SHE MUST BE SERIOUSLY STRESSED.

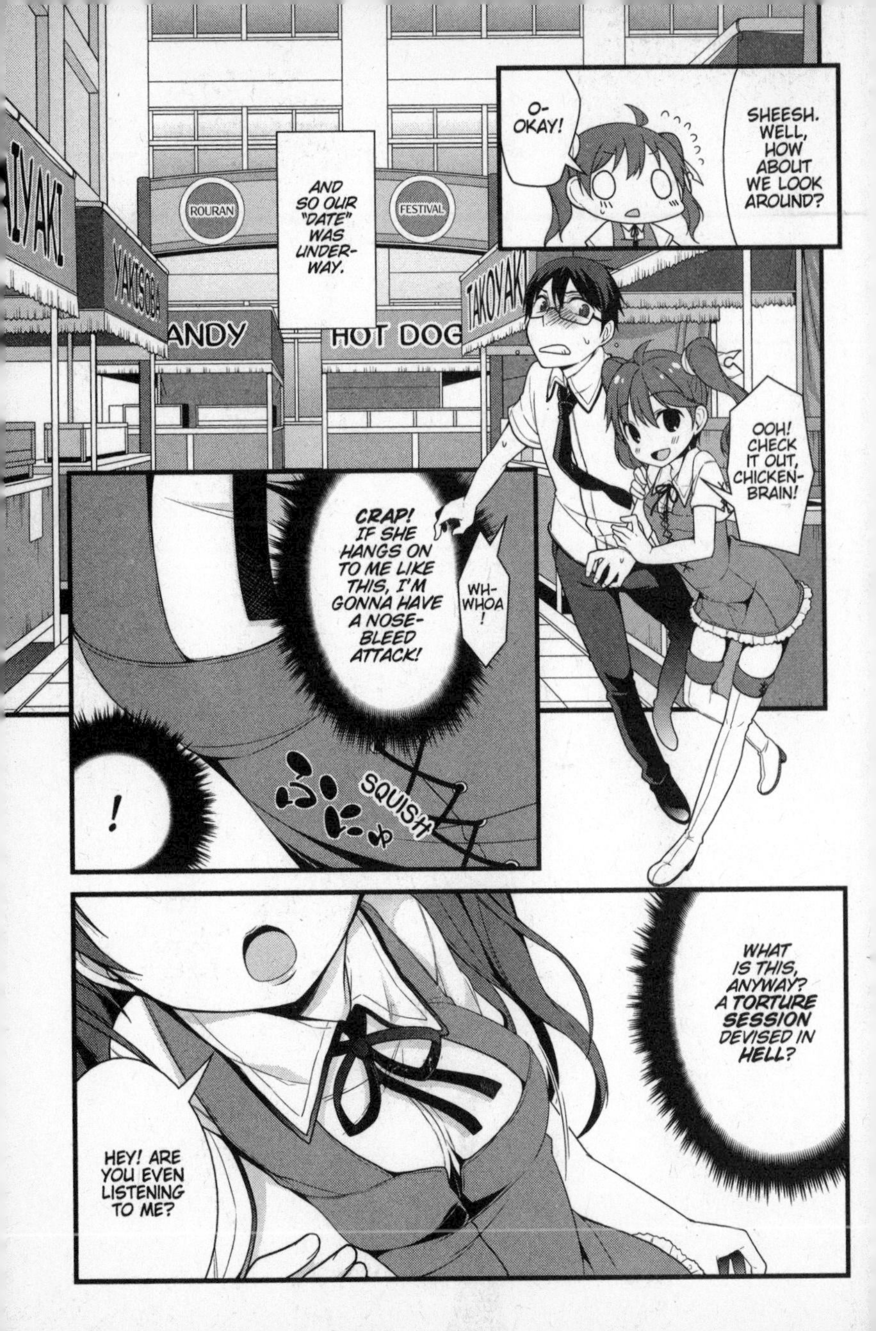
SHEESH. WELL, HOW ABOUT WE LOOK AROUND?
O-OKAY!
AND SO OUR "DATE" WAS UNDERWAY.
ROURAN
FESTIVAL
AIYAKI
YAKISOBA
ANDY
HOT DOG
TAKOYAKI
OOH! CHECK IT OUT, CHICKEN-BRAIN!
WH-WHOA!
CRAP! IF SHE HANGS ON TO ME LIKE THIS, I'M GONNA HAVE A NOSE-BLEED ATTACK!
SQUISH
!
WHAT IS THIS, ANYWAY? A TORTURE SESSION DEVISED IN HELL?
HEY! ARE YOU EVEN LISTENING TO ME?

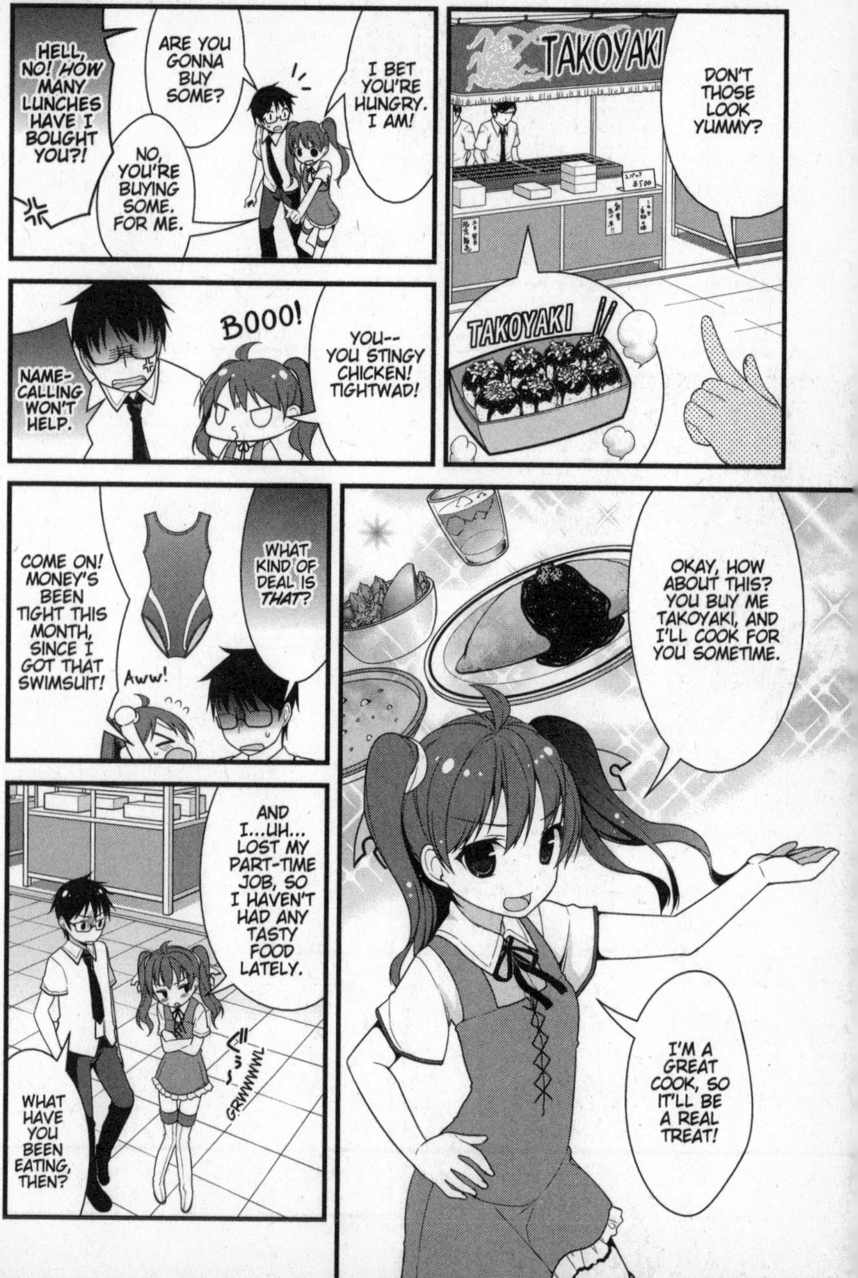
TAKOYAKI
DON'T THOSE LOOK YUMMY?
TAKOYAKI
I BET YOU'RE HUNGRY. I AM!
ARE YOU GONNA BUY SOME?
NO, YOU'RE BUYING SOME. FOR ME.
HELL, NO! *HOW* MANY LUNCHES HAVE I BOUGHT YOU?!
YOU-- YOU STINGY CHICKEN! TIGHTWAD!
BOOO!
NAME-CALLING WON'T HELP.
OKAY, HOW ABOUT THIS? YOU BUY ME TAKOYAKI, AND I'LL COOK FOR YOU SOMETIME.
I'M A GREAT COOK, SO IT'LL BE A REAL TREAT!
WHAT KIND OF DEAL IS *THAT*?
COME ON! MONEY'S BEEN TIGHT THIS MONTH, SINCE I GOT THAT SWIMSUIT!
Aww!
AND I...UH... LOST MY PART-TIME JOB, SO I HAVEN'T HAD ANY TASTY FOOD LATELY.
GRWWWWL
WHAT HAVE YOU BEEN EATING, THEN?

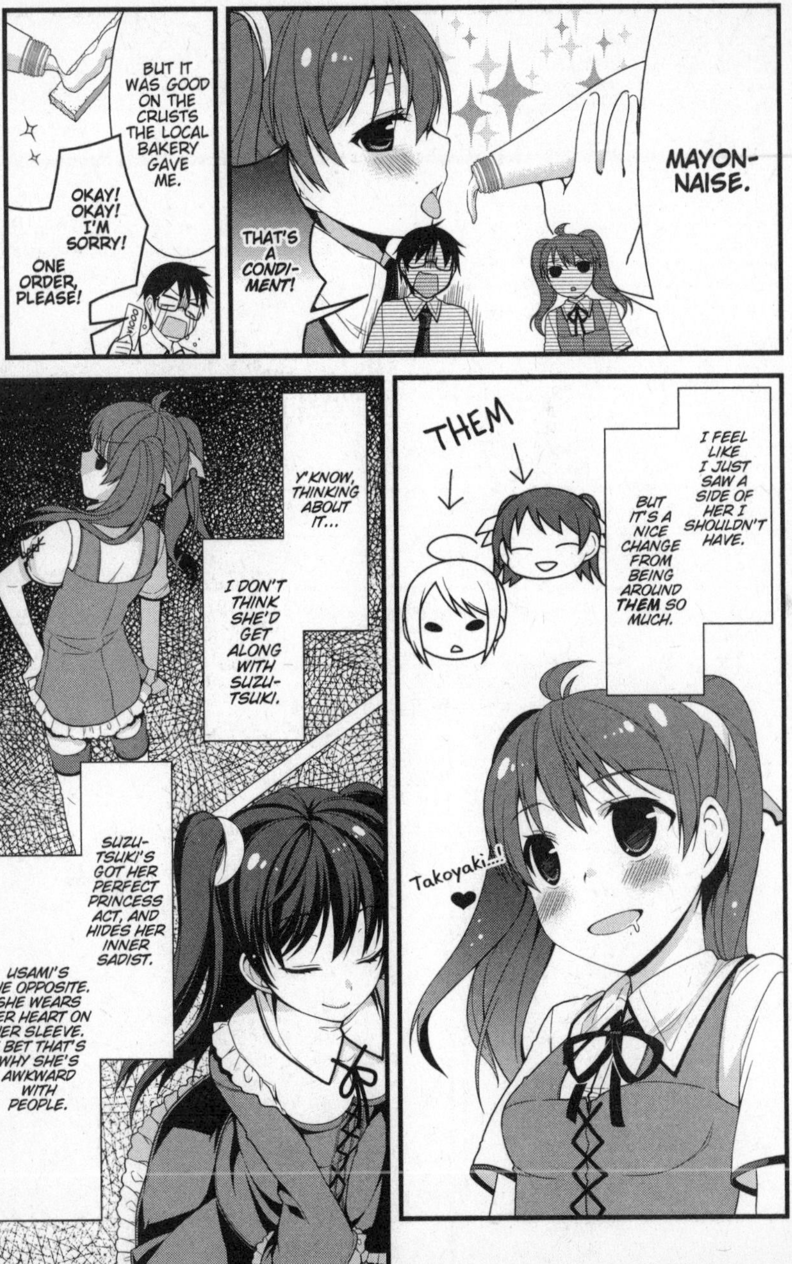
MAYON-NAISE.
THAT'S A CONDI-MENT!
BUT IT WAS GOOD ON THE CRUSTS THE LOCAL BAKERY GAVE ME.
OKAY! OKAY! I'M SORRY!
ONE ORDER, PLEASE!
I FEEL LIKE I JUST SAW A SIDE OF HER I SHOULDN'T HAVE.
BUT IT'S A NICE CHANGE FROM BEING AROUND THEM SO MUCH.
THEM
Takoyaki...!
Y'KNOW, THINKING ABOUT IT...
I DON'T THINK SHE'D GET ALONG WITH SUZU-TSUKI.
SUZU-TSUKI'S GOT HER PERFECT PRINCESS ACT, AND HIDES HER INNER SADIST.
USAMI'S THE OPPOSITE. SHE WEARS HER HEART ON HER SLEEVE. I BET THAT'S WHY SHE'S AWKWARD WITH PEOPLE.

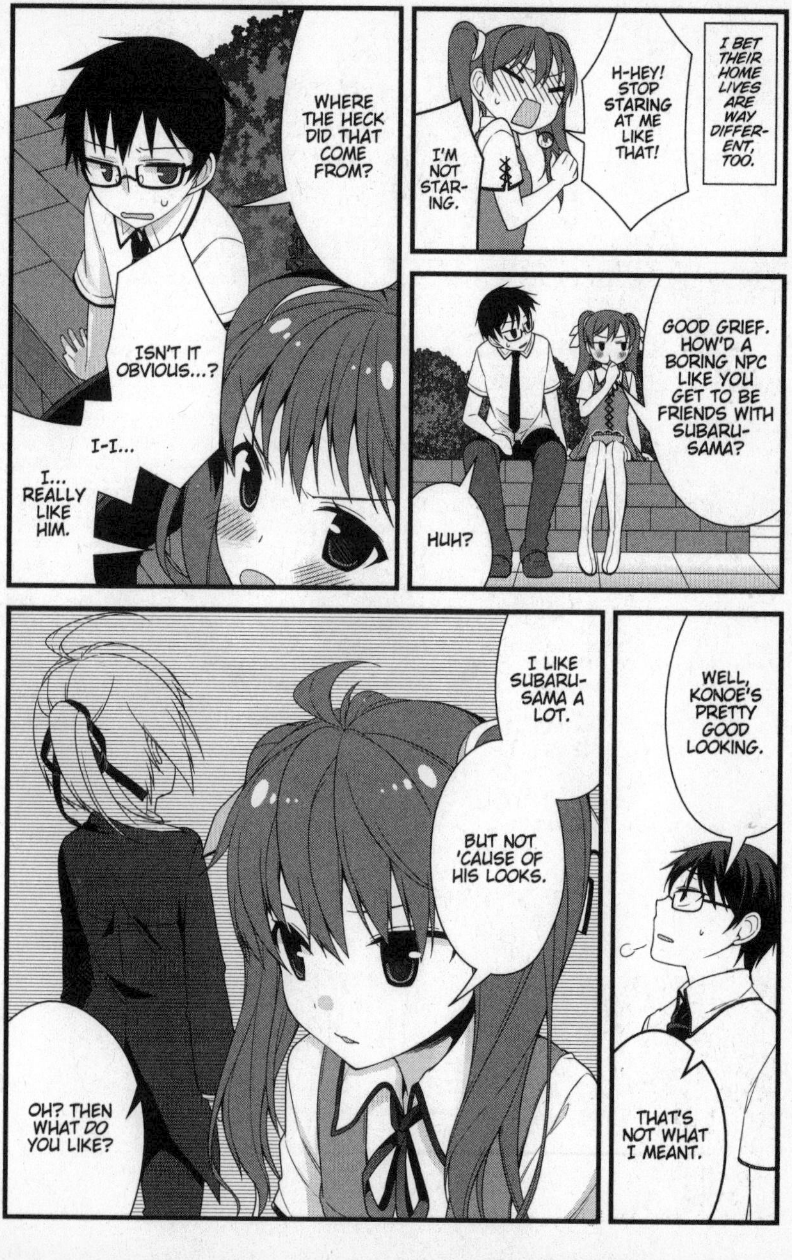
I BET THEIR HOME LIVES ARE WAY DIFFERENT, TOO.
H-HEY! STOP STARING AT ME LIKE THAT!
I'M NOT STARING.
GOOD GRIEF. HOW'D A BORING NPC LIKE YOU GET TO BE FRIENDS WITH SUBARU-SAMA?
HUH?
WHERE THE HECK DID THAT COME FROM?
ISN'T IT OBVIOUS...?
I-I...
I... REALLY LIKE HIM.
WELL, KONOE'S PRETTY GOOD LOOKING.
THAT'S NOT WHAT I MEANT.
I LIKE SUBARU-SAMA A LOT.
BUT NOT 'CAUSE OF HIS LOOKS.
OH? THEN WHAT DO YOU LIKE?

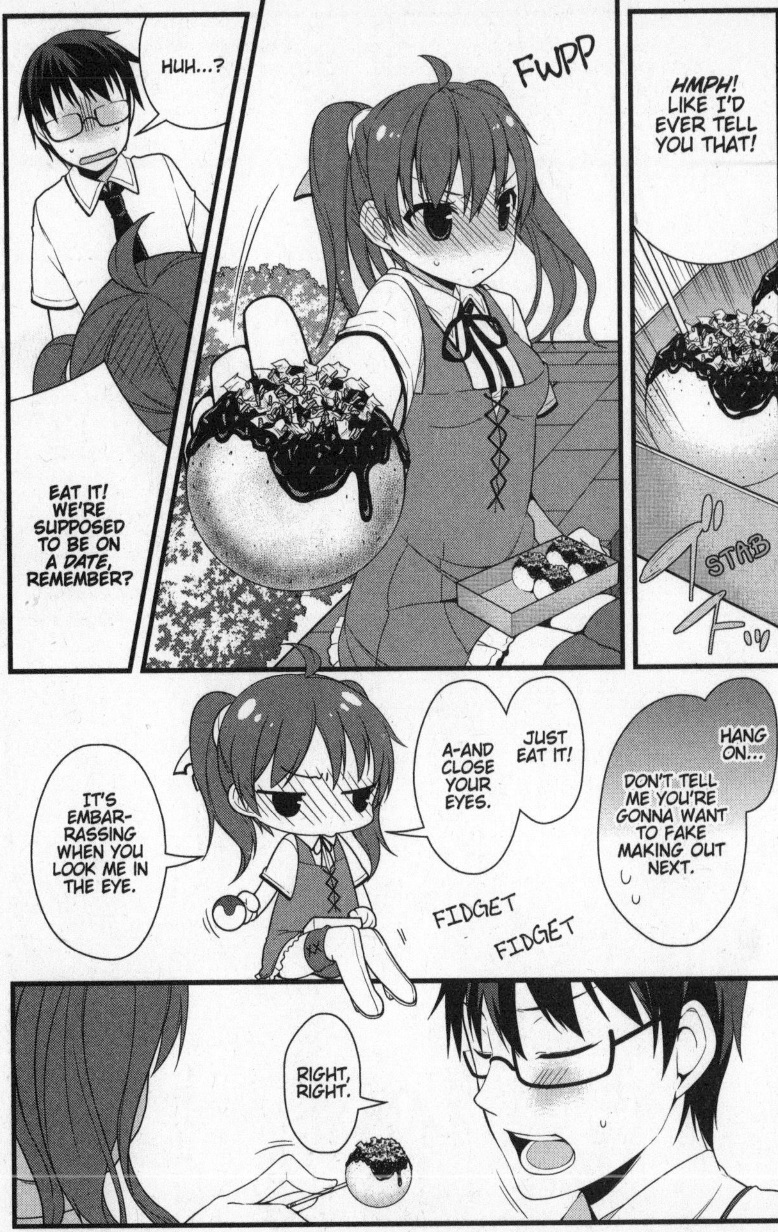
HMPH! LIKE I'D EVER TELL YOU THAT!
STAB
FWPP
HUH...?
EAT IT! WE'RE SUPPOSED TO BE ON A DATE, REMEMBER?
HANG ON...
DON'T TELL ME YOU'RE GONNA WANT TO FAKE MAKING OUT NEXT.
JUST EAT IT!
A-AND CLOSE YOUR EYES.
IT'S EMBARRASSING WHEN YOU LOOK ME IN THE EYE.
FIDGET
FIDGET
RIGHT, RIGHT.

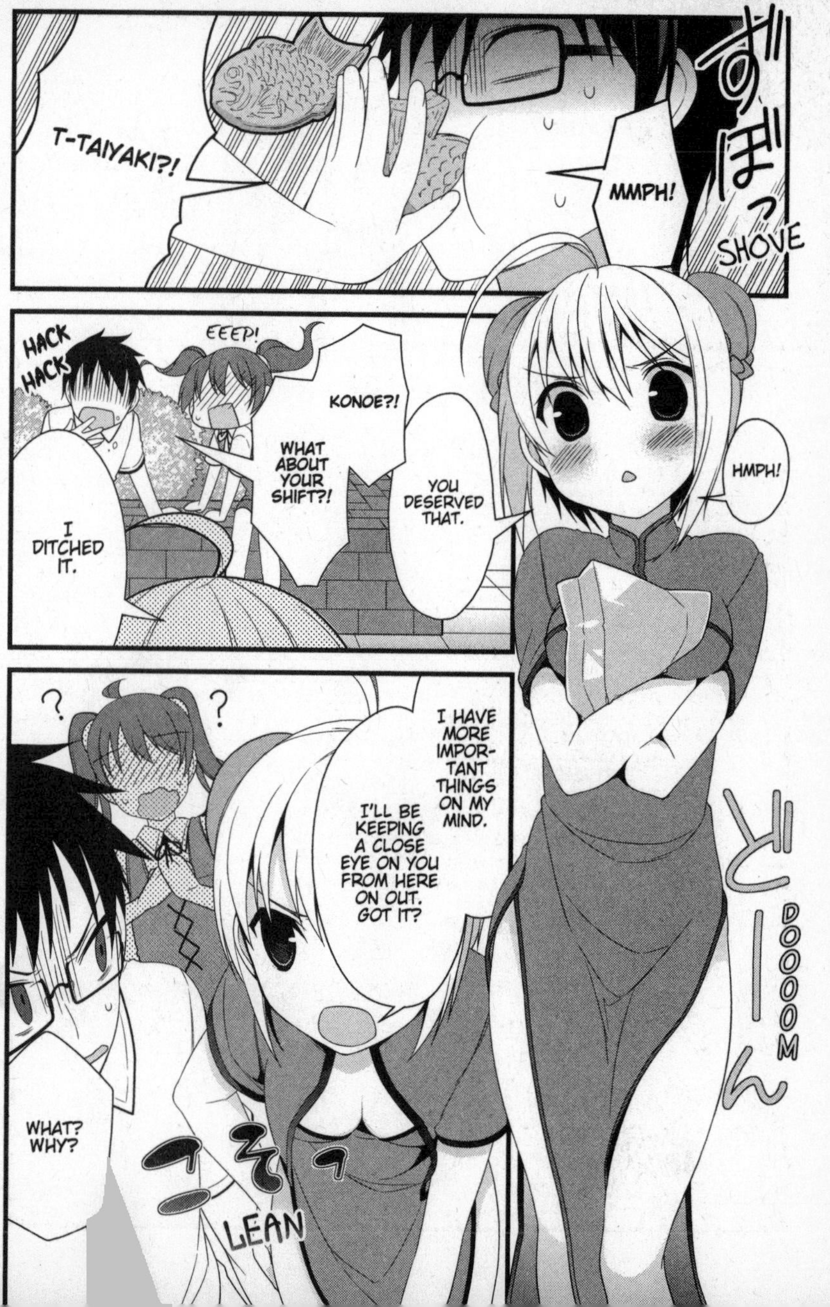
ずぼっ
SHOVE
MMPH!
T-TAIYAKI?!
HMPH!
YOU DESERVED THAT.
KONOE?!
WHAT ABOUT YOUR SHIFT?!
EEEP!
HACK HACK
I DITCHED IT.
どーん
DOOOOM
I HAVE MORE IMPORTANT THINGS ON MY MIND.
I'LL BE KEEPING A CLOSE EYE ON YOU FROM HERE ON OUT. GOT IT?
? ?
WHAT? WHY?
LEAN

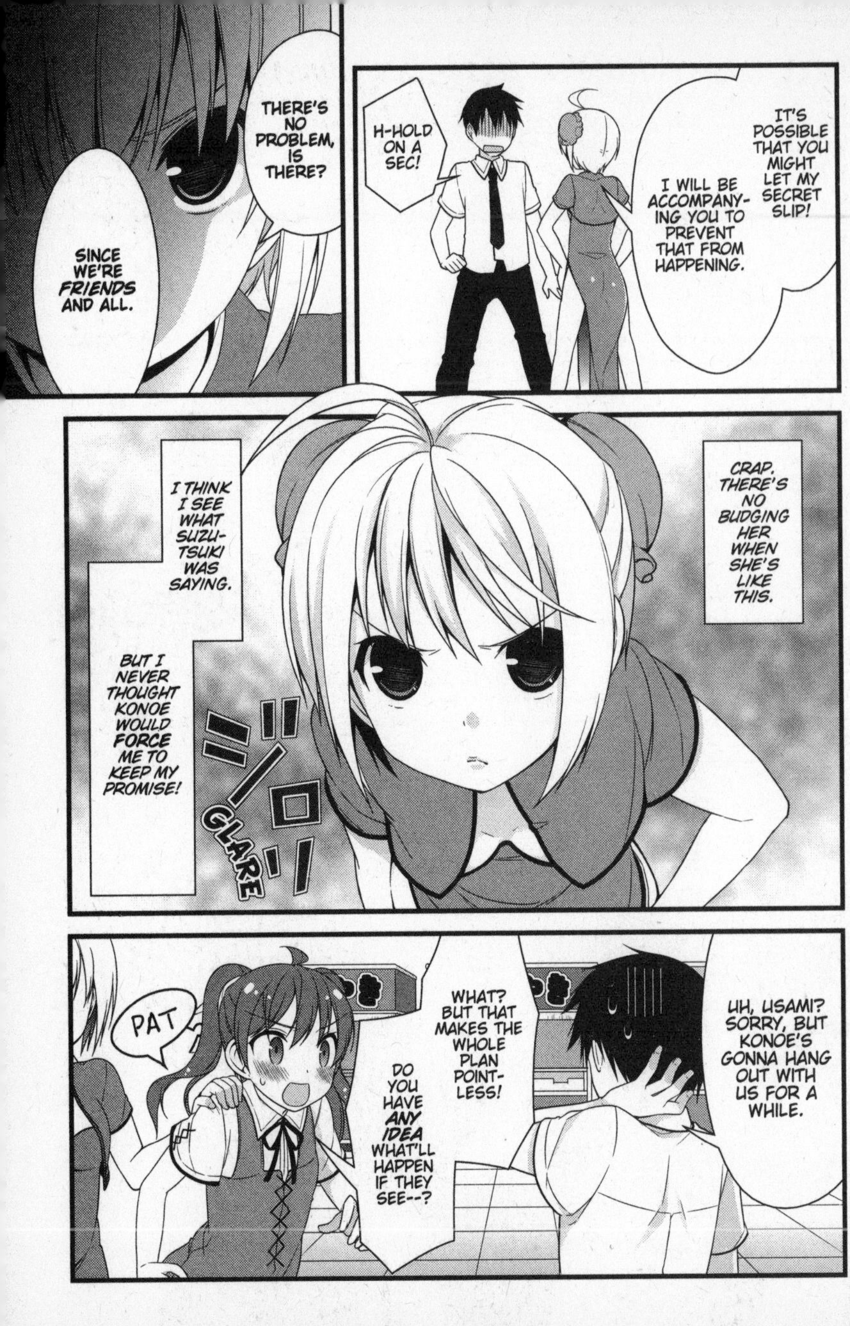
IT'S POSSIBLE THAT YOU MIGHT LET MY SECRET SLIP!
I WILL BE ACCOMPANYING YOU TO PREVENT THAT FROM HAPPENING.
H-HOLD ON A SEC!
THERE'S NO PROBLEM, IS THERE?
SINCE WE'RE *FRIENDS* AND ALL.
CRAP. THERE'S NO BUDGING HER WHEN SHE'S LIKE THIS.
I THINK I SEE WHAT SUZUTSUKI WAS SAYING.
*BUT I NEVER THOUGHT KONOE WOULD **FORCE** ME TO KEEP MY PROMISE!*
GLARE
UH, USAMI? SORRY, BUT KONOE'S GONNA HANG OUT WITH US FOR A WHILE.
WHAT? BUT THAT MAKES THE WHOLE PLAN POINTLESS!
DO YOU HAVE *ANY IDEA* WHAT'LL HAPPEN IF THEY SEE--?
PAT

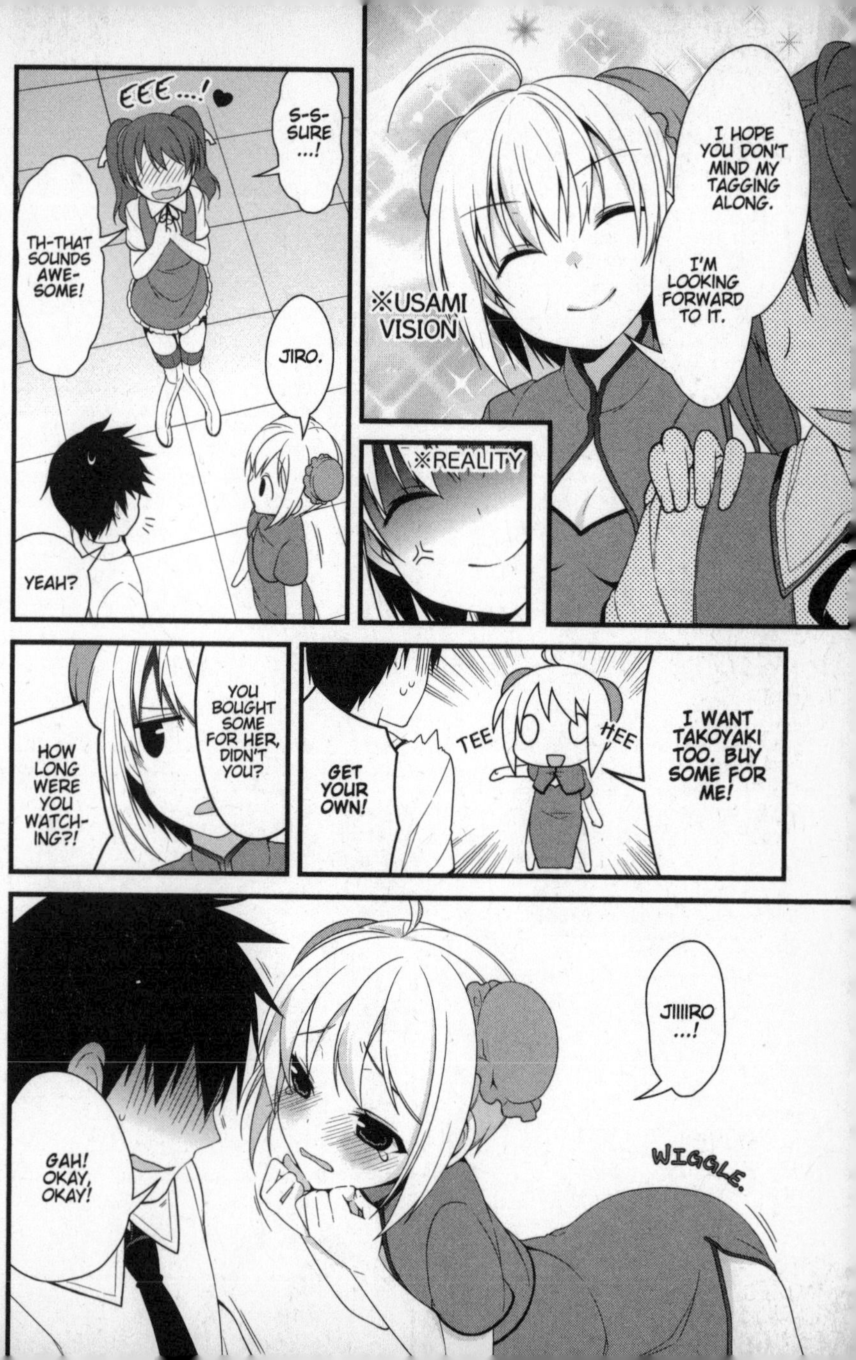
I HOPE YOU DON'T MIND MY TAGGING ALONG.
I'M LOOKING FORWARD TO IT.
※USAMI VISION
※REALITY
EEE...!♥
S-S-SURE ...!
TH-THAT SOUNDS AWE-SOME!
JIRO.
YEAH?
I WANT TAKOYAKI TOO. BUY SOME FOR ME!
TEE HEE
GET YOUR OWN!
YOU BOUGHT SOME FOR HER, DIDN'T YOU?
HOW LONG WERE YOU WATCHING?!
JIIIIRO ...!
WIGGLE.
GAH! OKAY, OKAY!

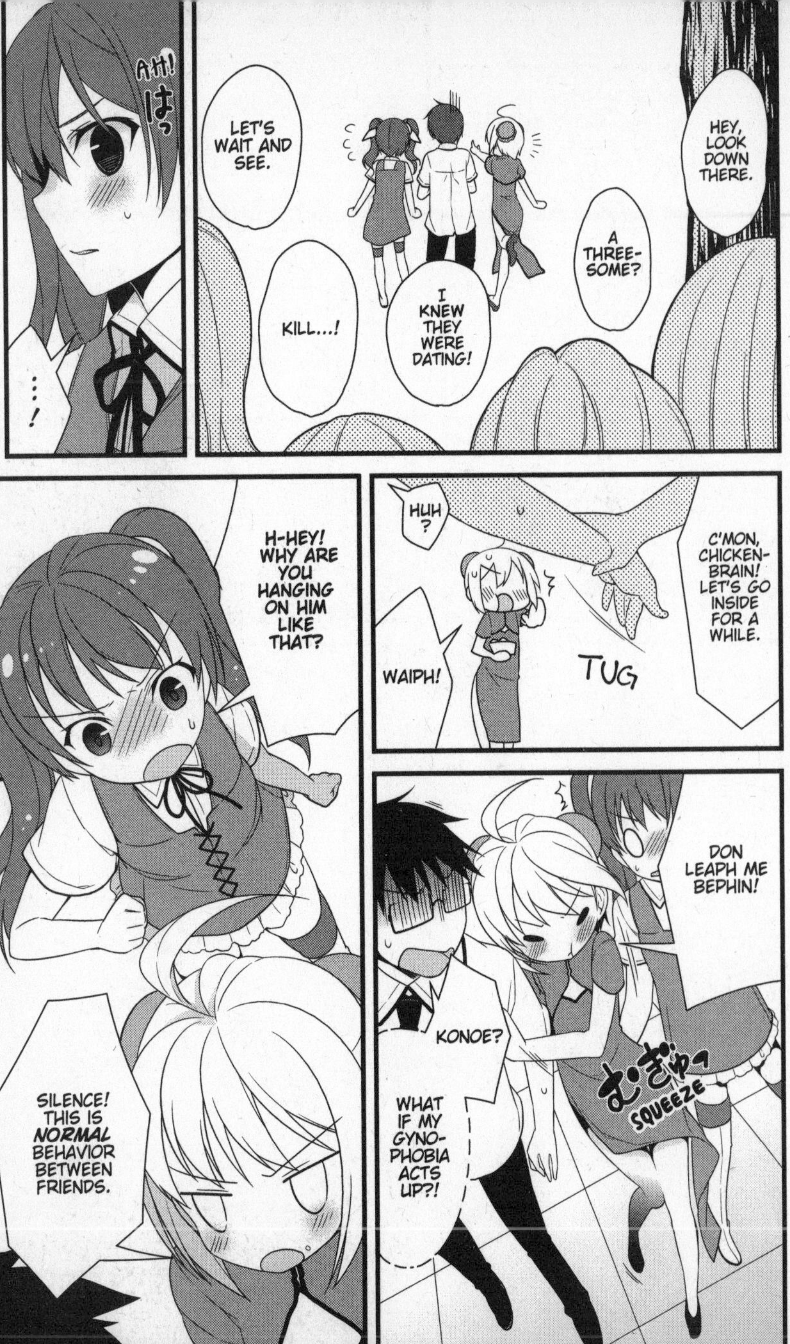
HEY, LOOK DOWN THERE.
A THREE-SOME?
LET'S WAIT AND SEE.
I KNEW THEY WERE DATING!
KILL...!
AH! はっ
...!
C'MON, CHICKEN-BRAIN! LET'S GO INSIDE FOR A WHILE.
HUH?
TUG
WAIPH!
DON LEAPH ME BEPHIN!
KONOE?
むぎゅっ SQUEEZE
WHAT IF MY GYNO-PHOBIA ACTS UP?!
H-HEY! WHY ARE YOU HANGING ON HIM LIKE THAT?
SILENCE! THIS IS *NORMAL* BEHAVIOR BETWEEN FRIENDS.

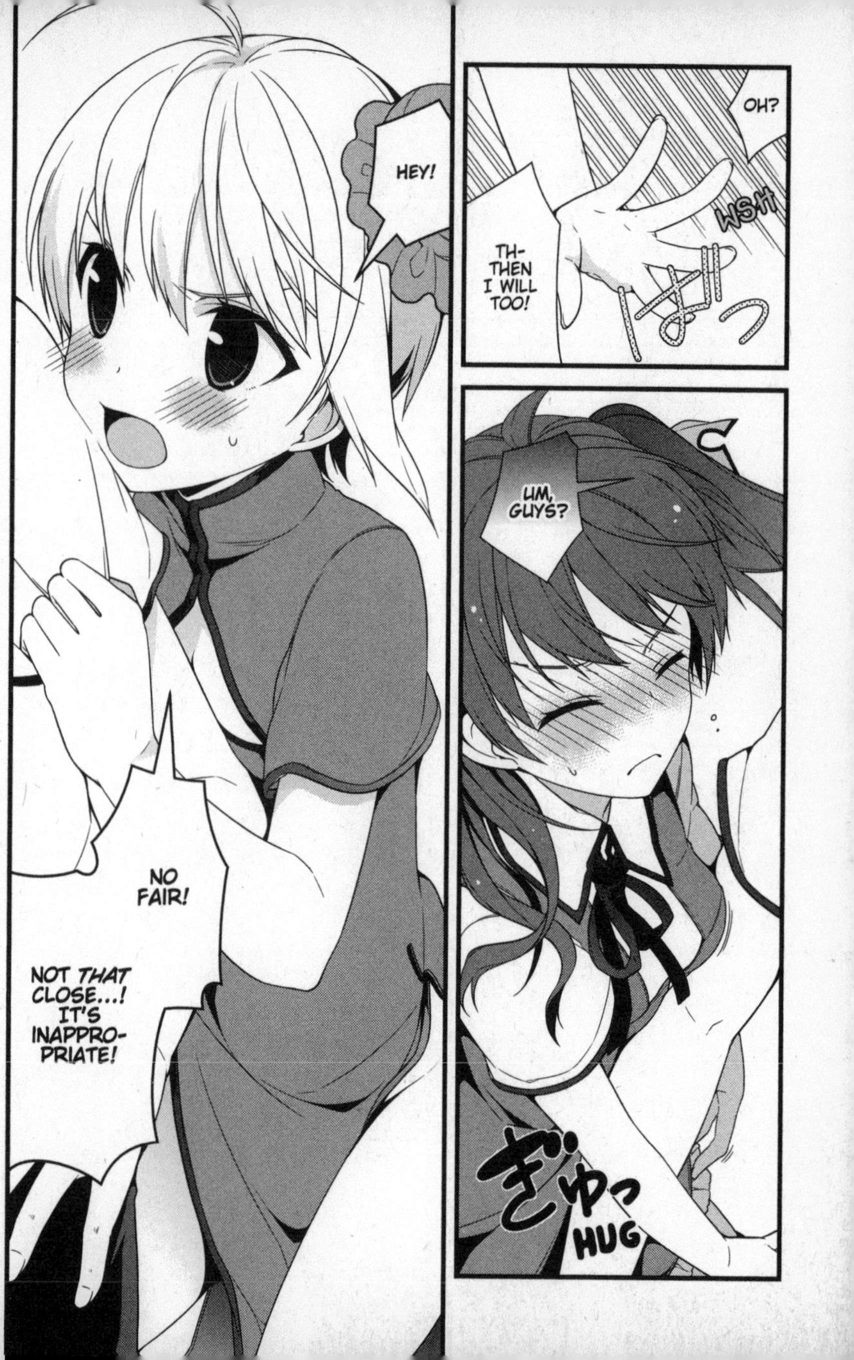
OH?
WSH
TH-THEN I WILL TOO!
UM, GUYS?
ぎゅっ
HUG
HEY!
NO FAIR!
NOT *THAT* CLOSE...! IT'S INAPPROPRIATE!

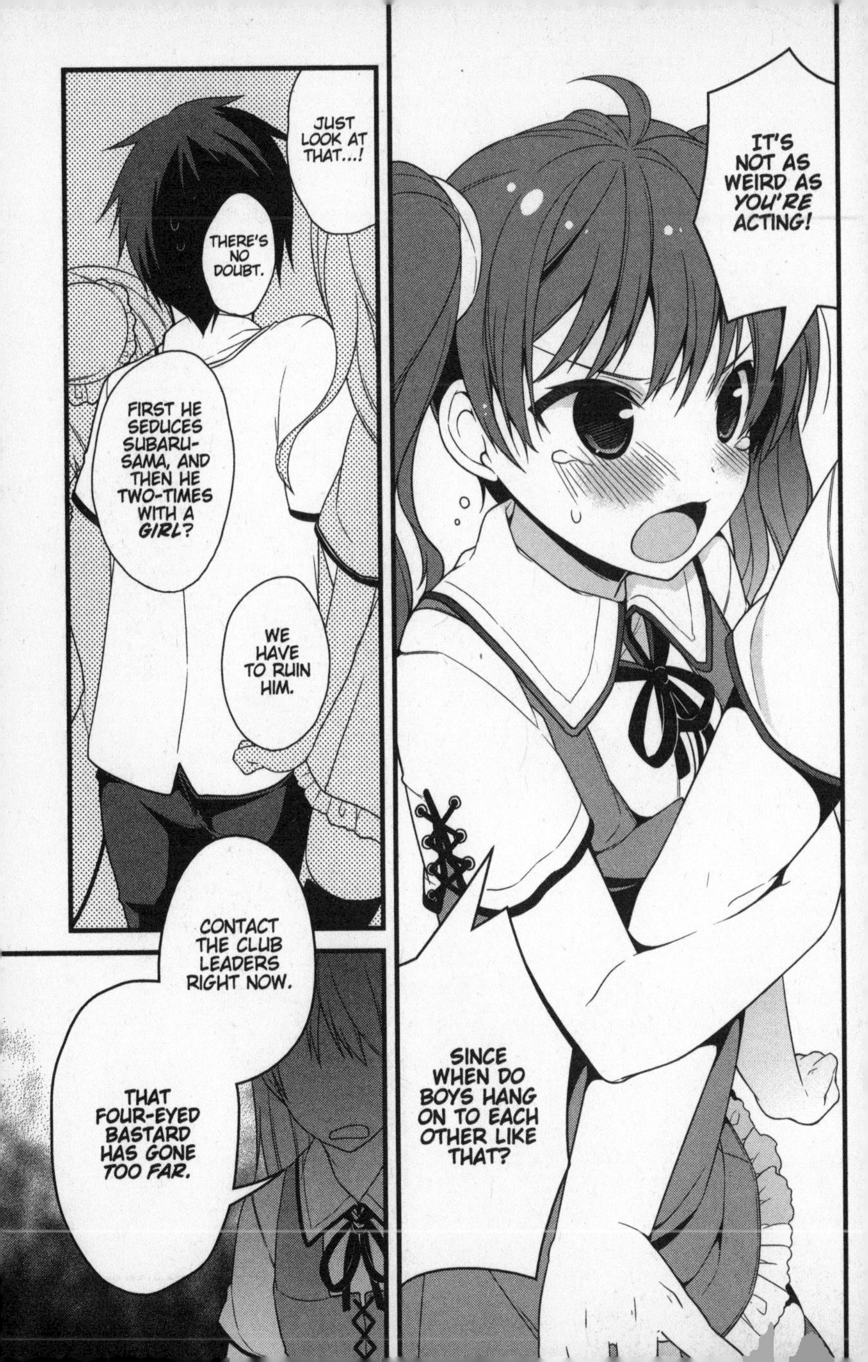
IT'S NOT AS WEIRD AS *YOU'RE* ACTING!
SINCE WHEN DO BOYS HANG ON TO EACH OTHER LIKE THAT?
JUST LOOK AT THAT...!
THERE'S NO DOUBT.
FIRST HE SEDUCES SUBARU-SAMA, AND THEN HE TWO-TIMES WITH A *GIRL*?
WE HAVE TO RUIN HIM.
CONTACT THE CLUB LEADERS RIGHT NOW.
THAT FOUR-EYED BASTARD HAS GONE *TOO FAR*.

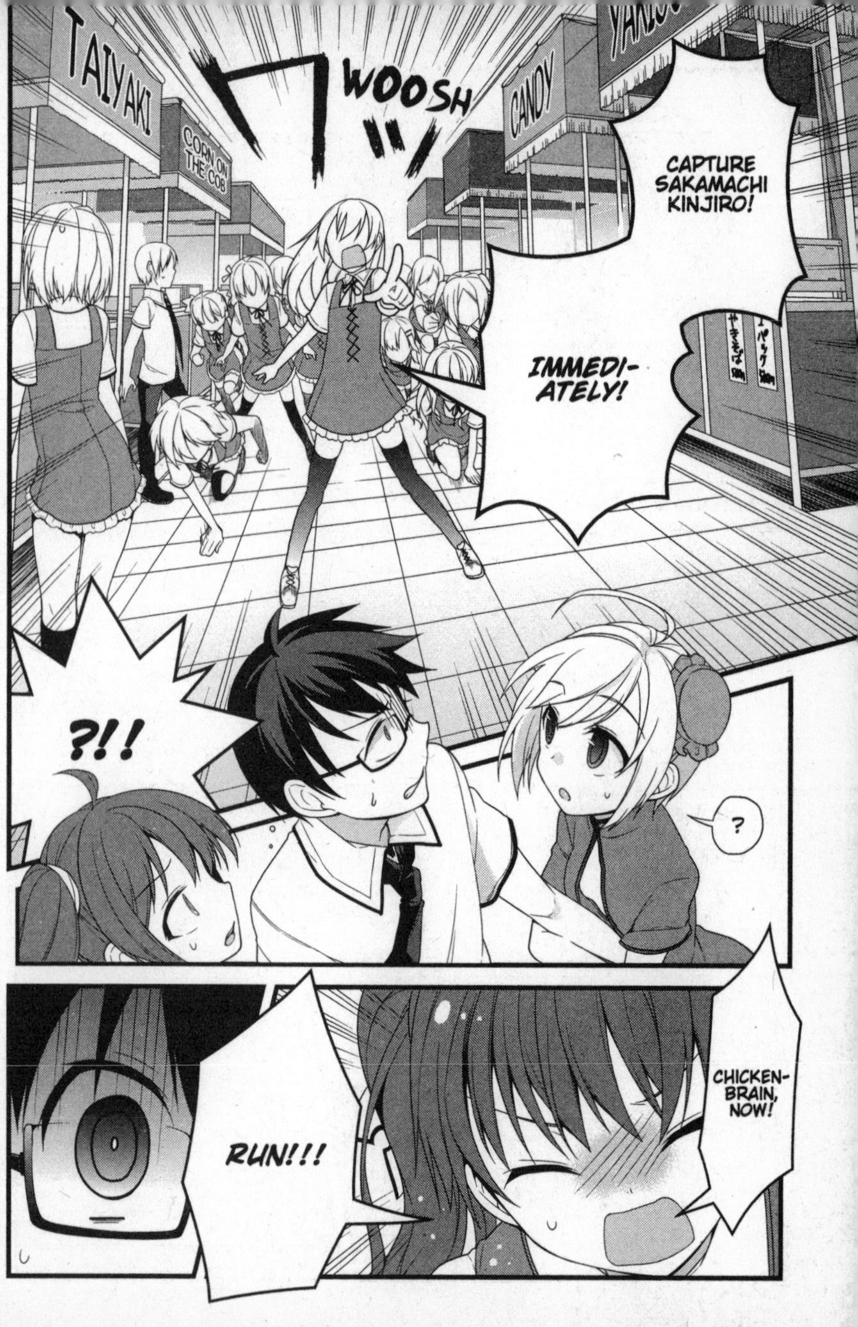
CANDY
CAPTURE SAKAMACHI KINJIRO!
WOOSH
TAIYAKI
CORN ON THE COB
IMMEDI-ATELY!
?
?!!
CHICKEN-BRAIN, NOW!
RUN!!!

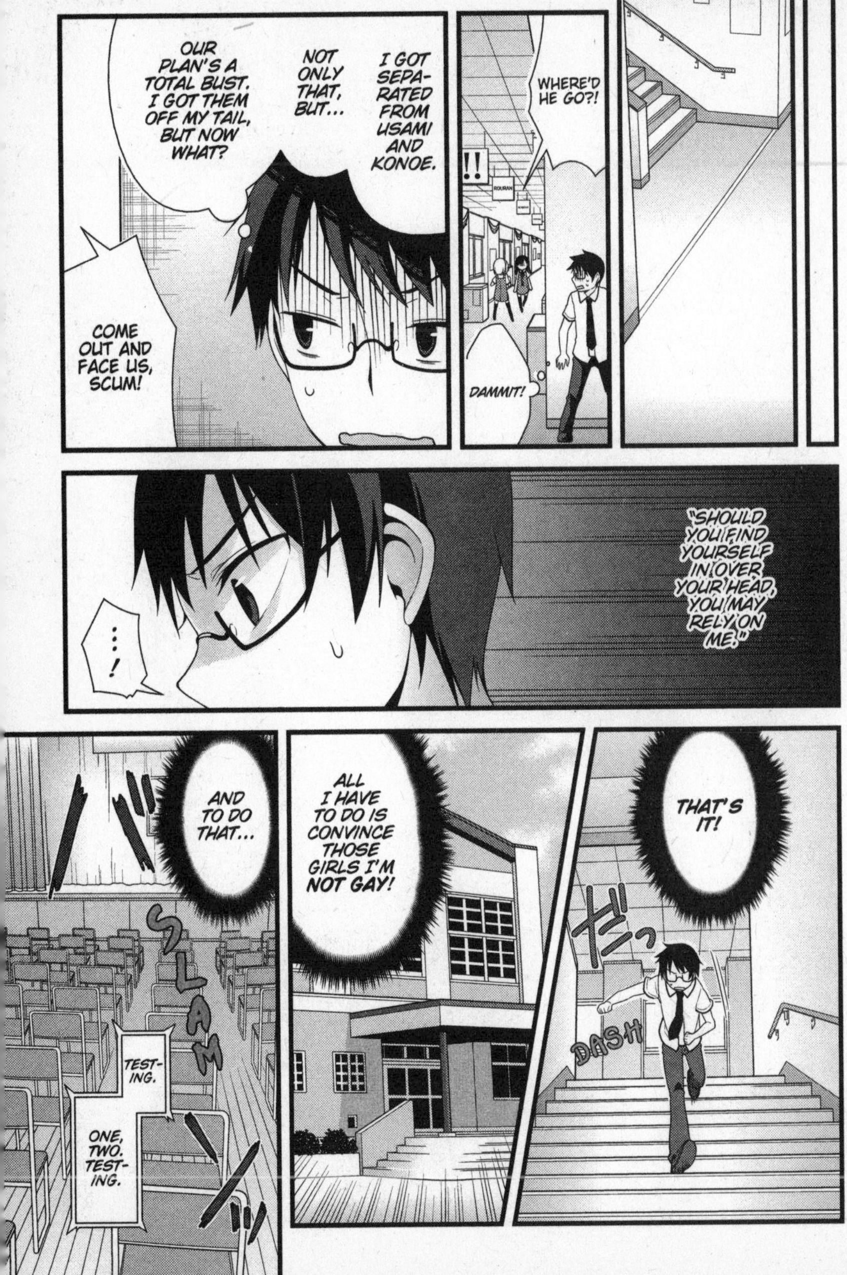
WHERE'D HE GO?!
!!
ROURAN
DAMMIT!
OUR PLAN'S A TOTAL BUST. I GOT THEM OFF MY TAIL, BUT NOW WHAT?
NOT ONLY THAT, BUT…
I GOT SEPARATED FROM USAMI AND KONOE.
COME OUT AND FACE US, SCUM!
"SHOULD YOU FIND YOURSELF IN OVER YOUR HEAD, YOU MAY RELY ON ME."
…!
THAT'S IT!
DASH
ALL I HAVE TO DO IS CONVINCE THOSE GIRLS I'M NOT GAY!
AND TO DO THAT…
SLAM
TESTING.
ONE, TWO. TESTING.

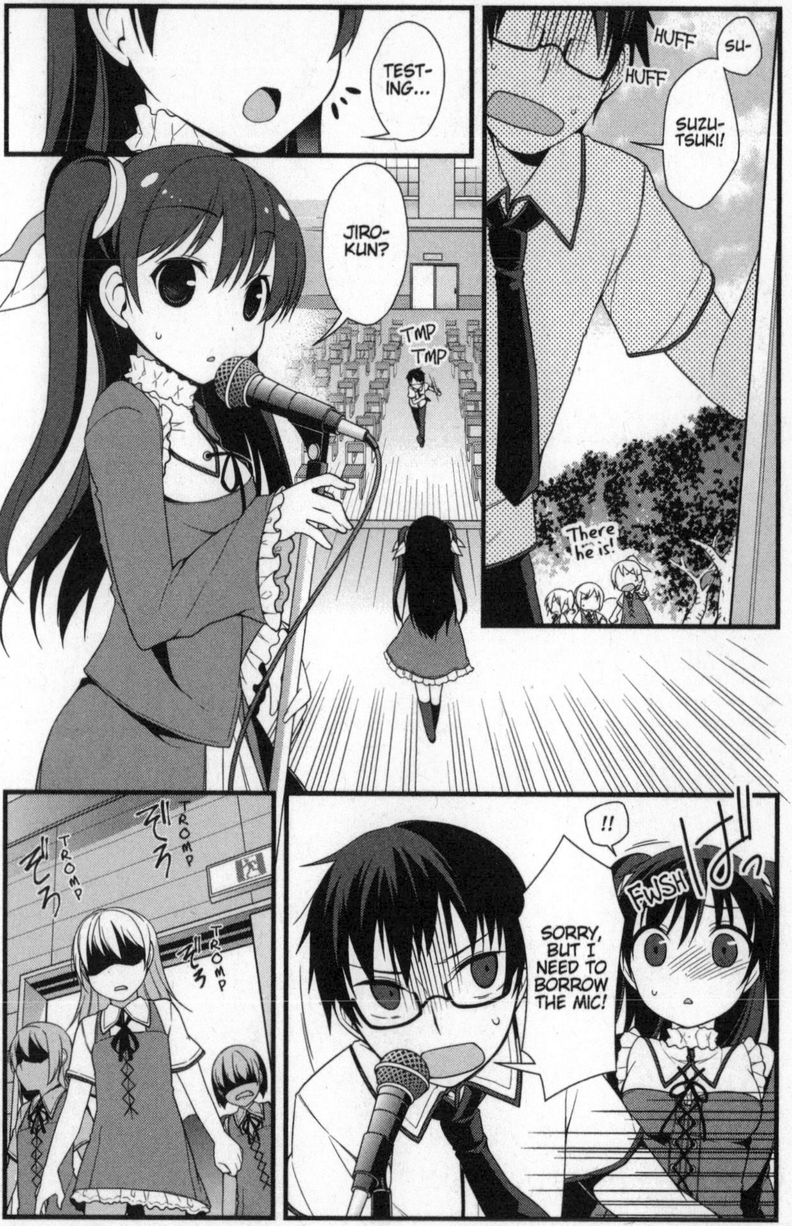

SU-
HUFF
HUFF
SUZU-TSUKI!
There he is!
TEST-ING...
JIRO-KUN?
TMP TMP
!!
FWSH
SORRY, BUT I NEED TO BORROW THE MIC!
TROMP
TROMP
TROMP

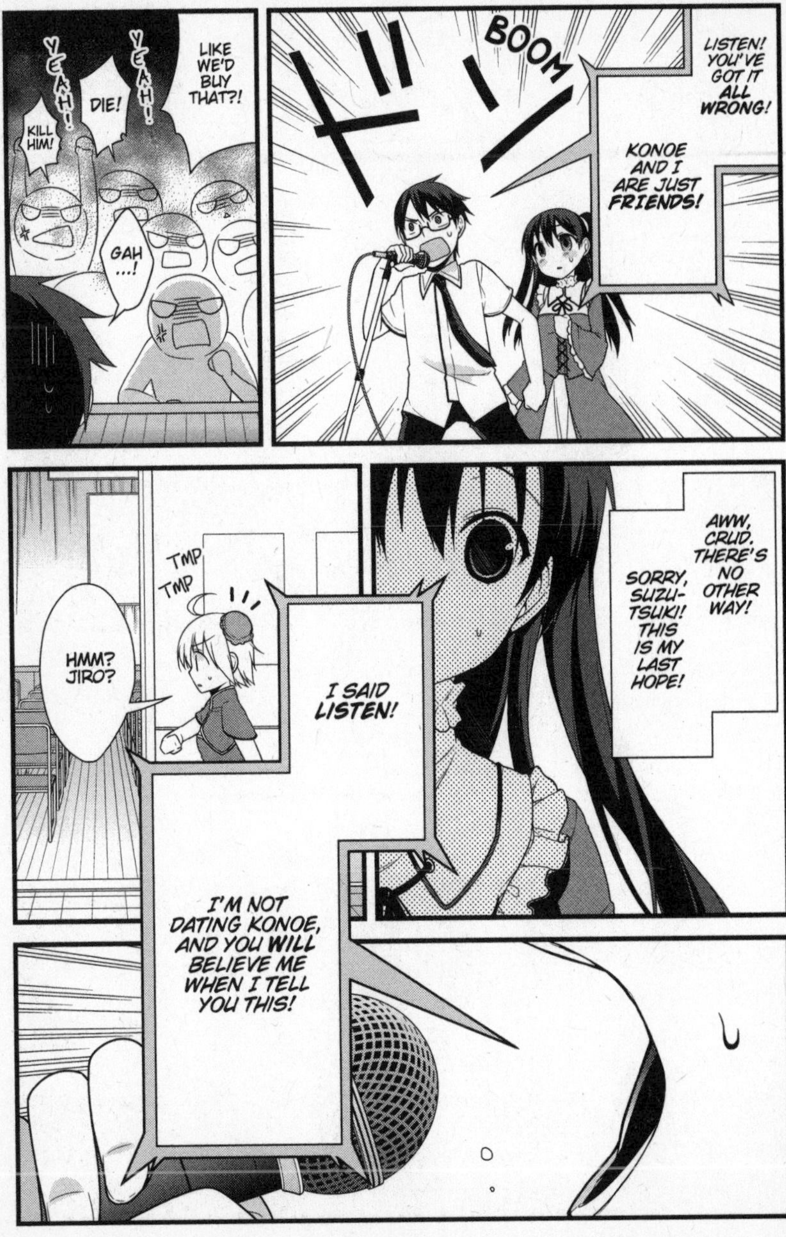
BOOM
LISTEN! YOU'VE GOT IT ALL WRONG!
KONOE AND I ARE JUST FRIENDS!
LIKE WE'D BUY THAT?!
YEAH!
DIE!
YEAH!
KILL HIM!
GAH ...!
AWW, CRUD. THERE'S NO OTHER WAY!
SORRY, SUZUTSUKI! THIS IS MY LAST HOPE!
I SAID LISTEN!
TMP TMP
HMM? JIRO?
I'M NOT DATING KONOE, AND YOU WILL BELIEVE ME WHEN I TELL YOU THIS!

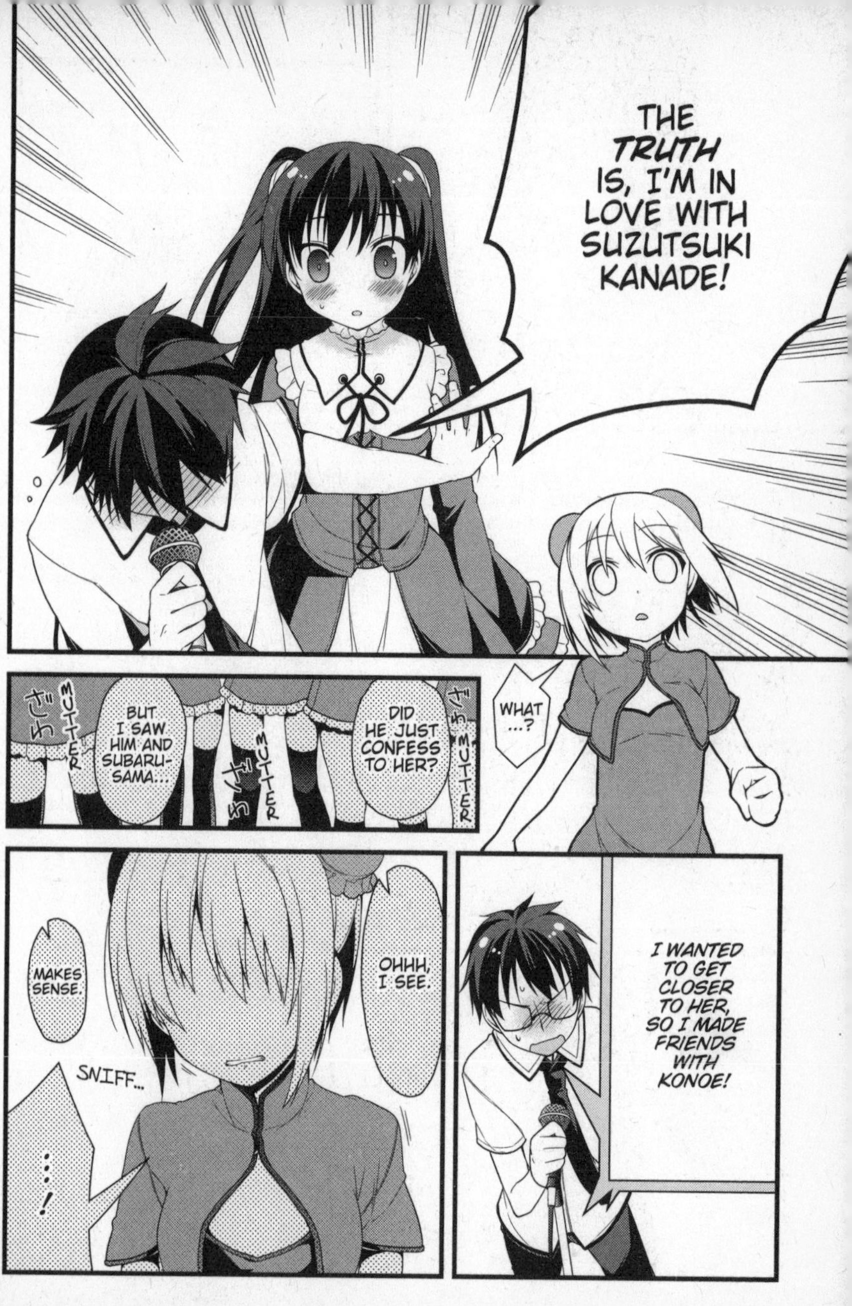
THE *TRUTH* IS, I'M IN LOVE WITH SUZUTSUKI KANADE!
WHAT ...?
ざわ MUTTER
DID HE JUST CONFESS TO HER?
ざわ MUTTER
BUT I SAW HIM AND SUBARU-SAMA...
ざわ MUTTER
I WANTED TO GET CLOSER TO HER, SO I MADE FRIENDS WITH KONOE!
OHHH, I SEE.
MAKES SENSE.
SNIFF...
...!

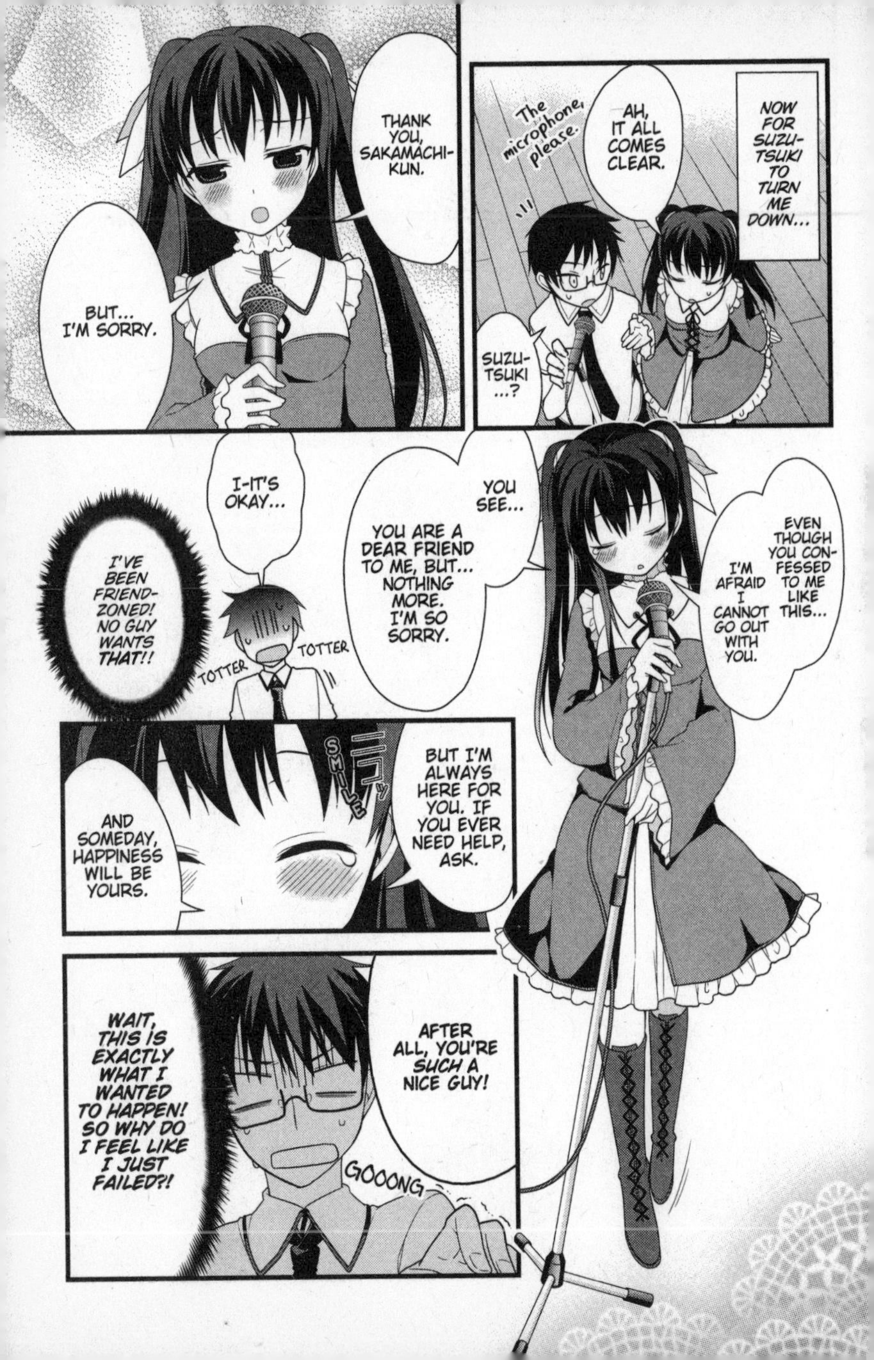
NOW FOR SUZUTSUKI TO TURN ME DOWN...
AH, IT ALL COMES CLEAR.
The microphone, please.
SUZUTSUKI ...?
THANK YOU, SAKAMACHI-KUN.
BUT... I'M SORRY.
EVEN THOUGH YOU CONFESSED TO ME LIKE THIS...
I'M AFRAID I CANNOT GO OUT WITH YOU.
YOU SEE...
YOU ARE A DEAR FRIEND TO ME, BUT... NOTHING MORE. I'M SO SORRY.
I-IT'S OKAY...
I'VE BEEN FRIEND-ZONED! NO GUY WANTS THAT!!
TOTTER
TOTTER
SMILE
BUT I'M ALWAYS HERE FOR YOU. IF YOU EVER NEED HELP, ASK.
AND SOMEDAY, HAPPINESS WILL BE YOURS.
AFTER ALL, YOU'RE SUCH A NICE GUY!
WAIT, THIS IS EXACTLY WHAT I WANTED TO HAPPEN! SO WHY DO I FEEL LIKE I JUST FAILED?!
GOOONG

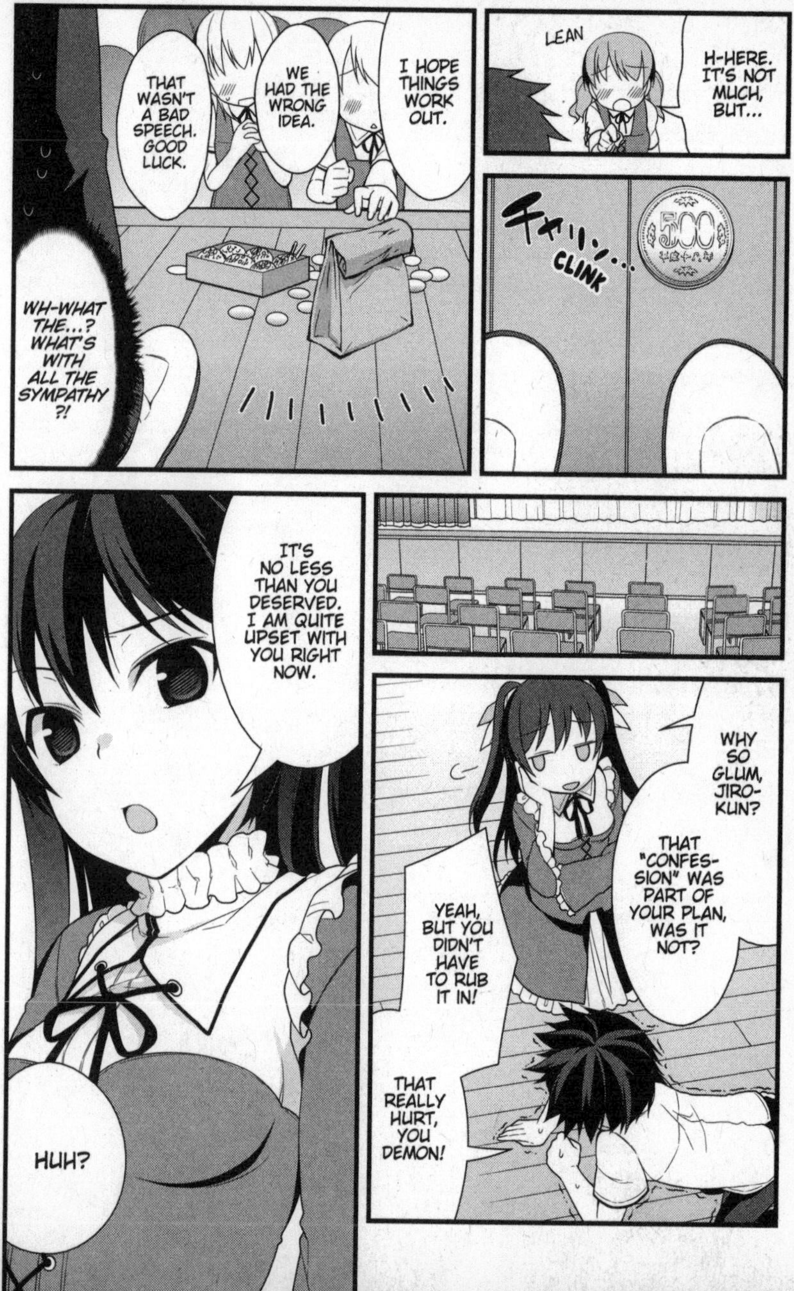
LEAN
H-HERE. IT'S NOT MUCH, BUT...
500
CLINK
I HOPE THINGS WORK OUT.
WE HAD THE WRONG IDEA.
THAT WASN'T A BAD SPEECH. GOOD LUCK.
WH-WHAT THE...? WHAT'S WITH ALL THE SYMPATHY?!
WHY SO GLUM, JIRO-KUN?
THAT "CONFESSION" WAS PART OF YOUR PLAN, WAS IT NOT?
YEAH, BUT YOU DIDN'T HAVE TO RUB IT IN!
THAT REALLY HURT, YOU DEMON!
IT'S NO LESS THAN YOU DESERVED. I AM QUITE UPSET WITH YOU RIGHT NOW.
HUH?

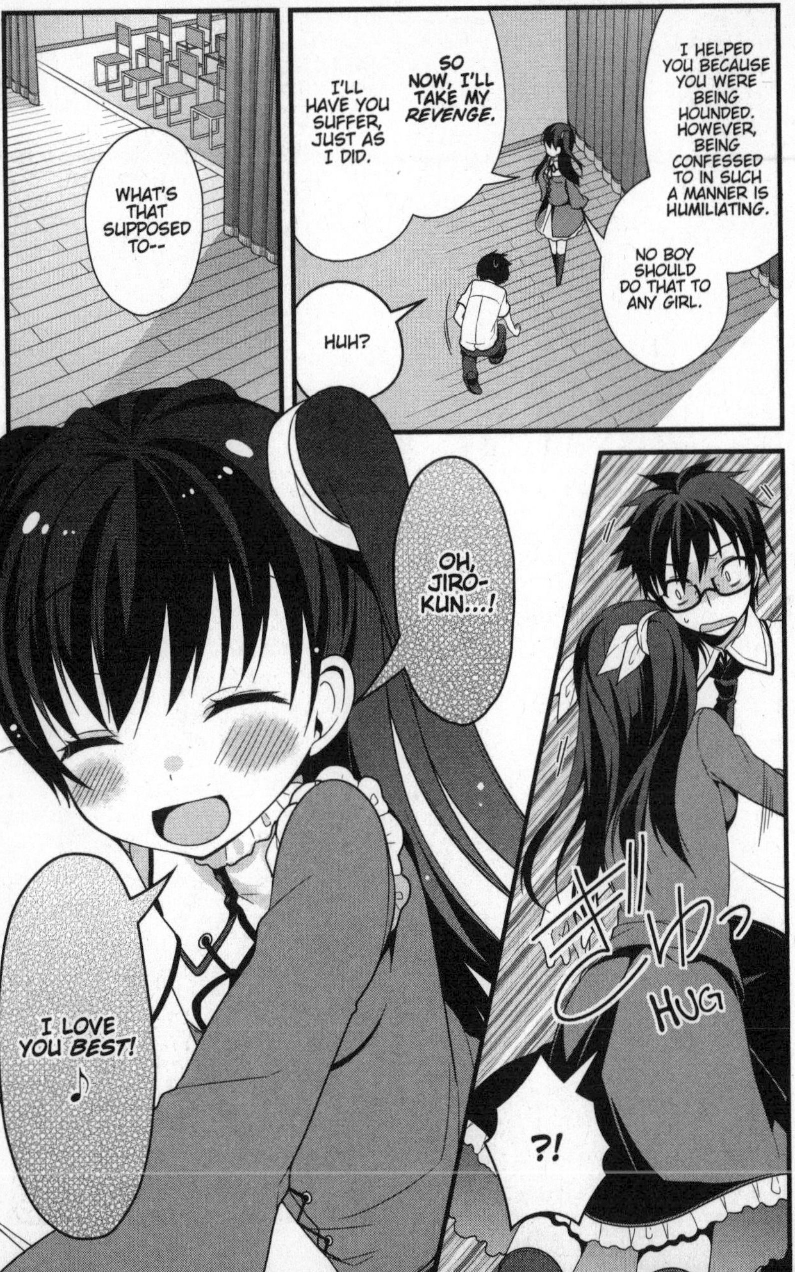
I HELPED YOU BECAUSE YOU WERE BEING HOUNDED. HOWEVER, BEING CONFESSED TO IN SUCH A MANNER IS HUMILIATING.
NO BOY SHOULD DO THAT TO ANY GIRL.
SO NOW, I'LL TAKE MY *REVENGE.*
I'LL HAVE YOU SUFFER, JUST AS I DID.
HUH?
WHAT'S THAT SUPPOSED TO--
ぎゅっ
HUG
?!
OH, JIRO-KUN...!
I LOVE YOU *BEST!* ♪

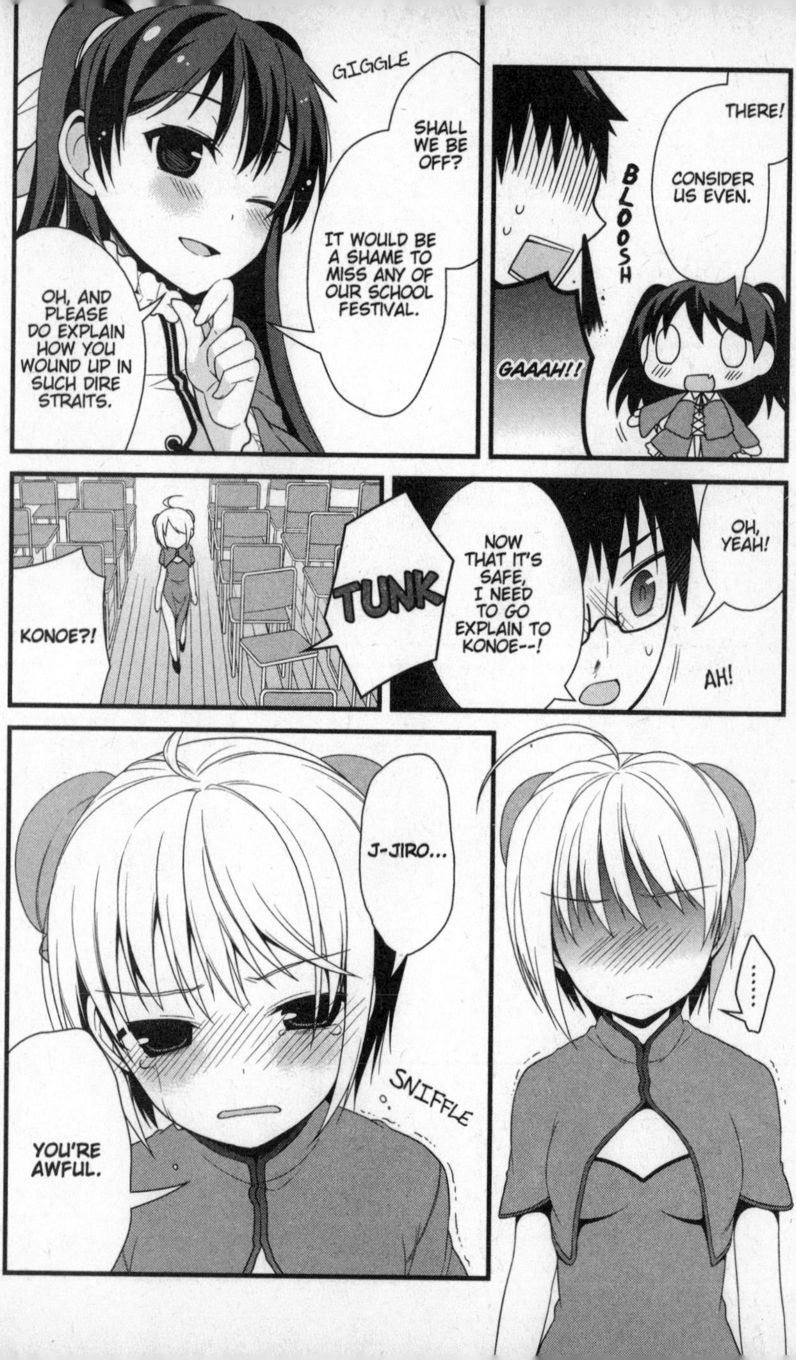
THERE!
CONSIDER US EVEN.
BLOOSH
GAAAH!!
GIGGLE
SHALL WE BE OFF?
IT WOULD BE A SHAME TO MISS ANY OF OUR SCHOOL FESTIVAL.
OH, AND PLEASE DO EXPLAIN HOW YOU WOUND UP IN SUCH DIRE STRAITS.
OH, YEAH!
NOW THAT IT'S SAFE, I NEED TO GO EXPLAIN TO KONOE--!
AH!
TUNK
KONOE?!
......
J-JIRO...
SNIFFLE
YOU'RE AWFUL.

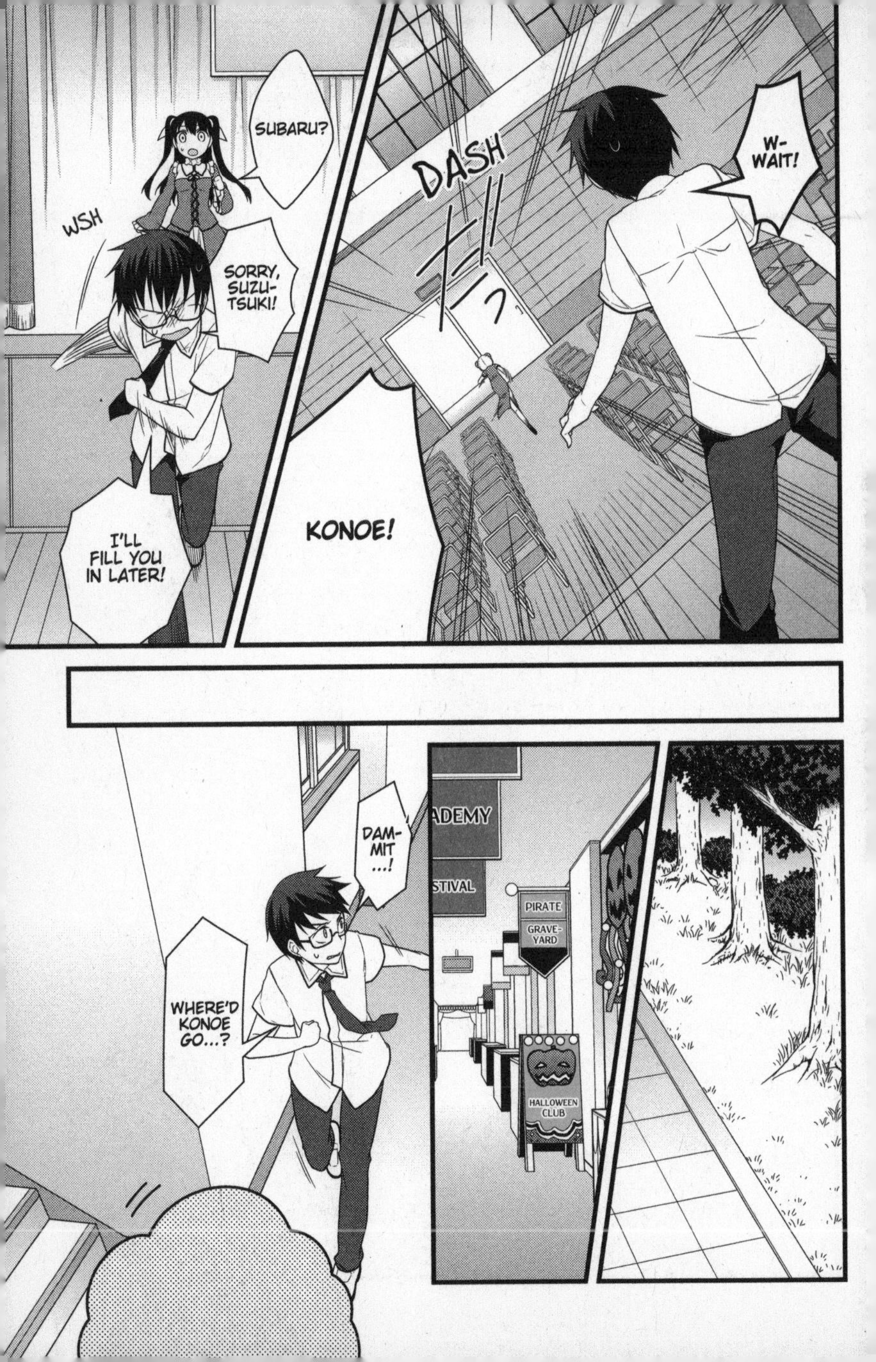
W-WAIT!
DASH
KONOE!
SUBARU?
WSH
SORRY, SUZU-TSUKI!
I'LL FILL YOU IN LATER!
ADEMY
STIVAL
PIRATE
GRAVE-YARD
HALLOWEEN CLUB
DAM-MIT ...!
WHERE'D KONOE GO...?

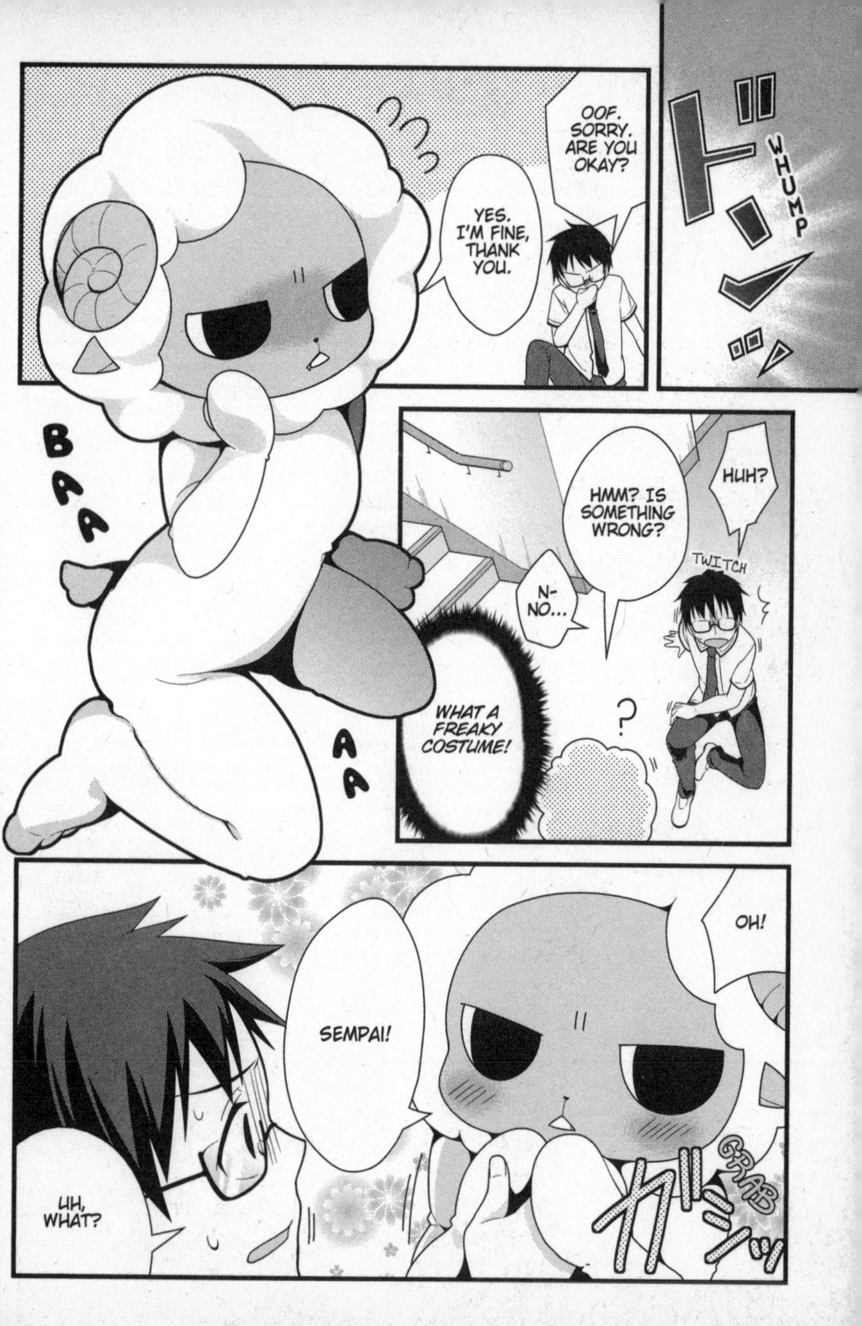
WHUMP
OOF. SORRY. ARE YOU OKAY?
YES. I'M FINE, THANK YOU.
BAAAA
HUH?
TWITCH
HMM? IS SOMETHING WRONG?
N-NO...
WHAT A FREAKY COSTUME!
?
OH!
SEMPAI!
GRAB
UH, WHAT?

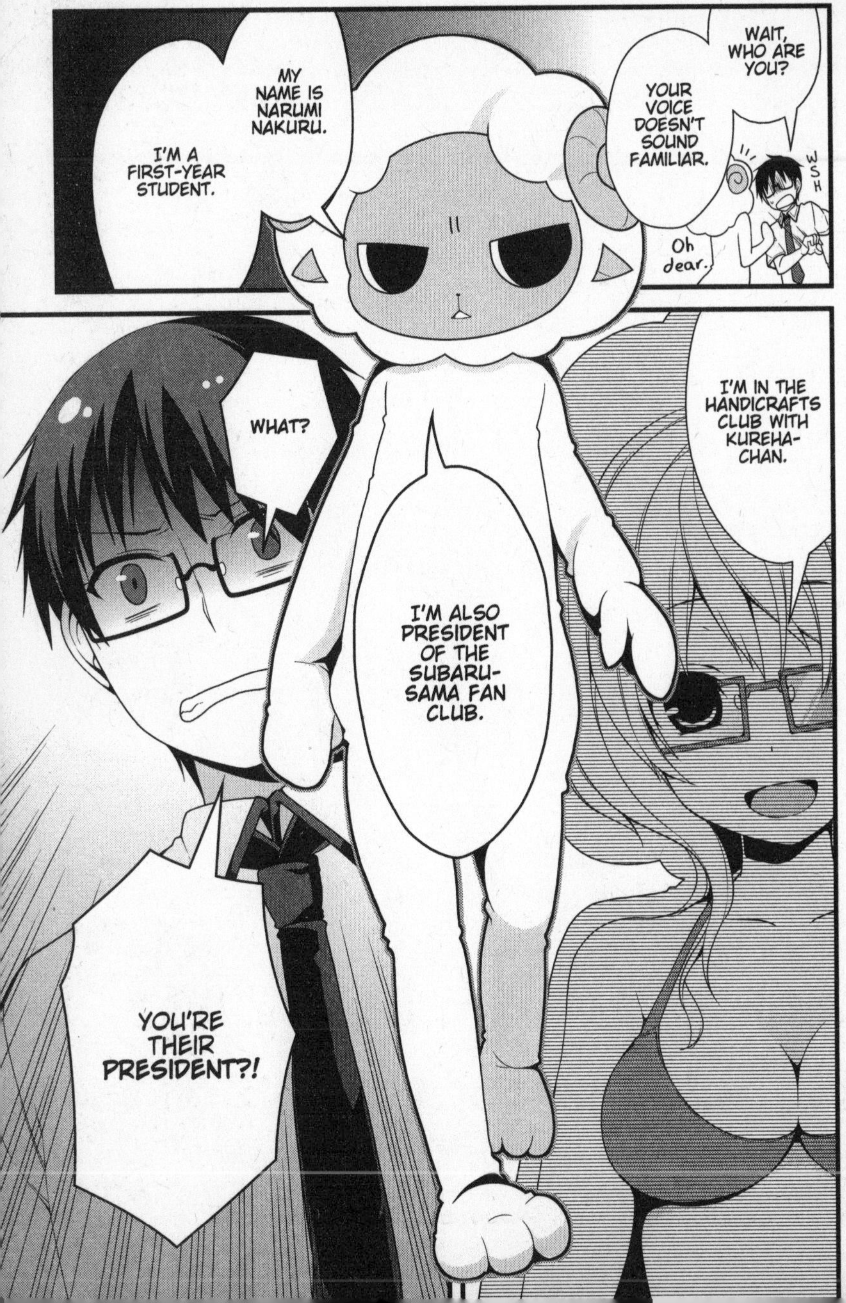
WAIT, WHO ARE YOU?
YOUR VOICE DOESN'T SOUND FAMILIAR.
WSH
Oh dear.
MY NAME IS NARUMI NAKURU.
I'M A FIRST-YEAR STUDENT.
I'M IN THE HANDICRAFTS CLUB WITH KUREHA-CHAN.
I'M ALSO PRESIDENT OF THE SUBARU-SAMA FAN CLUB.
WHAT?
YOU'RE THEIR PRESIDENT?!

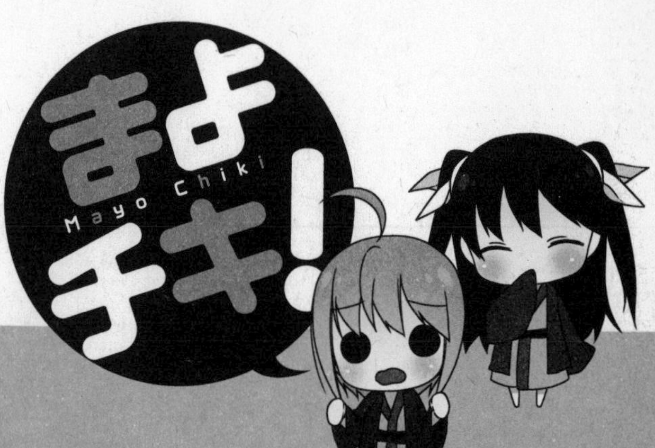
まよチキ!
Mayo Chiki

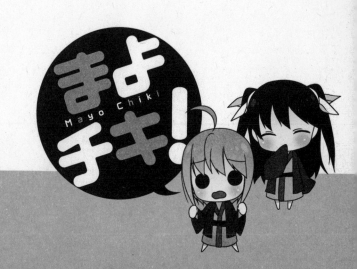

chapter 12 liar, liar

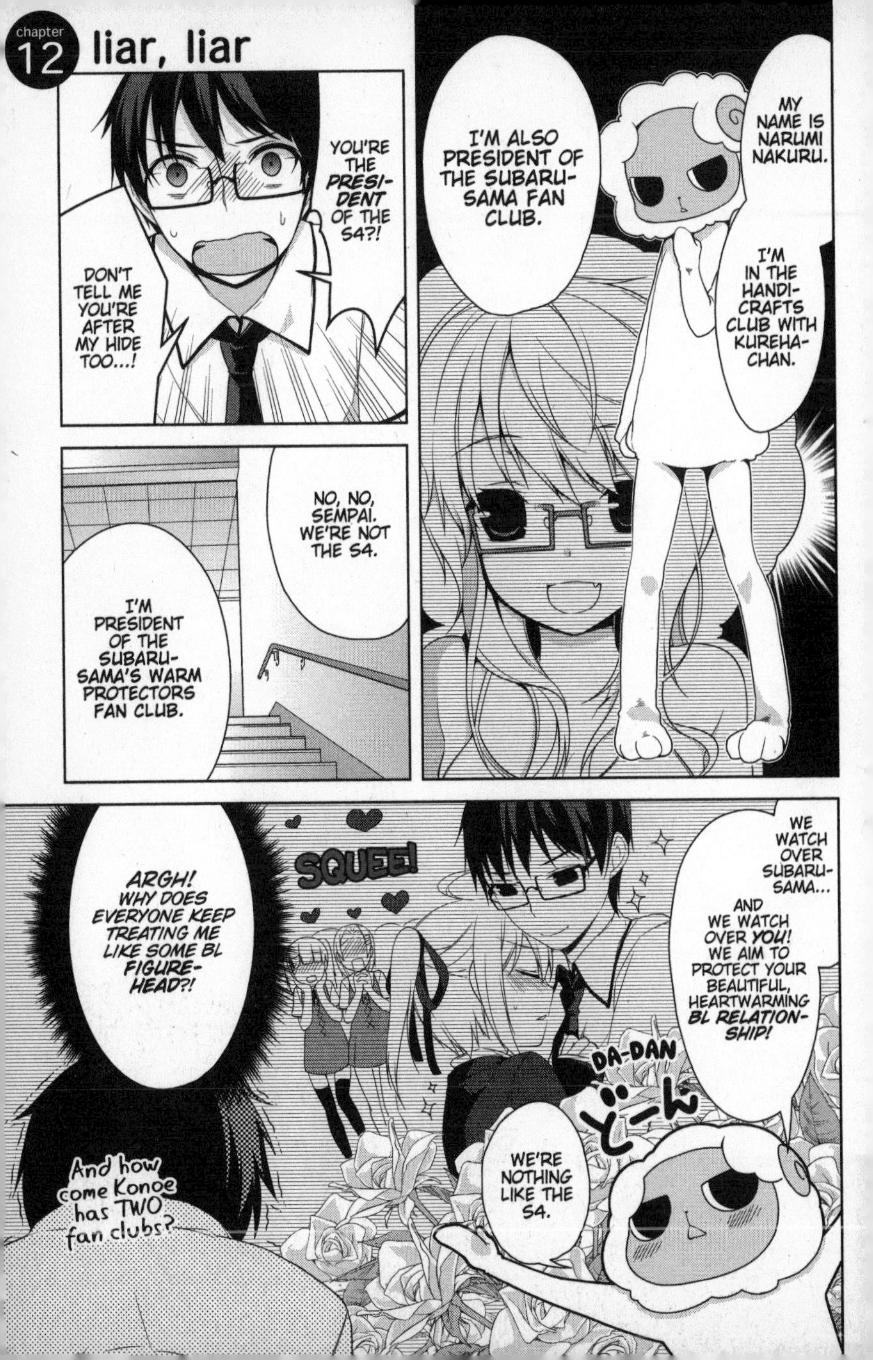
MY NAME IS NARUMI NAKURU.
I'M IN THE HANDICRAFTS CLUB WITH KUREHA-CHAN.
I'M ALSO PRESIDENT OF THE SUBARU-SAMA FAN CLUB.
YOU'RE THE PRESIDENT OF THE S4?!
DON'T TELL ME YOU'RE AFTER MY HIDE TOO...!
NO, NO, SEMPAI. WE'RE NOT THE S4.
I'M PRESIDENT OF THE SUBARU-SAMA'S WARM PROTECTORS FAN CLUB.
WE WATCH OVER SUBARU-SAMA... AND WE WATCH OVER YOU! WE AIM TO PROTECT YOUR BEAUTIFUL, HEARTWARMING BL RELATIONSHIP!
DA-DAN
どーん
WE'RE NOTHING LIKE THE S4.
SQUEE!
ARGH! WHY DOES EVERYONE KEEP TREATING ME LIKE SOME BL FIGUREHEAD?!
And how come Konoe has TWO fan clubs?

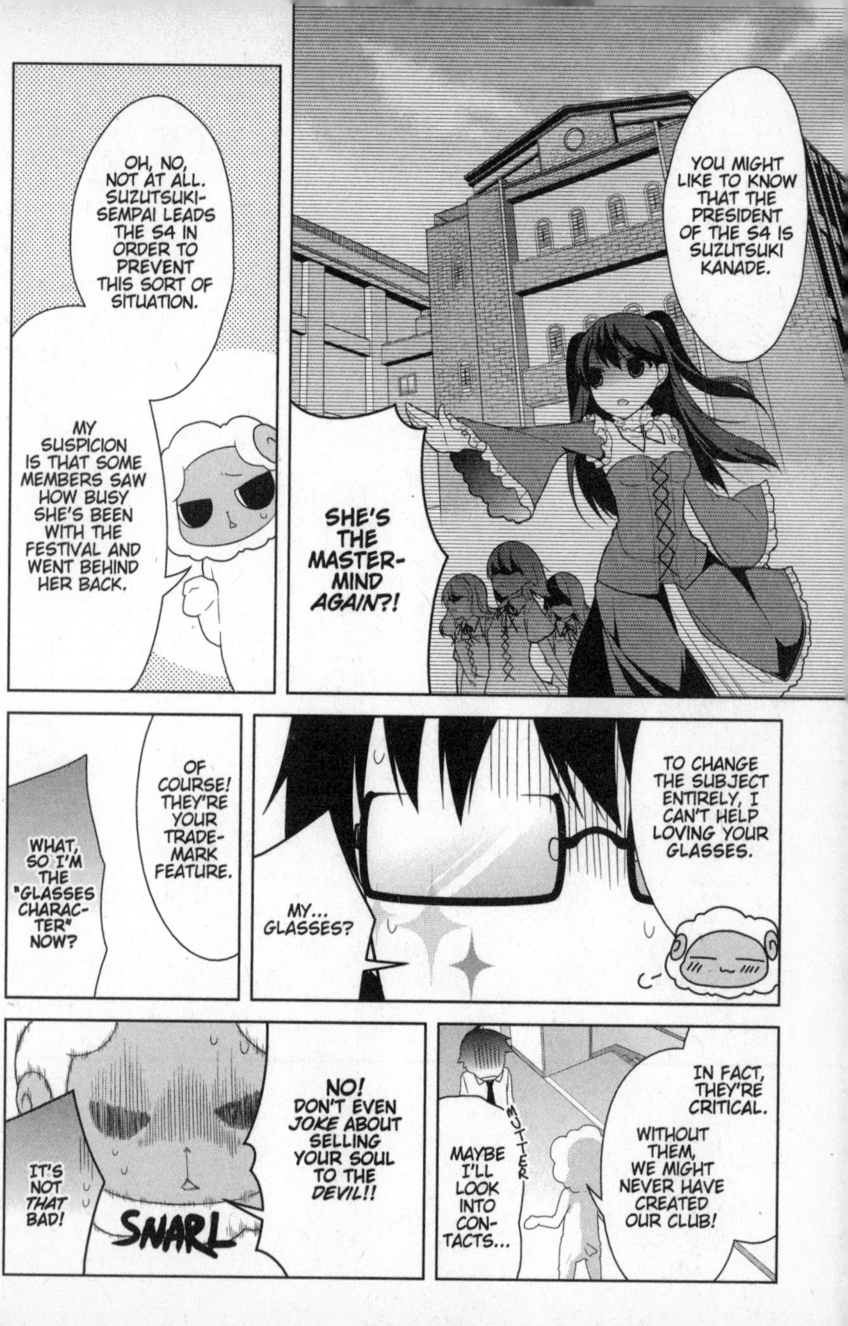
YOU MIGHT LIKE TO KNOW THAT THE PRESIDENT OF THE S4 IS SUZUTSUKI KANADE.
SHE'S THE MASTER-MIND *AGAIN*?!
OH, NO, NOT AT ALL. SUZUTSUKI-SEMPAI LEADS THE S4 IN ORDER TO PREVENT THIS SORT OF SITUATION.
MY SUSPICION IS THAT SOME MEMBERS SAW HOW BUSY SHE'S BEEN WITH THE FESTIVAL AND WENT BEHIND HER BACK.
TO CHANGE THE SUBJECT ENTIRELY, I CAN'T HELP LOVING YOUR GLASSES.
MY... GLASSES?
OF COURSE! THEY'RE YOUR TRADE-MARK FEATURE.
WHAT, SO I'M THE "GLASSES CHARAC-TER" NOW?
IN FACT, THEY'RE CRITICAL.
WITHOUT THEM, WE MIGHT NEVER HAVE CREATED OUR CLUB!
MUTTER
MAYBE I'LL LOOK INTO CON-TACTS...
NO! DON'T EVEN *JOKE* ABOUT SELLING YOUR SOUL TO THE *DEVIL*!!
SNARL
IT'S NOT *THAT* BAD!

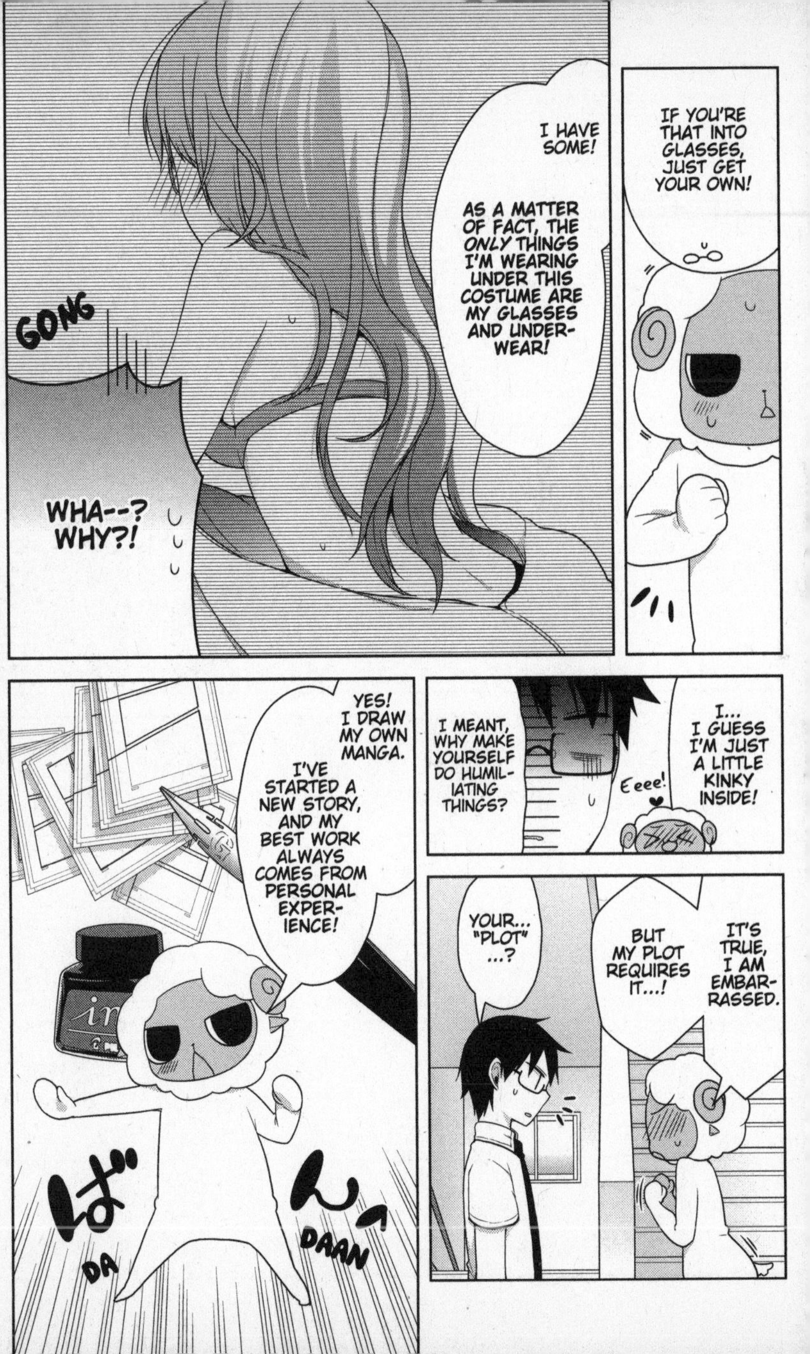
IF YOU'RE THAT INTO GLASSES, JUST GET YOUR OWN!
I HAVE SOME!
AS A MATTER OF FACT, THE *ONLY* THINGS I'M WEARING UNDER THIS COSTUME ARE MY GLASSES AND UNDER-WEAR!
GONG
WHA--? WHY?!
I... I GUESS I'M JUST A LITTLE KINKY INSIDE!
Eeee!
I MEANT, WHY MAKE YOURSELF DO HUMIL-IATING THINGS?
IT'S TRUE, I AM EMBAR-RASSED.
BUT MY PLOT REQUIRES IT...!
YOUR... "PLOT" ...?
YES! I DRAW MY OWN MANGA.
I'VE STARTED A NEW STORY, AND MY BEST WORK ALWAYS COMES FROM PERSONAL EXPER-IENCE!
ばん
DA DAAN

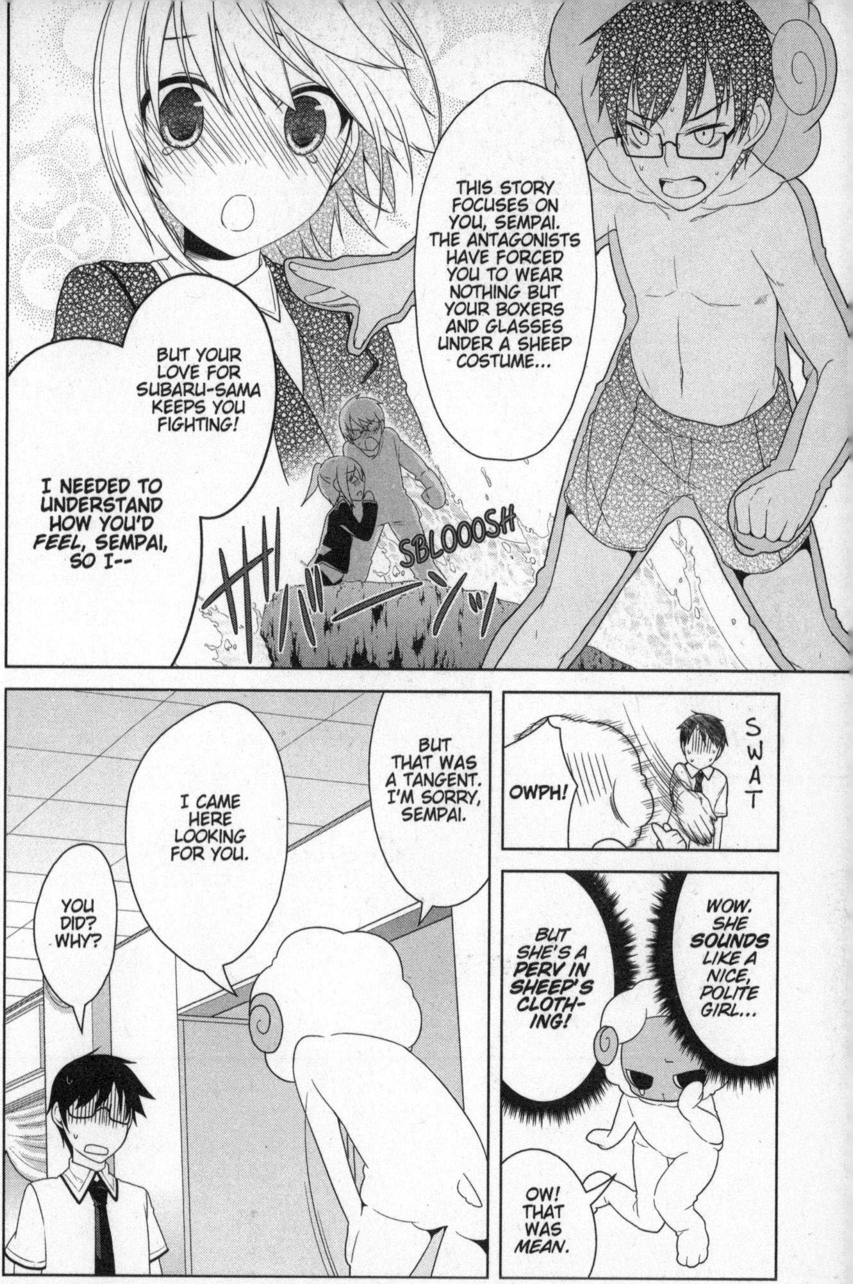
THIS STORY FOCUSES ON YOU, SEMPAI. THE ANTAGONISTS HAVE FORCED YOU TO WEAR NOTHING BUT YOUR BOXERS AND GLASSES UNDER A SHEEP COSTUME...
BUT YOUR LOVE FOR SUBARU-SAMA KEEPS YOU FIGHTING!
SBLOOOSH
I NEEDED TO UNDERSTAND HOW YOU'D *FEEL*, SEMPAI, SO I--
SWAT
OWPH!
WOW. SHE **SOUNDS** LIKE A NICE, POLITE GIRL...
BUT SHE'S A **PERV IN SHEEP'S CLOTHING!**
OW! THAT WAS MEAN.
BUT THAT WAS A TANGENT. I'M SORRY, SEMPAI.
I CAME HERE LOOKING FOR YOU.
YOU DID? WHY?

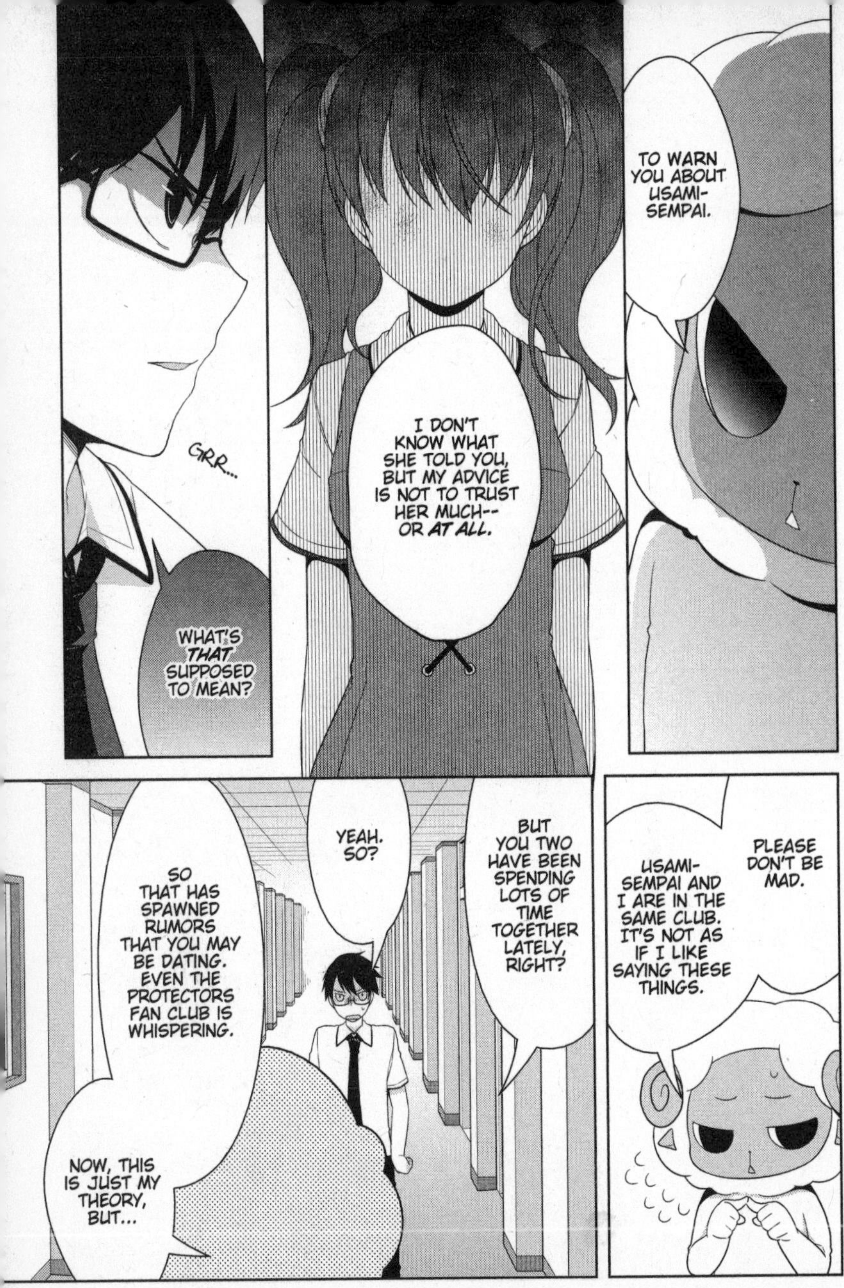
TO WARN YOU ABOUT USAMI-SEMPAI.
I DON'T KNOW WHAT SHE TOLD YOU, BUT MY ADVICE IS NOT TO TRUST HER MUCH-- OR AT ALL.
GRR...
WHAT'S THAT SUPPOSED TO MEAN?
PLEASE DON'T BE MAD.
USAMI-SEMPAI AND I ARE IN THE SAME CLUB. IT'S NOT AS IF I LIKE SAYING THESE THINGS.
BUT YOU TWO HAVE BEEN SPENDING LOTS OF TIME TOGETHER LATELY, RIGHT?
YEAH. SO?
SO THAT HAS SPAWNED RUMORS THAT YOU MAY BE DATING. EVEN THE PROTECTORS FAN CLUB IS WHISPERING.
NOW, THIS IS JUST MY THEORY, BUT...

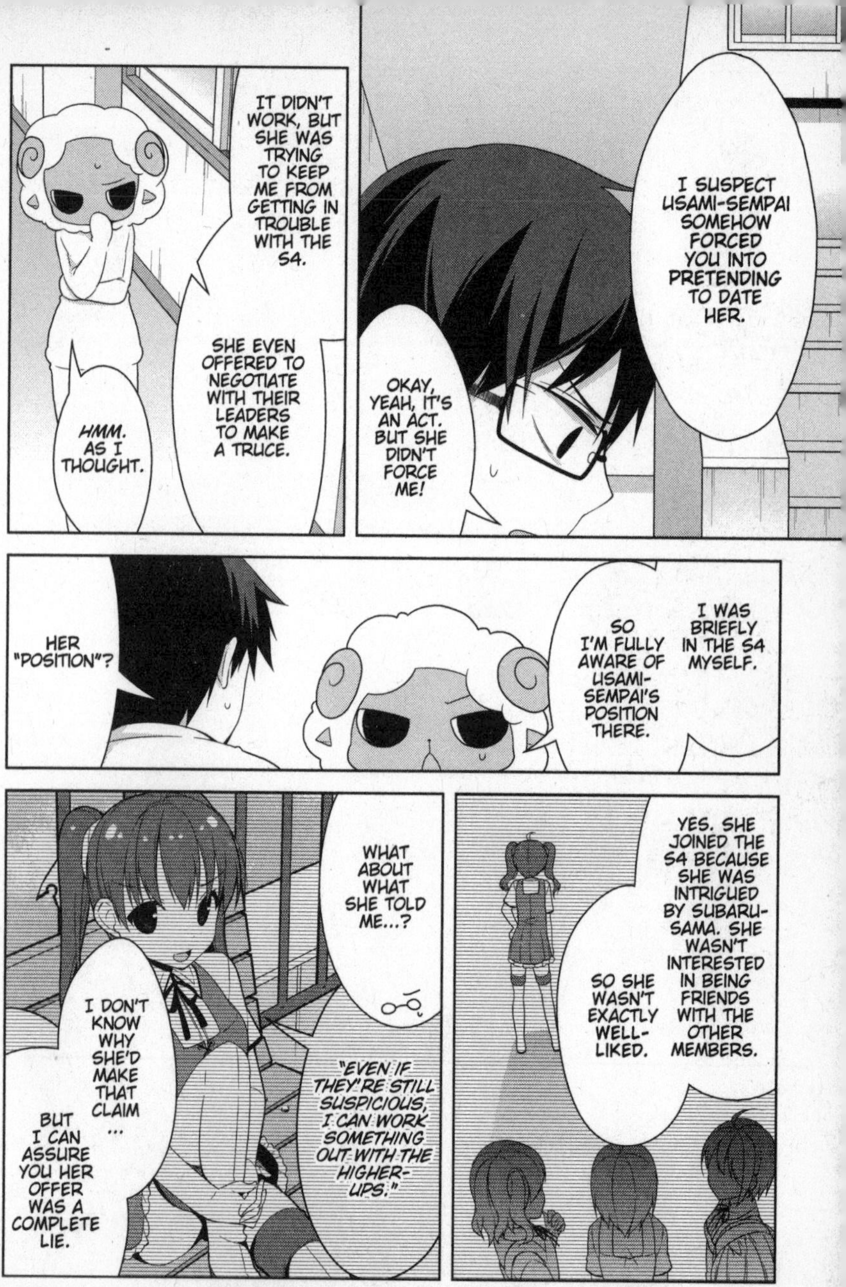
I SUSPECT USAMI-SEMPAI SOMEHOW FORCED YOU INTO PRETENDING TO DATE HER.
OKAY, YEAH, IT'S AN ACT. BUT SHE DIDN'T FORCE ME!
IT DIDN'T WORK, BUT SHE WAS TRYING TO KEEP ME FROM GETTING IN TROUBLE WITH THE S4.
SHE EVEN OFFERED TO NEGOTIATE WITH THEIR LEADERS TO MAKE A TRUCE.
HMM. AS I THOUGHT.
I WAS BRIEFLY IN THE S4 MYSELF.
SO I'M FULLY AWARE OF USAMI-SEMPAI'S POSITION THERE.
HER "POSITION"?
YES. SHE JOINED THE S4 BECAUSE SHE WAS INTRIGUED BY SUBARU-SAMA. SHE WASN'T INTERESTED IN BEING FRIENDS WITH THE OTHER MEMBERS.
SO SHE WASN'T EXACTLY WELL-LIKED.
WHAT ABOUT WHAT SHE TOLD ME...?
"EVEN IF THEY'RE STILL SUSPICIOUS, I CAN WORK SOMETHING OUT WITH THE HIGHER-UPS."
I DON'T KNOW WHY SHE'D MAKE THAT CLAIM... BUT I CAN ASSURE YOU HER OFFER WAS A COMPLETE LIE.

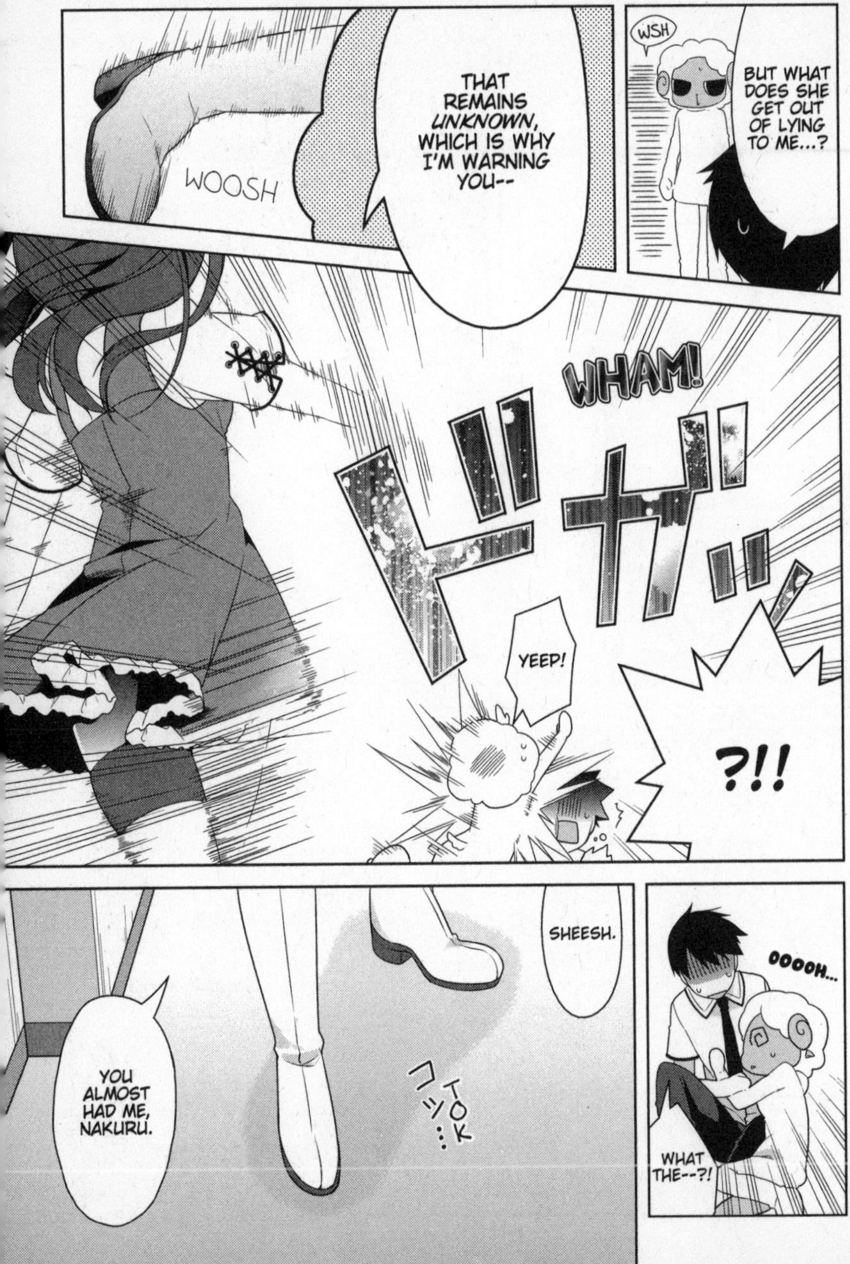
WSH
BUT WHAT DOES SHE GET OUT OF LYING TO ME...?
THAT REMAINS *UNKNOWN*, WHICH IS WHY I'M WARNING YOU--
WOOSH
WHAM!
ドガッ
YEEP!
?!!
OOOOH...
WHAT THE--?!
SHEESH.
YOU ALMOST HAD ME, NAKURU.
TOK
コツ…

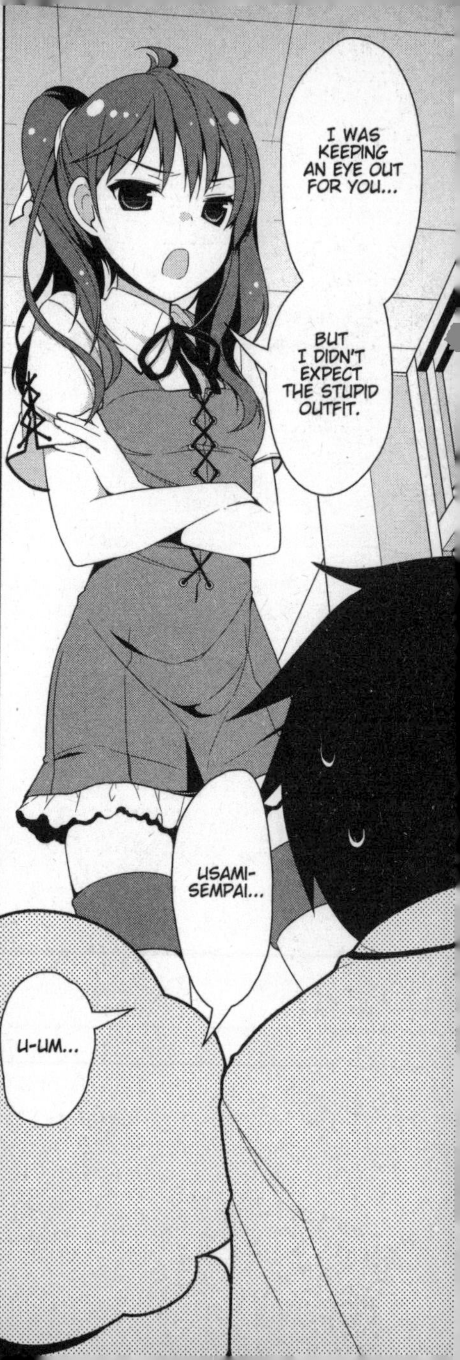
I WAS KEEPING AN EYE OUT FOR YOU...
BUT I DIDN'T EXPECT THE STUPID OUTFIT.
USAMI-SEMPAI...
U-UM...
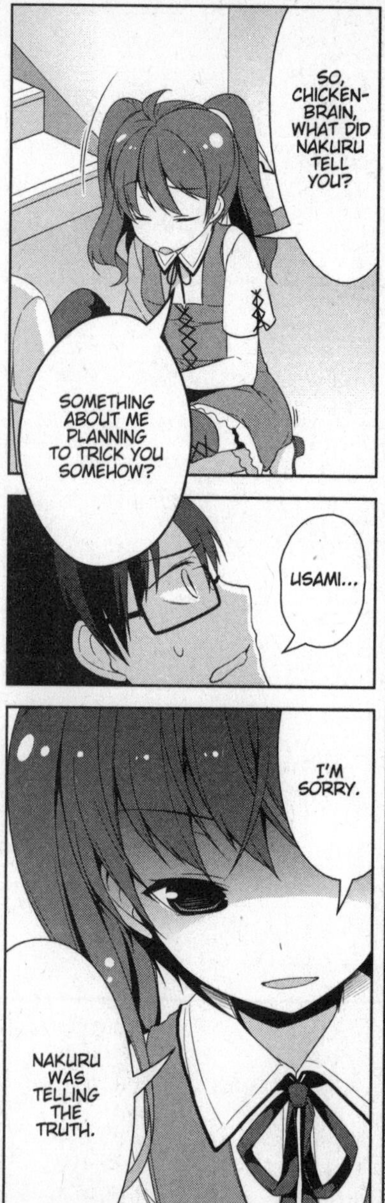
SO, CHICKEN-BRAIN, WHAT DID NAKURU TELL YOU?
SOMETHING ABOUT ME PLANNING TO TRICK YOU SOMEHOW?
USAMI...
I'M SORRY.
NAKURU WAS TELLING THE TRUTH.

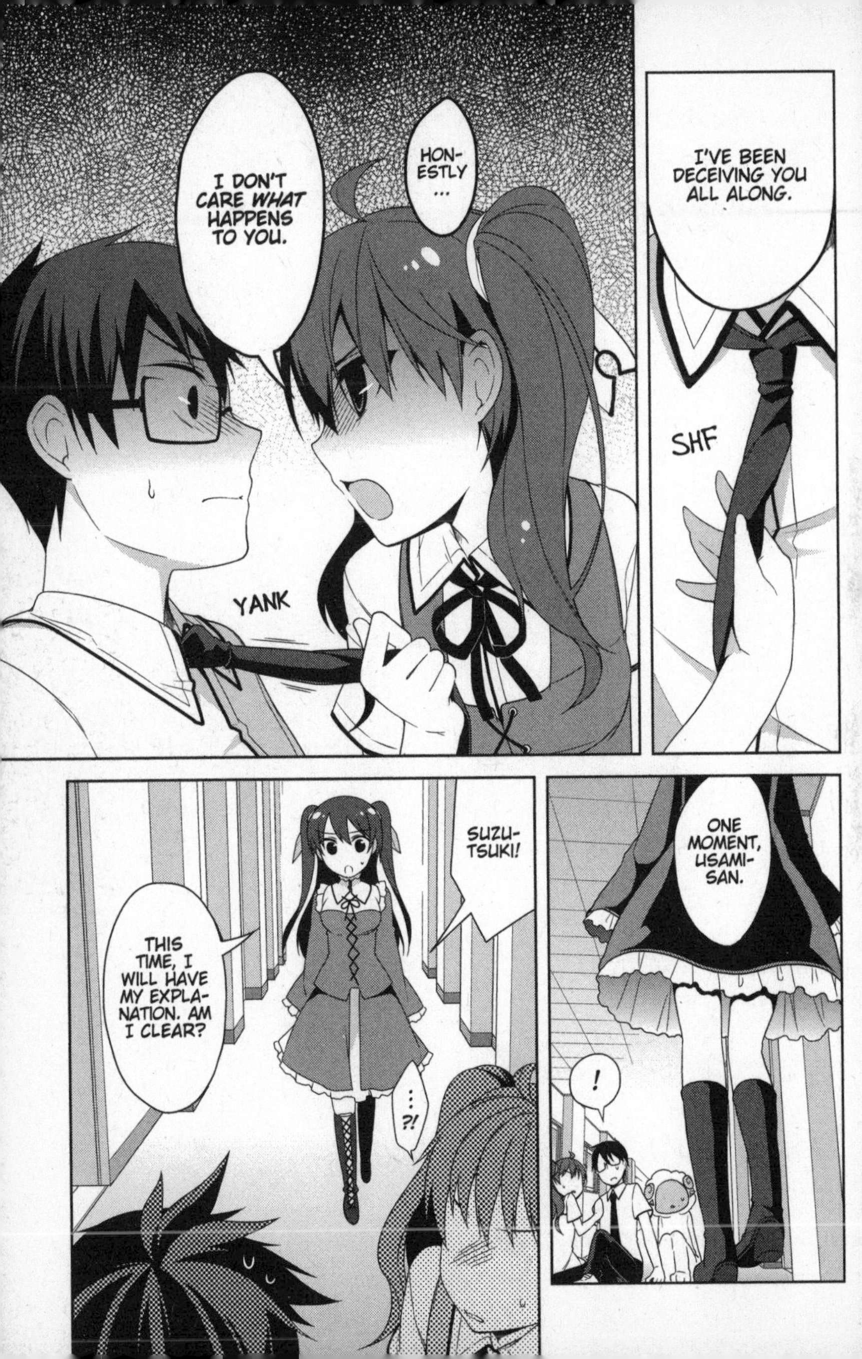
I'VE BEEN DECEIVING YOU ALL ALONG.
SHF
HON-ESTLY ...
I DON'T CARE *WHAT* HAPPENS TO YOU.
YANK
ONE MOMENT, USAMI-SAN.
!
SUZU-TSUKI!
THIS TIME, I WILL HAVE MY EXPLA-NATION. AM I CLEAR?
...?!

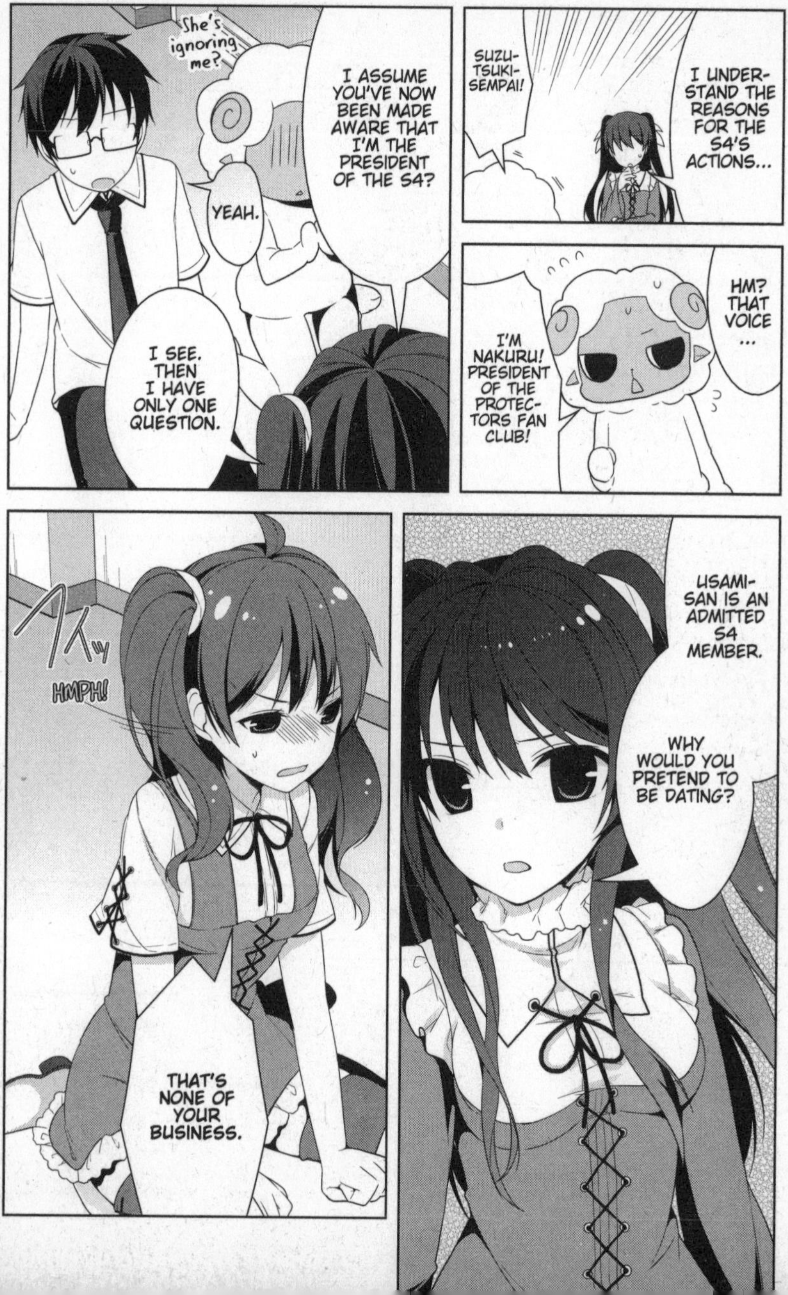
I UNDERSTAND THE REASONS FOR THE S4'S ACTIONS...
SUZUTSUKI-SEMPAI!
HM? THAT VOICE ...
I'M NAKURU! PRESIDENT OF THE PROTECTORS FAN CLUB!
I ASSUME YOU'VE NOW BEEN MADE AWARE THAT I'M THE PRESIDENT OF THE S4?
She's ignoring me?
YEAH.
I SEE. THEN I HAVE ONLY ONE QUESTION.
USAMI-SAN IS AN ADMITTED S4 MEMBER.
WHY WOULD YOU PRETEND TO BE DATING?
フイッ
HMPH!
THAT'S NONE OF YOUR BUSINESS.

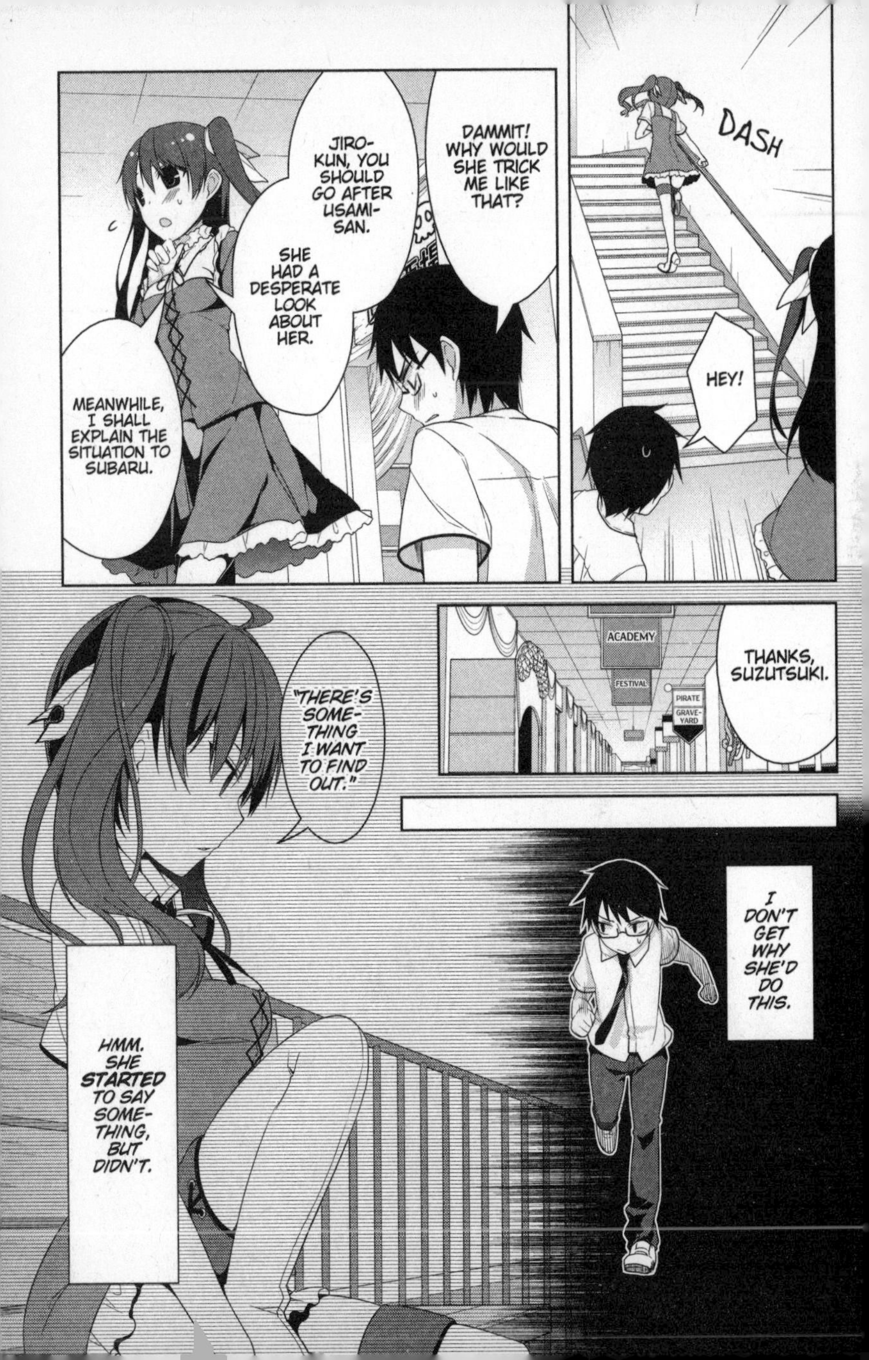
DASH
HEY!
DAMMIT! WHY WOULD SHE TRICK ME LIKE THAT?
JIRO-KUN, YOU SHOULD GO AFTER USAMI-SAN.
SHE HAD A DESPERATE LOOK ABOUT HER.
MEANWHILE, I SHALL EXPLAIN THE SITUATION TO SUBARU.
THANKS, SUZUTSUKI.
ACADEMY
FESTIVAL
PIRATE GRAVE-YARD
I DON'T GET WHY SHE'D DO THIS.
"THERE'S SOMETHING I WANT TO FIND OUT."
HMM. SHE STARTED TO SAY SOMETHING, BUT DIDN'T.

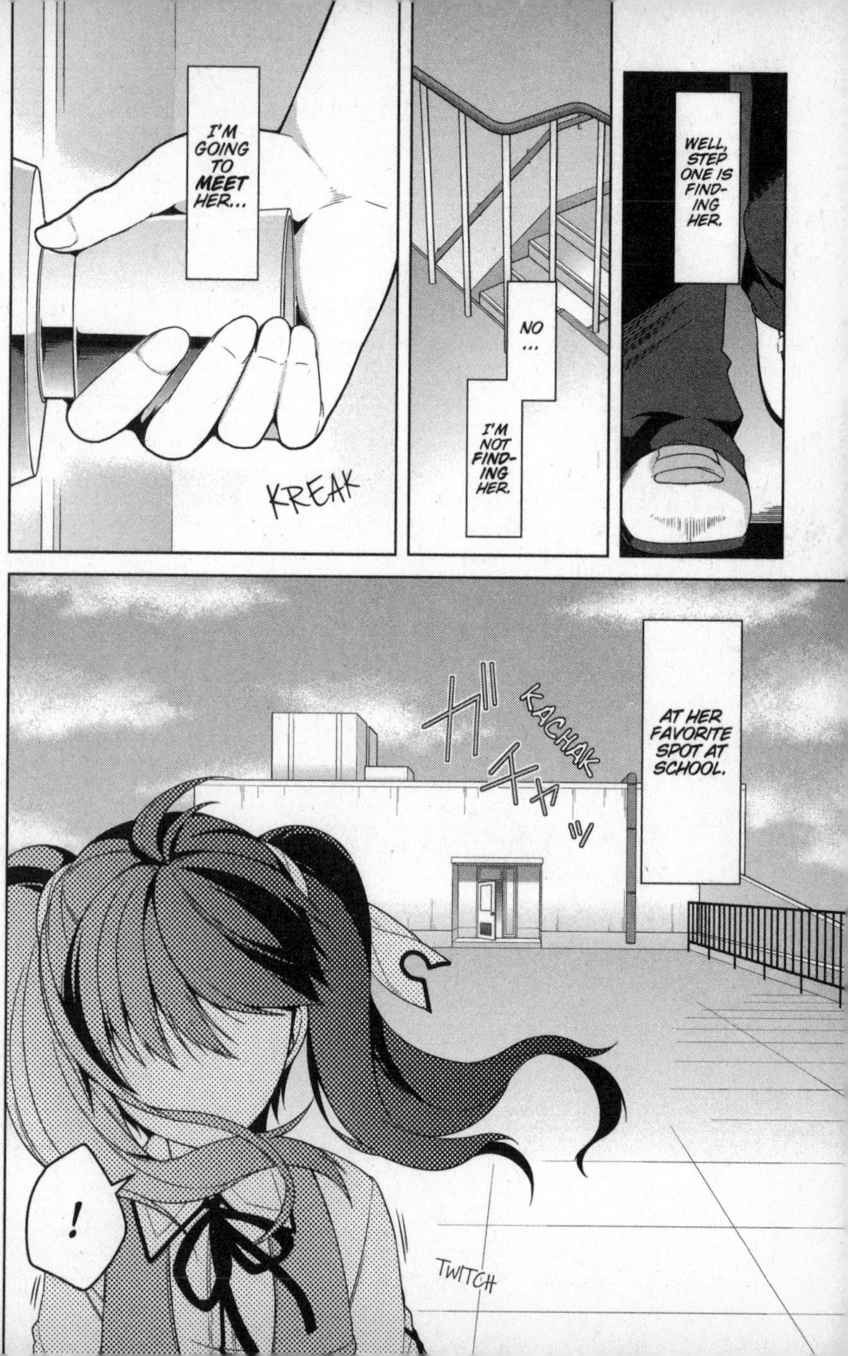
WELL, STEP ONE IS FINDING HER.
NO...
I'M NOT FINDING HER.
I'M GOING TO MEET HER...
KREAK
AT HER FAVORITE SPOT AT SCHOOL.
KACHAK
!
TWITCH

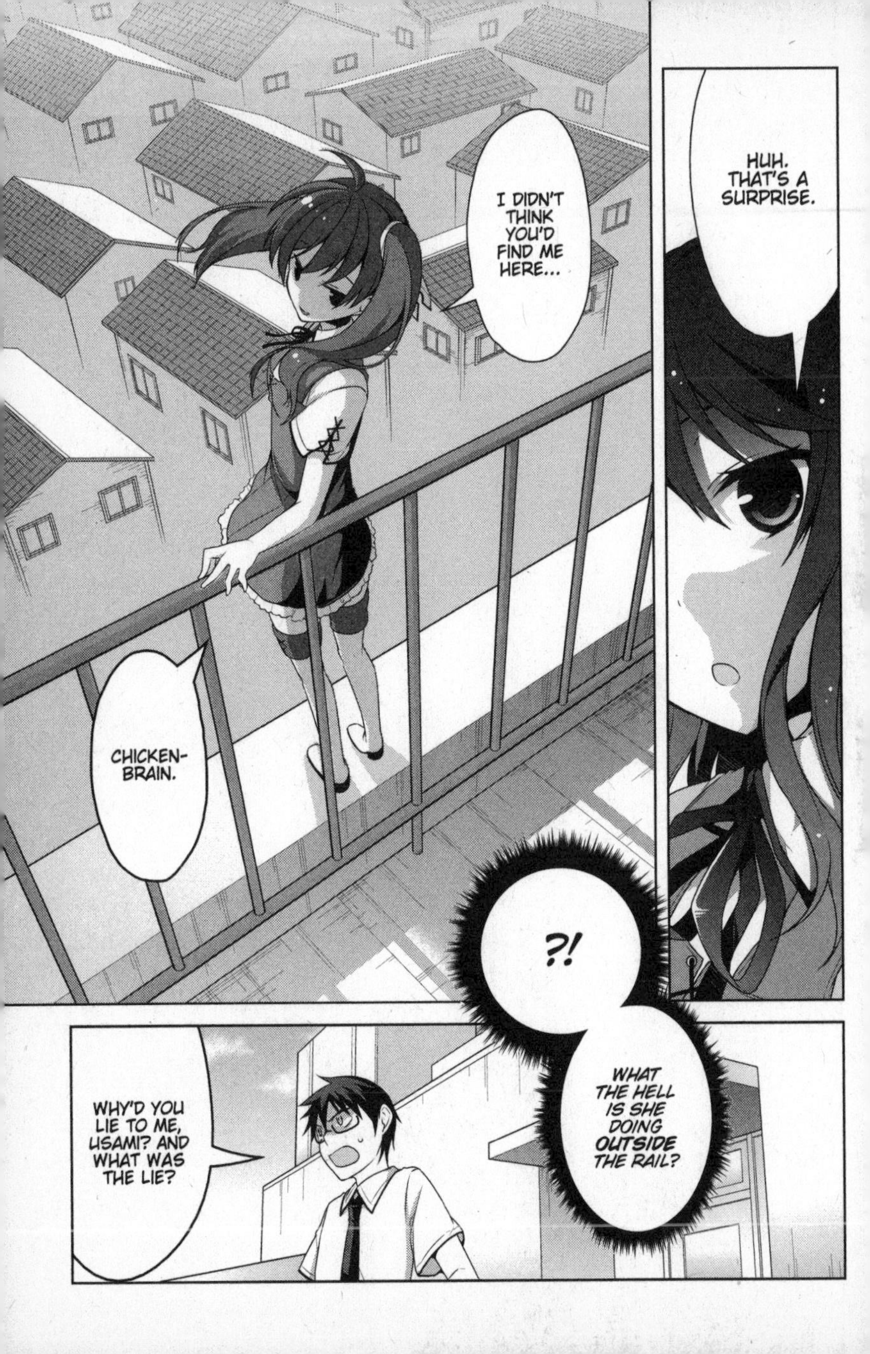
HUH. THAT'S A SURPRISE.
I DIDN'T THINK YOU'D FIND ME HERE...
CHICKEN-BRAIN.
?!
WHAT THE HELL IS SHE DOING OUTSIDE THE RAIL?
WHY'D YOU LIE TO ME, USAMI? AND WHAT WAS THE LIE?

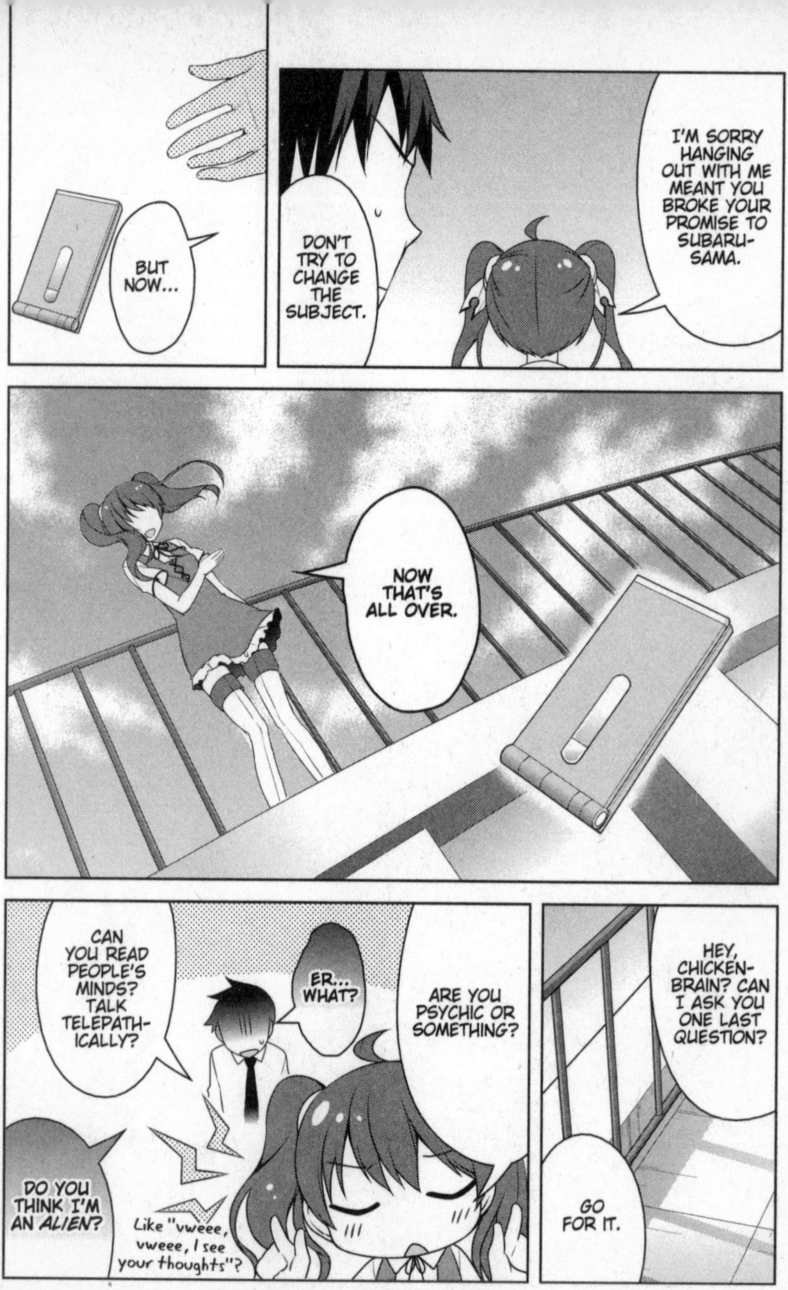
I'M SORRY HANGING OUT WITH ME MEANT YOU BROKE YOUR PROMISE TO SUBARU-SAMA.
DON'T TRY TO CHANGE THE SUBJECT.
BUT NOW...
NOW THAT'S ALL OVER.
HEY, CHICKEN-BRAIN? CAN I ASK YOU ONE LAST QUESTION?
GO FOR IT.
ARE YOU PSYCHIC OR SOMETHING?
ER... WHAT?
CAN YOU READ PEOPLE'S MINDS? TALK TELEPATH-ICALLY?
Like "vweee, vweee, I see your thoughts"?
DO YOU THINK I'M AN *ALIEN*?

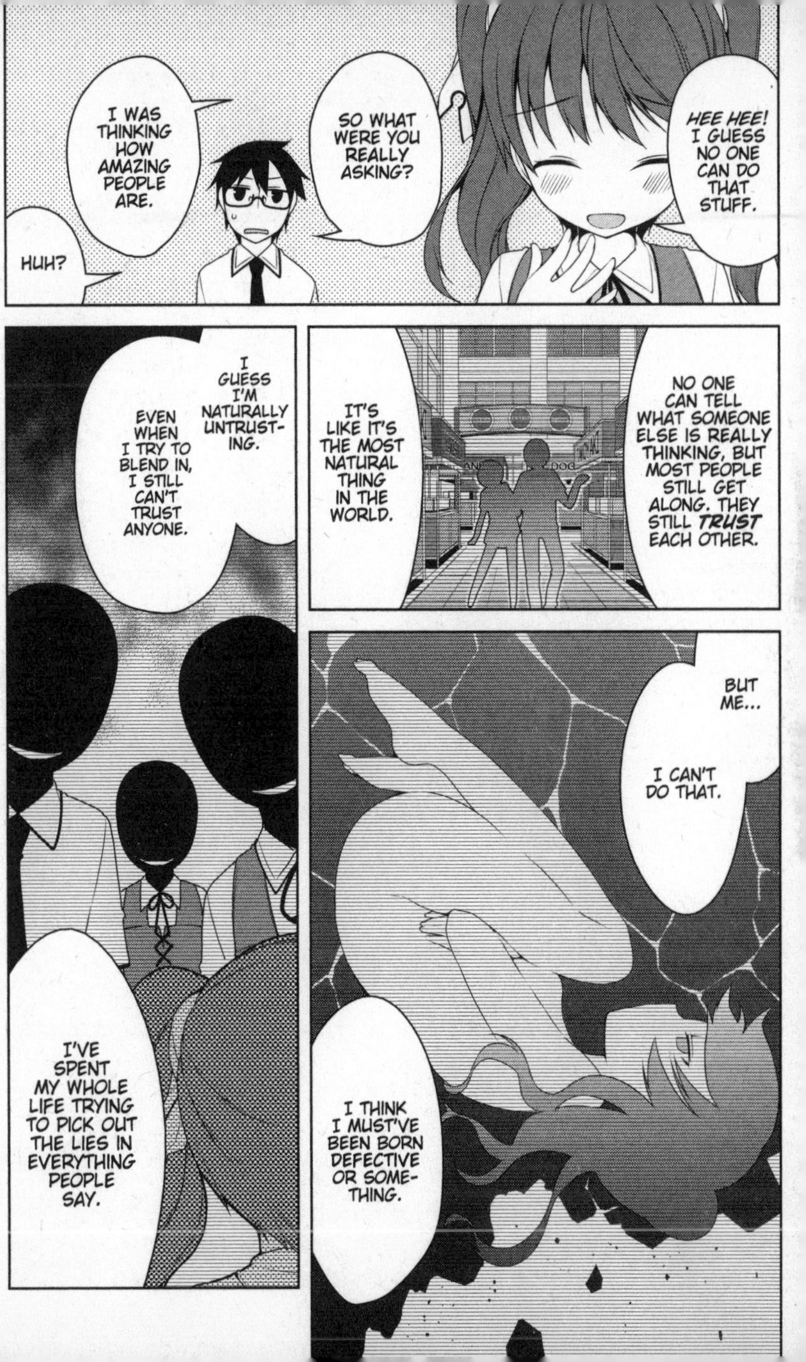
HEE HEE! I GUESS NO ONE CAN DO THAT STUFF.
SO WHAT WERE YOU REALLY ASKING?
I WAS THINKING HOW AMAZING PEOPLE ARE.
HUH?
NO ONE CAN TELL WHAT SOMEONE ELSE IS REALLY THINKING, BUT MOST PEOPLE STILL GET ALONG. THEY STILL *TRUST* EACH OTHER.
IT'S LIKE IT'S THE MOST NATURAL THING IN THE WORLD.
BUT ME...
I CAN'T DO THAT.
I THINK I MUST'VE BEEN BORN DEFECTIVE OR SOME-THING.
I GUESS I'M NATURALLY UNTRUST-ING.
EVEN WHEN I TRY TO BLEND IN, I STILL CAN'T TRUST ANYONE.
I'VE SPENT MY WHOLE LIFE TRYING TO PICK OUT THE LIES IN EVERYTHING PEOPLE SAY.

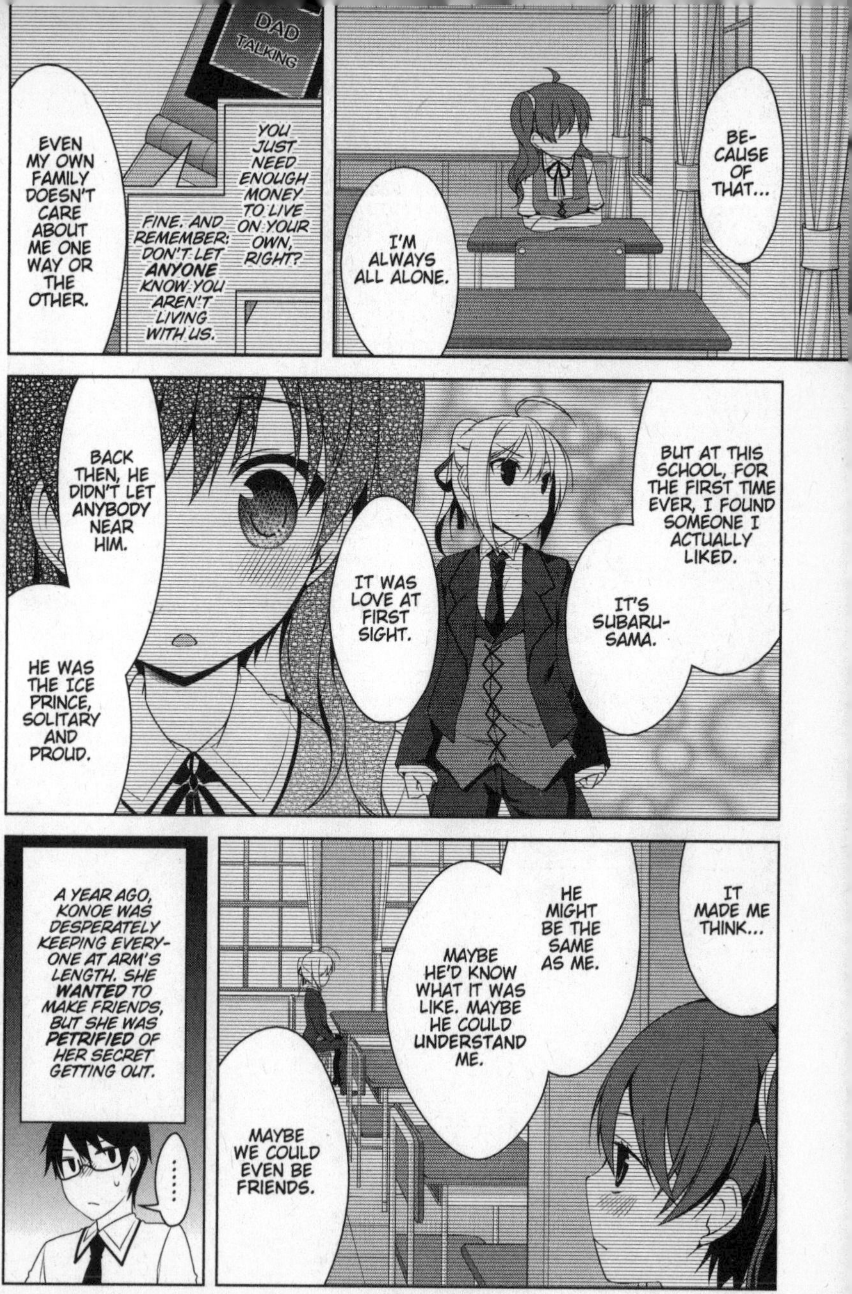
BE-CAUSE OF THAT...
I'M ALWAYS ALL ALONE.
DAD TALKING
YOU JUST NEED ENOUGH MONEY TO LIVE ON YOUR OWN, RIGHT?
FINE. AND REMEMBER: DON'T LET ANYONE KNOW YOU AREN'T LIVING WITH US.
EVEN MY OWN FAMILY DOESN'T CARE ABOUT ME ONE WAY OR THE OTHER.
BUT AT THIS SCHOOL, FOR THE FIRST TIME EVER, I FOUND SOMEONE I ACTUALLY LIKED.
IT'S SUBARU-SAMA.
IT WAS LOVE AT FIRST SIGHT.
BACK THEN, HE DIDN'T LET ANYBODY NEAR HIM.
HE WAS THE ICE PRINCE, SOLITARY AND PROUD.
IT MADE ME THINK...
HE MIGHT BE THE SAME AS ME.
MAYBE HE'D KNOW WHAT IT WAS LIKE. MAYBE HE COULD UNDERSTAND ME.
MAYBE WE COULD EVEN BE FRIENDS.
A YEAR AGO, KONOE WAS DESPERATELY KEEPING EVERY-ONE AT ARM'S LENGTH. SHE WANTED TO MAKE FRIENDS, BUT SHE WAS PETRIFIED OF HER SECRET GETTING OUT.
......

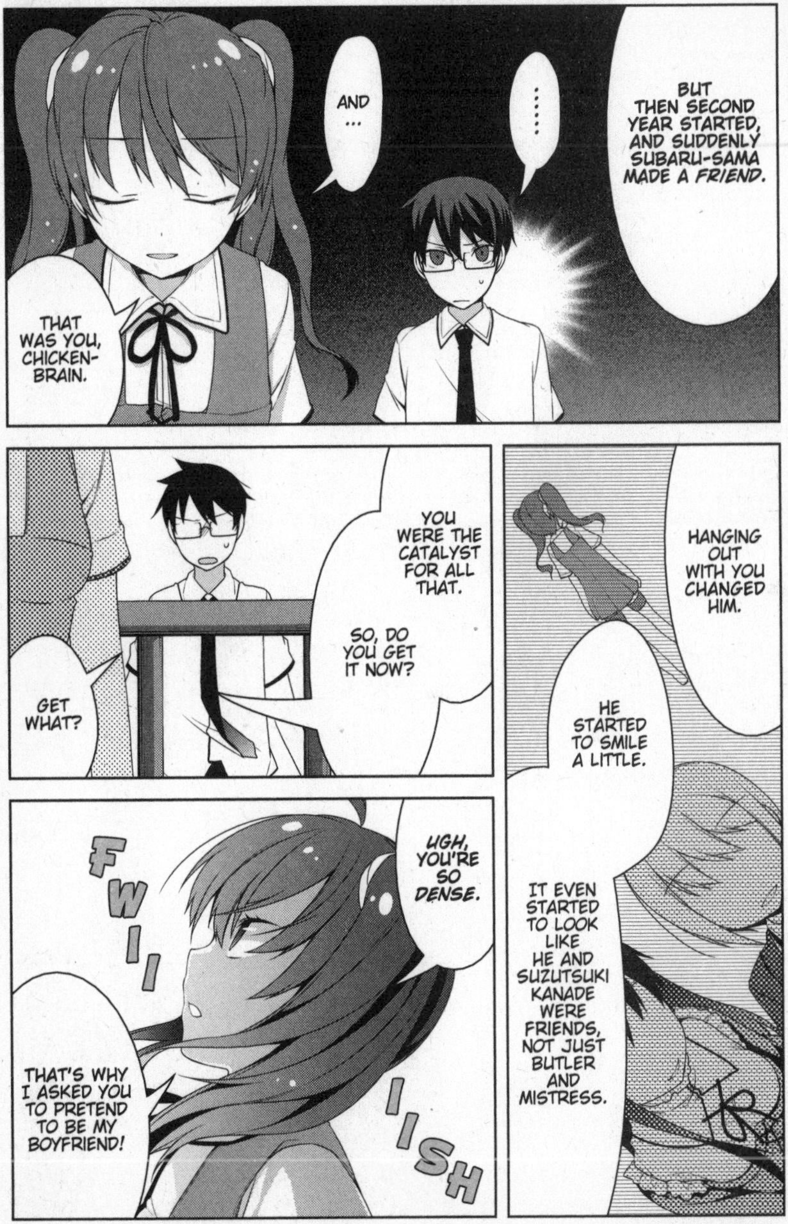
BUT THEN SECOND YEAR STARTED, AND SUDDENLY SUBARU-SAMA MADE A *FRIEND*.
......
AND ...
THAT WAS YOU, CHICKEN-BRAIN.
HANGING OUT WITH YOU CHANGED HIM.
HE STARTED TO SMILE A LITTLE.
IT EVEN STARTED TO LOOK LIKE HE AND SUZUTSUKI KANADE WERE FRIENDS, NOT JUST BUTLER AND MISTRESS.
YOU WERE THE CATALYST FOR ALL THAT.
SO, DO YOU GET IT NOW?
GET WHAT?
UGH, YOU'RE SO *DENSE*.
FWIIIISH
THAT'S WHY I ASKED YOU TO PRETEND TO BE MY BOYFRIEND!

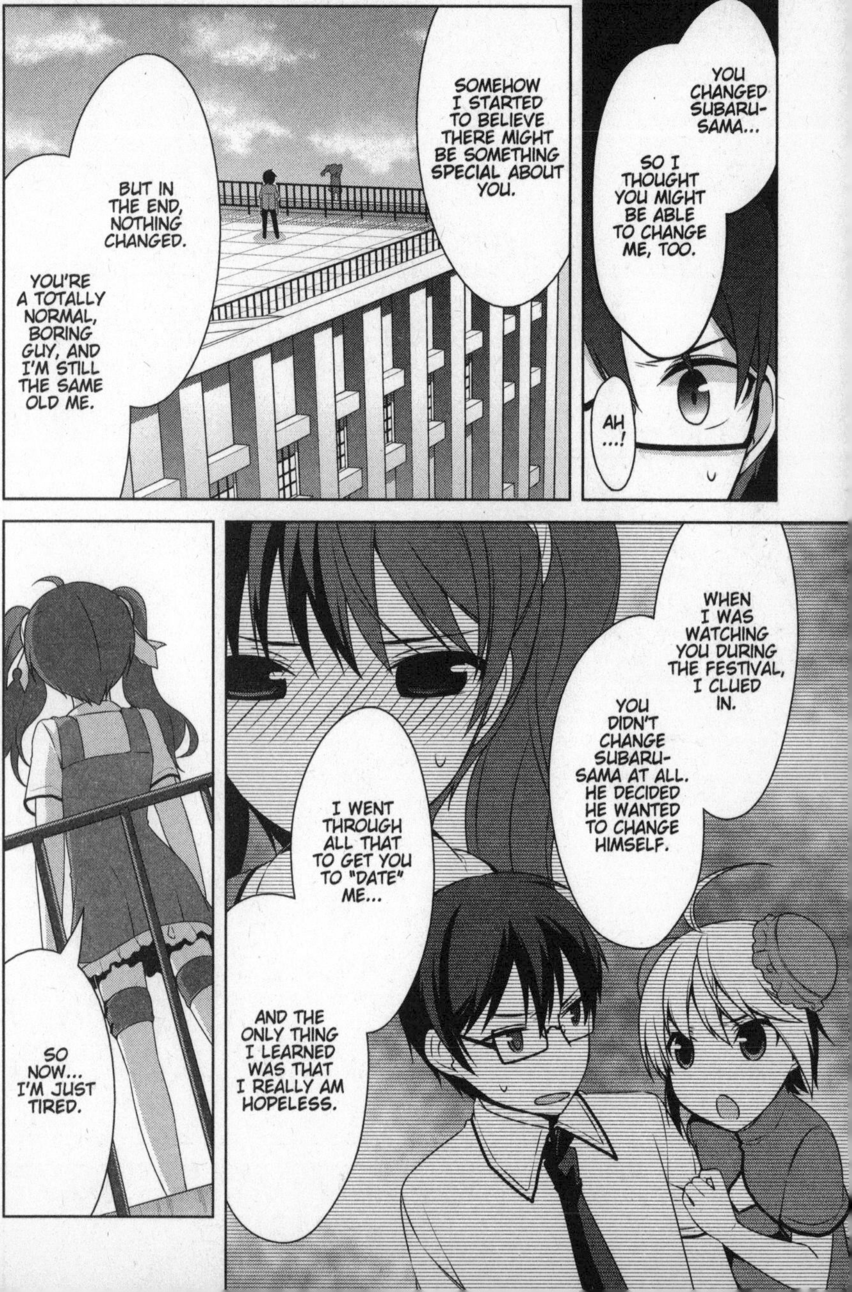
YOU CHANGED SUBARU-SAMA...
SO I THOUGHT YOU MIGHT BE ABLE TO CHANGE ME, TOO.
AH ...!
SOMEHOW I STARTED TO BELIEVE THERE MIGHT BE SOMETHING SPECIAL ABOUT YOU.
BUT IN THE END, NOTHING CHANGED.
YOU'RE A TOTALLY NORMAL, BORING GUY, AND I'M STILL THE SAME OLD ME.
WHEN I WAS WATCHING YOU DURING THE FESTIVAL, I CLUED IN.
YOU DIDN'T CHANGE SUBARU-SAMA AT ALL. HE DECIDED HE WANTED TO CHANGE HIMSELF.
I WENT THROUGH ALL THAT TO GET YOU TO "DATE" ME...
AND THE ONLY THING I LEARNED WAS THAT I REALLY AM HOPELESS.
SO NOW... I'M JUST TIRED.

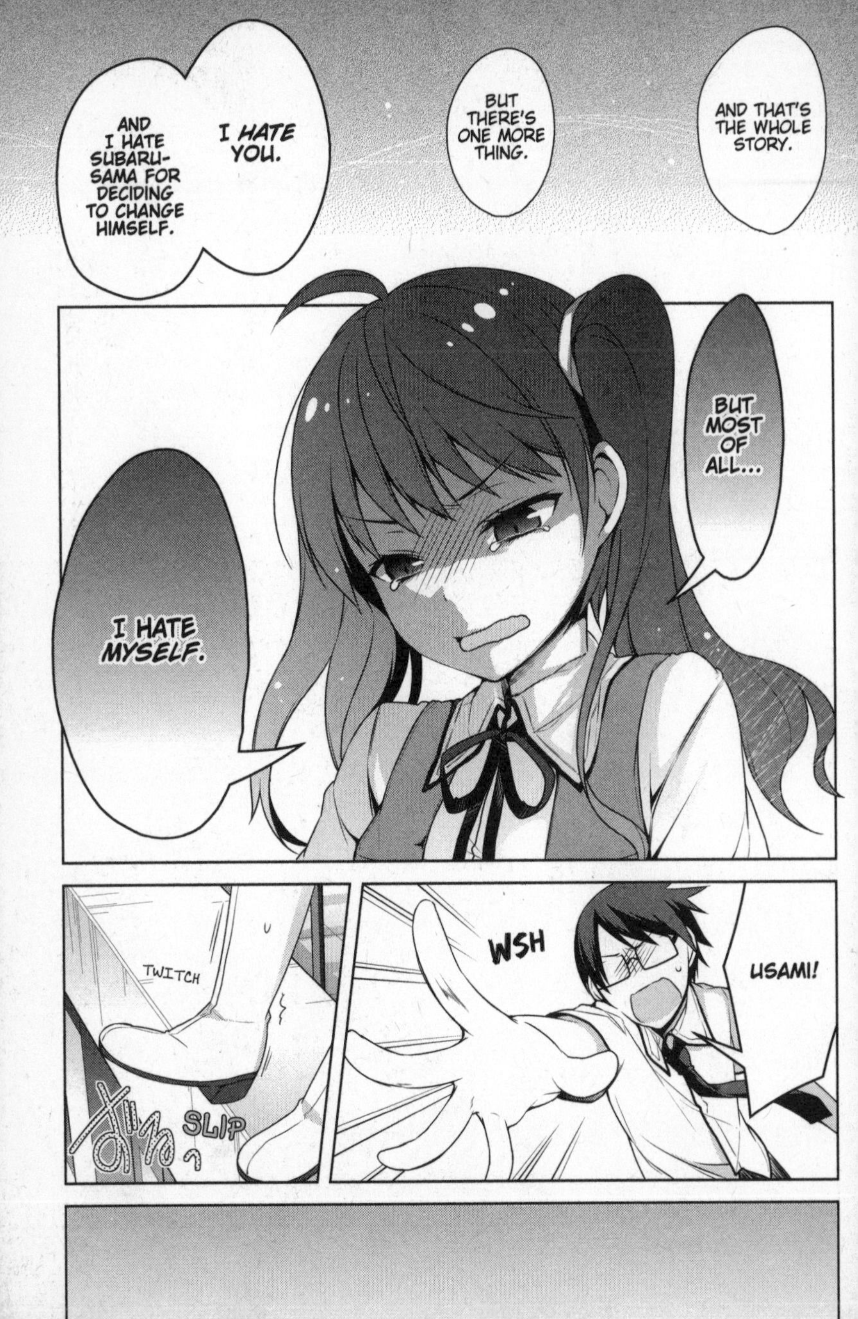
AND THAT'S THE WHOLE STORY.
BUT THERE'S ONE MORE THING.
I HATE YOU.
AND I HATE SUBARU-SAMA FOR DECIDING TO CHANGE HIMSELF.
BUT MOST OF ALL...
I HATE MYSELF.
USAMI!
WSH
TWITCH
SLIP

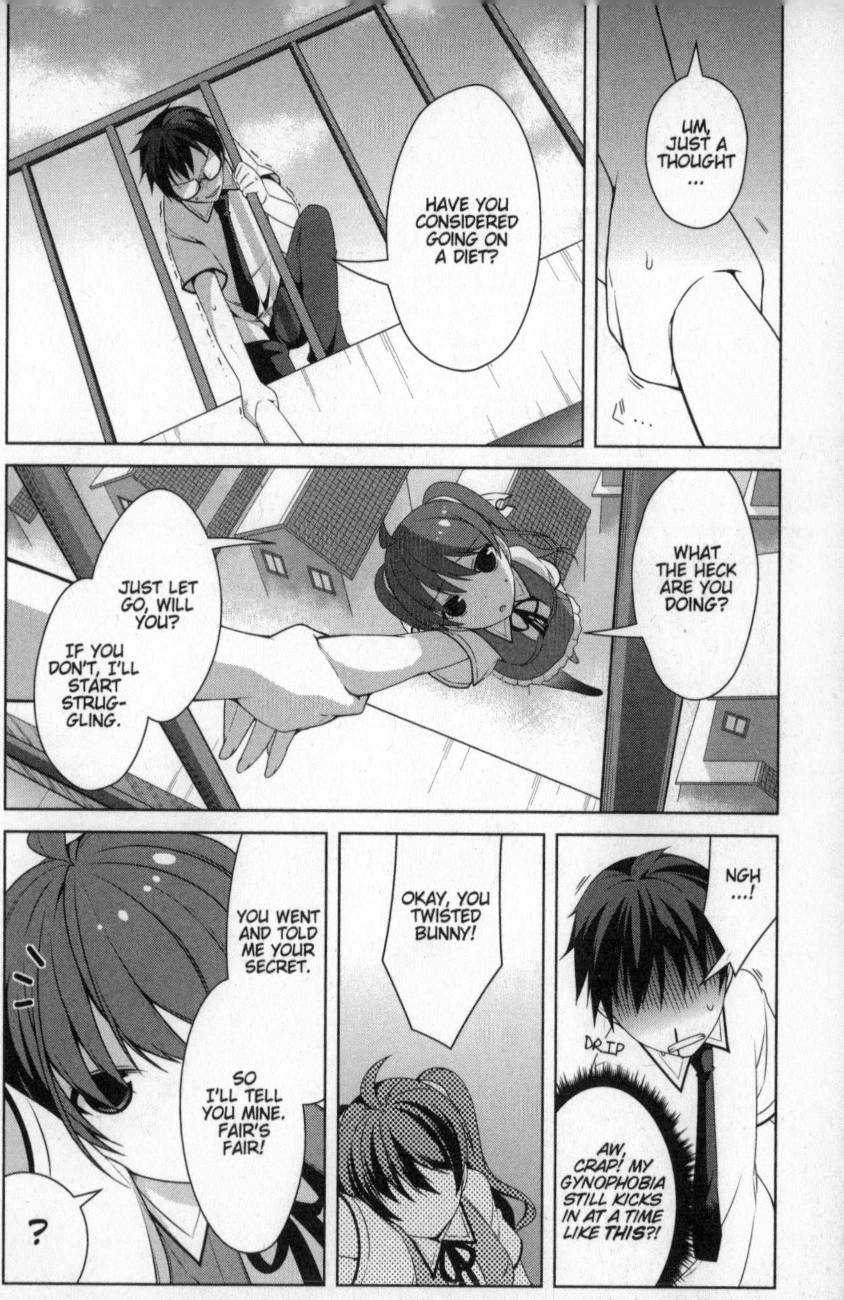
UM, JUST A THOUGHT ...
ぐ...
HAVE YOU CONSIDERED GOING ON A DIET?
WHAT THE HECK ARE YOU DOING?
JUST LET GO, WILL YOU?
IF YOU DON'T, I'LL START STRUG-GLING.
NGH ...!
DRIP
AW, CRAP! MY GYNOPHOBIA STILL KICKS IN AT A TIME LIKE THIS?!
OKAY, YOU TWISTED BUNNY!
YOU WENT AND TOLD ME YOUR SECRET.
SO I'LL TELL YOU MINE. FAIR'S FAIR!
?

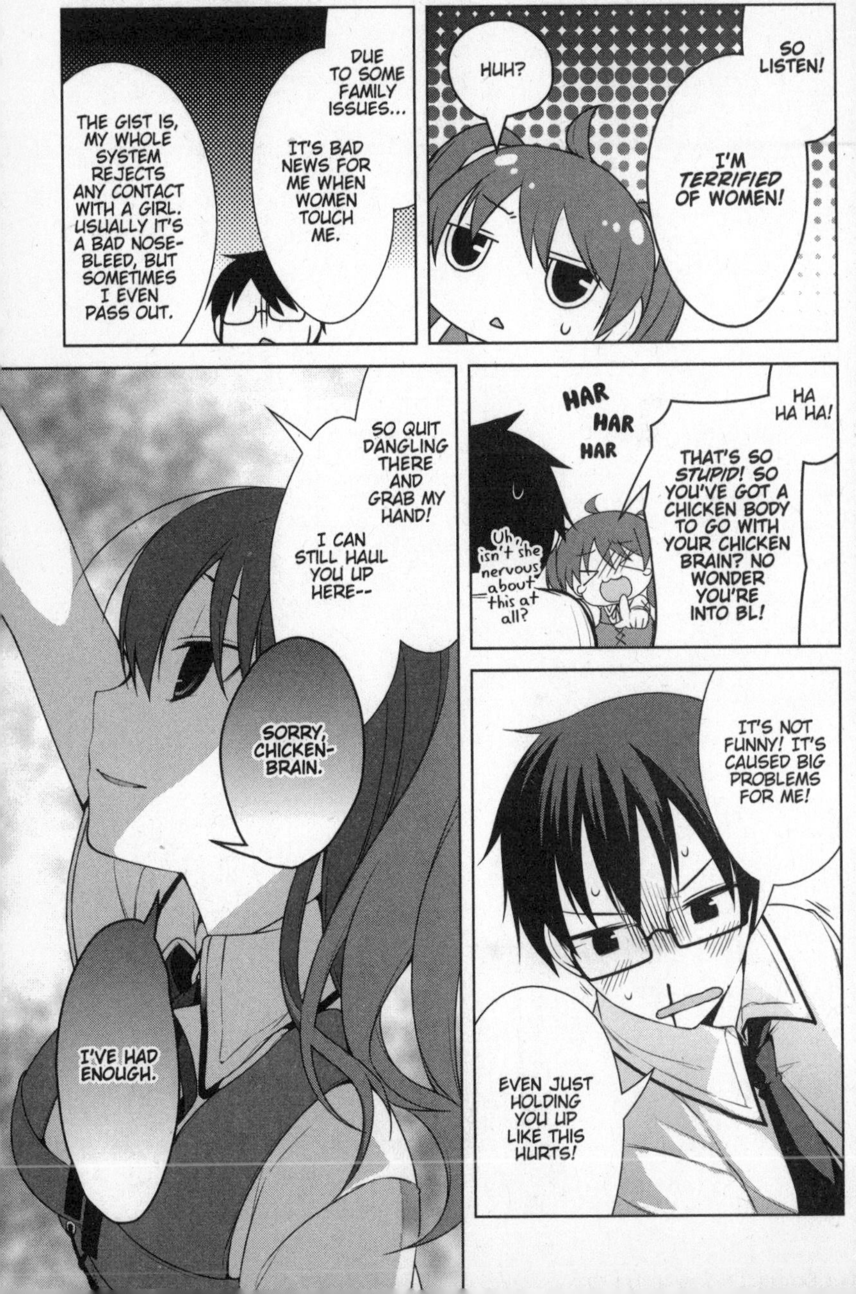
SO LISTEN!
I'M TERRIFIED OF WOMEN!
HUH?
DUE TO SOME FAMILY ISSUES...
IT'S BAD NEWS FOR ME WHEN WOMEN TOUCH ME.
THE GIST IS, MY WHOLE SYSTEM REJECTS ANY CONTACT WITH A GIRL. USUALLY IT'S A BAD NOSE-BLEED, BUT SOMETIMES I EVEN PASS OUT.
HA HA HA!
THAT'S SO STUPID! SO YOU'VE GOT A CHICKEN BODY TO GO WITH YOUR CHICKEN BRAIN? NO WONDER YOU'RE INTO BL!
HAR HAR HAR
Uh, isn't she nervous about this at all?
IT'S NOT FUNNY! IT'S CAUSED BIG PROBLEMS FOR ME!
EVEN JUST HOLDING YOU UP LIKE THIS HURTS!
SO QUIT DANGLING THERE AND GRAB MY HAND!
I CAN STILL HAUL YOU UP HERE--
SORRY, CHICKEN-BRAIN.
I'VE HAD ENOUGH.

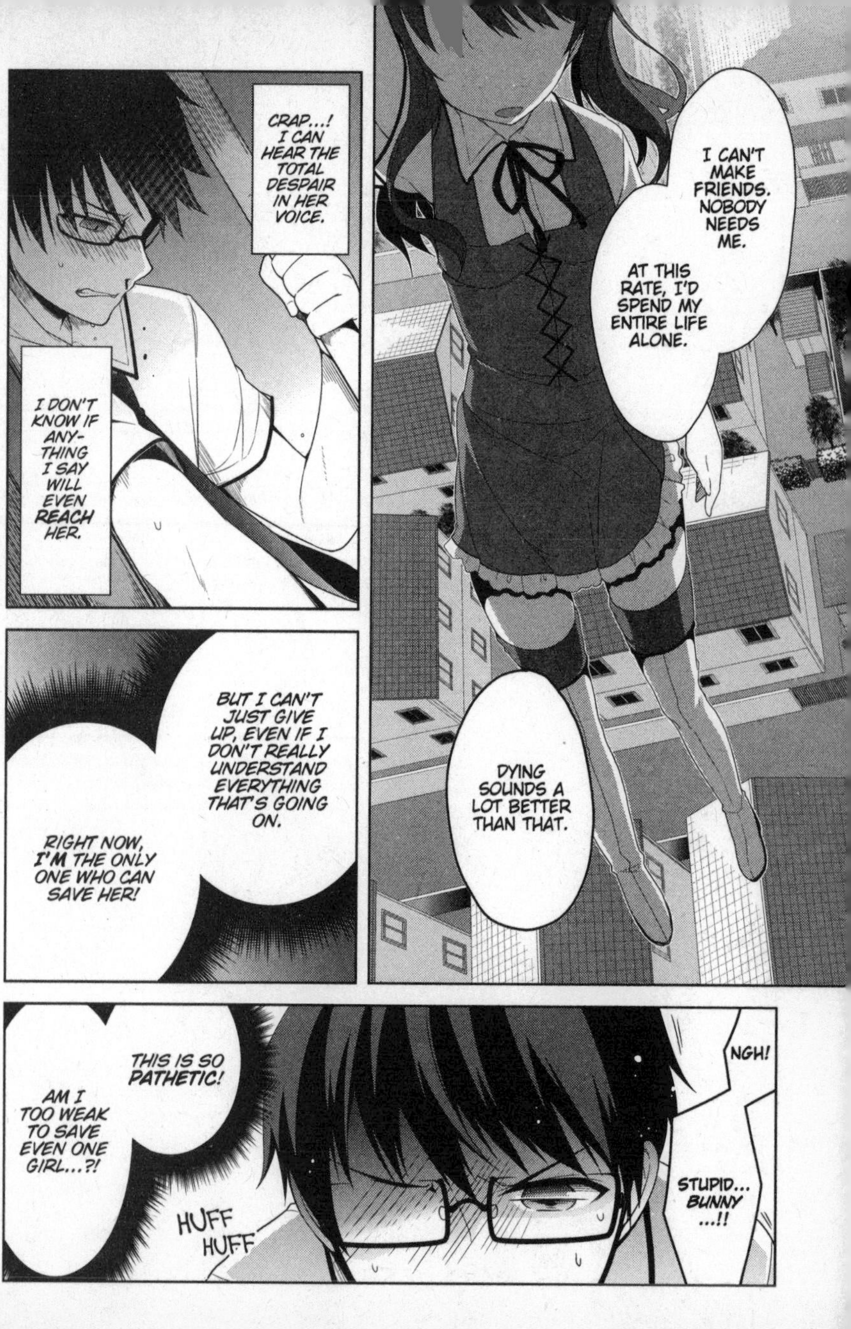
I CAN'T MAKE FRIENDS. NOBODY NEEDS ME.
AT THIS RATE, I'D SPEND MY ENTIRE LIFE ALONE.
DYING SOUNDS A LOT BETTER THAN THAT.
CRAP...! I CAN HEAR THE TOTAL DESPAIR IN HER VOICE.
I DON'T KNOW IF ANY-THING I SAY WILL EVEN REACH HER.
BUT I CAN'T JUST GIVE UP, EVEN IF I DON'T REALLY UNDERSTAND EVERYTHING THAT'S GOING ON.
RIGHT NOW, I'M THE ONLY ONE WHO CAN SAVE HER!
NGH!
STUPID... BUNNY ...!!
THIS IS SO PATHETIC!
AM I TOO WEAK TO SAVE EVEN ONE GIRL...?!
HUFF HUFF

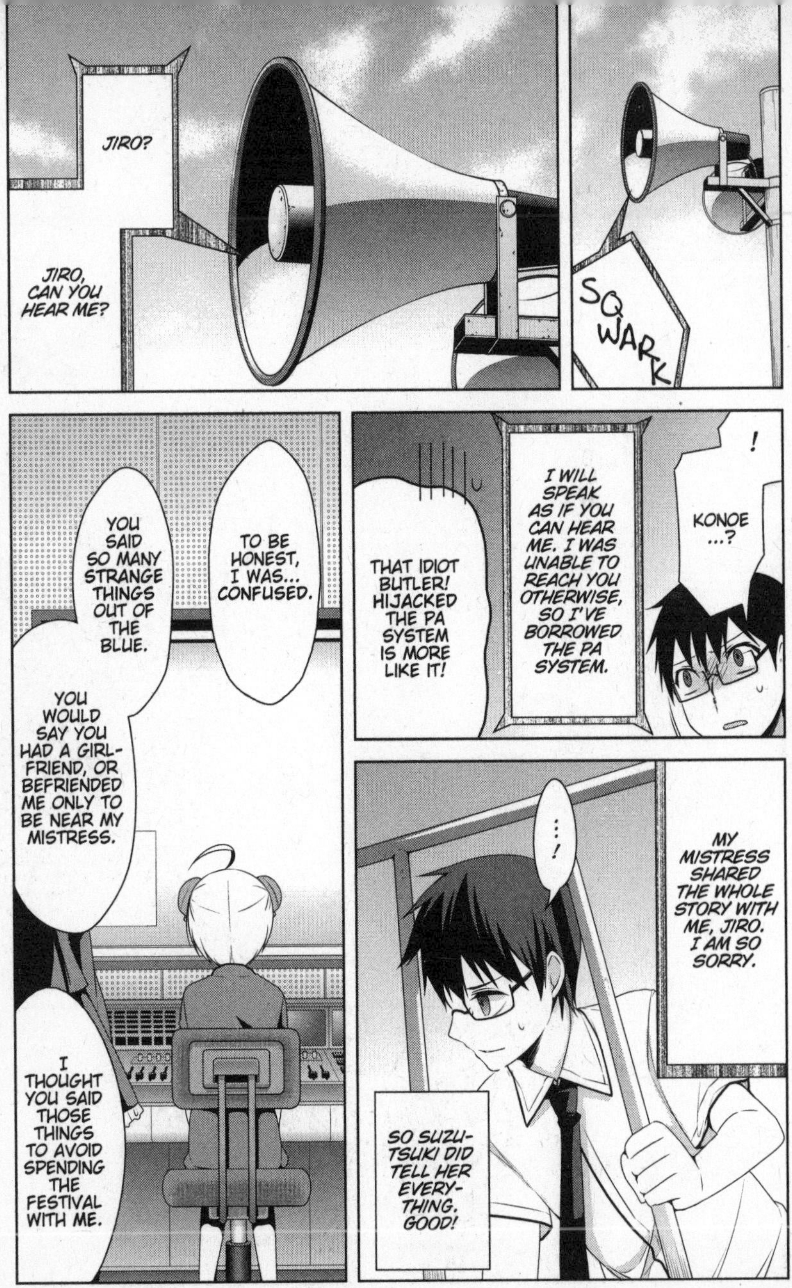
SQWARK
JIRO?
JIRO, CAN YOU HEAR ME?
!
KONOE ...?
I WILL SPEAK AS IF YOU CAN HEAR ME. I WAS UNABLE TO REACH YOU OTHERWISE, SO I'VE BORROWED THE PA SYSTEM.
THAT IDIOT BUTLER! HIJACKED THE PA SYSTEM IS MORE LIKE IT!
MY MISTRESS SHARED THE WHOLE STORY WITH ME, JIRO. I AM SO SORRY.
...!
SO SUZUTSUKI DID TELL HER EVERYTHING. GOOD!
TO BE HONEST, I WAS... CONFUSED.
YOU SAID SO MANY STRANGE THINGS OUT OF THE BLUE.
YOU WOULD SAY YOU HAD A GIRLFRIEND, OR BEFRIENDED ME ONLY TO BE NEAR MY MISTRESS.
I THOUGHT YOU SAID THOSE THINGS TO AVOID SPENDING THE FESTIVAL WITH ME.

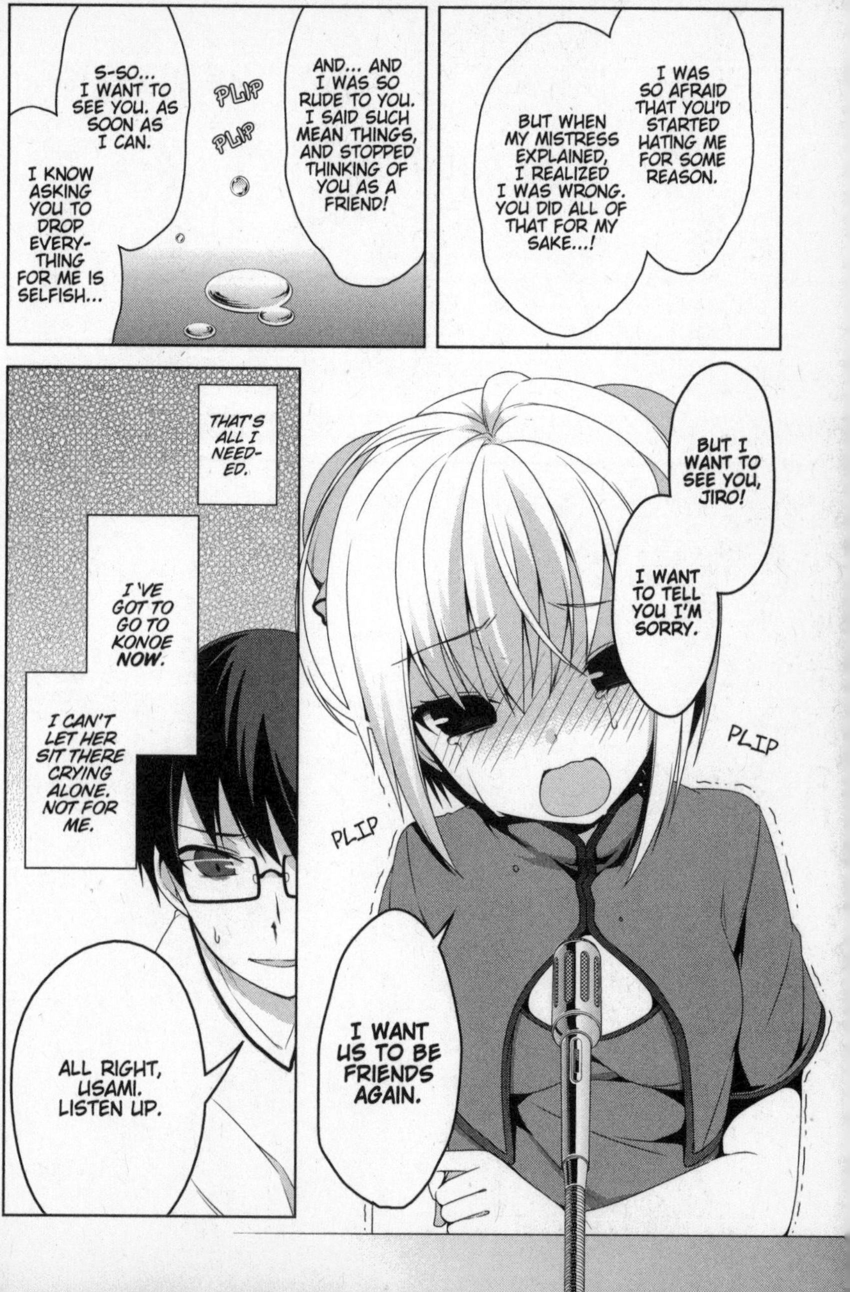
I WAS SO AFRAID THAT YOU'D STARTED HATING ME FOR SOME REASON.
BUT WHEN MY MISTRESS EXPLAINED, I REALIZED I WAS WRONG. YOU DID ALL OF THAT FOR MY SAKE...!
AND... AND I WAS SO RUDE TO YOU. I SAID SUCH MEAN THINGS, AND STOPPED THINKING OF YOU AS A FRIEND!
PLIP
PLIP
S-SO... I WANT TO SEE YOU. AS SOON AS I CAN.
I KNOW ASKING YOU TO DROP EVERY-THING FOR ME IS SELFISH...
BUT I WANT TO SEE YOU, JIRO!
I WANT TO TELL YOU I'M SORRY.
PLIP
PLIP
I WANT US TO BE FRIENDS AGAIN.
THAT'S ALL I NEEDED.
I'VE GOT TO GO TO KONOE NOW.
I CAN'T LET HER SIT THERE CRYING ALONE. NOT FOR ME.
ALL RIGHT, USAMI. LISTEN UP.

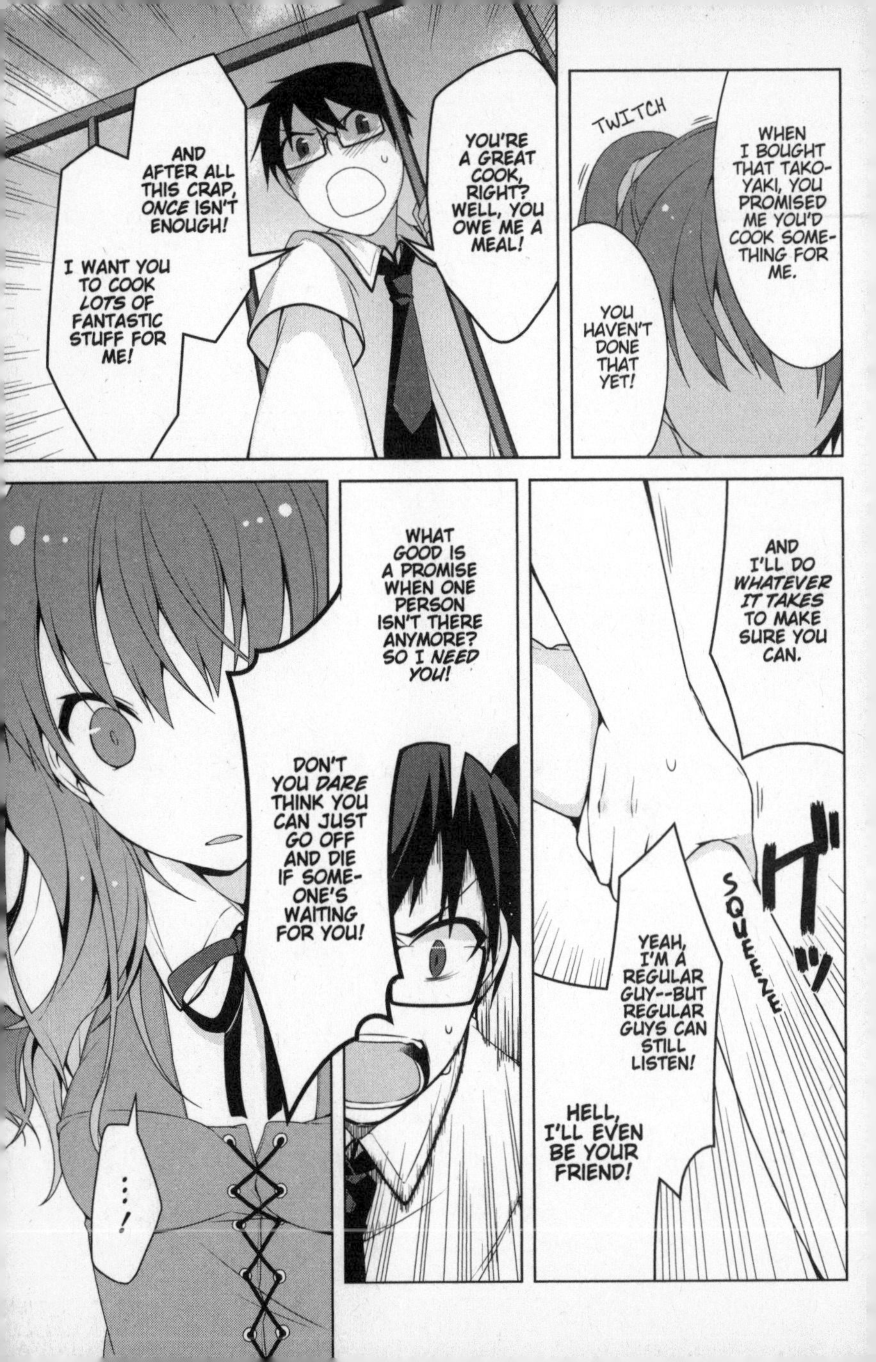
TWITCH
WHEN I BOUGHT THAT TAKO-YAKI, YOU PROMISED ME YOU'D COOK SOME-THING FOR ME.
YOU HAVEN'T DONE THAT YET!
YOU'RE A GREAT COOK, RIGHT? WELL, YOU OWE ME A MEAL!
AND AFTER ALL THIS CRAP, *ONCE* ISN'T ENOUGH!
I WANT YOU TO COOK *LOTS* OF FANTASTIC STUFF FOR ME!
AND I'LL DO *WHATEVER IT TAKES* TO MAKE SURE YOU CAN.
SQUEEZE
YEAH, I'M A REGULAR GUY--BUT REGULAR GUYS CAN STILL LISTEN!
HELL, I'LL EVEN BE YOUR FRIEND!
WHAT GOOD IS A PROMISE WHEN ONE PERSON ISN'T THERE ANYMORE? SO I *NEED* YOU!
DON'T YOU *DARE* THINK YOU CAN JUST GO OFF AND DIE IF SOME-ONE'S WAITING FOR YOU!
...!

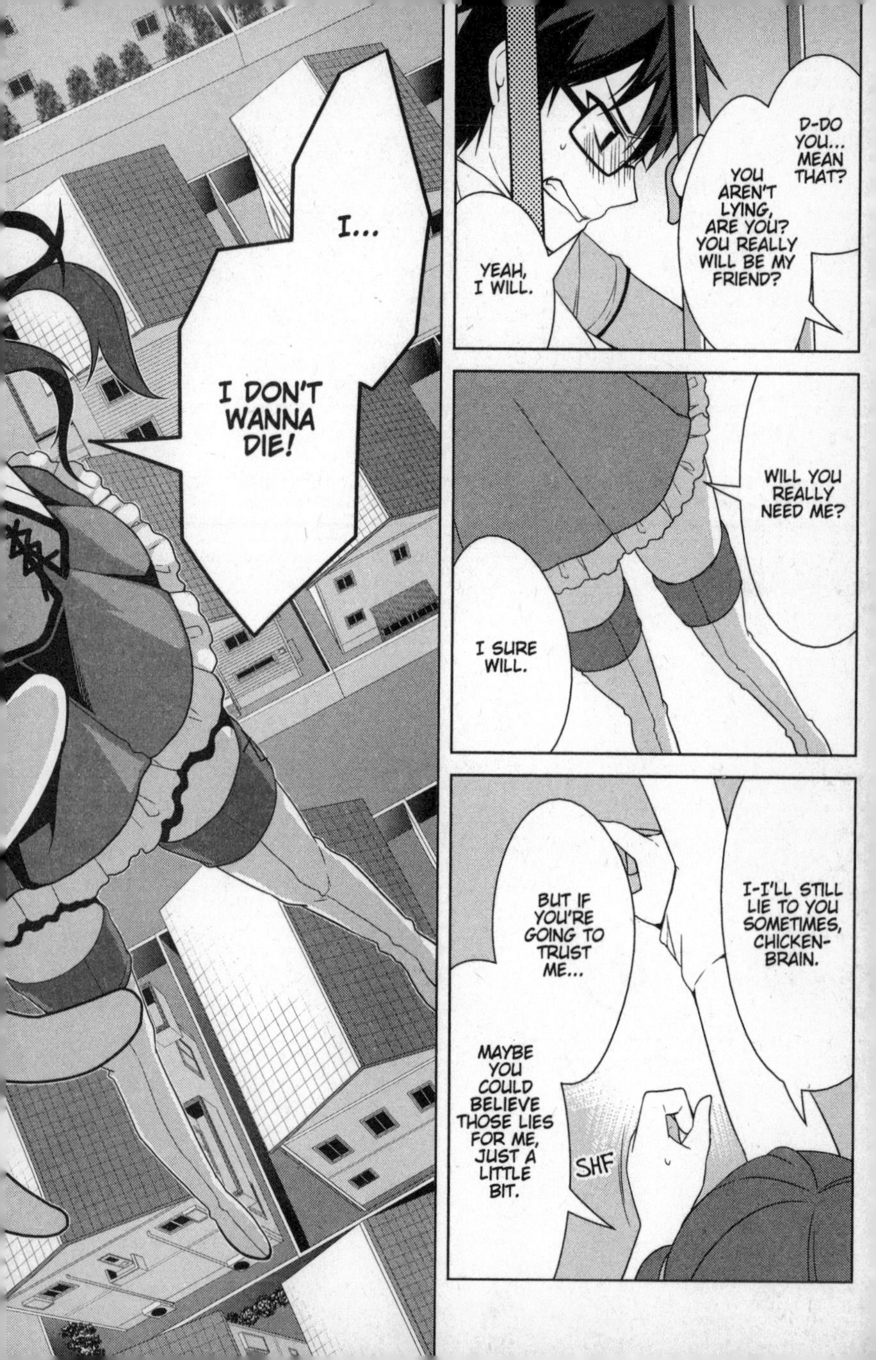
D-DO YOU... MEAN THAT?
YOU AREN'T LYING, ARE YOU? YOU REALLY WILL BE MY FRIEND?
YEAH, I WILL.
WILL YOU REALLY NEED ME?
I SURE WILL.
I-I'LL STILL LIE TO YOU SOMETIMES, CHICKEN-BRAIN.
BUT IF YOU'RE GOING TO TRUST ME...
MAYBE YOU COULD BELIEVE THOSE LIES FOR ME, JUST A LITTLE BIT.
SHF
I...
I DON'T WANNA DIE!

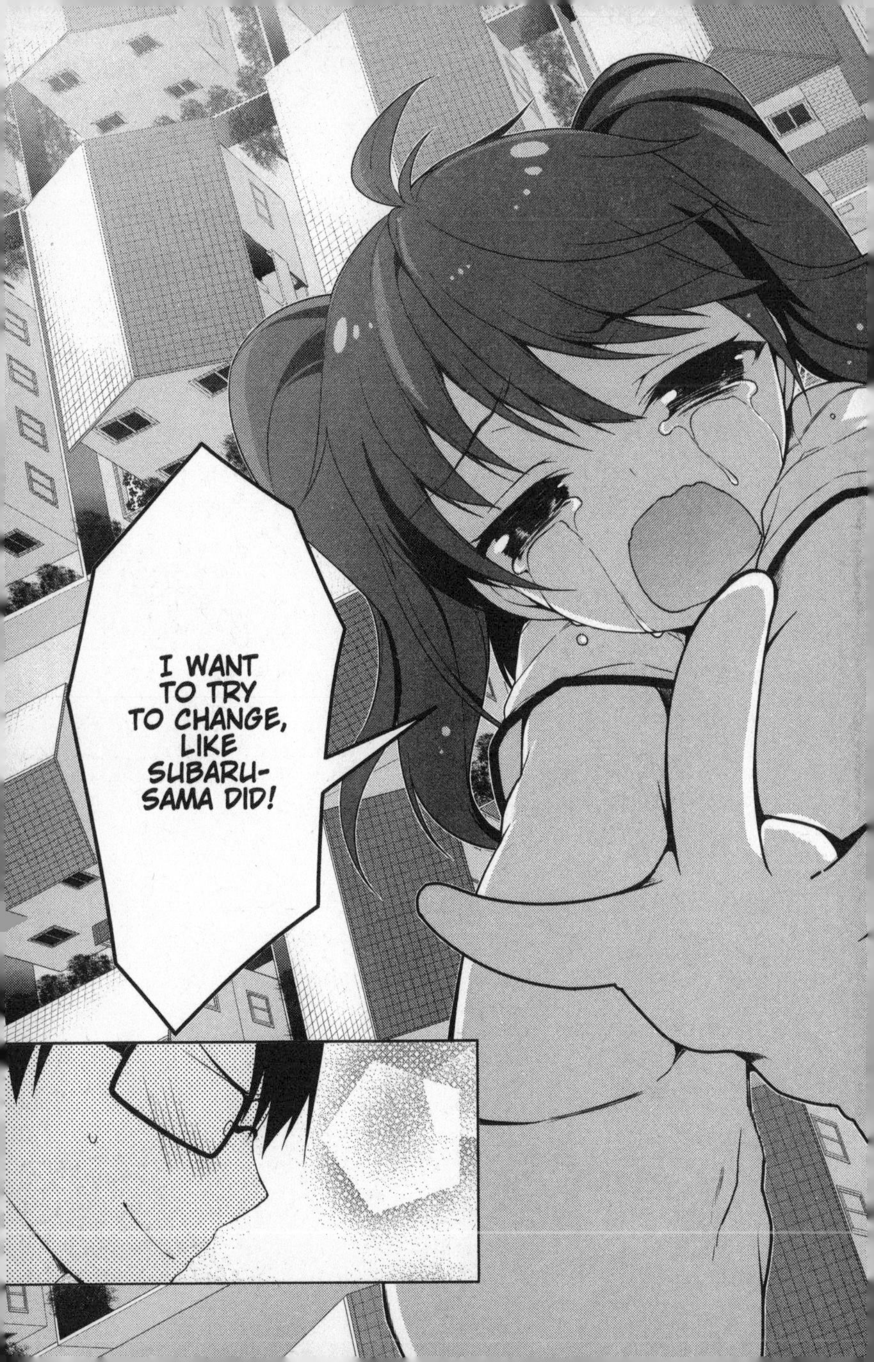
I WANT TO TRY TO CHANGE, LIKE SUBARU-SAMA DID!

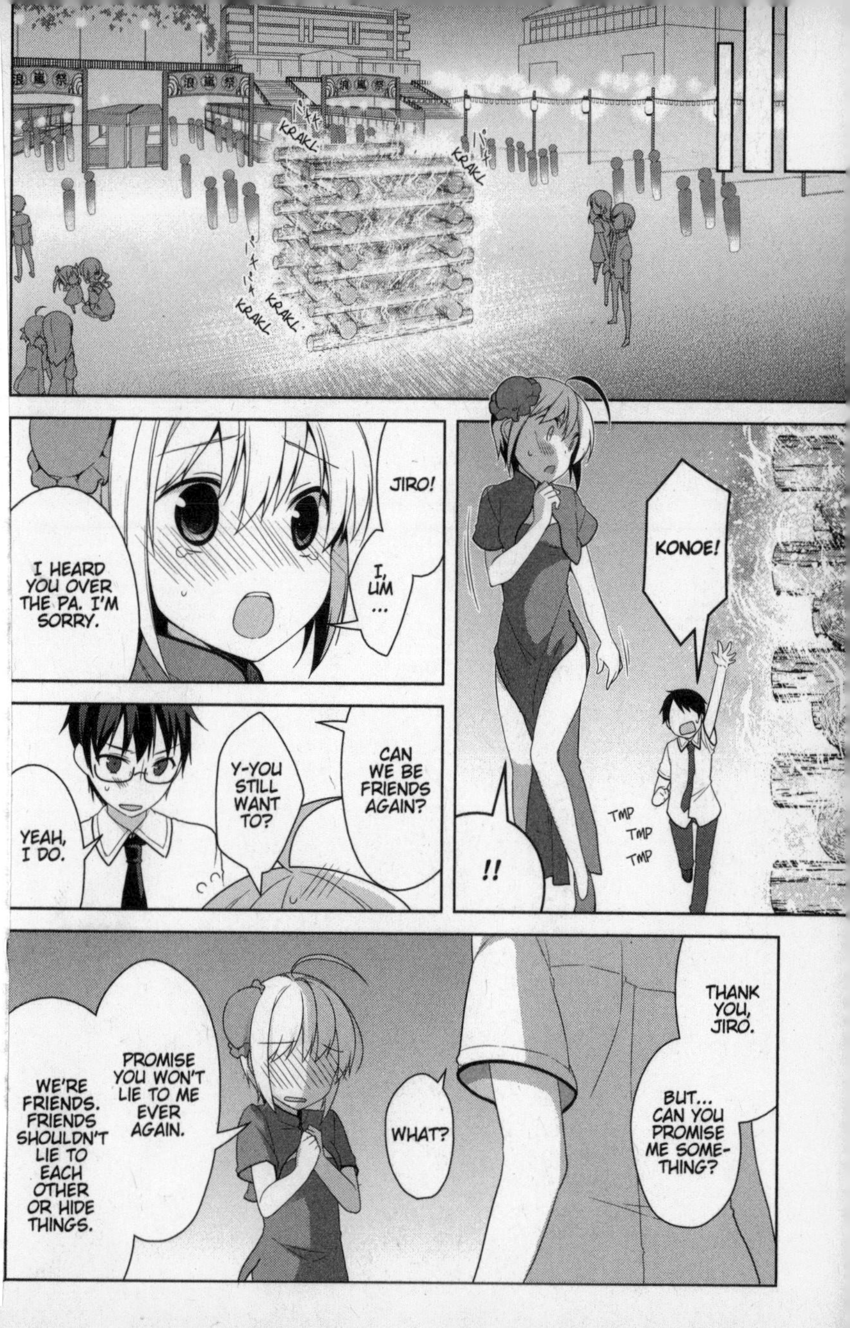
KRAKL
KRAKL
KRAKL
KRAKL
KONOE!
TMP
TMP
TMP
!!
JIRO!
I, UM...
I HEARD YOU OVER THE PA. I'M SORRY.
CAN WE BE FRIENDS AGAIN?
Y-YOU STILL WANT TO?
YEAH, I DO.
THANK YOU, JIRO.
BUT... CAN YOU PROMISE ME SOME-THING?
WHAT?
PROMISE YOU WON'T LIE TO ME EVER AGAIN.
WE'RE FRIENDS. FRIENDS SHOULDN'T LIE TO EACH OTHER OR HIDE THINGS.

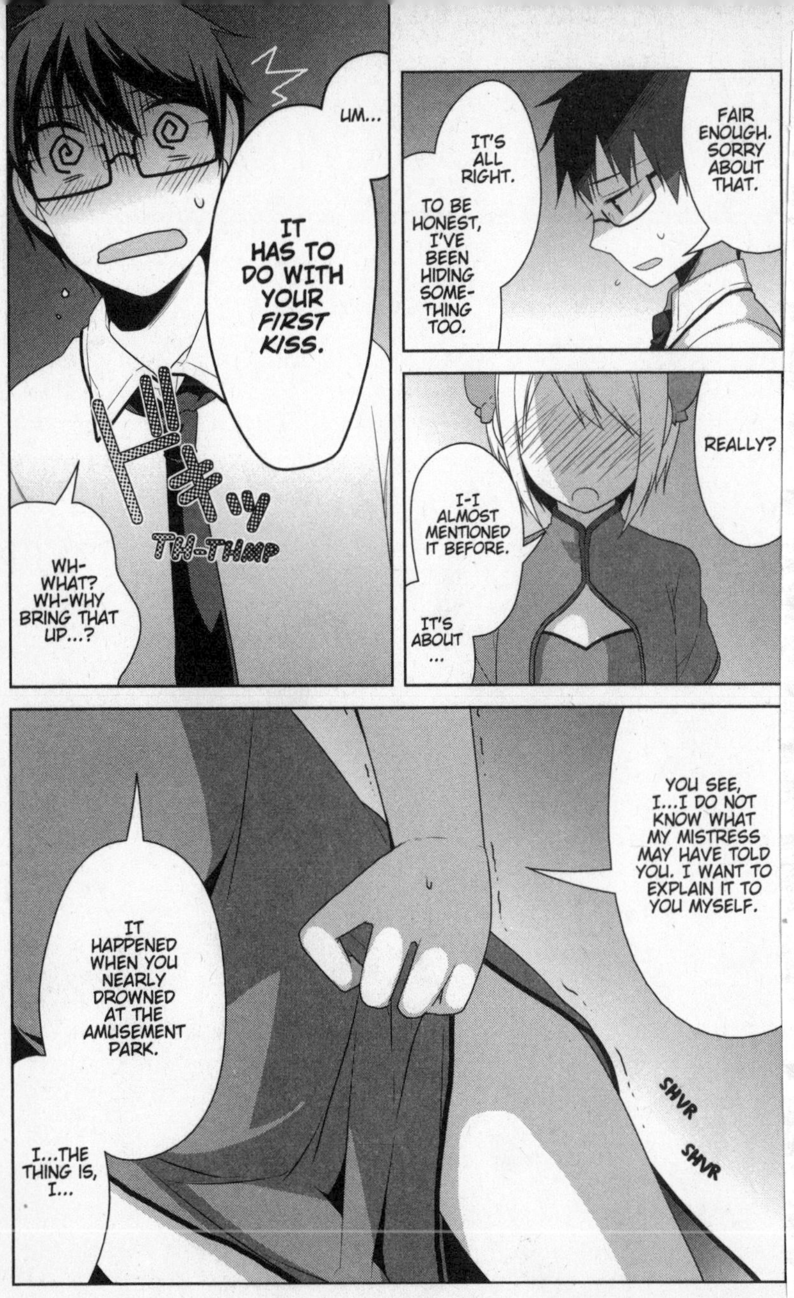
FAIR ENOUGH. SORRY ABOUT THAT.
IT'S ALL RIGHT.
TO BE HONEST, I'VE BEEN HIDING SOME-THING TOO.
REALLY?
I-I ALMOST MENTIONED IT BEFORE.
IT'S ABOUT ...
UM...
IT HAS TO DO WITH YOUR *FIRST KISS.*
ドキッ
TH-THMP
WH-WHAT? WH-WHY BRING THAT UP...?
YOU SEE, I...I DO NOT KNOW WHAT MY MISTRESS MAY HAVE TOLD YOU. I WANT TO EXPLAIN IT TO YOU MYSELF.
SHVR
SHVR
IT HAPPENED WHEN YOU NEARLY DROWNED AT THE AMUSEMENT PARK.
I...THE THING IS, I...

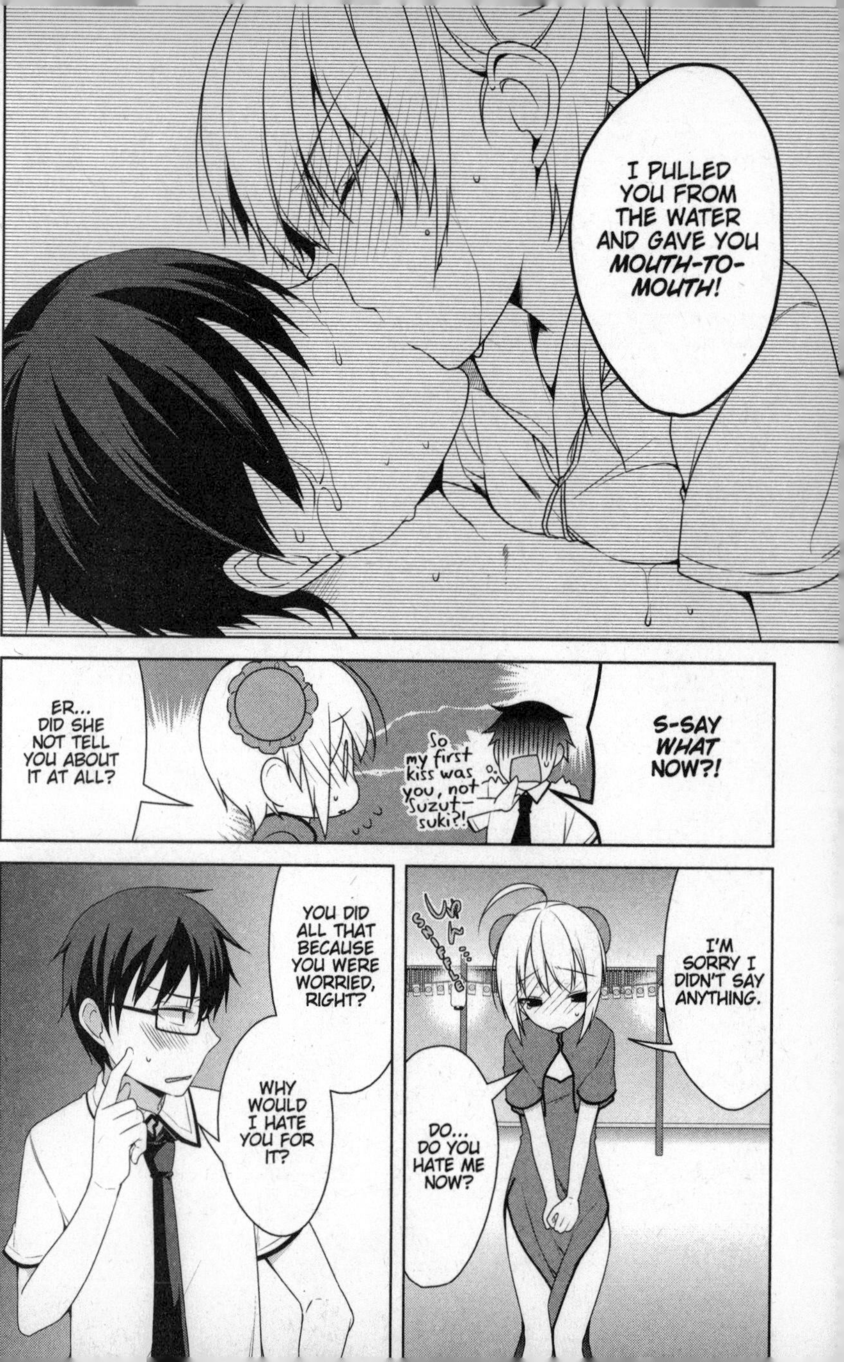
I PULLED YOU FROM THE WATER AND GAVE YOU MOUTH-TO-MOUTH!
S-SAY WHAT NOW?!
So my first kiss was you, not Suzutsuki?!
ER... DID SHE NOT TELL YOU ABOUT IT AT ALL?
I'M SORRY I DIDN'T SAY ANYTHING.
DO... DO YOU HATE ME NOW?
YOU DID ALL THAT BECAUSE YOU WERE WORRIED, RIGHT?
WHY WOULD I HATE YOU FOR IT?

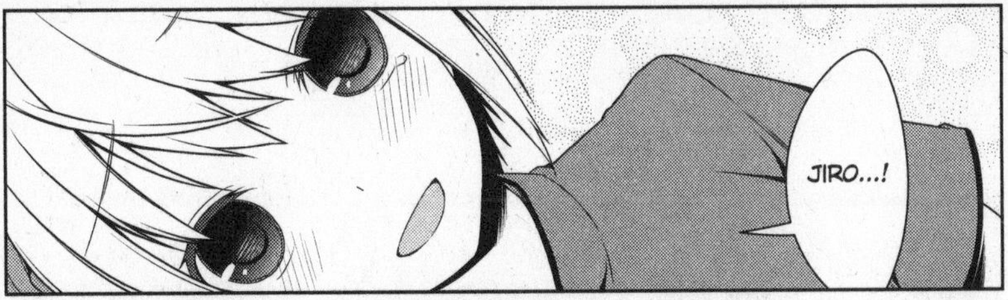
JIRO...!

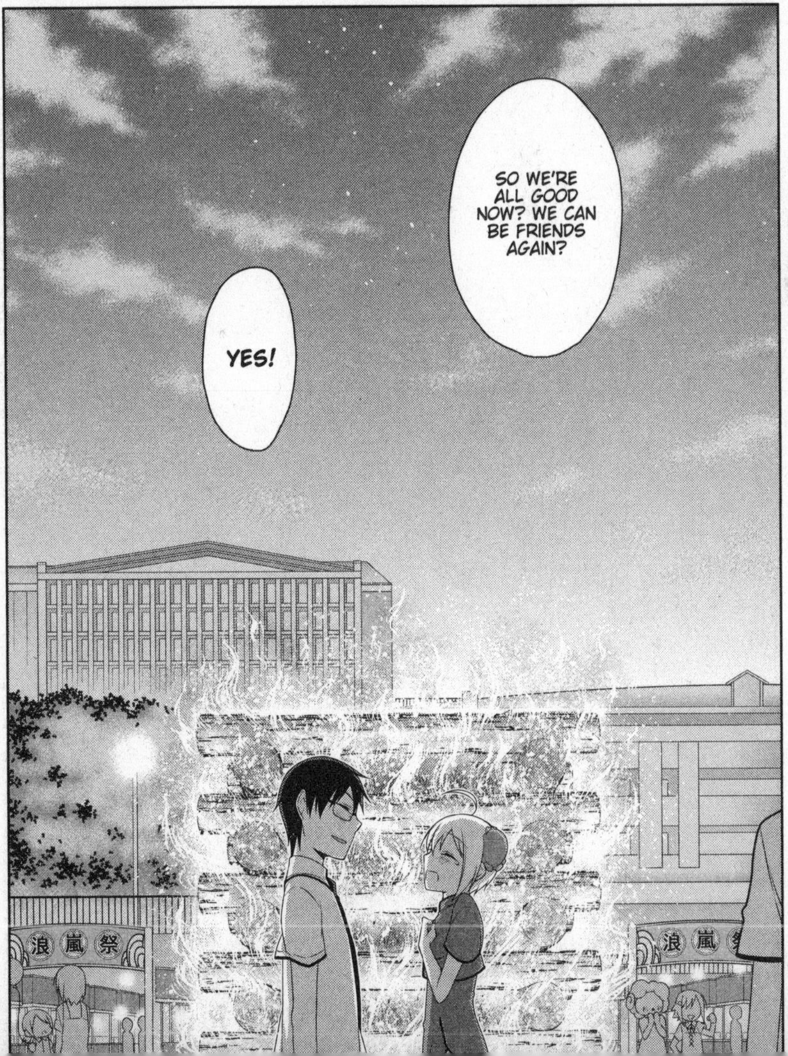
SO WE'RE ALL GOOD NOW? WE CAN BE FRIENDS AGAIN?
YES!
浪嵐祭

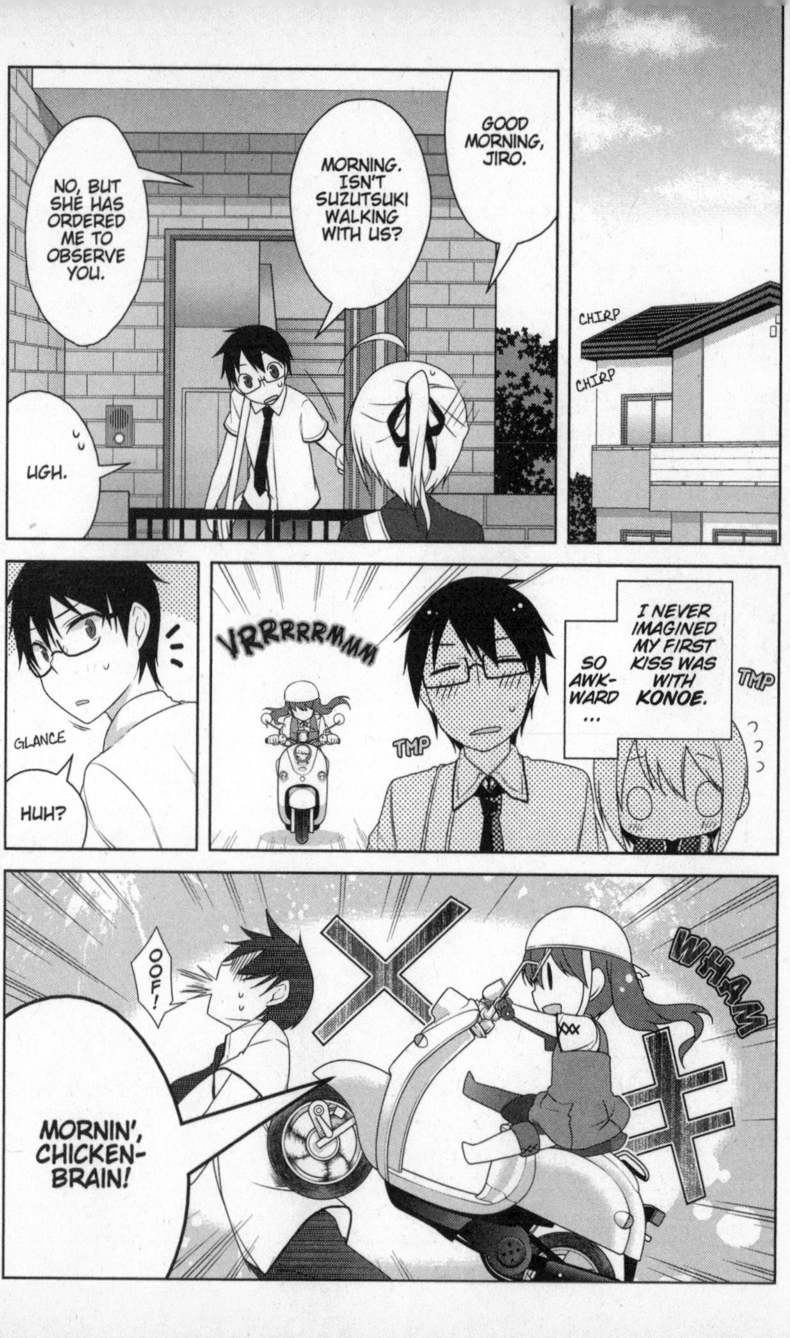
CHIRP
CHIRP
GOOD MORNING, JIRO.
MORNING. ISN'T SUZUTSUKI WALKING WITH US?
NO, BUT SHE HAS ORDERED ME TO OBSERVE YOU.
UGH.
TMP
I NEVER IMAGINED MY FIRST KISS WAS WITH KONOE.
SO AWK-WARD ...
TMP
VRRRRRMMM
GLANCE
HUH?
WHAM
OOF!
MORNIN', CHICKEN-BRAIN!

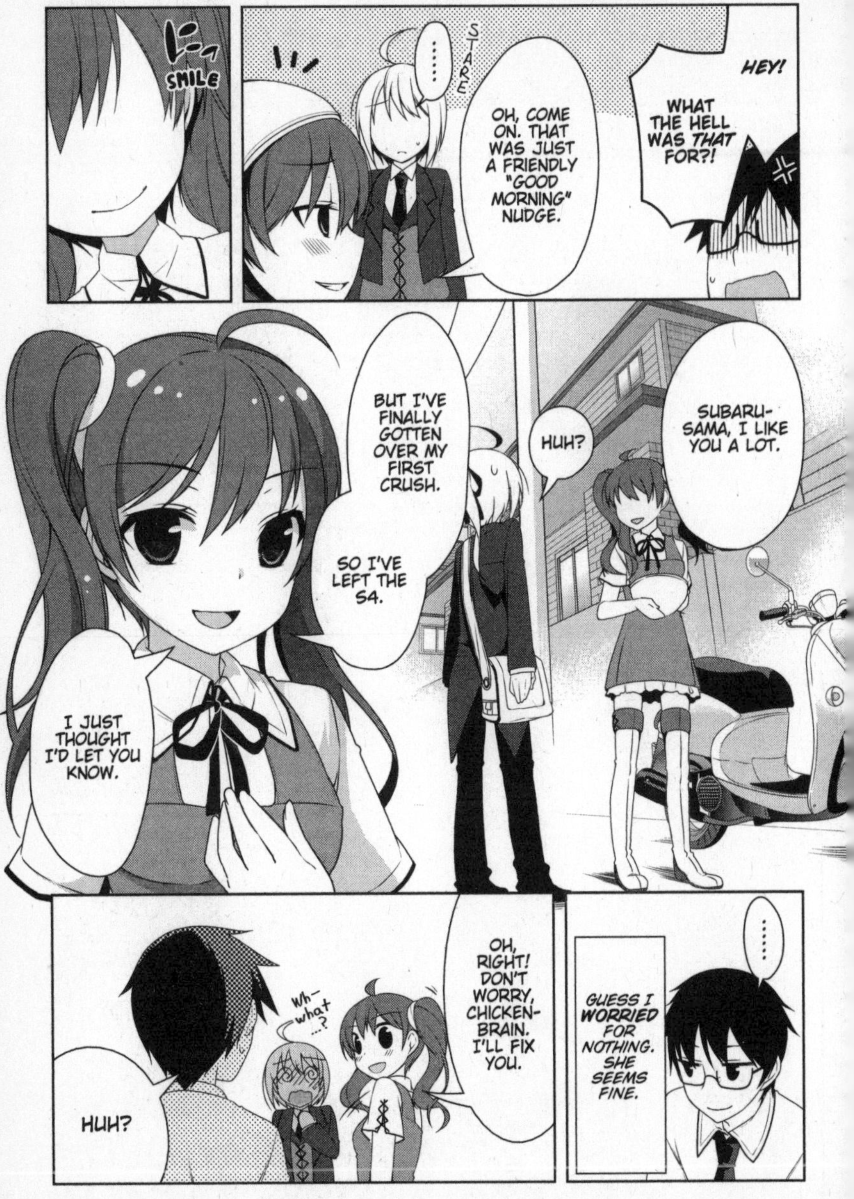
HEY!
WHAT THE HELL WAS THAT FOR?!
STARE
......
OH, COME ON. THAT WAS JUST A FRIENDLY "GOOD MORNING" NUDGE.
SMILE
SUBARU-SAMA, I LIKE YOU A LOT.
HUH?
BUT I'VE FINALLY GOTTEN OVER MY FIRST CRUSH.
SO I'VE LEFT THE S4.
I JUST THOUGHT I'D LET YOU KNOW.
......
GUESS I WORRIED FOR NOTHING. SHE SEEMS FINE.
OH, RIGHT! DON'T WORRY, CHICKEN-BRAIN. I'LL FIX YOU.
Wh-what...?
HUH?

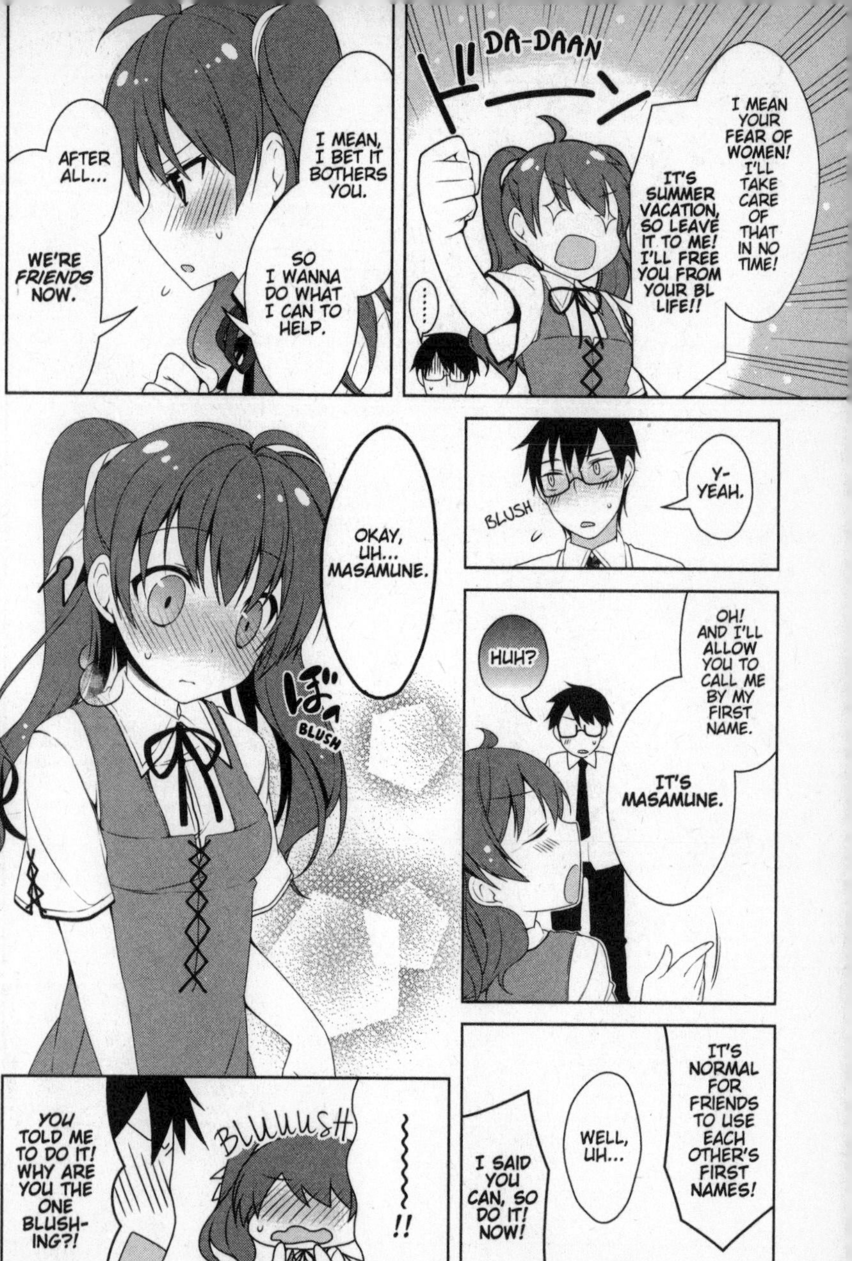
DA-DAAN
I MEAN YOUR FEAR OF WOMEN! I'LL TAKE CARE OF THAT IN NO TIME!
IT'S SUMMER VACATION, SO LEAVE IT TO ME! I'LL FREE YOU FROM YOUR BL LIFE!!
......
I MEAN, I BET IT BOTHERS YOU.
SO I WANNA DO WHAT I CAN TO HELP.
AFTER ALL...
WE'RE FRIENDS NOW.
Y-YEAH.
BLUSH
OH! AND I'LL ALLOW YOU TO CALL ME BY MY FIRST NAME.
HUH?
IT'S MASAMUNE.
IT'S NORMAL FOR FRIENDS TO USE EACH OTHER'S FIRST NAMES!
WELL, UH...
I SAID YOU CAN, SO DO IT! NOW!
OKAY, UH... MASAMUNE.
ぼっ
BLUSH
~~~~!!
BLUUUSH
YOU TOLD ME TO DO IT! WHY ARE YOU THE ONE BLUSH-ING?!
~~~~

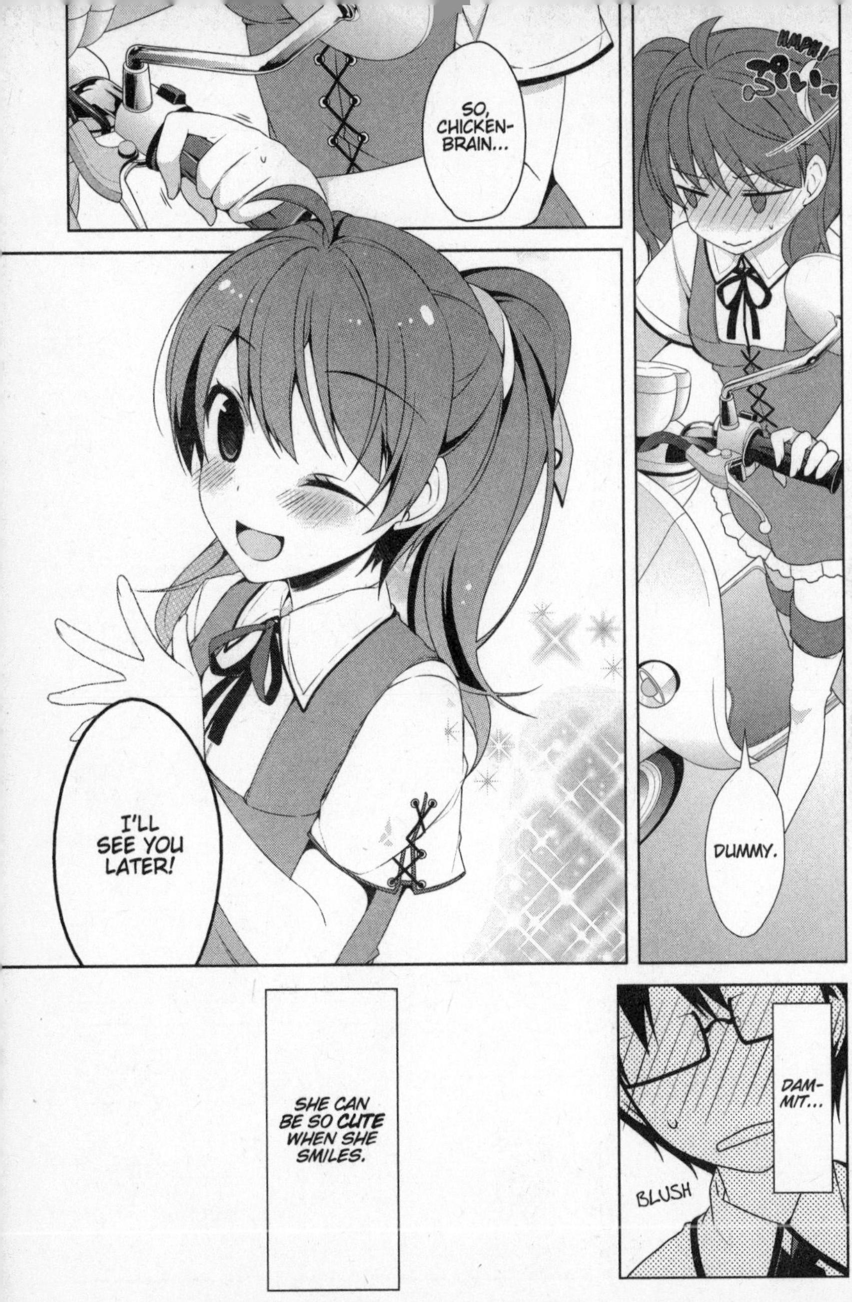
HMPH!
DUMMY.
SO, CHICKEN-BRAIN...
I'LL SEE YOU LATER!
DAM-MIT...
BLUSH
SHE CAN BE SO CUTE WHEN SHE SMILES.

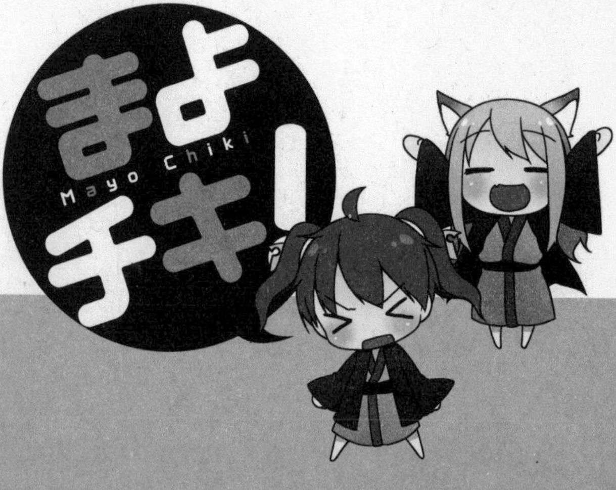
まよチキ!
Mayo Chiki

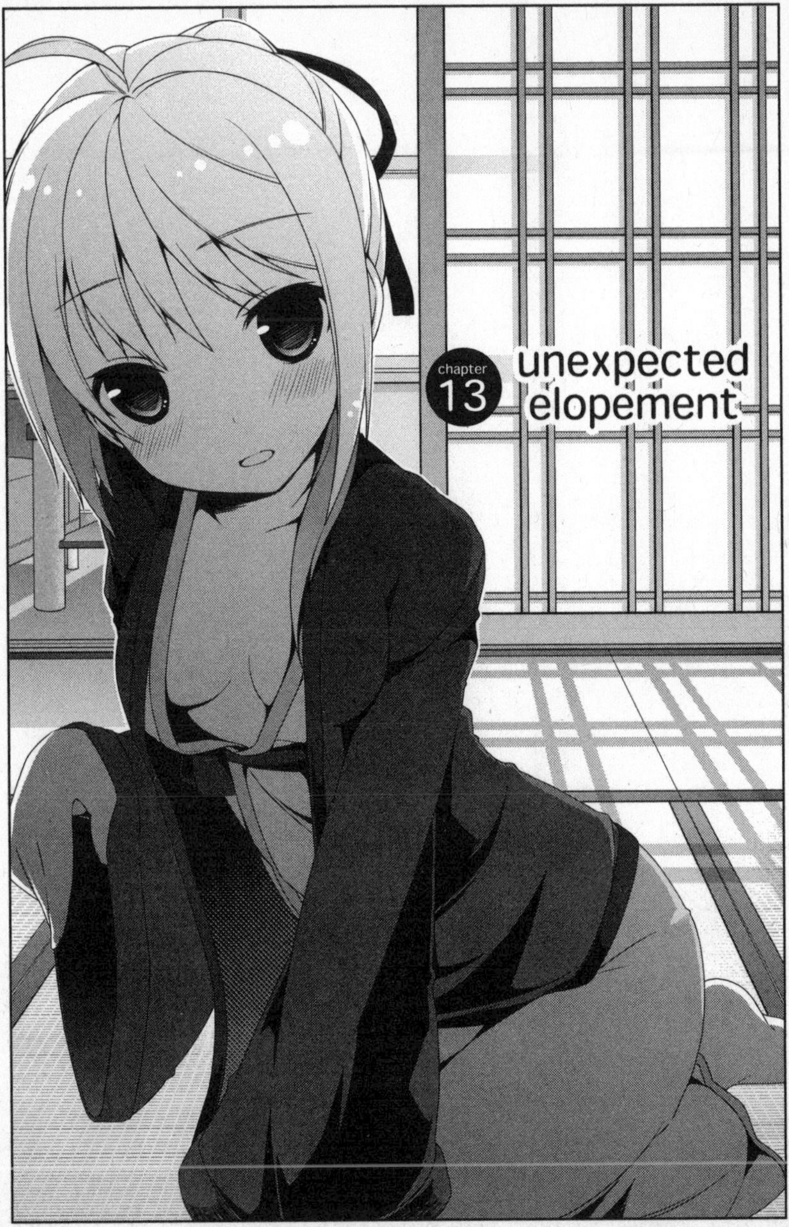
chapter
13
unexpected elopement

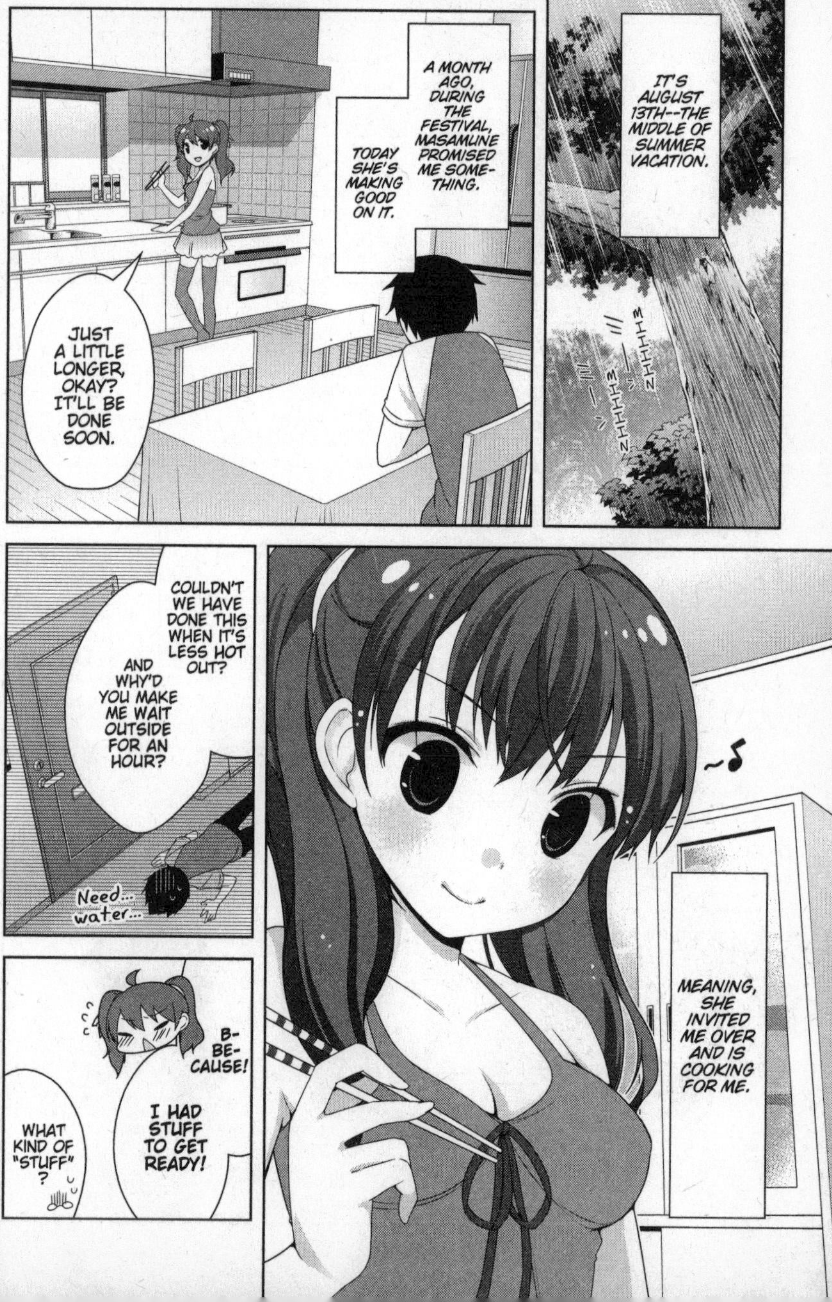
IT'S AUGUST 13TH--THE MIDDLE OF SUMMER VACATION.
MIIIIIN
MIIIIIN
A MONTH AGO, DURING THE FESTIVAL, MASAMUNE PROMISED ME SOME-THING.
TODAY SHE'S MAKING GOOD ON IT.
JUST A LITTLE LONGER, OKAY? IT'LL BE DONE SOON.
~♪
MEANING, SHE INVITED ME OVER AND IS COOKING FOR ME.
COULDN'T WE HAVE DONE THIS WHEN IT'S LESS HOT OUT?
AND WHY'D YOU MAKE ME WAIT OUTSIDE FOR AN HOUR?
Need... water...
B-BE-CAUSE!
I HAD STUFF TO GET READY!
WHAT KIND OF "STUFF"?

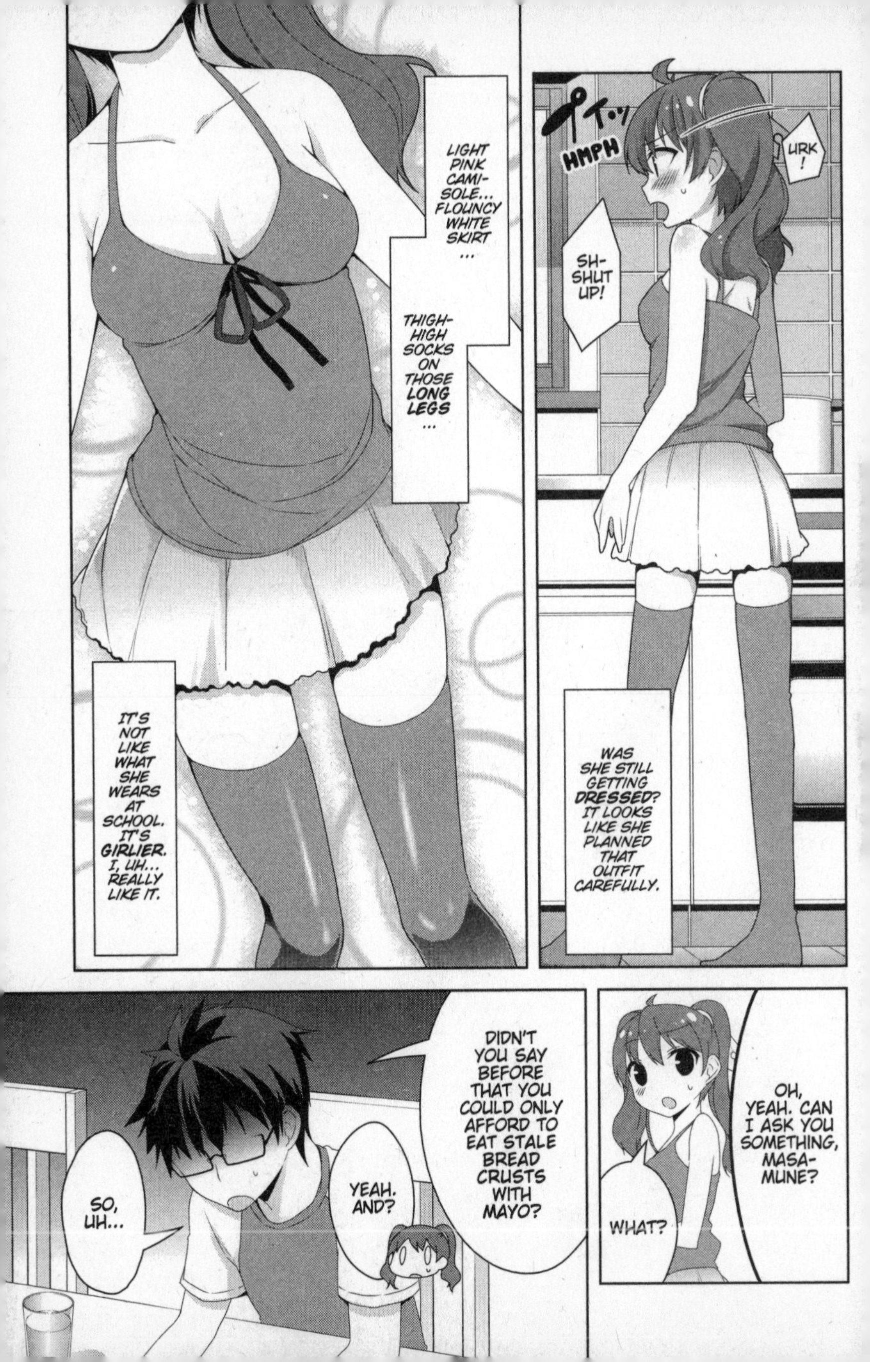
URK!
HMPH
SH-SHUT UP!
WAS SHE STILL GETTING DRESSED? IT LOOKS LIKE SHE PLANNED THAT OUTFIT CAREFULLY.
LIGHT PINK CAMISOLE... FLOUNCY WHITE SKIRT...
THIGH-HIGH SOCKS ON THOSE LONG LEGS...
IT'S NOT LIKE WHAT SHE WEARS AT SCHOOL. IT'S GIRLIER. I, UH... REALLY LIKE IT.
OH, YEAH. CAN I ASK YOU SOMETHING, MASAMUNE?
WHAT?
DIDN'T YOU SAY BEFORE THAT YOU COULD ONLY AFFORD TO EAT STALE BREAD CRUSTS WITH MAYO?
YEAH. AND?
SO, UH...

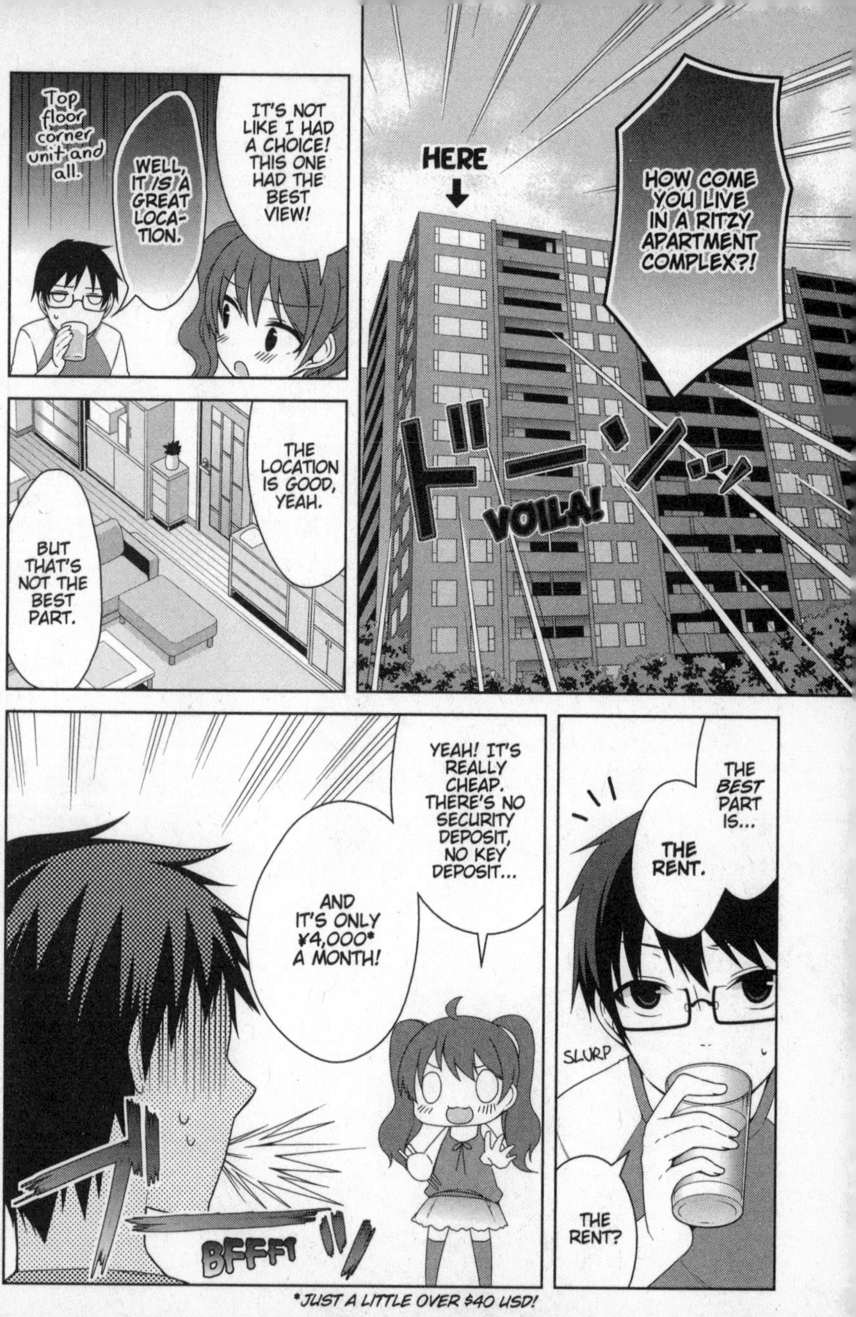
HOW COME YOU LIVE IN A RITZY APARTMENT COMPLEX?!
HERE
VOILA!
IT'S NOT LIKE I HAD A CHOICE! THIS ONE HAD THE BEST VIEW!
WELL, IT IS A GREAT LOCA- TION.
Top floor corner unit and all.
THE LOCATION IS GOOD, YEAH.
BUT THAT'S NOT THE BEST PART.
THE BEST PART IS...
THE RENT.
SLURP
THE RENT?
YEAH! IT'S REALLY CHEAP. THERE'S NO SECURITY DEPOSIT, NO KEY DEPOSIT...
AND IT'S ONLY ¥4,000* A MONTH!
BFFF!

*JUST A LITTLE OVER $40 USD!

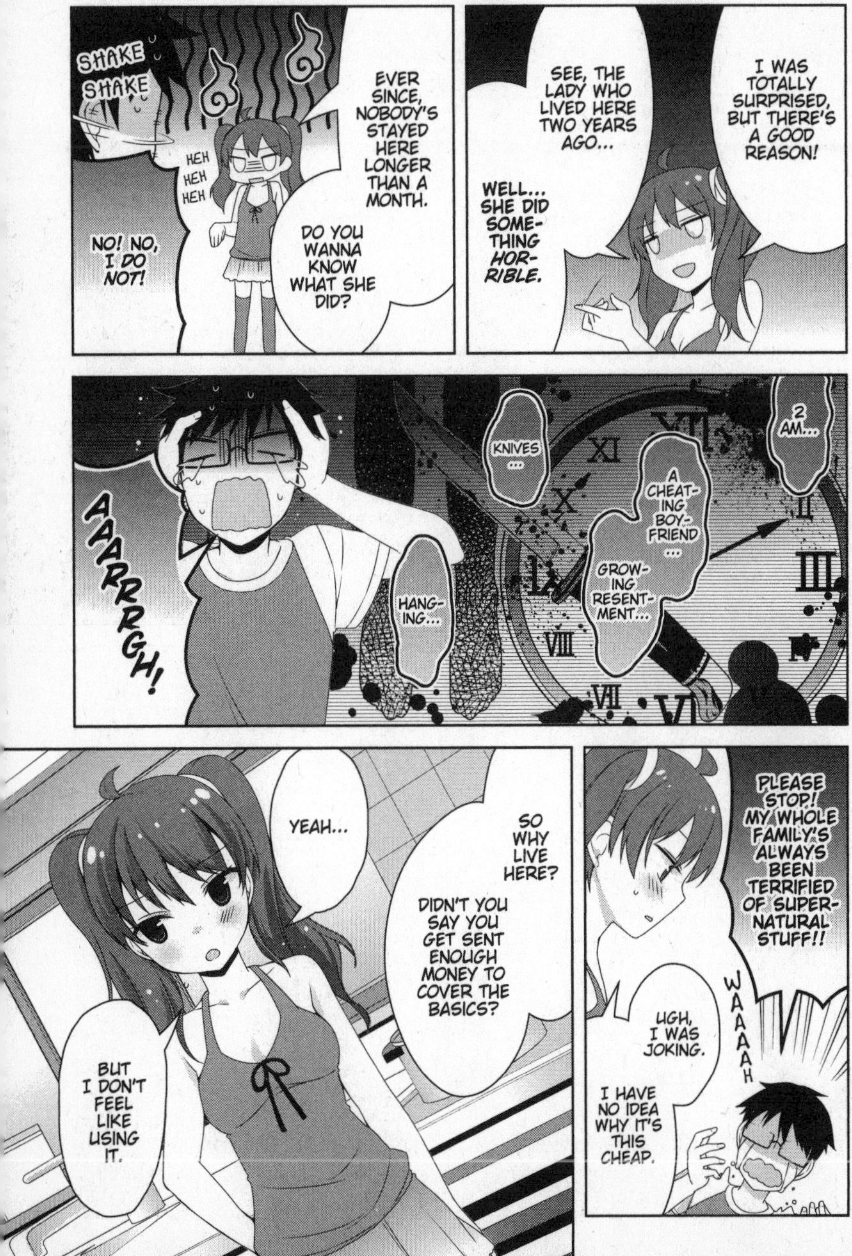
I WAS TOTALLY SURPRISED, BUT THERE'S A GOOD REASON!
SEE, THE LADY WHO LIVED HERE TWO YEARS AGO...
WELL... SHE DID SOMETHING *HORRIBLE*.
EVER SINCE, NOBODY'S STAYED HERE LONGER THAN A MONTH.
SHAKE SHAKE
HEH HEH HEH
DO YOU WANNA KNOW WHAT SHE DID?
NO! NO, I DO *NOT*!
2 AM...
A CHEATING BOYFRIEND...
KNIVES...
GROWING RESENTMENT...
HANGING...
AAARRRGH!
PLEASE STOP! MY WHOLE FAMILY'S ALWAYS BEEN TERRIFIED OF SUPERNATURAL STUFF!!
WAAAAAH
UGH, I WAS JOKING.
I HAVE NO IDEA WHY IT'S THIS CHEAP.
YEAH...
SO WHY LIVE HERE?
DIDN'T YOU SAY YOU GET SENT ENOUGH MONEY TO COVER THE BASICS?
BUT I DON'T FEEL LIKE USING IT.

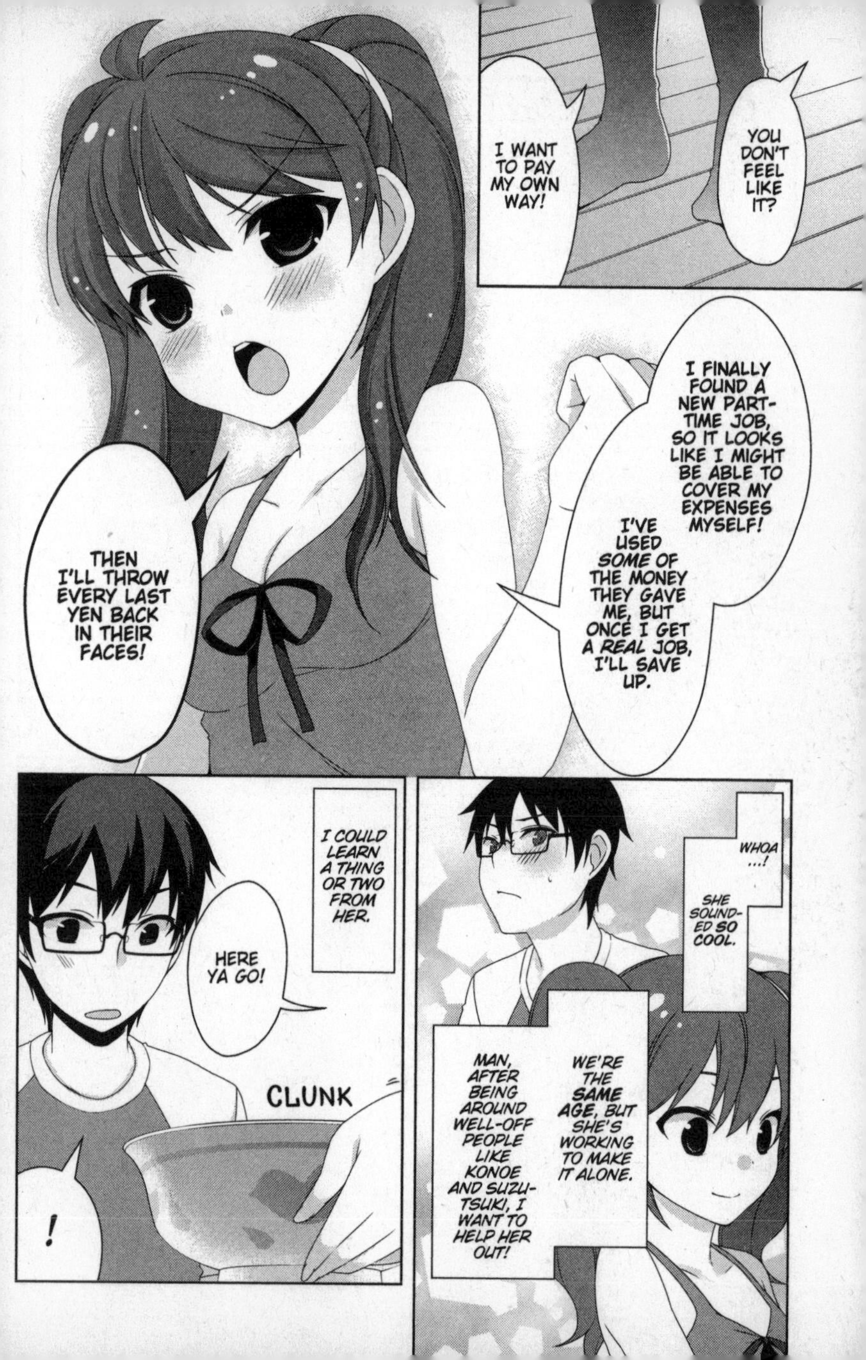
YOU DON'T FEEL LIKE IT?
I WANT TO PAY MY OWN WAY!
I FINALLY FOUND A NEW PART-TIME JOB, SO IT LOOKS LIKE I MIGHT BE ABLE TO COVER MY EXPENSES MYSELF!
I'VE USED *SOME* OF THE MONEY THEY GAVE ME, BUT ONCE I GET A *REAL* JOB, I'LL SAVE UP.
THEN I'LL THROW EVERY LAST YEN BACK IN THEIR FACES!
WHOA ...!
SHE SOUNDED SO COOL.
WE'RE THE SAME AGE, BUT SHE'S WORKING TO MAKE IT ALONE.
MAN, AFTER BEING AROUND WELL-OFF PEOPLE LIKE KONOE AND SUZUTSUKI, I WANT TO HELP HER OUT!
I COULD LEARN A THING OR TWO FROM HER.
HERE YA GO!
CLUNK
!

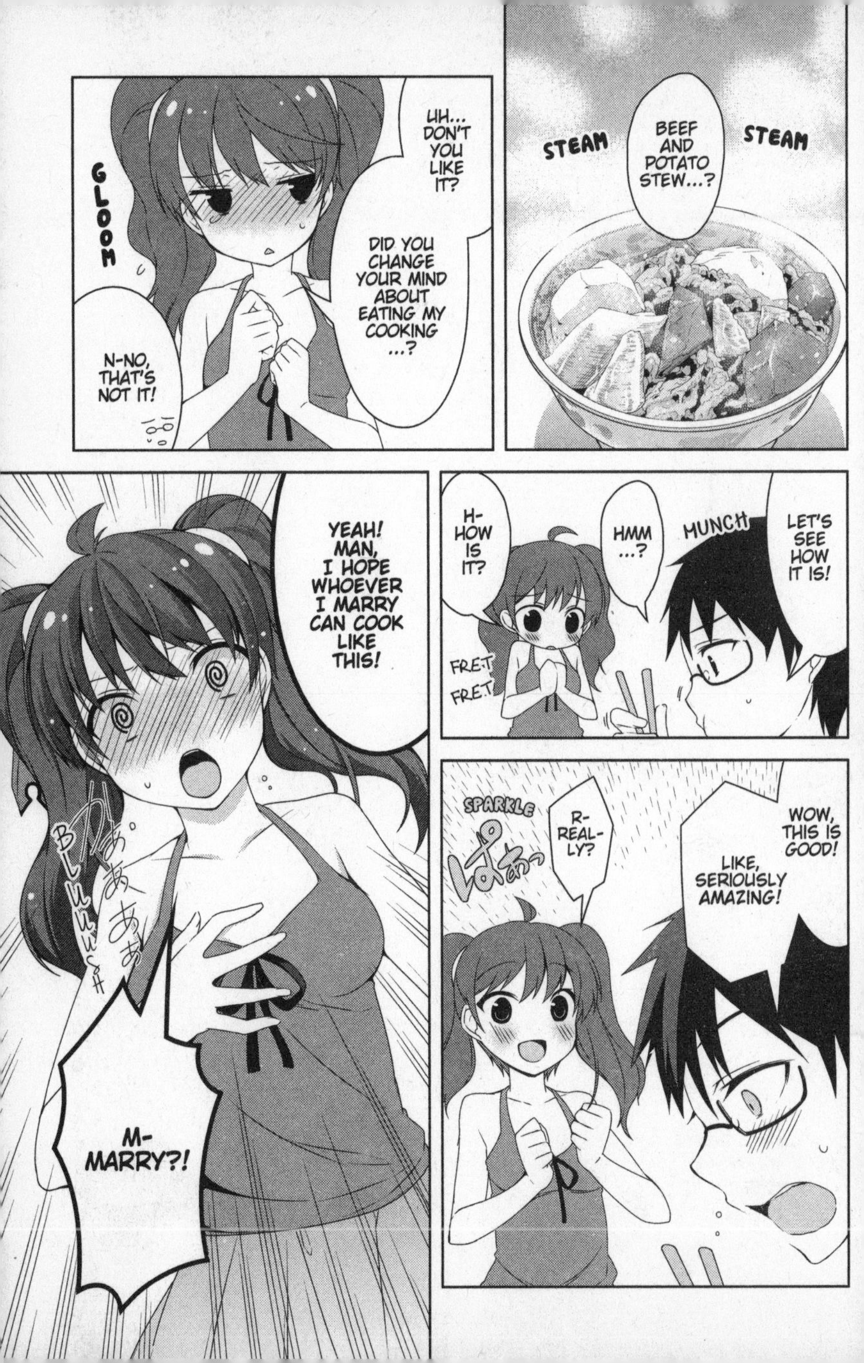
STEAM
BEEF AND POTATO STEW...?
STEAM
UH... DON'T YOU LIKE IT?
DID YOU CHANGE YOUR MIND ABOUT EATING MY COOKING ...?
GLOOM
N-NO, THAT'S NOT IT!
LET'S SEE HOW IT IS!
MUNCH
HMM ...?
H-HOW IS IT?
FRET FRET
WOW, THIS IS GOOD!
LIKE, SERIOUSLY AMAZING!
R-REAL-LY?
SPARKLE
YEAH! MAN, I HOPE WHOEVER I MARRY CAN COOK LIKE THIS!
BLUUUSH
M-MARRY?!

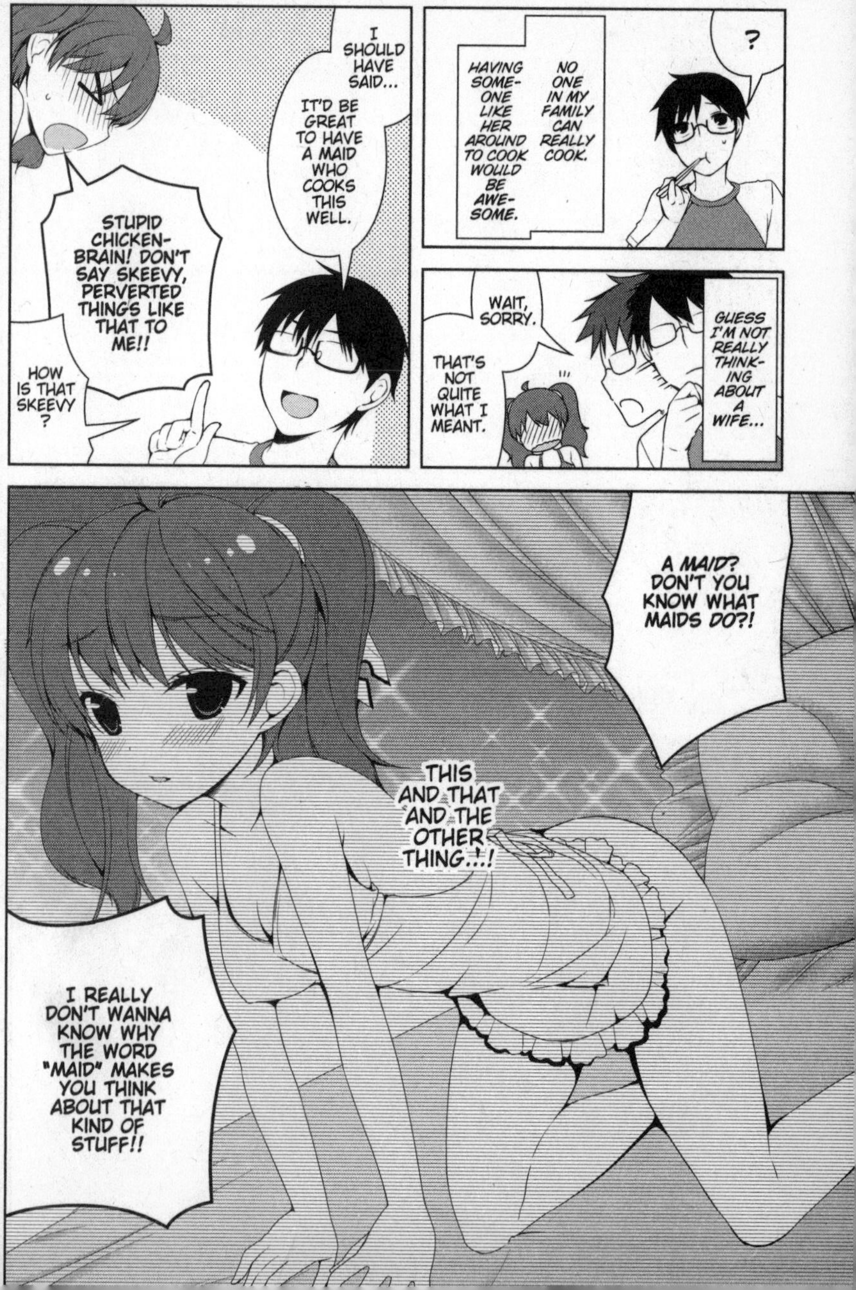
?
NO ONE IN MY FAMILY CAN REALLY COOK.
HAVING SOMEONE LIKE HER AROUND TO COOK WOULD BE AWESOME.
GUESS I'M NOT REALLY THINKING ABOUT A WIFE...
WAIT, SORRY.
THAT'S NOT QUITE WHAT I MEANT.
I SHOULD HAVE SAID...
IT'D BE GREAT TO HAVE A MAID WHO COOKS THIS WELL.
STUPID CHICKEN-BRAIN! DON'T SAY SKEEVY, PERVERTED THINGS LIKE THAT TO ME!!
HOW IS THAT SKEEVY?
A MAID? DON'T YOU KNOW WHAT MAIDS DO?!
THIS AND THAT AND THE OTHER THING...!
I REALLY DON'T WANNA KNOW WHY THE WORD "MAID" MAKES YOU THINK ABOUT THAT KIND OF STUFF!!

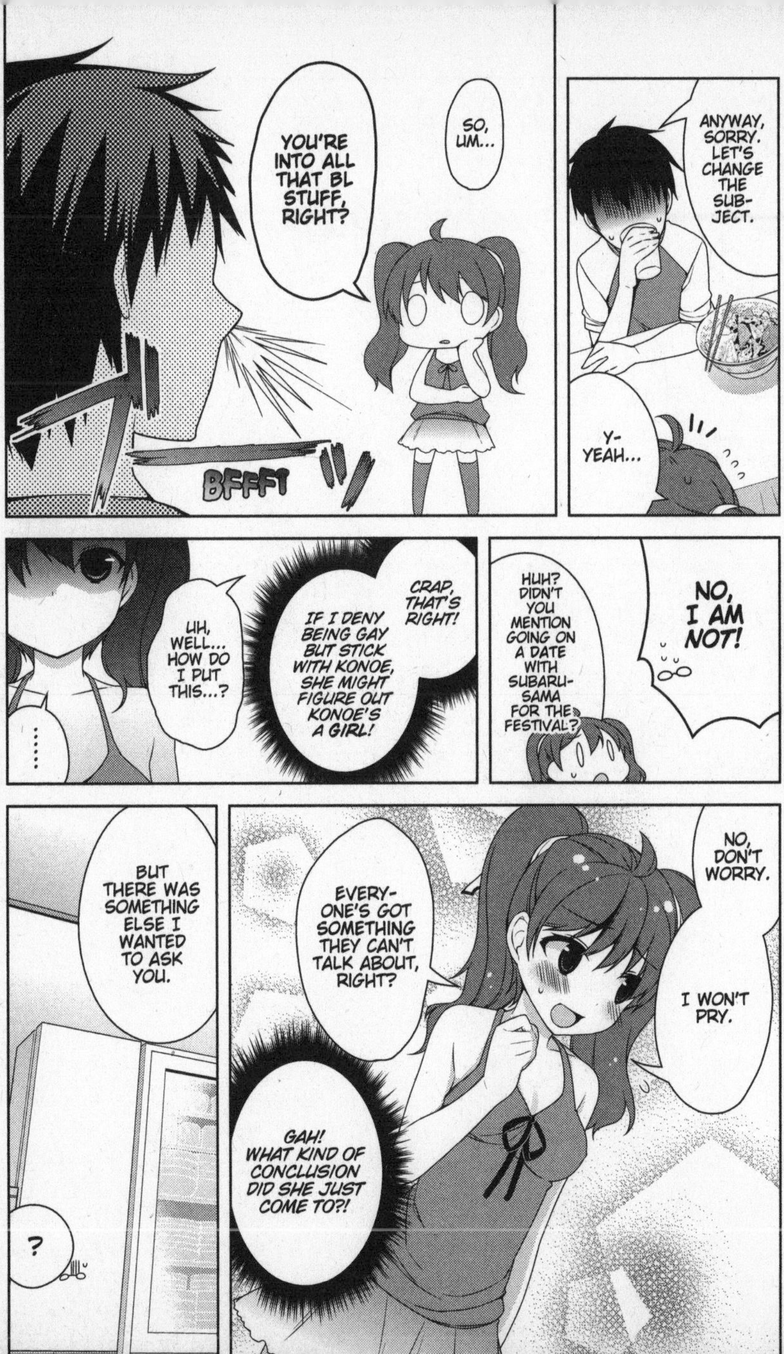
ANYWAY, SORRY. LET'S CHANGE THE SUB-JECT.
Y-YEAH...
SO, UM...
YOU'RE INTO ALL THAT BL STUFF, RIGHT?
BFFFT
NO, I AM NOT!
HUH? DIDN'T YOU MENTION GOING ON A DATE WITH SUBARU-SAMA FOR THE FESTIVAL?
CRAP, THAT'S RIGHT!
IF I DENY BEING GAY BUT STICK WITH KONOE, SHE MIGHT FIGURE OUT KONOE'S A GIRL!
UH, WELL... HOW DO I PUT THIS...?
......
NO, DON'T WORRY.
I WON'T PRY.
EVERY-ONE'S GOT SOMETHING THEY CAN'T TALK ABOUT, RIGHT?
GAH! WHAT KIND OF CONCLUSION DID SHE JUST COME TO?!
BUT THERE WAS SOMETHING ELSE I WANTED TO ASK YOU.
?

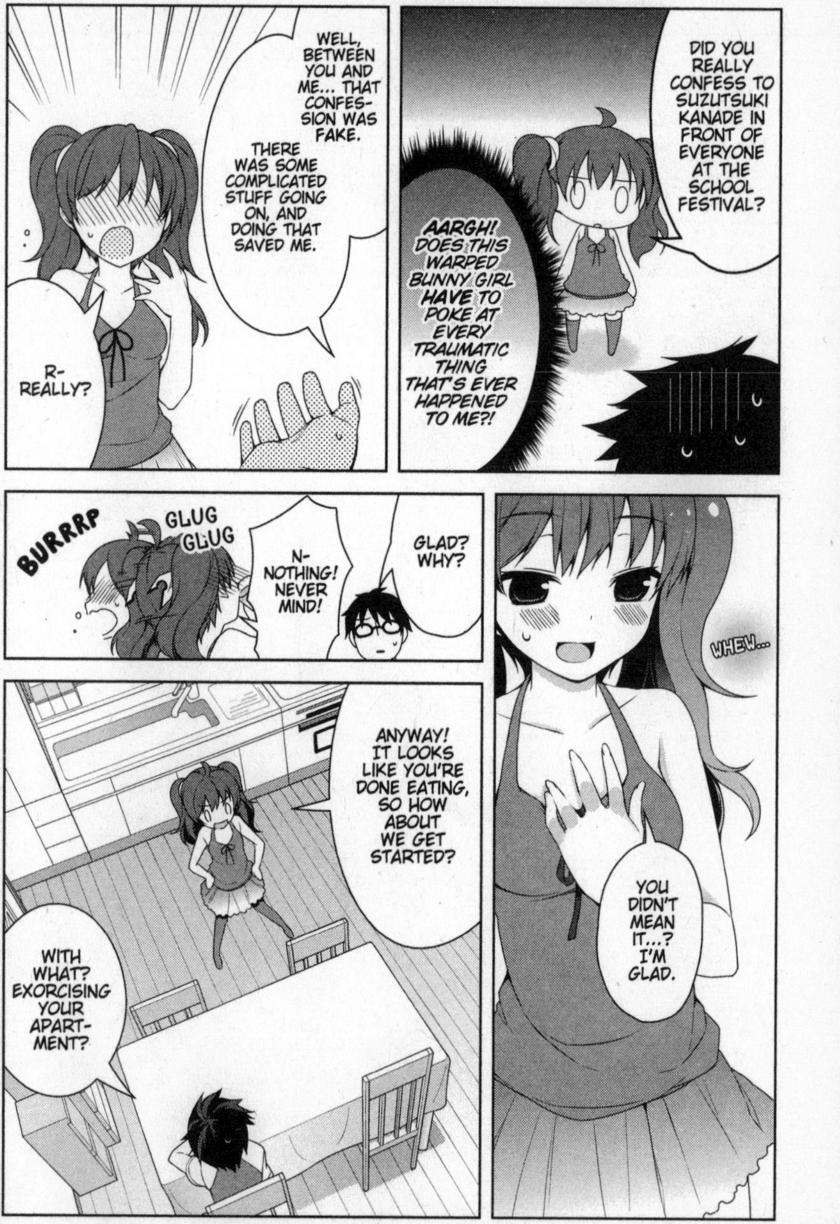
DID YOU REALLY CONFESS TO SUZUTSUKI KANADE IN FRONT OF EVERYONE AT THE SCHOOL FESTIVAL?
AARGH! DOES THIS WARPED BUNNY GIRL HAVE TO POKE AT EVERY TRAUMATIC THING THAT'S EVER HAPPENED TO ME?!
WELL, BETWEEN YOU AND ME... THAT CONFESSION WAS FAKE.
THERE WAS SOME COMPLICATED STUFF GOING ON, AND DOING THAT SAVED ME.
R-REALLY?
WHEW...
YOU DIDN'T MEAN IT...? I'M GLAD.
GLAD? WHY?
N-NOTHING! NEVER MIND!
GLUG GLUG
BURRRP
ANYWAY! IT LOOKS LIKE YOU'RE DONE EATING, SO HOW ABOUT WE GET STARTED?
WITH WHAT? EXORCISING YOUR APARTMENT?

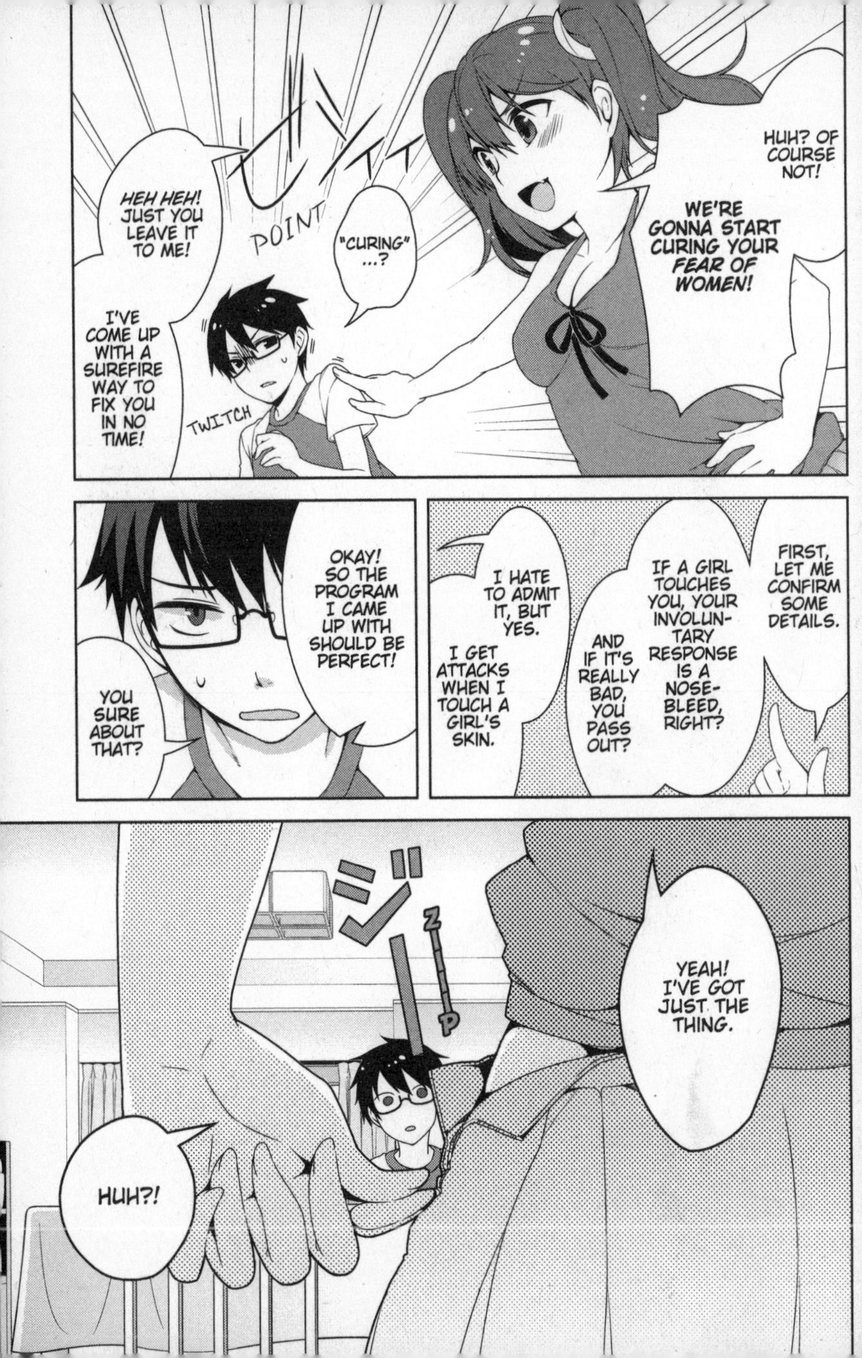
HUH? OF COURSE NOT!
WE'RE GONNA START CURING YOUR FEAR OF WOMEN!
"CURING" ...?
HEH HEH! JUST YOU LEAVE IT TO ME!
POINT
I'VE COME UP WITH A SUREFIRE WAY TO FIX YOU IN NO TIME!
TWITCH
FIRST, LET ME CONFIRM SOME DETAILS.
IF A GIRL TOUCHES YOU, YOUR INVOLUNTARY RESPONSE IS A NOSE-BLEED, RIGHT?
AND IF IT'S REALLY BAD, YOU PASS OUT?
I HATE TO ADMIT IT, BUT YES.
I GET ATTACKS WHEN I TOUCH A GIRL'S SKIN.
OKAY! SO THE PROGRAM I CAME UP WITH SHOULD BE PERFECT!
YOU SURE ABOUT THAT?
YEAH! I'VE GOT JUST THE THING.
ZIIIP
HUH?!

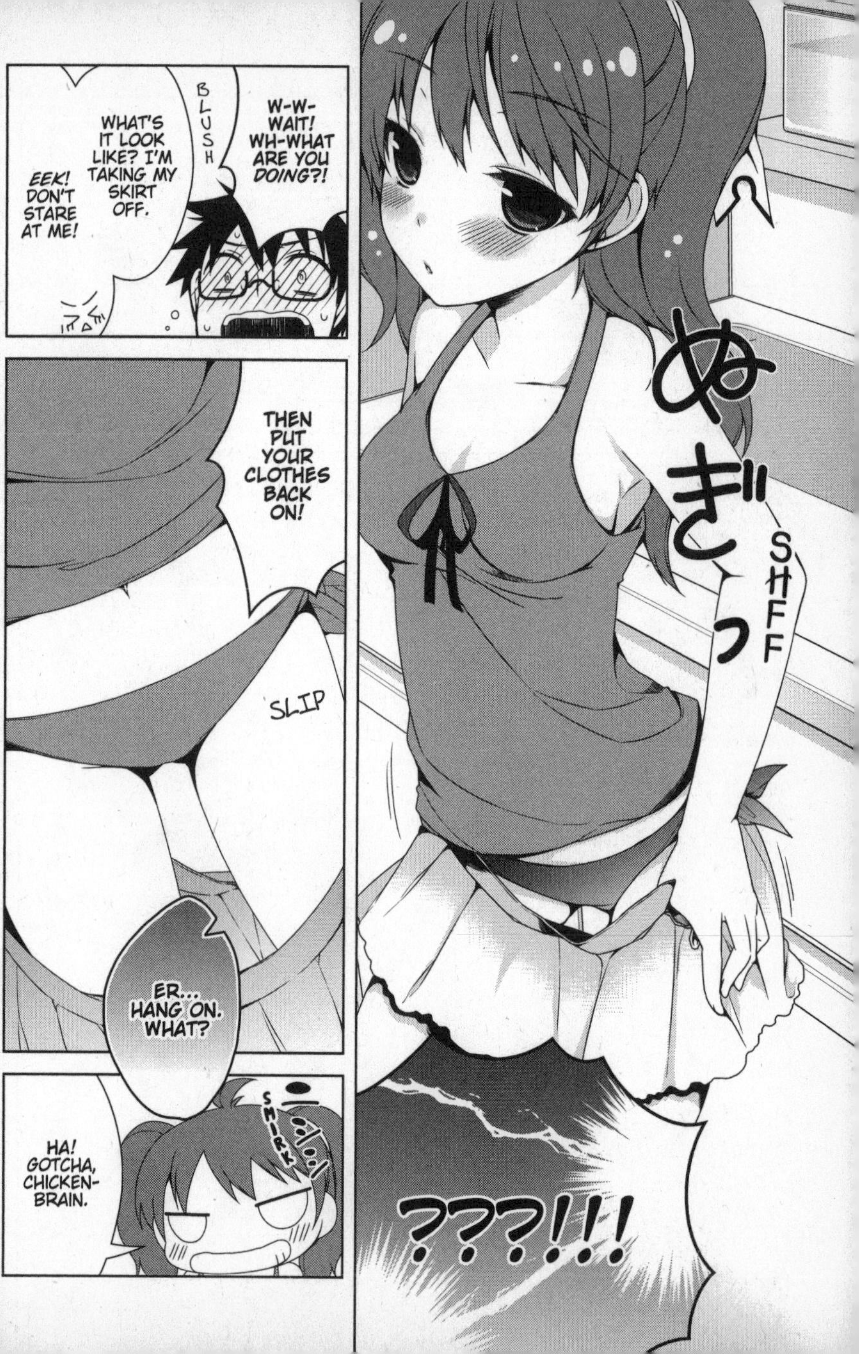
ぬぎっ
SHFF
???!!!
W-W-WAIT! WH-WHAT ARE YOU DOING?!
BLUSH
WHAT'S IT LOOK LIKE? I'M TAKING MY SKIRT OFF.
EEK! DON'T STARE AT ME!
THEN PUT YOUR CLOTHES BACK ON!
SLIP
ER... HANG ON. WHAT?
SMIRK
HA! GOTCHA, CHICKEN-BRAIN.

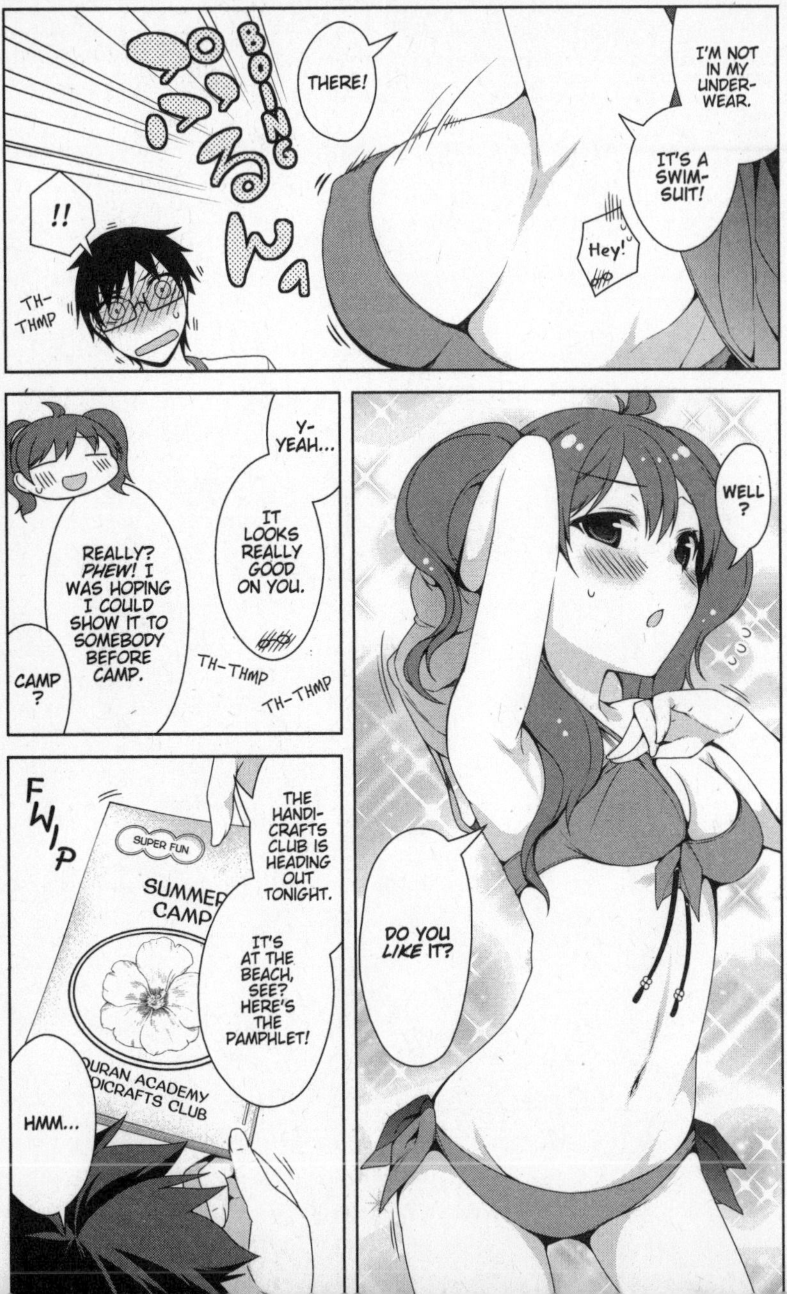
I'M NOT IN MY UNDER-WEAR.
IT'S A SWIM-SUIT!
Hey!
THERE!
BOING
!!
TH-THMP
WELL?
DO YOU LIKE IT?
Y-YEAH...
IT LOOKS REALLY GOOD ON YOU.
REALLY? PHEW! I WAS HOPING I COULD SHOW IT TO SOMEBODY BEFORE CAMP.
TH-THMP
TH-THMP
CAMP?
THE HANDI-CRAFTS CLUB IS HEADING OUT TONIGHT.
IT'S AT THE BEACH, SEE? HERE'S THE PAMPHLET!
FWIP
SUPER FUN
SUMMER CAMP
URAN ACADEMY
DICRAFTS CLUB
HMM...

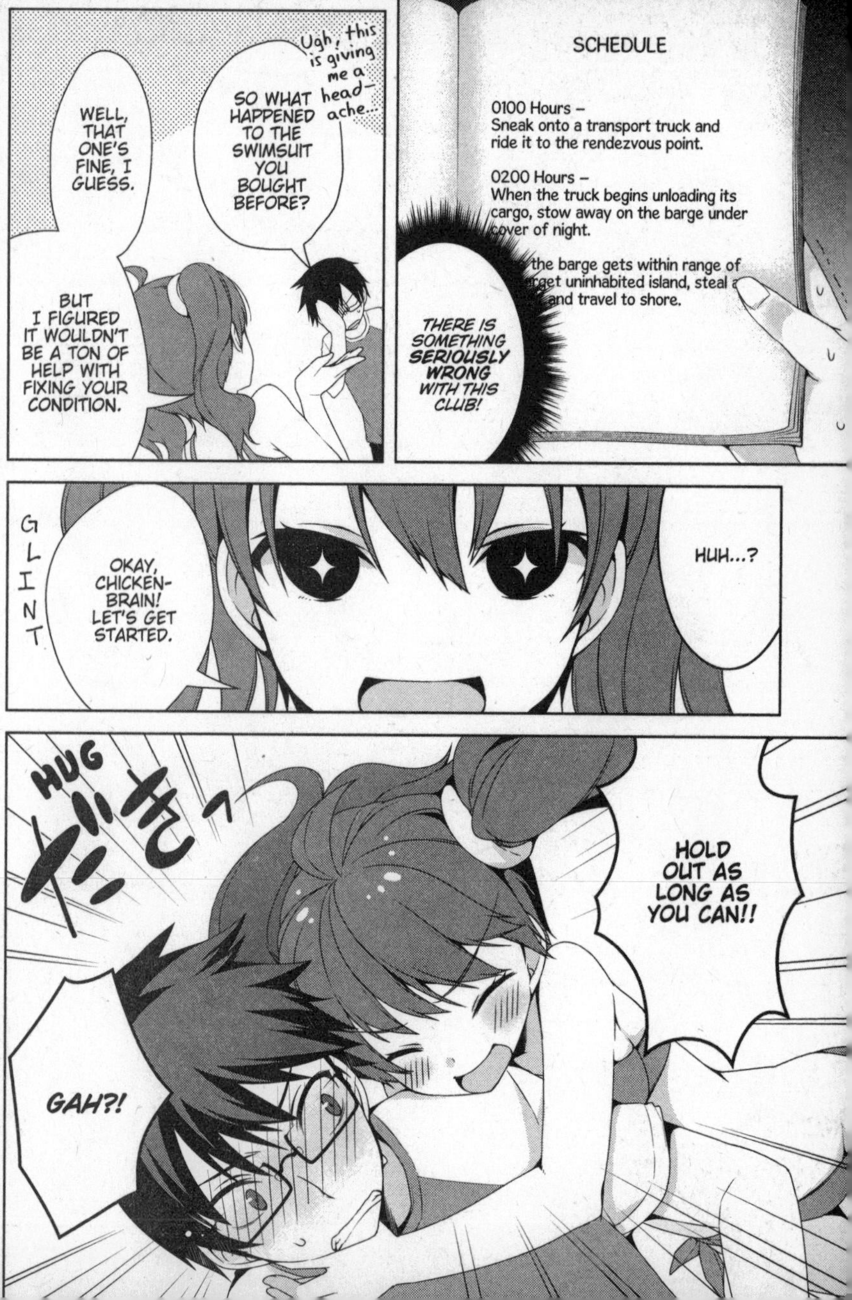
SCHEDULE
0100 Hours –
Sneak onto a transport truck and ride it to the rendezvous point.
0200 Hours –
When the truck begins unloading its cargo, stow away on the barge under cover of night.
the barge gets within range of
uninhabited island, steal
and travel to shore.
THERE IS SOMETHING SERIOUSLY WRONG WITH THIS CLUB!
Ugh, this is giving me a headache...
SO WHAT HAPPENED TO THE SWIMSUIT YOU BOUGHT BEFORE?
WELL, THAT ONE'S FINE, I GUESS.
BUT I FIGURED IT WOULDN'T BE A TON OF HELP WITH FIXING YOUR CONDITION.
HUH...?
GLINT
OKAY, CHICKEN-BRAIN! LET'S GET STARTED.
HOLD OUT AS LONG AS YOU CAN!!
HUG
GAH?!

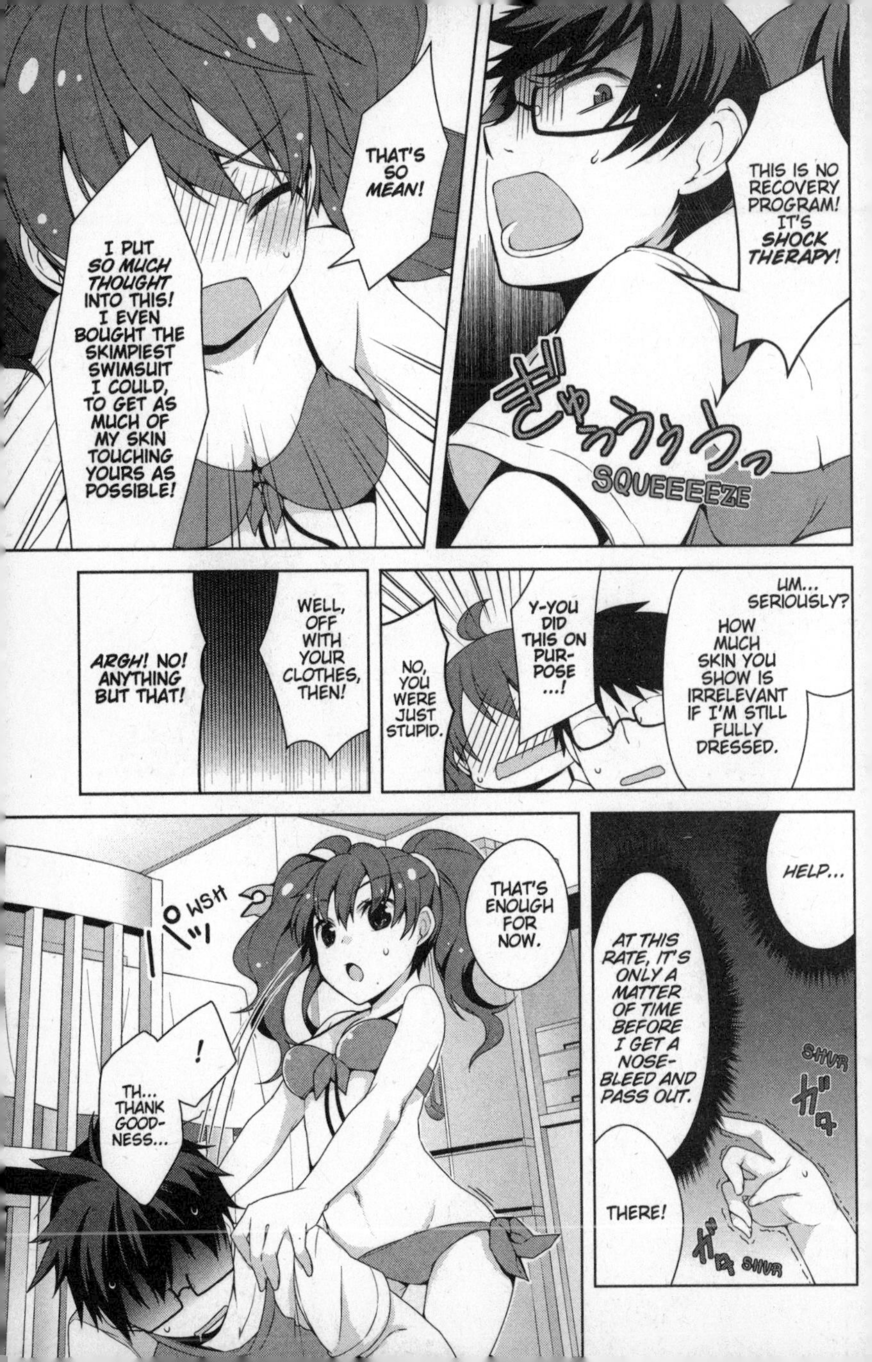
THIS IS NO RECOVERY PROGRAM! IT'S SHOCK THERAPY!
SQUEEEEEZE
THAT'S SO MEAN!
I PUT SO MUCH THOUGHT INTO THIS! I EVEN BOUGHT THE SKIMPIEST SWIMSUIT I COULD, TO GET AS MUCH OF MY SKIN TOUCHING YOURS AS POSSIBLE!
UM... SERIOUSLY?
HOW MUCH SKIN YOU SHOW IS IRRELEVANT IF I'M STILL FULLY DRESSED.
Y-YOU DID THIS ON PUR-POSE ...!
NO, YOU WERE JUST STUPID.
WELL, OFF WITH YOUR CLOTHES, THEN!
ARGH! NO! ANYTHING BUT THAT!
HELP...
AT THIS RATE, IT'S ONLY A MATTER OF TIME BEFORE I GET A NOSE-BLEED AND PASS OUT.
SHIVR
THERE!
SHIVR
THAT'S ENOUGH FOR NOW.
WSH
!
TH... THANK GOOD-NESS...

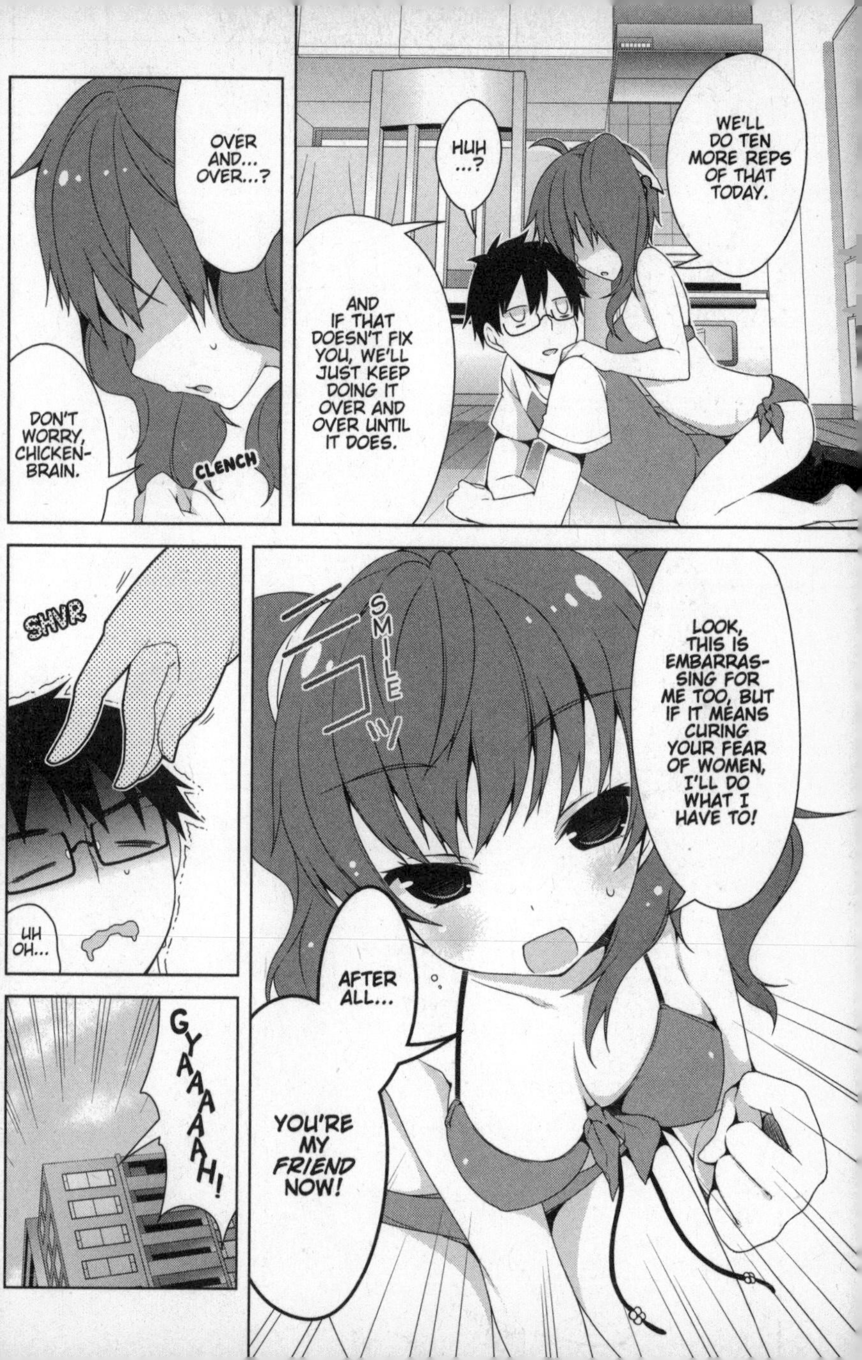
WE'LL DO TEN MORE REPS OF THAT TODAY.
HUH ...?
AND IF THAT DOESN'T FIX YOU, WE'LL JUST KEEP DOING IT OVER AND OVER UNTIL IT DOES.
OVER AND... OVER...?
DON'T WORRY, CHICKEN-BRAIN.
CLENCH
SMILE
LOOK, THIS IS EMBARRASSING FOR ME TOO, BUT IF IT MEANS CURING YOUR FEAR OF WOMEN, I'LL DO WHAT I HAVE TO!
AFTER ALL...
YOU'RE MY FRIEND NOW!
SHVR
UH OH...
GYAAAAAH!

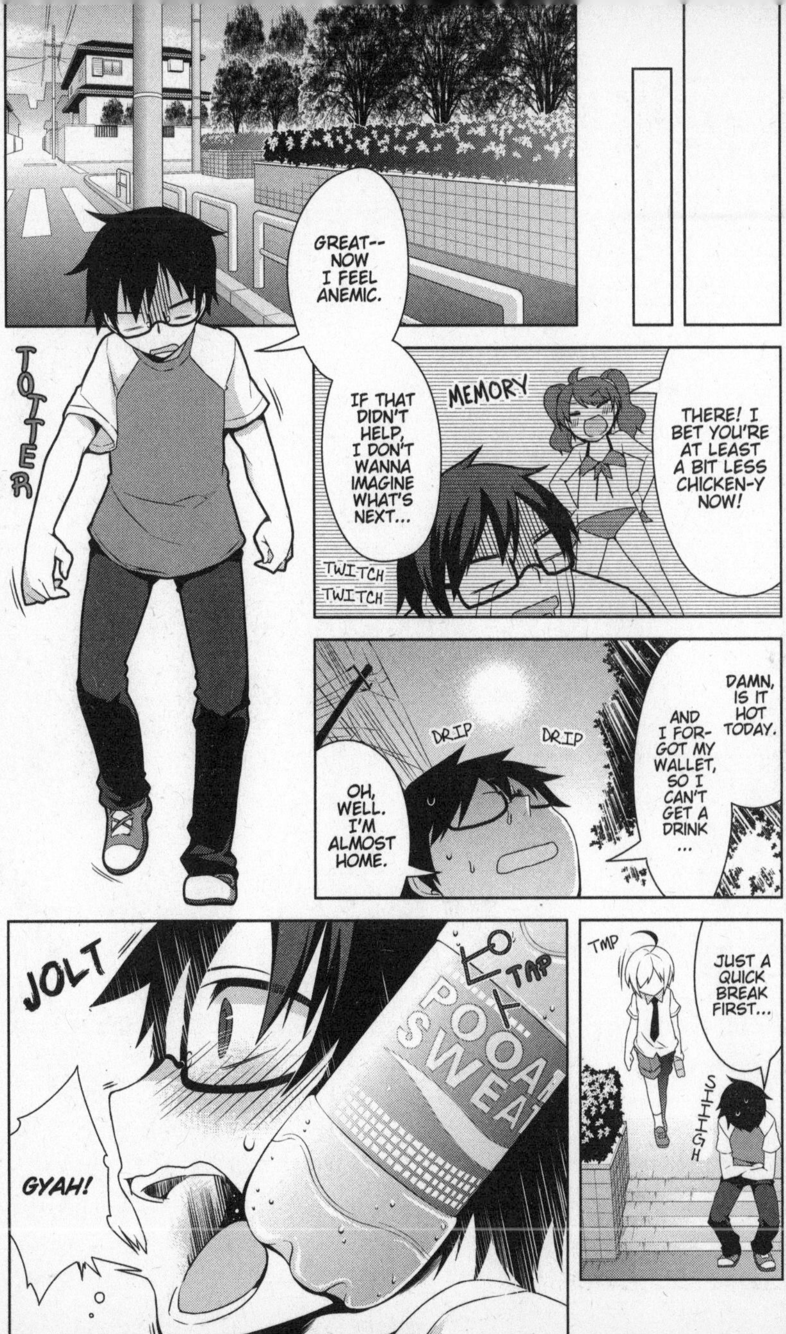
THERE! I BET YOU'RE AT LEAST A BIT LESS CHICKEN-Y NOW!
MEMORY
IF THAT DIDN'T HELP, I DON'T WANNA IMAGINE WHAT'S NEXT...
TWITCH
TWITCH
DAMN, IS IT HOT TODAY.
AND I FORGOT MY WALLET, SO I CAN'T GET A DRINK...
DRIP
DRIP
OH, WELL. I'M ALMOST HOME.
GREAT-- NOW I FEEL ANEMIC.
TOTTER
JUST A QUICK BREAK FIRST...
TMP
SIIIGH
TAP
POCA SWEA
JOLT
GYAH!

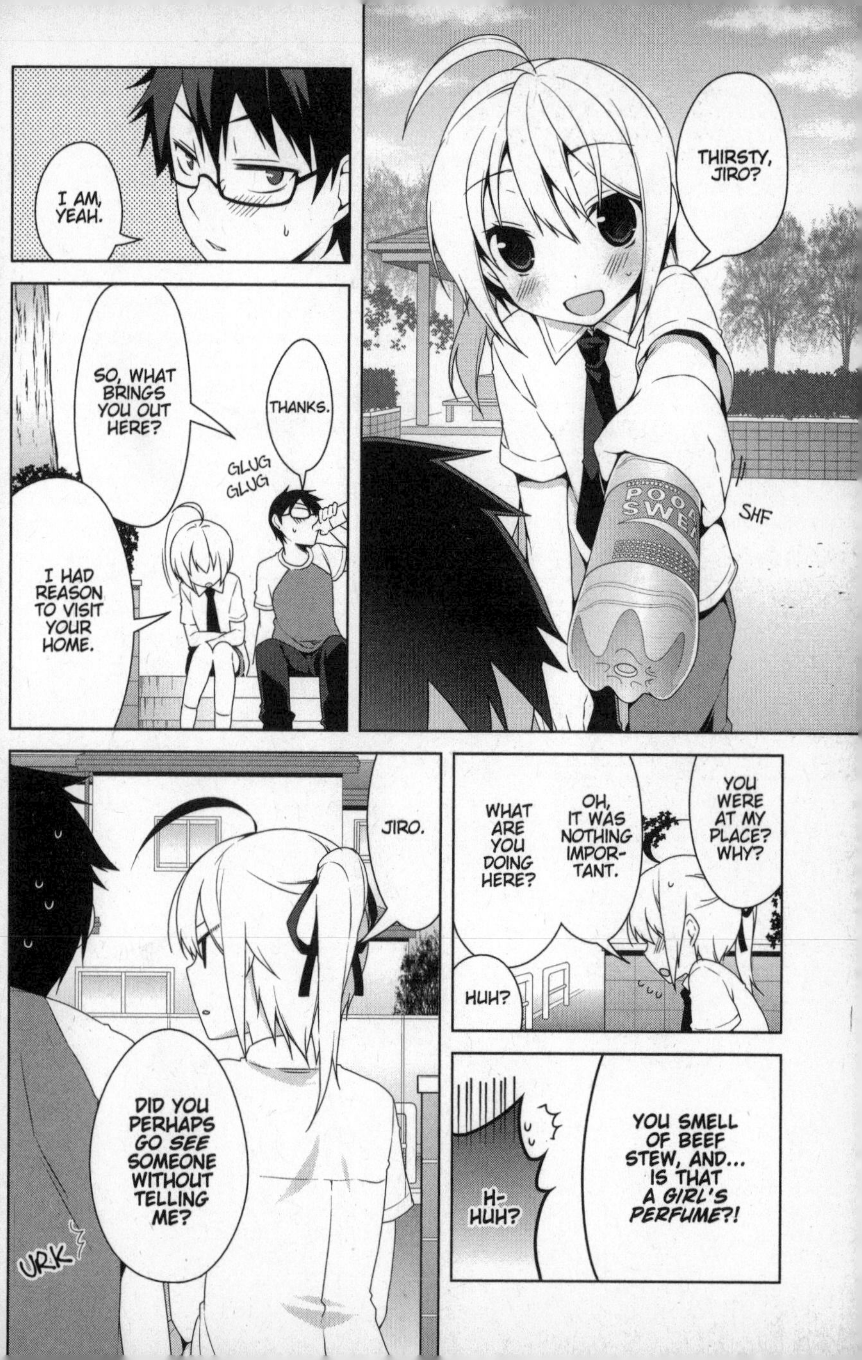
THIRSTY, JIRO?
SHF
I AM, YEAH.
THANKS.
GLUG GLUG
SO, WHAT BRINGS YOU OUT HERE?
I HAD REASON TO VISIT YOUR HOME.
YOU WERE AT MY PLACE? WHY?
OH, IT WAS NOTHING IMPORTANT.
WHAT ARE YOU DOING HERE?
HUH?
YOU SMELL OF BEEF STEW, AND... IS THAT A *GIRL'S PERFUME*?!
H-HUH?
JIRO.
DID YOU PERHAPS GO *SEE* SOMEONE WITHOUT TELLING ME?
URK

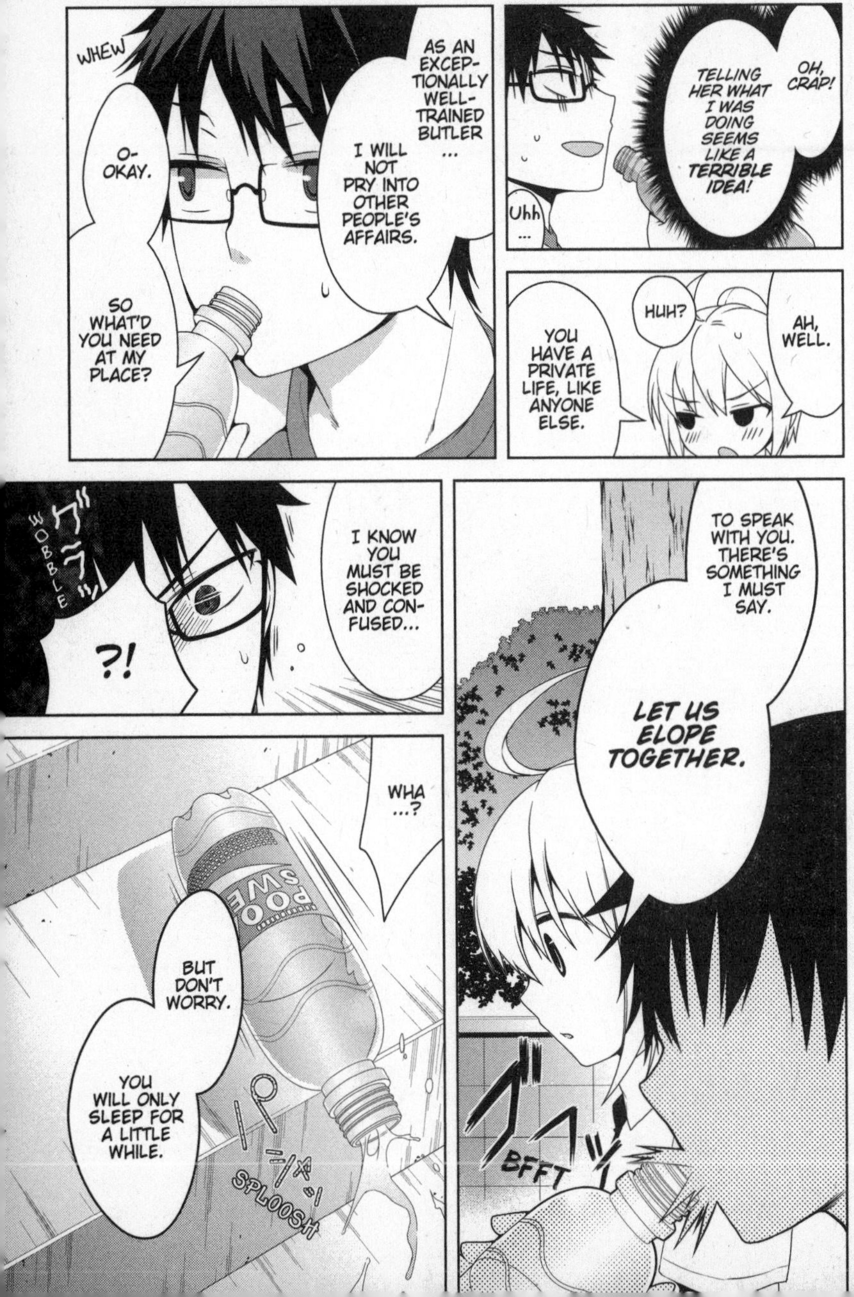
OH, CRAP!
TELLING HER WHAT I WAS DOING SEEMS LIKE A TERRIBLE IDEA!
Uhh ...
AH, WELL.
HUH?
YOU HAVE A PRIVATE LIFE, LIKE ANYONE ELSE.
AS AN EXCEPTIONALLY WELL-TRAINED BUTLER ...
I WILL NOT PRY INTO OTHER PEOPLE'S AFFAIRS.
WHEW
O-OKAY.
SO WHAT'D YOU NEED AT MY PLACE?
TO SPEAK WITH YOU. THERE'S SOMETHING I MUST SAY.
LET US ELOPE TOGETHER.
BFFT
I KNOW YOU MUST BE SHOCKED AND CONFUSED...
WOBBLE
?!
WHA ...?
BUT DON'T WORRY.
YOU WILL ONLY SLEEP FOR A LITTLE WHILE.
SPLOOSH

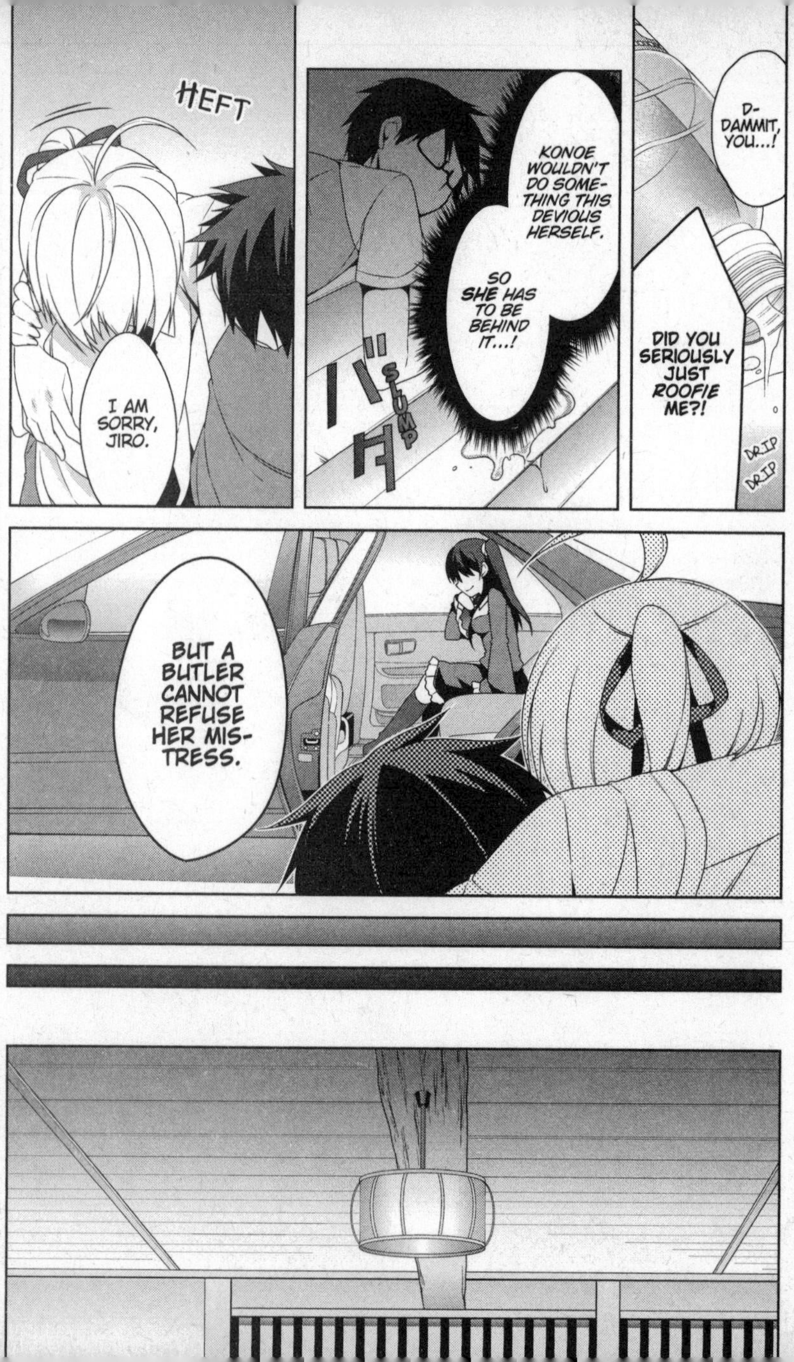
D-DAMMIT, YOU...!
DID YOU SERIOUSLY JUST ROOFIE ME?!
DRIP DRIP
KONOE WOULDN'T DO SOMETHING THIS DEVIOUS HERSELF.
SO SHE HAS TO BE BEHIND IT...!
SLUMP
HEFT
I AM SORRY, JIRO.
BUT A BUTLER CANNOT REFUSE HER MISTRESS.

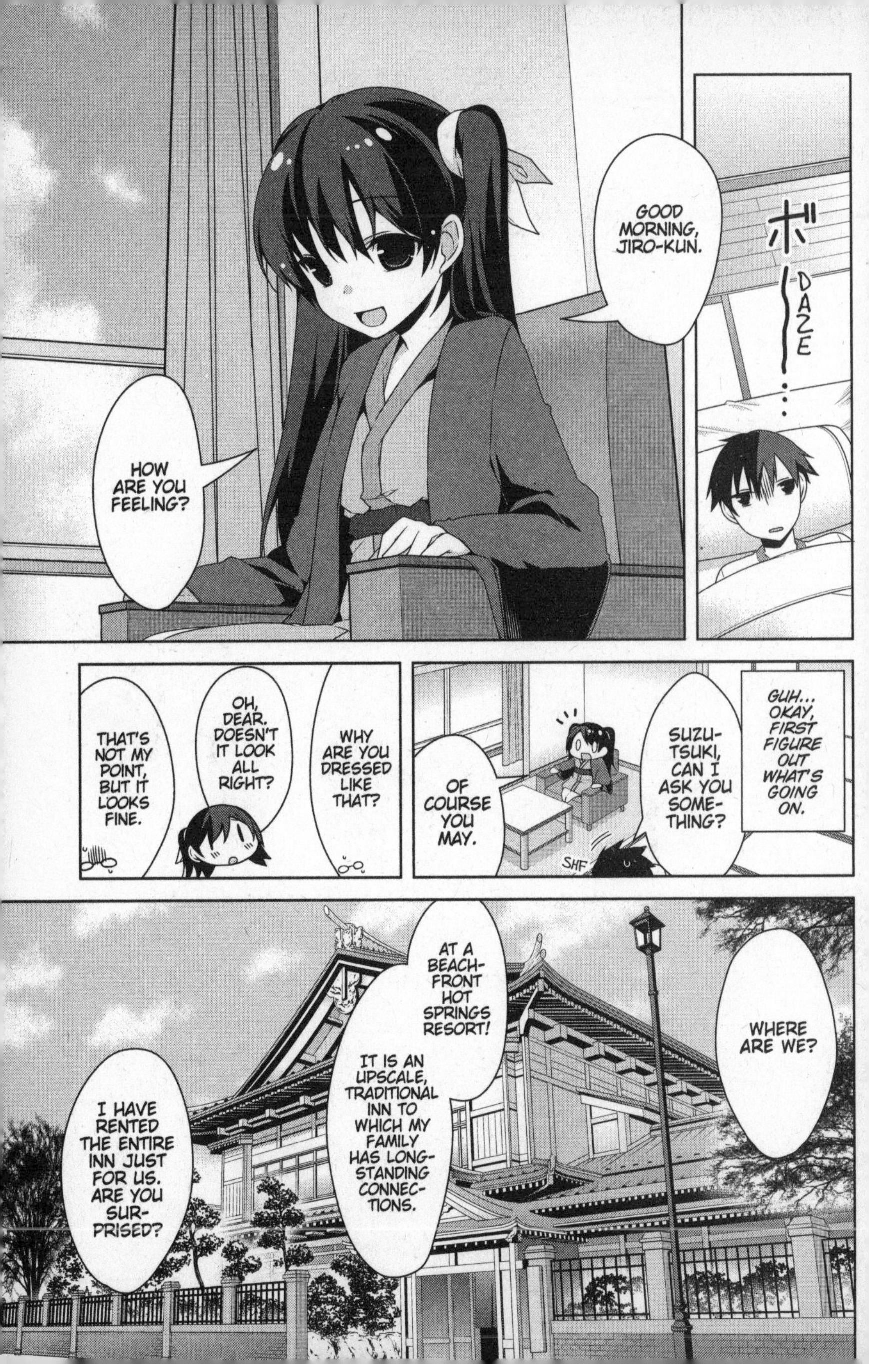
ボー…
DAZE
GOOD MORNING, JIRO-KUN.
HOW ARE YOU FEELING?
GUH... OKAY, FIRST FIGURE OUT WHAT'S GOING ON.
SUZUTSUKI, CAN I ASK YOU SOMETHING?
OF COURSE YOU MAY.
SHF
WHY ARE YOU DRESSED LIKE THAT?
OH, DEAR. DOESN'T IT LOOK ALL RIGHT?
THAT'S NOT MY POINT, BUT IT LOOKS FINE.
WHERE ARE WE?
AT A BEACH-FRONT HOT SPRINGS RESORT!
IT IS AN UPSCALE, TRADITIONAL INN TO WHICH MY FAMILY HAS LONG-STANDING CONNEC-TIONS.
I HAVE RENTED THE ENTIRE INN JUST FOR US. ARE YOU SUR-PRISED?

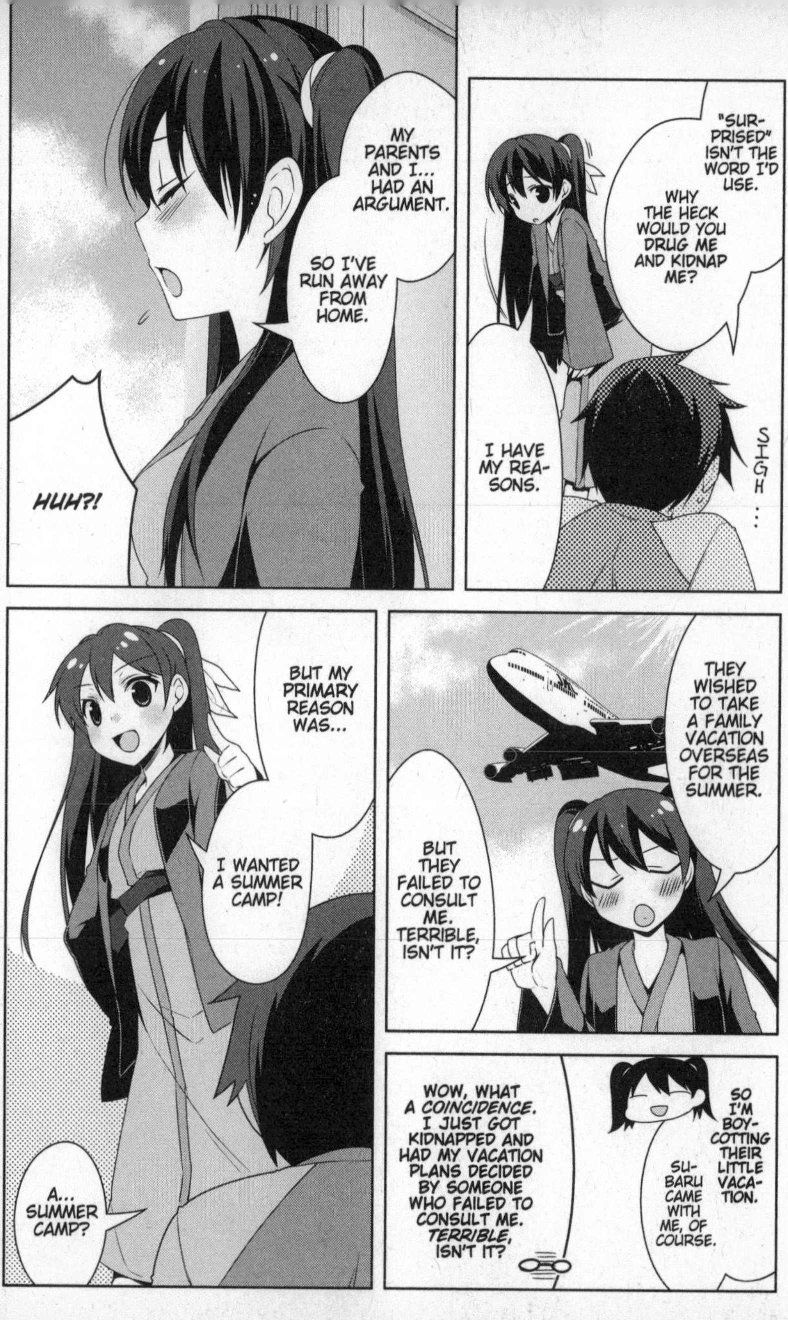

"SURPRISED" ISN'T THE WORD I'D USE.
WHY THE HECK WOULD YOU DRUG ME AND KIDNAP ME?
SIGH...
I HAVE MY REASONS.
MY PARENTS AND I... HAD AN ARGUMENT.
SO I'VE RUN AWAY FROM HOME.
HUH?!
THEY WISHED TO TAKE A FAMILY VACATION OVERSEAS FOR THE SUMMER.
BUT THEY FAILED TO CONSULT ME. TERRIBLE, ISN'T IT?
SO I'M BOYCOTTING THEIR LITTLE VACATION.
SUBARU CAME WITH ME, OF COURSE.
WOW, WHAT A *COINCIDENCE*. I JUST GOT KIDNAPPED AND HAD MY VACATION PLANS DECIDED BY SOMEONE WHO FAILED TO CONSULT ME. *TERRIBLE*, ISN'T IT?
BUT MY PRIMARY REASON WAS...
I WANTED A SUMMER CAMP!
A... SUMMER CAMP?

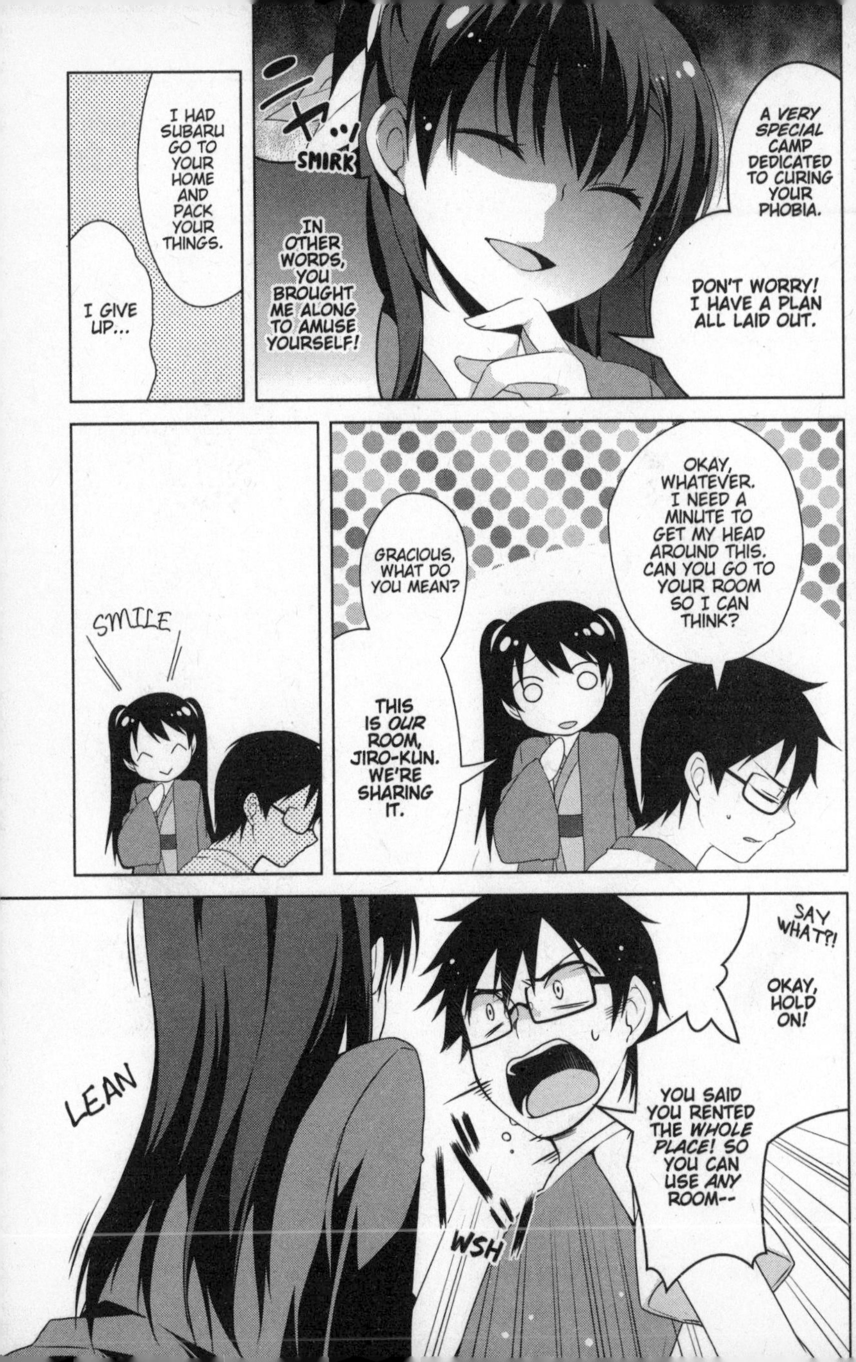
A VERY SPECIAL CAMP DEDICATED TO CURING YOUR PHOBIA.
DON'T WORRY! I HAVE A PLAN ALL LAID OUT.
SMIRK
IN OTHER WORDS, YOU BROUGHT ME ALONG TO AMUSE YOURSELF!
I HAD SUBARU GO TO YOUR HOME AND PACK YOUR THINGS.
I GIVE UP...
OKAY, WHATEVER. I NEED A MINUTE TO GET MY HEAD AROUND THIS. CAN YOU GO TO YOUR ROOM SO I CAN THINK?
GRACIOUS, WHAT DO YOU MEAN?
THIS IS *OUR* ROOM, JIRO-KUN. WE'RE SHARING IT.
SMILE
SAY WHAT?!
OKAY, HOLD ON!
YOU SAID YOU RENTED THE *WHOLE PLACE*! SO YOU CAN USE *ANY* ROOM--
LEAN
WSH

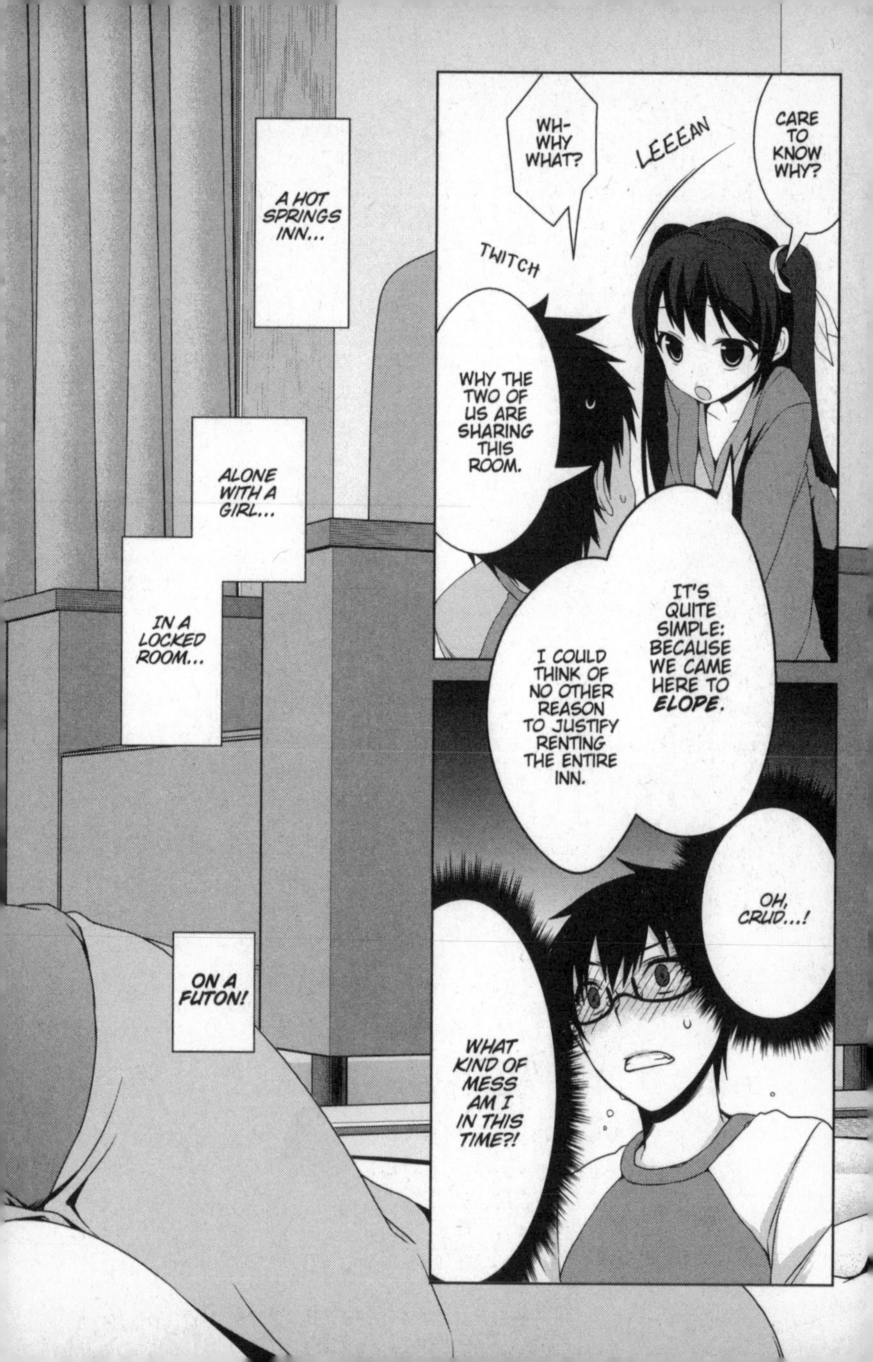
CARE TO KNOW WHY?
LEEEAN
WH- WHY WHAT?
TWITCH
WHY THE TWO OF US ARE SHARING THIS ROOM.
IT'S QUITE SIMPLE: BECAUSE WE CAME HERE TO ELOPE.
I COULD THINK OF NO OTHER REASON TO JUSTIFY RENTING THE ENTIRE INN.
OH, CRUD...!
WHAT KIND OF MESS AM I IN THIS TIME?!
A HOT SPRINGS INN...
ALONE WITH A GIRL...
IN A LOCKED ROOM...
ON A FUTON!

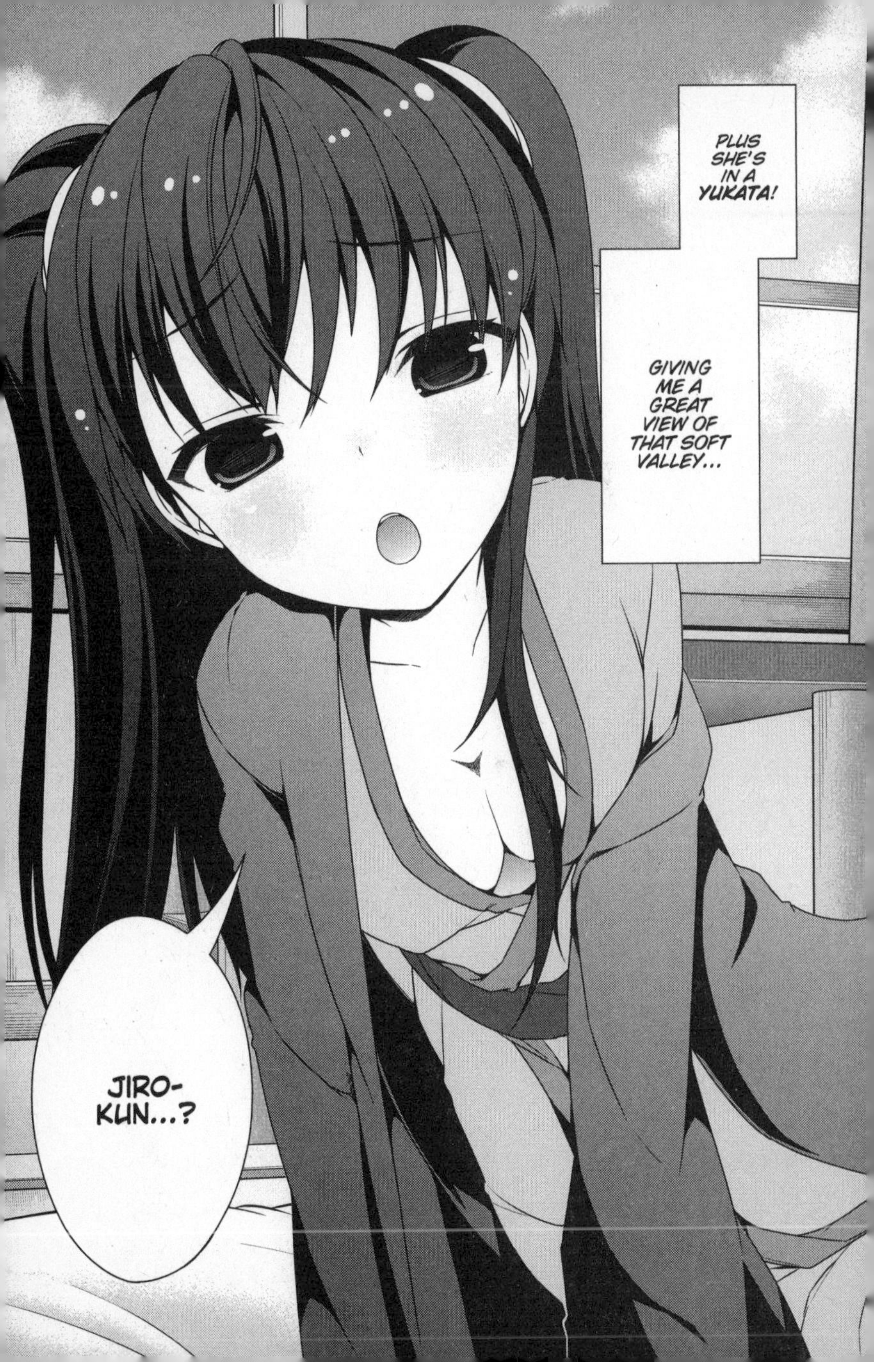
PLUS SHE'S IN A YUKATA!
GIVING ME A GREAT VIEW OF THAT SOFT VALLEY...
JIRO-KUN...?

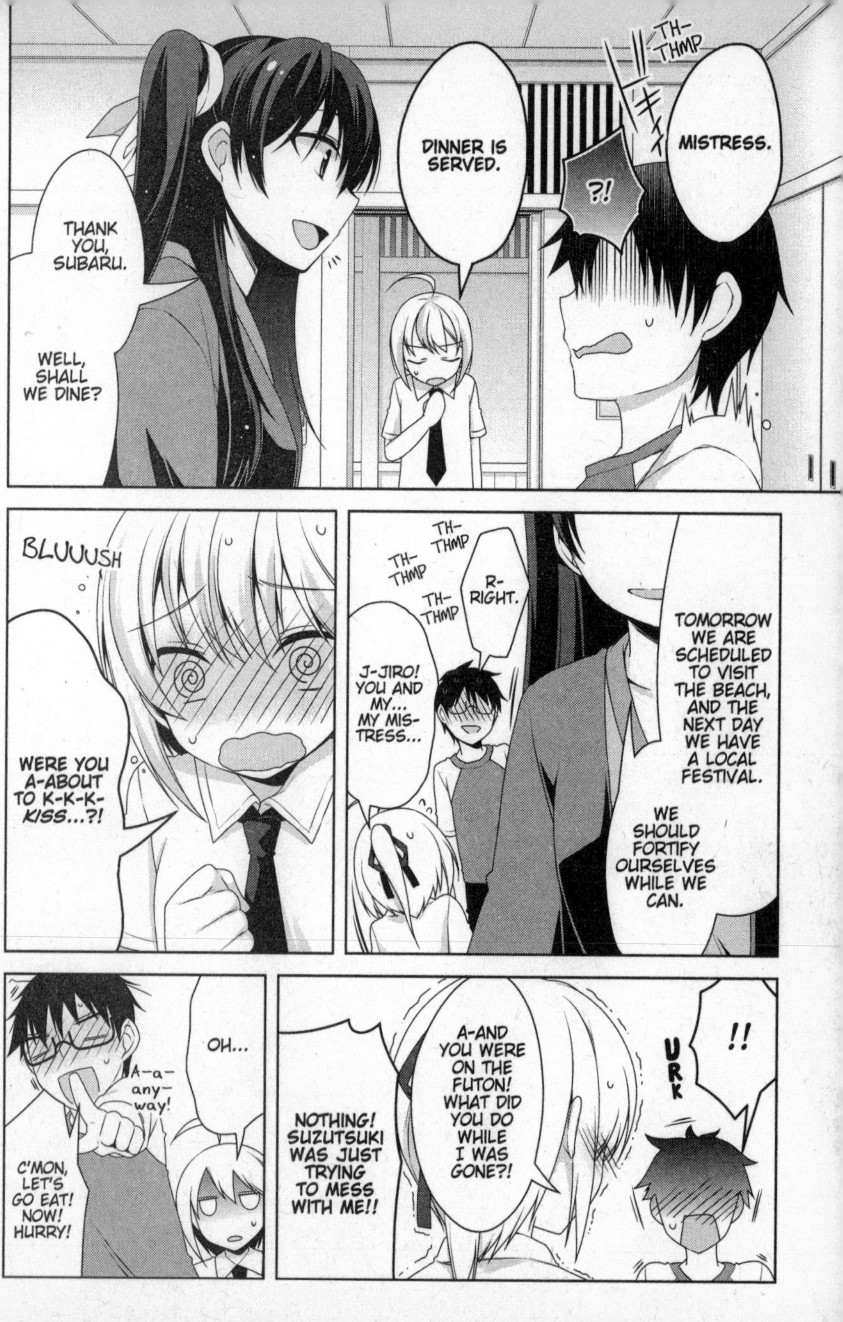
TH-THMP
MISTRESS.
?!
DINNER IS SERVED.
THANK YOU, SUBARU.
WELL, SHALL WE DINE?
TOMORROW WE ARE SCHEDULED TO VISIT THE BEACH, AND THE NEXT DAY WE HAVE A LOCAL FESTIVAL.
WE SHOULD FORTIFY OURSELVES WHILE WE CAN.
TH-THMP
R-RIGHT.
TH-THMP
TH-THMP
J-JIRO! YOU AND MY... MY MIS-TRESS...
BLUUUSH
WERE YOU A-ABOUT TO K-K-K-KISS...?!
!!
URK
A-AND YOU WERE ON THE FUTON! WHAT DID YOU DO WHILE I WAS GONE?!
NOTHING! SUZUTSUKI WAS JUST TRYING TO MESS WITH ME!!
OH...
A-a-any-way!
C'MON, LET'S GO EAT! NOW! HURRY!

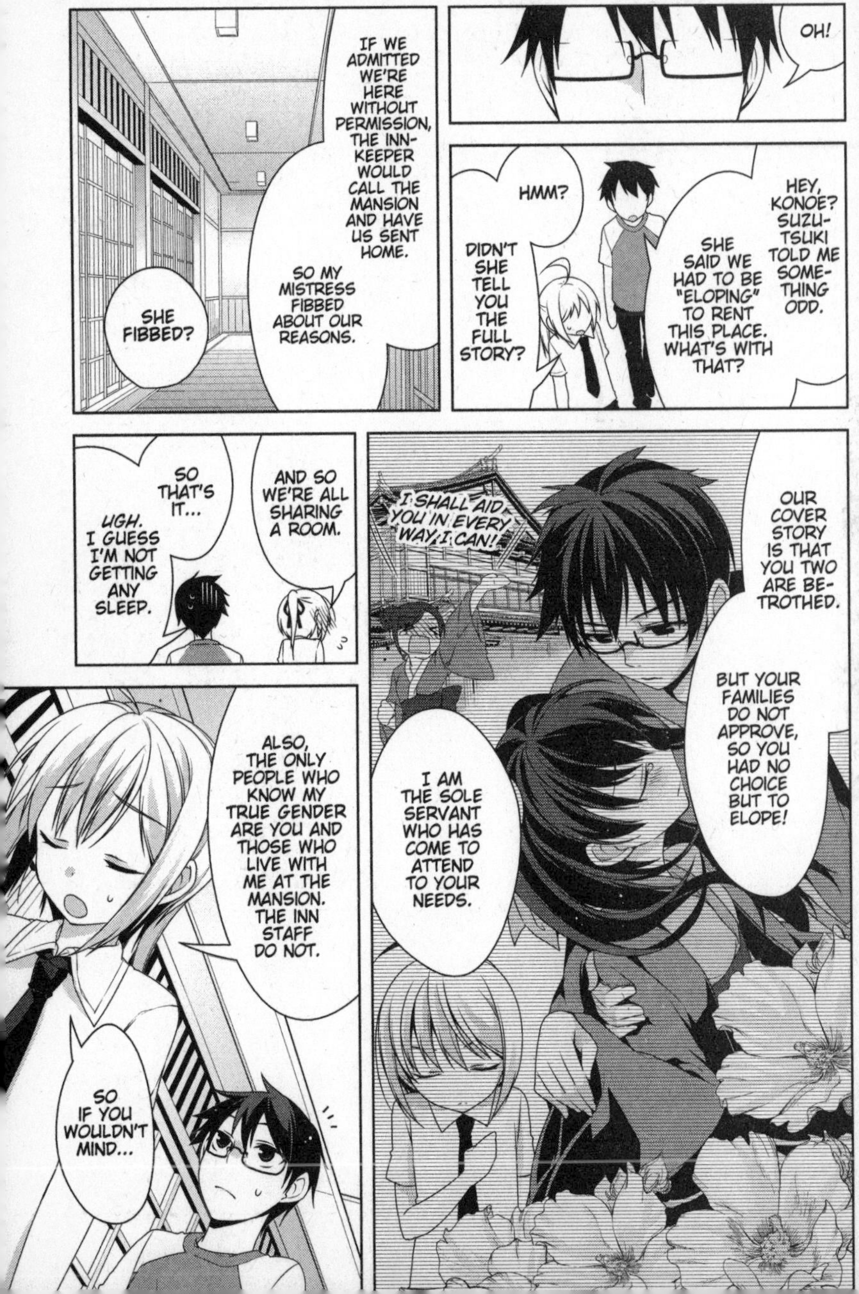
OH!
HEY, KONOE? SUZUTSUKI TOLD ME SOMETHING ODD.
SHE SAID WE HAD TO BE "ELOPING" TO RENT THIS PLACE. WHAT'S WITH THAT?
HMM?
DIDN'T SHE TELL YOU THE FULL STORY?
IF WE ADMITTED WE'RE HERE WITHOUT PERMISSION, THE INNKEEPER WOULD CALL THE MANSION AND HAVE US SENT HOME.
SO MY MISTRESS FIBBED ABOUT OUR REASONS.
SHE FIBBED?
OUR COVER STORY IS THAT YOU TWO ARE BETROTHED.
BUT YOUR FAMILIES DO NOT APPROVE, SO YOU HAD NO CHOICE BUT TO ELOPE!
I SHALL AID YOU IN EVERY WAY I CAN!
I AM THE SOLE SERVANT WHO HAS COME TO ATTEND TO YOUR NEEDS.
AND SO WE'RE ALL SHARING A ROOM.
SO THAT'S IT...
UGH. I GUESS I'M NOT GETTING ANY SLEEP.
ALSO, THE ONLY PEOPLE WHO KNOW MY TRUE GENDER ARE YOU AND THOSE WHO LIVE WITH ME AT THE MANSION. THE INN STAFF DO NOT.
SO IF YOU WOULDN'T MIND...

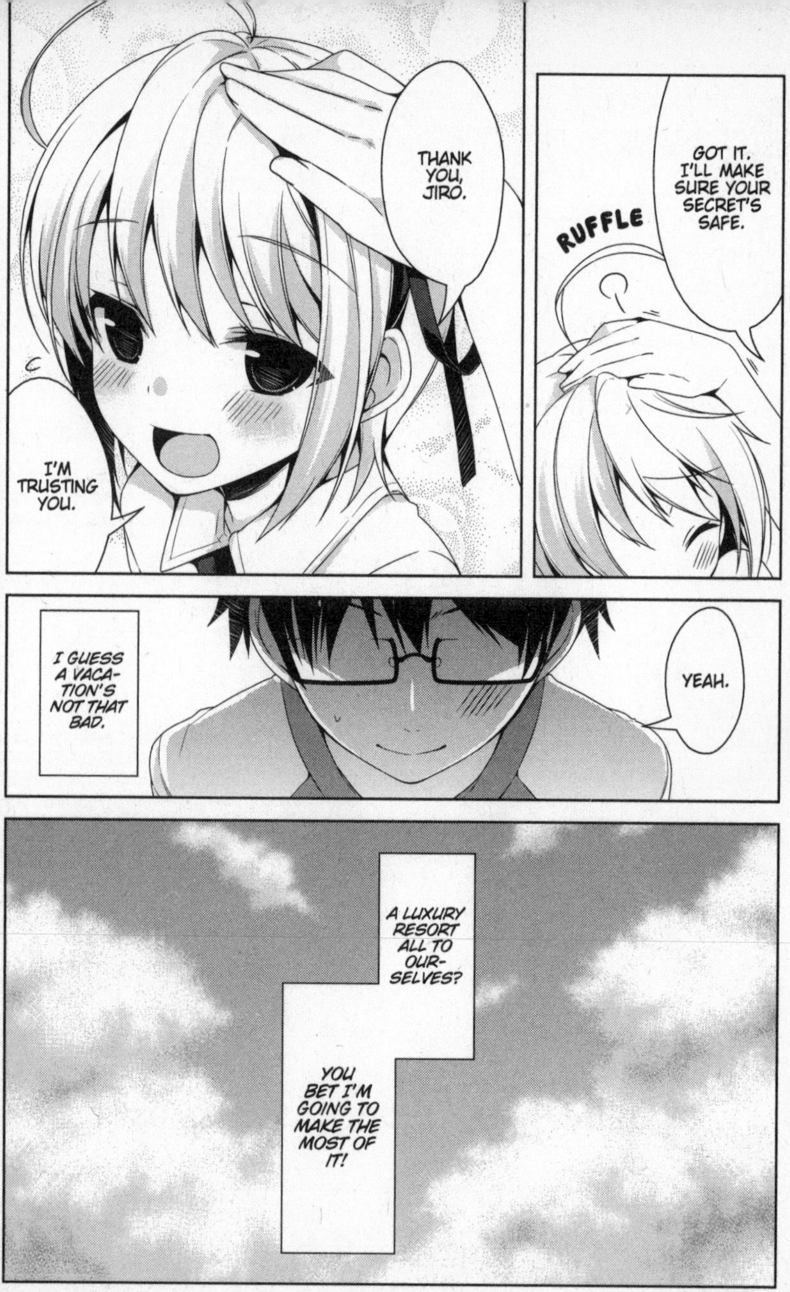
GOT IT. I'LL MAKE SURE YOUR SECRET'S SAFE.
RUFFLE
THANK YOU, JIRO.
I'M TRUSTING YOU.
YEAH.
I GUESS A VACATION'S NOT THAT BAD.
A LUXURY RESORT ALL TO OURSELVES?
YOU BET I'M GOING TO MAKE THE MOST OF IT!

chapter 14 bayside baby

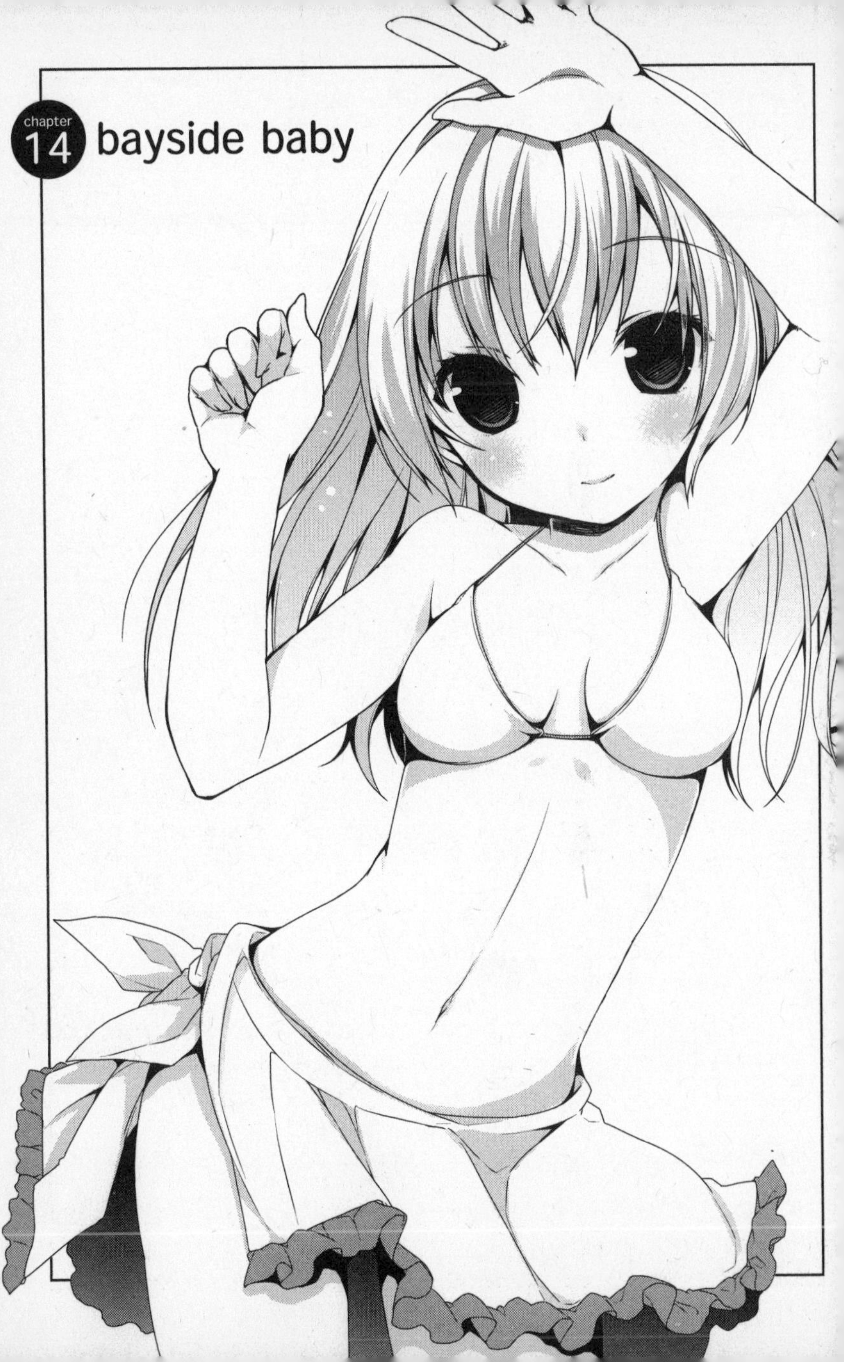

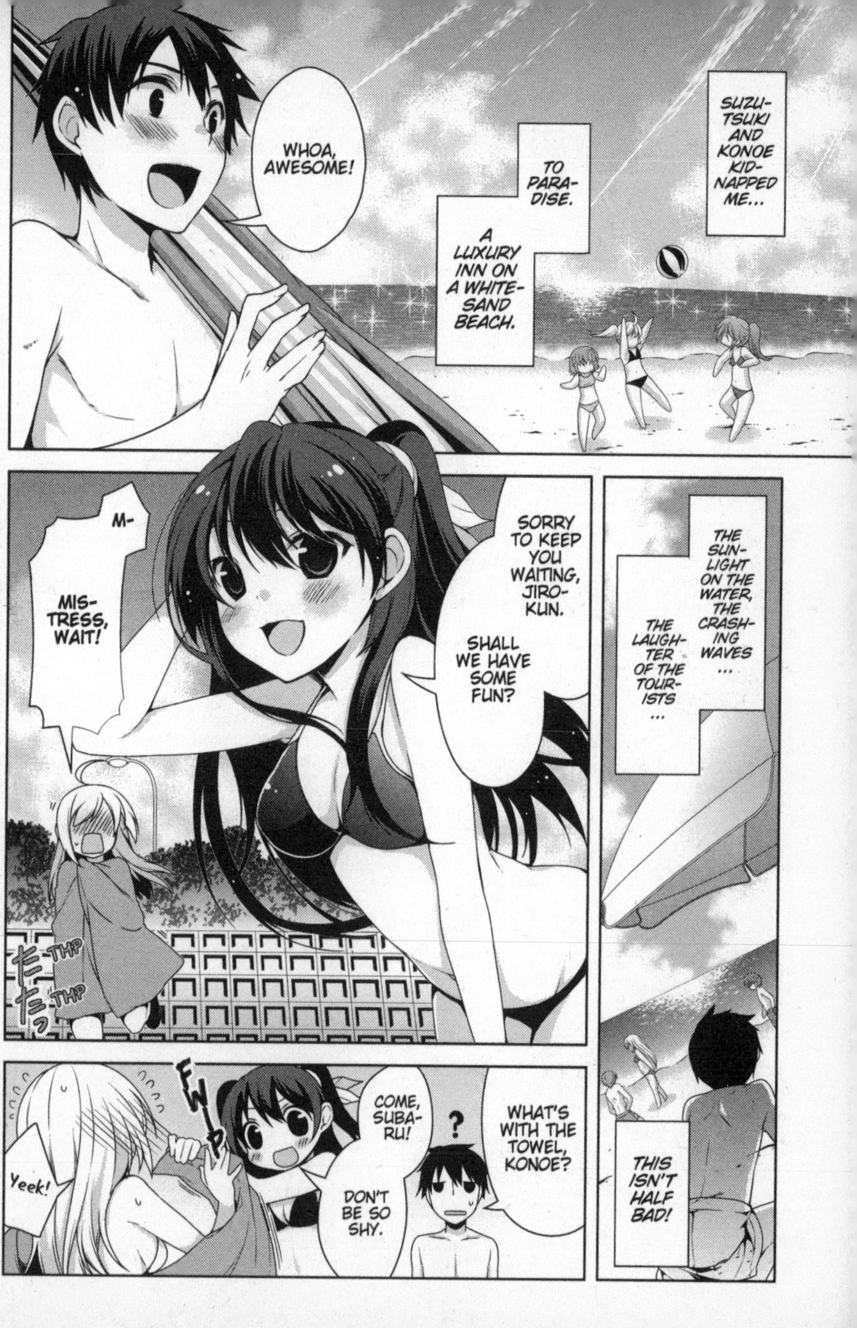
SUZUTSUKI AND KONOE KIDNAPPED ME...
TO PARADISE.
A LUXURY INN ON A WHITE-SAND BEACH.
WHOA, AWESOME!
THE SUNLIGHT ON THE WATER, THE CRASHING WAVES...
THE LAUGHTER OF THE TOURISTS...
THIS ISN'T HALF BAD!
SORRY TO KEEP YOU WAITING, JIRO-KUN.
SHALL WE HAVE SOME FUN?
M-
MISTRESS, WAIT!
THP
THP
WHAT'S WITH THE TOWEL, KONOE?
?
COME, SUBARU!
DON'T BE SO SHY.
FWIP
Yeek!

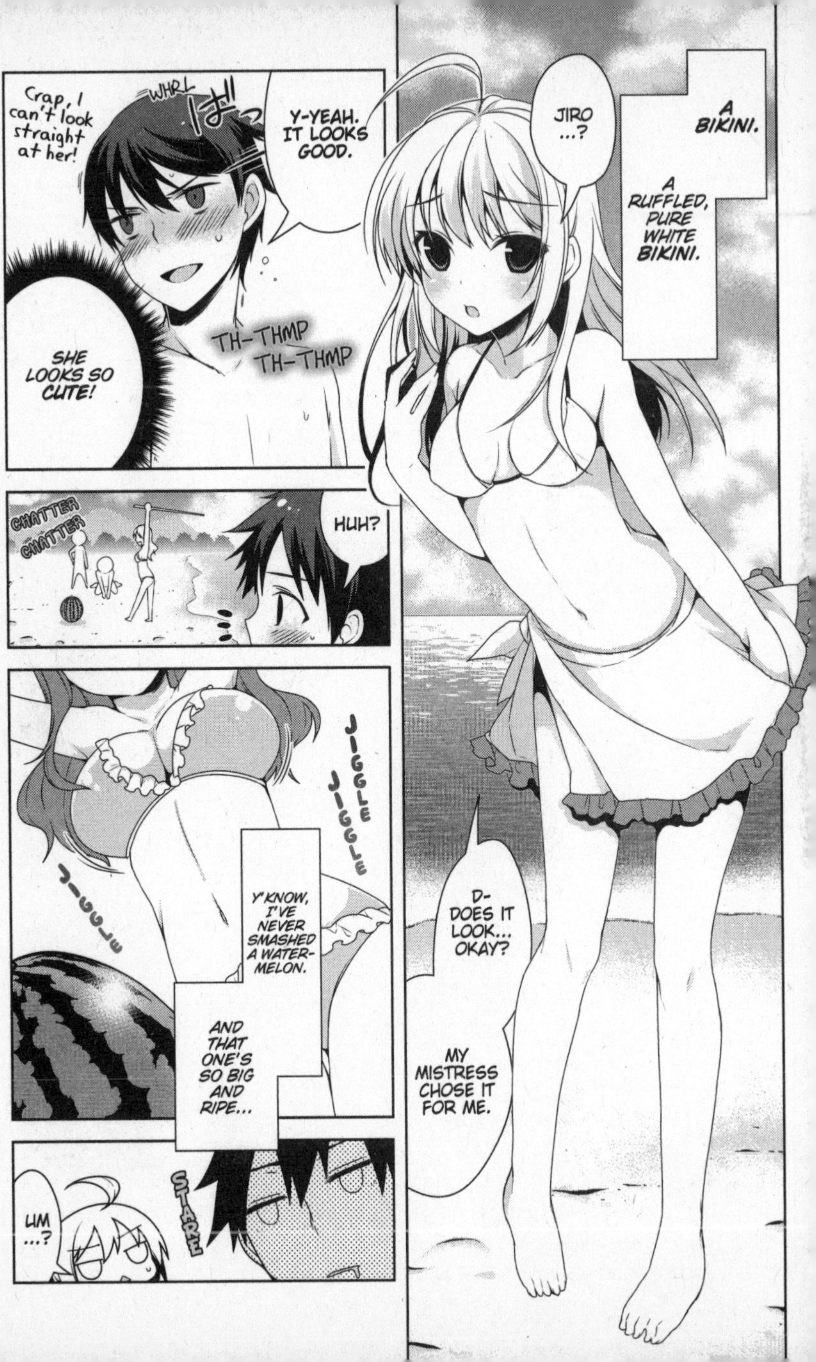
A BIKINI.
A RUFFLED, PURE WHITE BIKINI.
JIRO ...?
D- DOES IT LOOK... OKAY?
MY MISTRESS CHOSE IT FOR ME.
Y-YEAH. IT LOOKS GOOD.
WHRL
Crap, I can't look straight at her!
TH-THMP TH-THMP
SHE LOOKS SO CUTE!
HUH?
CHATTER CHATTER
JIGGLE JIGGLE
JIGGLE
Y'KNOW, I'VE NEVER SMASHED A WATER-MELON.
AND THAT ONE'S SO BIG AND RIPE...
STARE
UM ...?

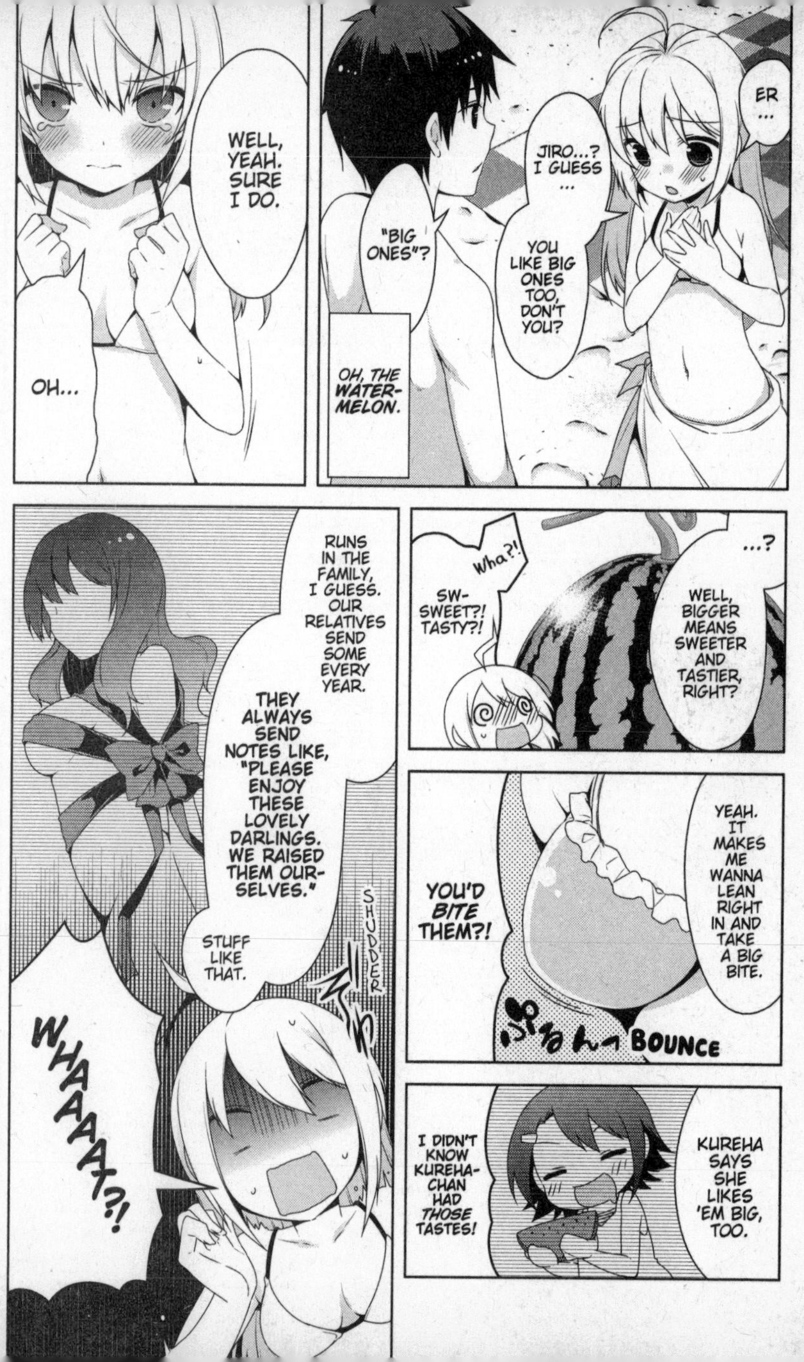
ER...
JIRO...? I GUESS...
YOU LIKE BIG ONES TOO, DON'T YOU?
"BIG ONES"?
OH, THE WATER-MELON.
WELL, YEAH. SURE I DO.
OH...
...?
WELL, BIGGER MEANS SWEETER AND TASTIER, RIGHT?
Wha?!
SW-SWEET?! TASTY?!
YEAH. IT MAKES ME WANNA LEAN RIGHT IN AND TAKE A BIG BITE.
YOU'D BITE THEM?!
ぷるんっ BOUNCE
KUREHA SAYS SHE LIKES 'EM BIG, TOO.
I DIDN'T KNOW KUREHA-CHAN HAD THOSE TASTES!
RUNS IN THE FAMILY, I GUESS. OUR RELATIVES SEND SOME EVERY YEAR.
THEY ALWAYS SEND NOTES LIKE, "PLEASE ENJOY THESE LOVELY DARLINGS. WE RAISED THEM OUR-SELVES."
STUFF LIKE THAT.
SHUDDER
WHAAAA?!

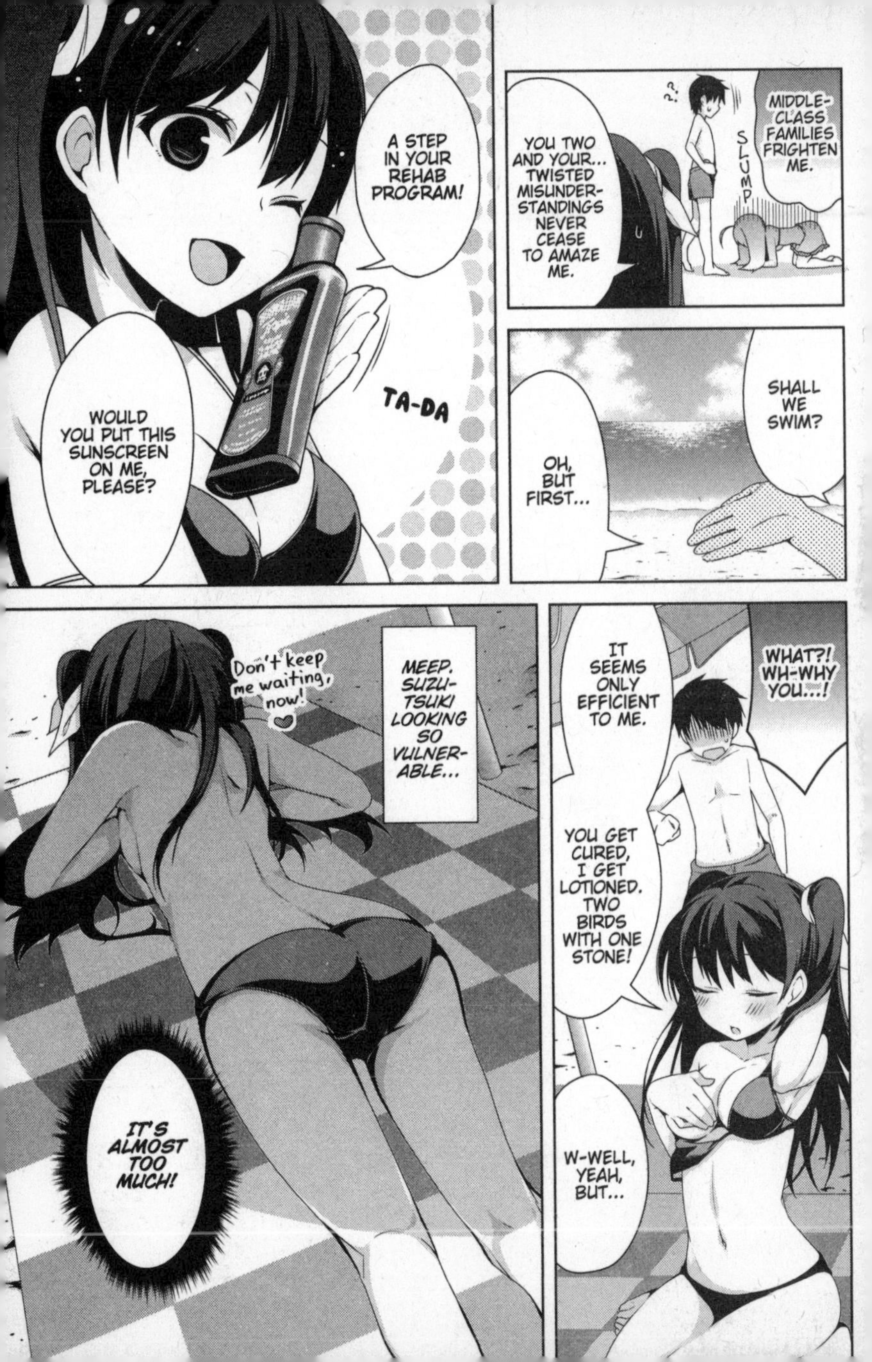
MIDDLE-CLASS FAMILIES FRIGHTEN ME.
SLUMP
??
YOU TWO AND YOUR... TWISTED MISUNDERSTANDINGS NEVER CEASE TO AMAZE ME.
SHALL WE SWIM?
OH, BUT FIRST...
A STEP IN YOUR REHAB PROGRAM!
TA-DA
WOULD YOU PUT THIS SUNSCREEN ON ME, PLEASE?
WHAT?! WH-WHY YOU...!
IT SEEMS ONLY EFFICIENT TO ME.
YOU GET CURED, I GET LOTIONED. TWO BIRDS WITH ONE STONE!
W-WELL, YEAH, BUT...
MEEP. SUZU-TSUKI LOOKING SO VULNERABLE...
Don't keep me waiting, now!
IT'S ALMOST TOO MUCH!

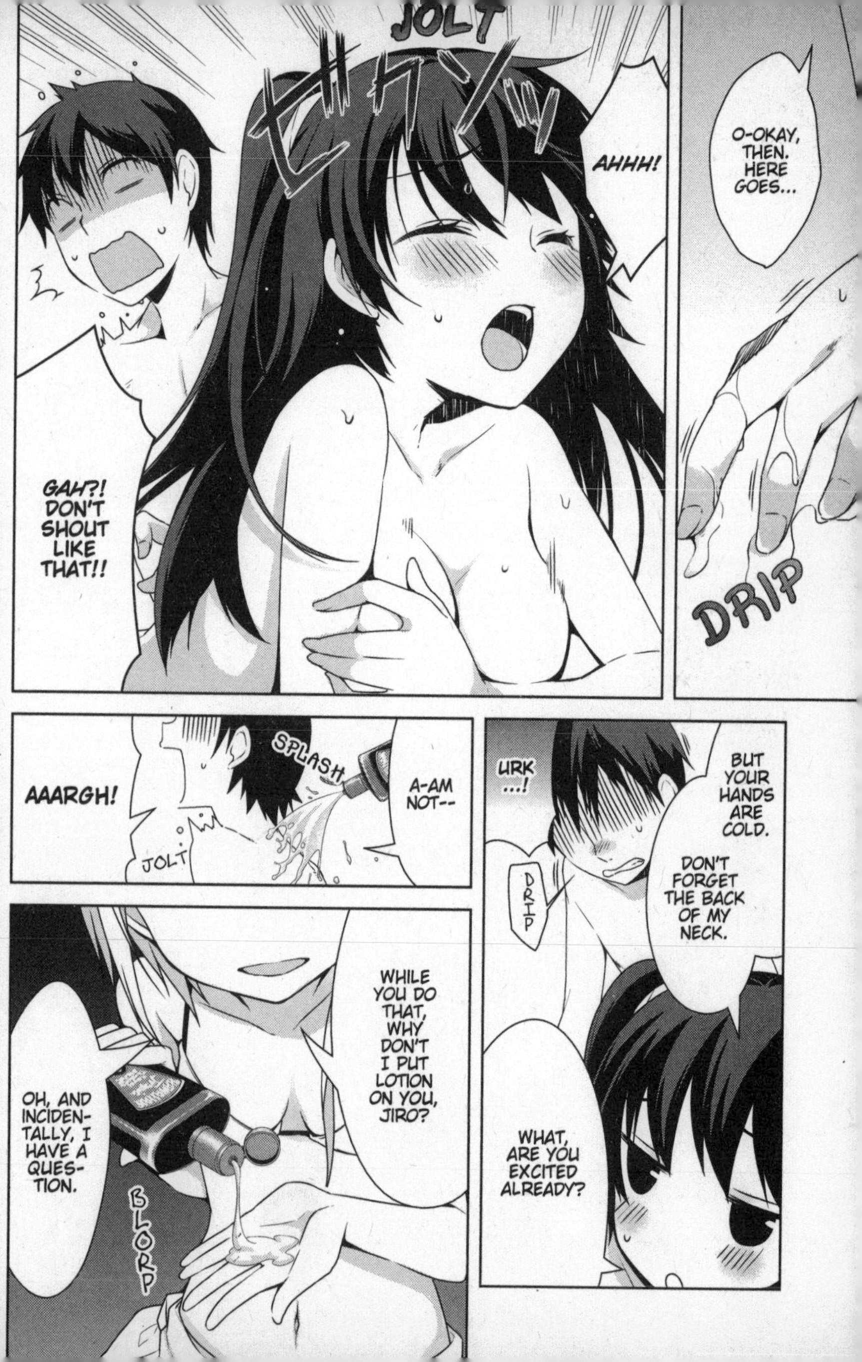
O-OKAY, THEN. HERE GOES...
DRIP
JOLT
AHHH!
GAH?! DON'T SHOUT LIKE THAT!!
BUT YOUR HANDS ARE COLD.
DON'T FORGET THE BACK OF MY NECK.
URK ...!
DRIP
WHAT, ARE YOU EXCITED ALREADY?
A-AM NOT--
SPLASH
AAARGH!
JOLT
WHILE YOU DO THAT, WHY DON'T I PUT LOTION ON YOU, JIRO?
OH, AND INCIDENTALLY, I HAVE A QUESTION.
BLORP

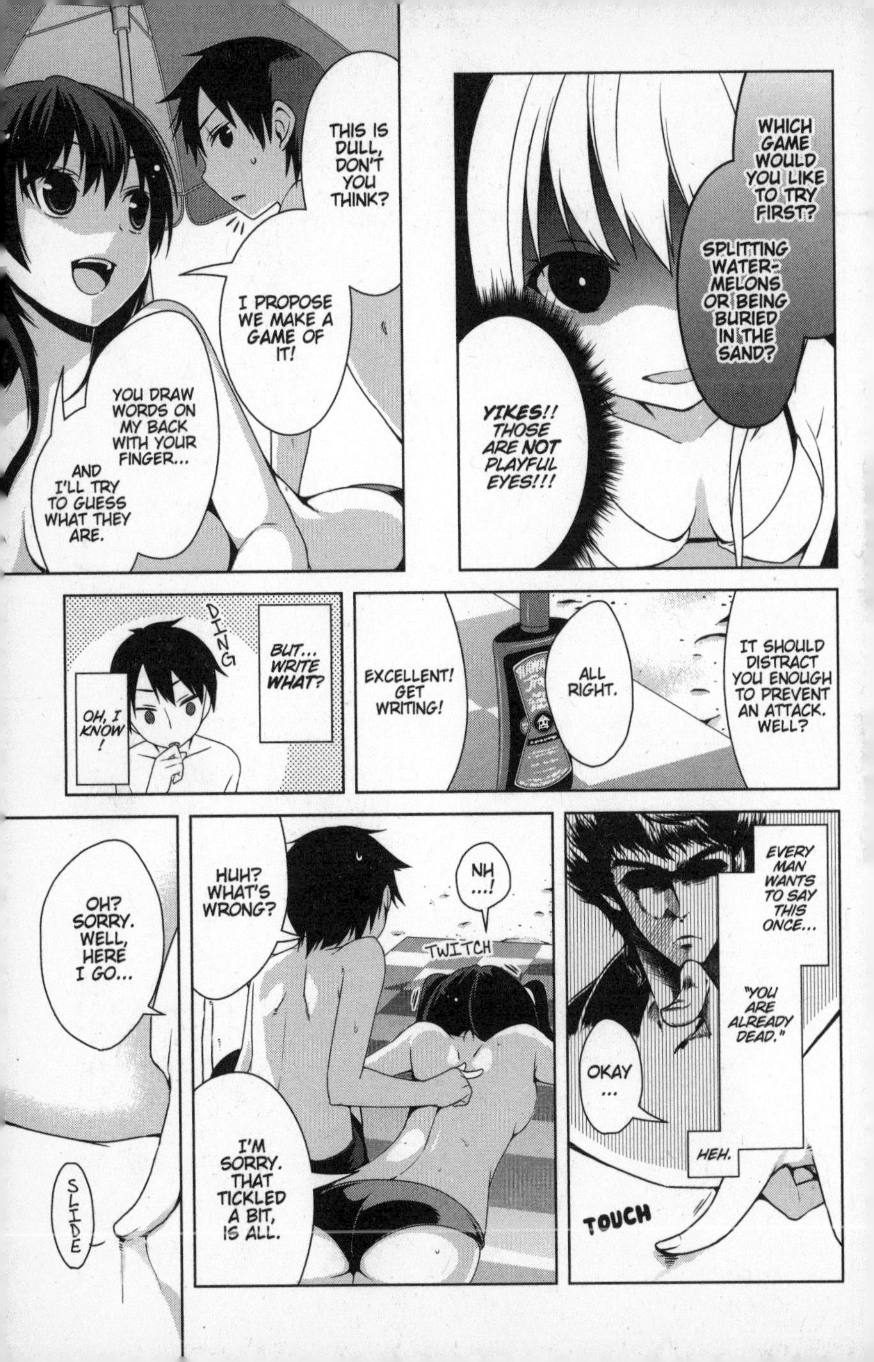
WHICH GAME WOULD YOU LIKE TO TRY FIRST?
SPLITTING WATERMELONS OR BEING BURIED IN THE SAND?
YIKES!! THOSE ARE NOT PLAYFUL EYES!!!
THIS IS DULL, DON'T YOU THINK?
I PROPOSE WE MAKE A GAME OF IT!
YOU DRAW WORDS ON MY BACK WITH YOUR FINGER...
AND I'LL TRY TO GUESS WHAT THEY ARE.
IT SHOULD DISTRACT YOU ENOUGH TO PREVENT AN ATTACK. WELL?
ALL RIGHT.
EXCELLENT! GET WRITING!
BUT... WRITE WHAT?
DING
OH, I KNOW!
EVERY MAN WANTS TO SAY THIS ONCE...
"YOU ARE ALREADY DEAD."
OKAY...
HEH.
TOUCH
NH...!
TWITCH
HUH? WHAT'S WRONG?
I'M SORRY. THAT TICKLED A BIT, IS ALL.
OH? SORRY. WELL, HERE I GO...
SLIDE

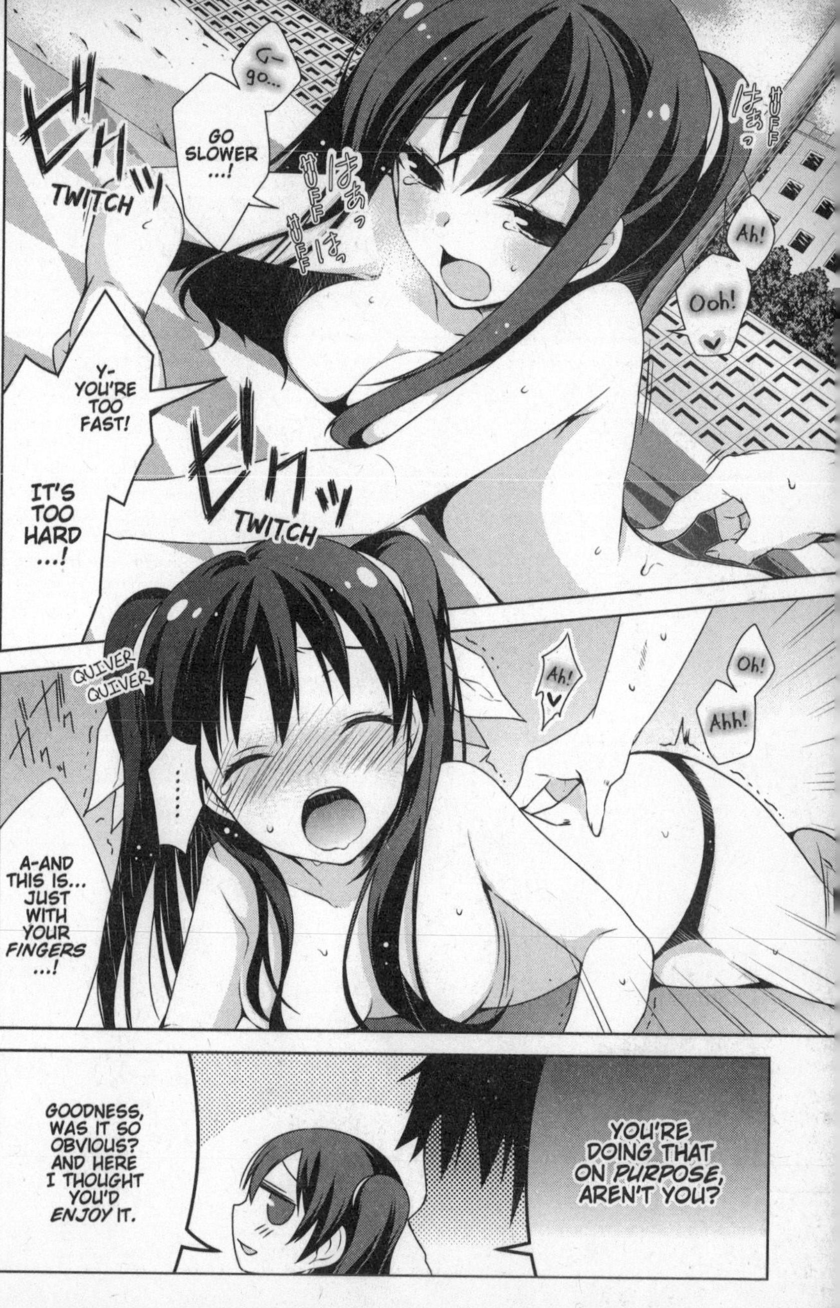
HUFF
Ah!
Ooh! ♥
G-go...
GO SLOWER...!
HUFF HUFF
TWITCH
Y-YOU'RE TOO FAST!
TWITCH
IT'S TOO HARD...!
Oh!
Ahh!
Ah! ♥
QUIVER QUIVER
......
A-AND THIS IS... JUST WITH YOUR *FINGERS*...!
YOU'RE DOING THAT ON *PURPOSE*, AREN'T YOU?
GOODNESS, WAS IT SO OBVIOUS? AND HERE I THOUGHT YOU'D *ENJOY* IT.

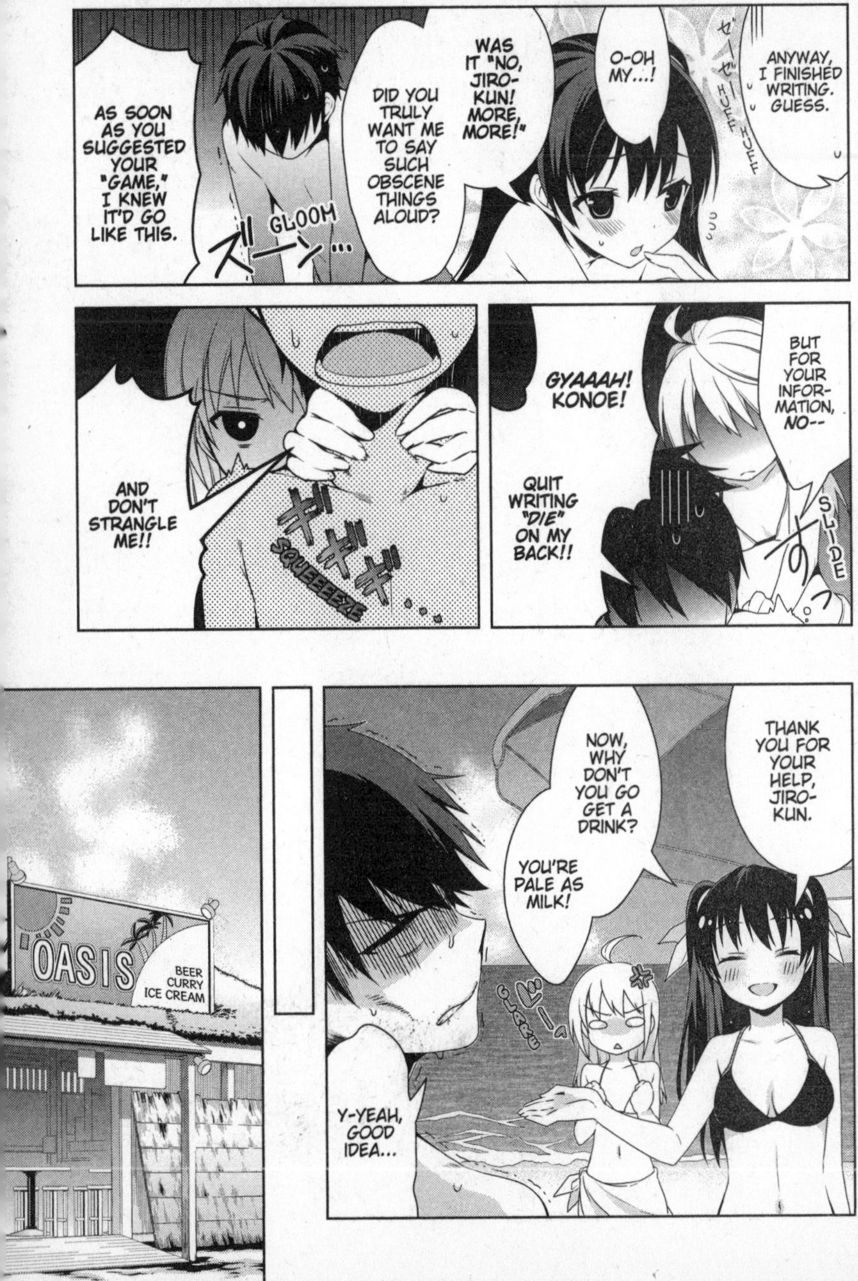
ANYWAY, I FINISHED WRITING. GUESS.
HUFF HUFF
O-OH MY...!
WAS IT "NO, JIRO-KUN! MORE, MORE!"
DID YOU TRULY WANT ME TO SAY SUCH OBSCENE THINGS ALOUD?
GLOOM
AS SOON AS YOU SUGGESTED YOUR "GAME," I KNEW IT'D GO LIKE THIS.
BUT FOR YOUR INFORMATION, NO--
SLIDE
GYAAAH! KONOE!
QUIT WRITING "DIE" ON MY BACK!!
SQUEEEEEZE
AND DON'T STRANGLE ME!!
THANK YOU FOR YOUR HELP, JIRO-KUN.
NOW, WHY DON'T YOU GO GET A DRINK?
YOU'RE PALE AS MILK!
GLARE
Y-YEAH, GOOD IDEA...
OASIS
BEER
CURRY
ICE CREAM

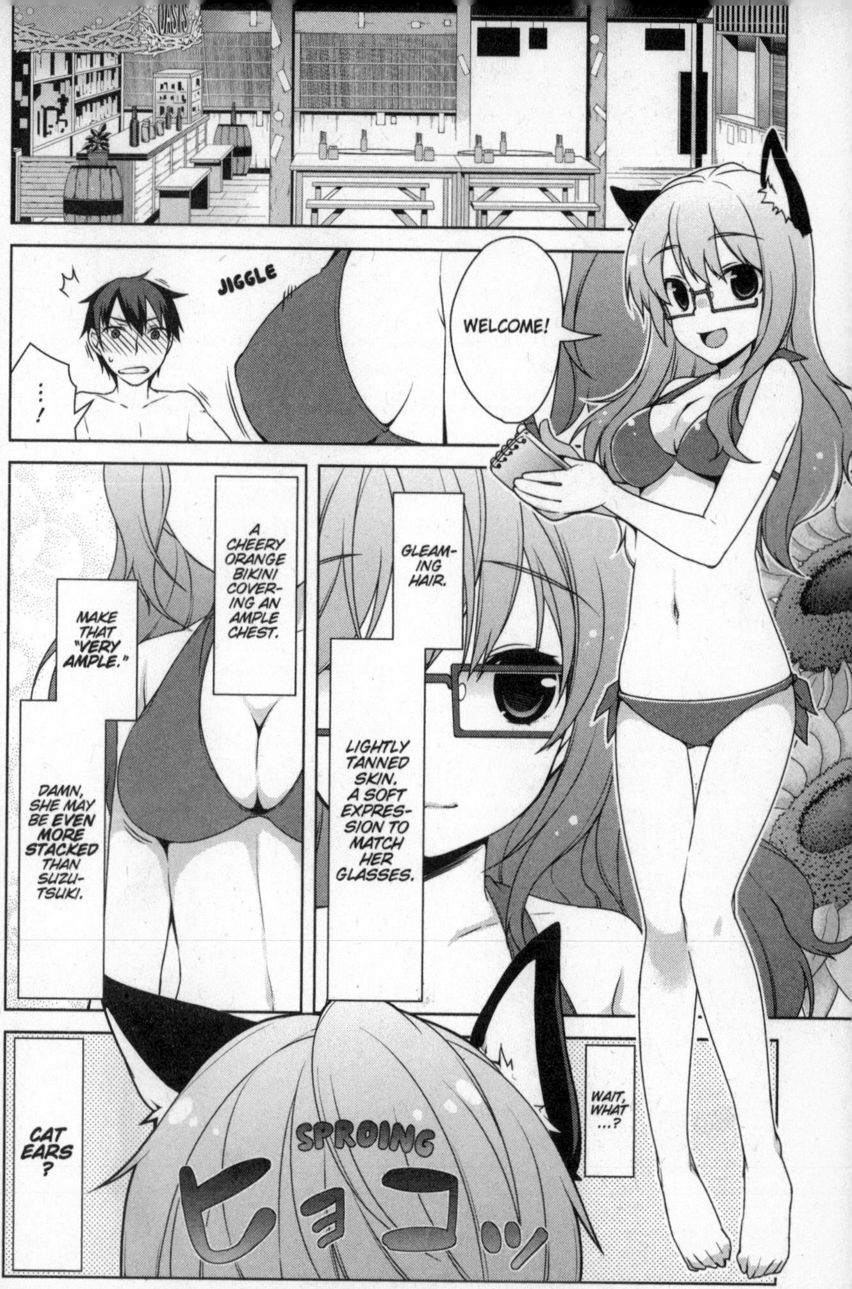
WELCOME!
JIGGLE
...!
GLEAMING-ING HAIR.
LIGHTLY TANNED SKIN. A SOFT EXPRESSION TO MATCH HER GLASSES.
A CHEERY ORANGE BIKINI COVERING AN AMPLE CHEST.
MAKE THAT "VERY AMPLE."
DAMN, SHE MAY BE EVEN MORE STACKED THAN SUZU-TSUKI.
WAIT, WHAT ...?
SPROING
ヒョコッ
CAT EARS?

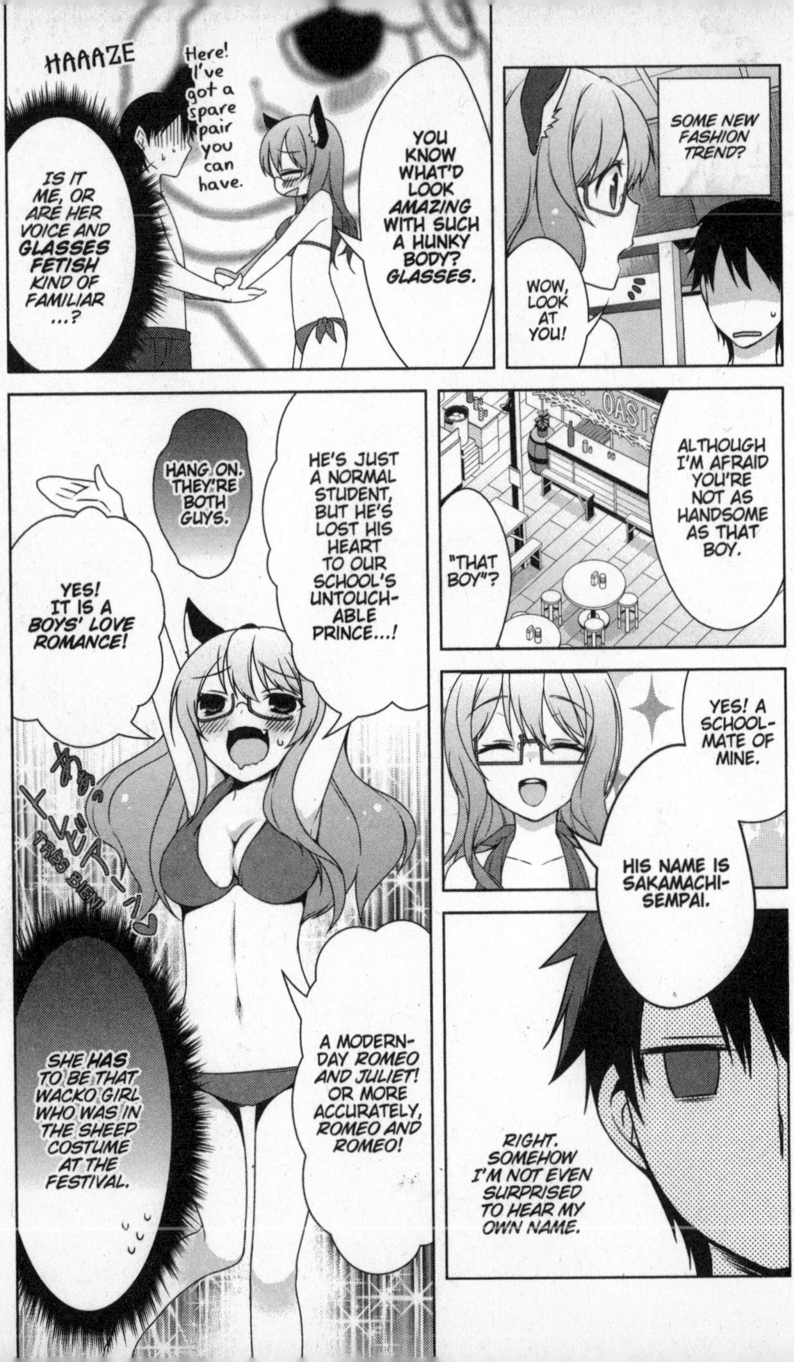
SOME NEW FASHION TREND?
WOW, LOOK AT YOU!
YOU KNOW WHAT'D LOOK *AMAZING* WITH SUCH A HUNKY BODY? *GLASSES.*
Here! I've got a spare pair you can have.
HAAAZE
IS IT ME, OR ARE HER VOICE AND **GLASSES FETISH** KIND OF FAMILIAR ...?
ALTHOUGH I'M AFRAID YOU'RE NOT AS HANDSOME AS THAT BOY.
"THAT BOY"?
YES! A SCHOOL-MATE OF MINE.
HIS NAME IS SAKAMACHI-SEMPAI.
RIGHT. SOMEHOW I'M NOT EVEN SURPRISED TO HEAR MY OWN NAME.
HE'S JUST A NORMAL STUDENT, BUT HE'S LOST HIS HEART TO OUR SCHOOL'S UNTOUCH-ABLE PRINCE...!
HANG ON. THEY'RE BOTH GUYS.
YES! IT IS A *BOYS' LOVE ROMANCE!*
TRES BIEN!
A MODERN-DAY *ROMEO AND JULIET!* OR MORE ACCURATELY, *ROMEO AND ROMEO!*
SHE **HAS** TO BE THAT WACKO GIRL WHO WAS IN THE SHEEP COSTUME AT THE FESTIVAL.

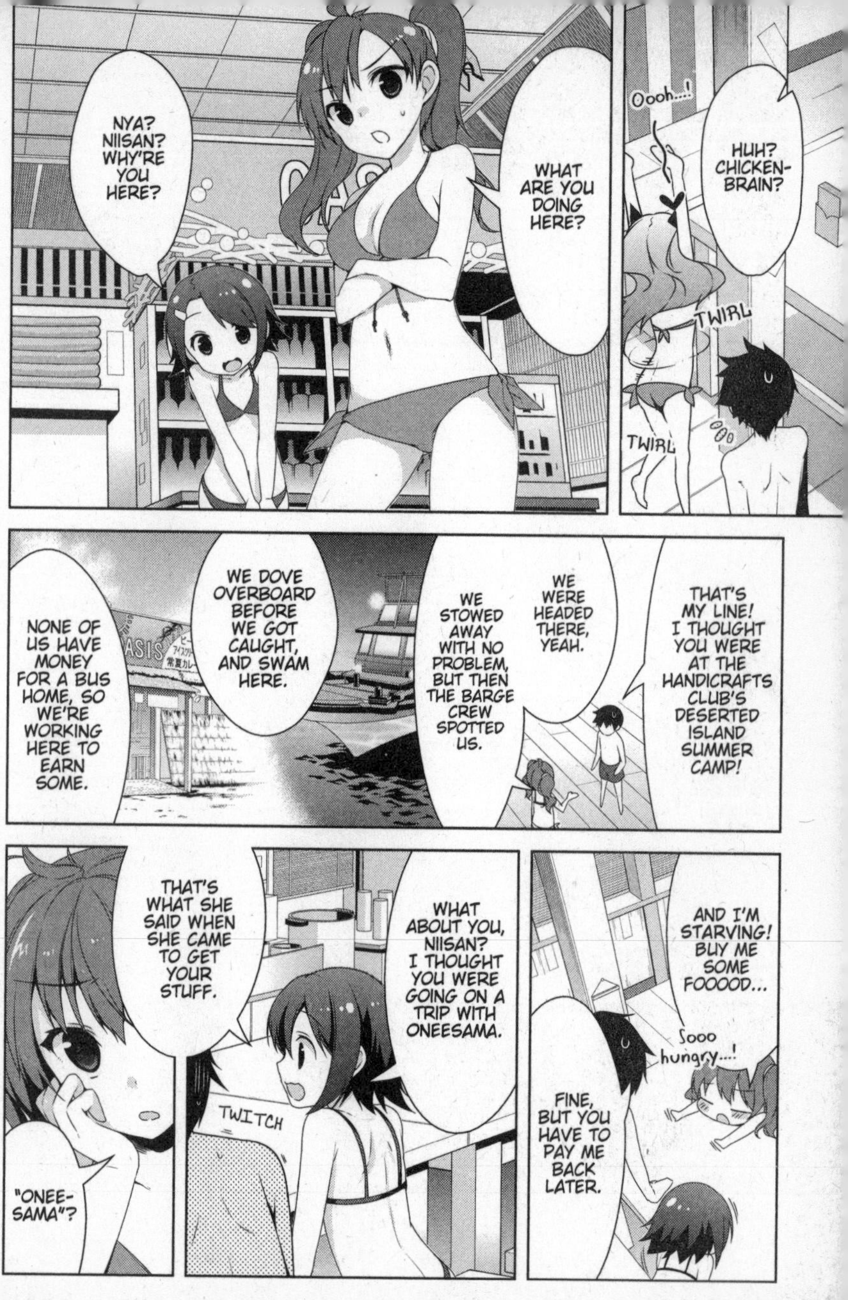
Oooh...!
HUH? CHICKEN-BRAIN?
TWIRL
TWIRL
WHAT ARE YOU DOING HERE?
NYA? NIISAN? WHY'RE YOU HERE?
THAT'S MY LINE! I THOUGHT YOU WERE AT THE HANDICRAFTS CLUB'S DESERTED ISLAND SUMMER CAMP!
WE WERE HEADED THERE, YEAH.
WE STOWED AWAY WITH NO PROBLEM, BUT THEN THE BARGE CREW SPOTTED US.
WE DOVE OVERBOARD BEFORE WE GOT CAUGHT, AND SWAM HERE.
NONE OF US HAVE MONEY FOR A BUS HOME, SO WE'RE WORKING HERE TO EARN SOME.
AND I'M STARVING! BUY ME SOME FOOOOD...
Sooo hungry...!
FINE, BUT YOU HAVE TO PAY ME BACK LATER.
WHAT ABOUT YOU, NIISAN? I THOUGHT YOU WERE GOING ON A TRIP WITH ONEESAMA.
TWITCH
THAT'S WHAT SHE SAID WHEN SHE CAME TO GET YOUR STUFF.
"ONEE-SAMA"?

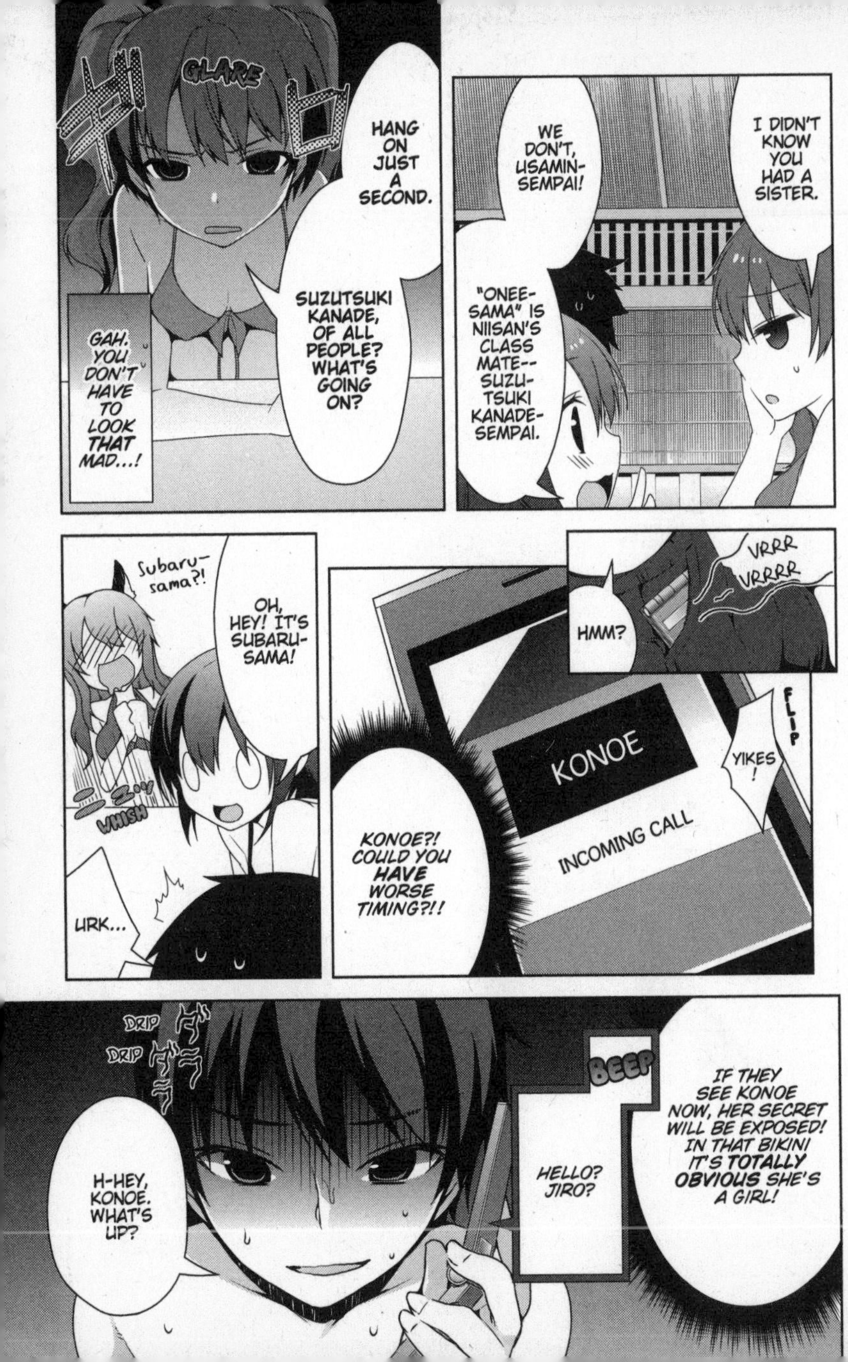
I DIDN'T KNOW YOU HAD A SISTER.
WE DON'T, USAMIN-SEMPAI!
"ONEE-SAMA" IS NIISAN'S CLASS MATE--SUZU-TSUKI KANADE-SEMPAI.
GLARE
HANG ON JUST A SECOND.
SUZUTSUKI KANADE, OF ALL PEOPLE? WHAT'S GOING ON?
GAH. YOU DON'T HAVE TO LOOK THAT MAD...!
VRRR
VRRRR
HMM?
FLIP
YIKES!
KONOE
INCOMING CALL
KONOE?! COULD YOU HAVE WORSE TIMING?!!
OH, HEY! IT'S SUBARU-SAMA!
Subaru-sama?!
WHISH
URK...
IF THEY SEE KONOE NOW, HER SECRET WILL BE EXPOSED! IN THAT BIKINI IT'S TOTALLY OBVIOUS SHE'S A GIRL!
BEEP
HELLO? JIRO?
DRIP
DRIP
H-HEY, KONOE. WHAT'S UP?

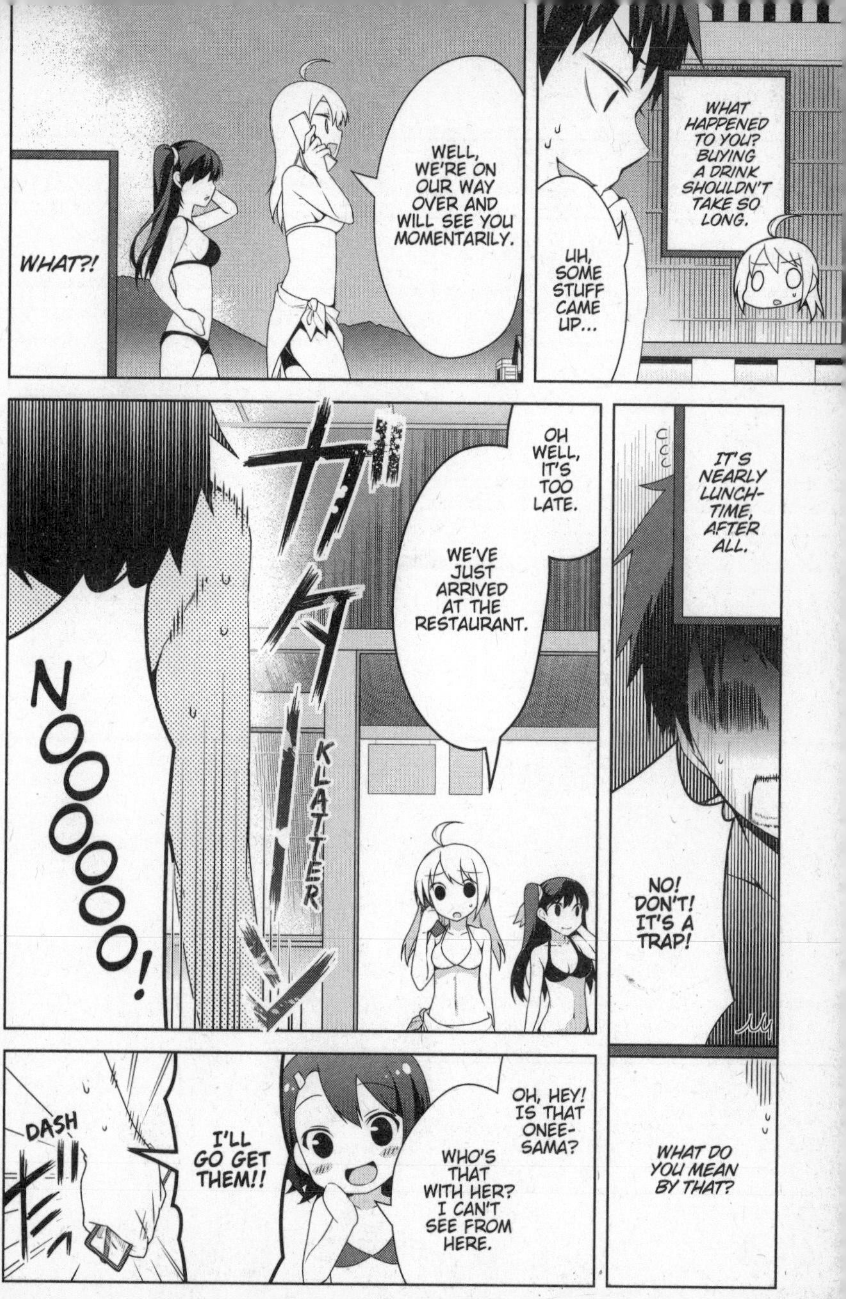
WHAT HAPPENED TO YOU? BUYING A DRINK SHOULDN'T TAKE SO LONG.
UH, SOME STUFF CAME UP...
WELL, WE'RE ON OUR WAY OVER AND WILL SEE YOU MOMENTARILY.
WHAT?!
IT'S NEARLY LUNCH-TIME, AFTER ALL.
NO! DON'T! IT'S A TRAP!
OH WELL, IT'S TOO LATE.
WE'VE JUST ARRIVED AT THE RESTAURANT.
KLATTER
NOOOOOO!
WHAT DO YOU MEAN BY THAT?
OH, HEY! IS THAT ONEE-SAMA?
WHO'S THAT WITH HER? I CAN'T SEE FROM HERE.
I'LL GO GET THEM!!
DASH

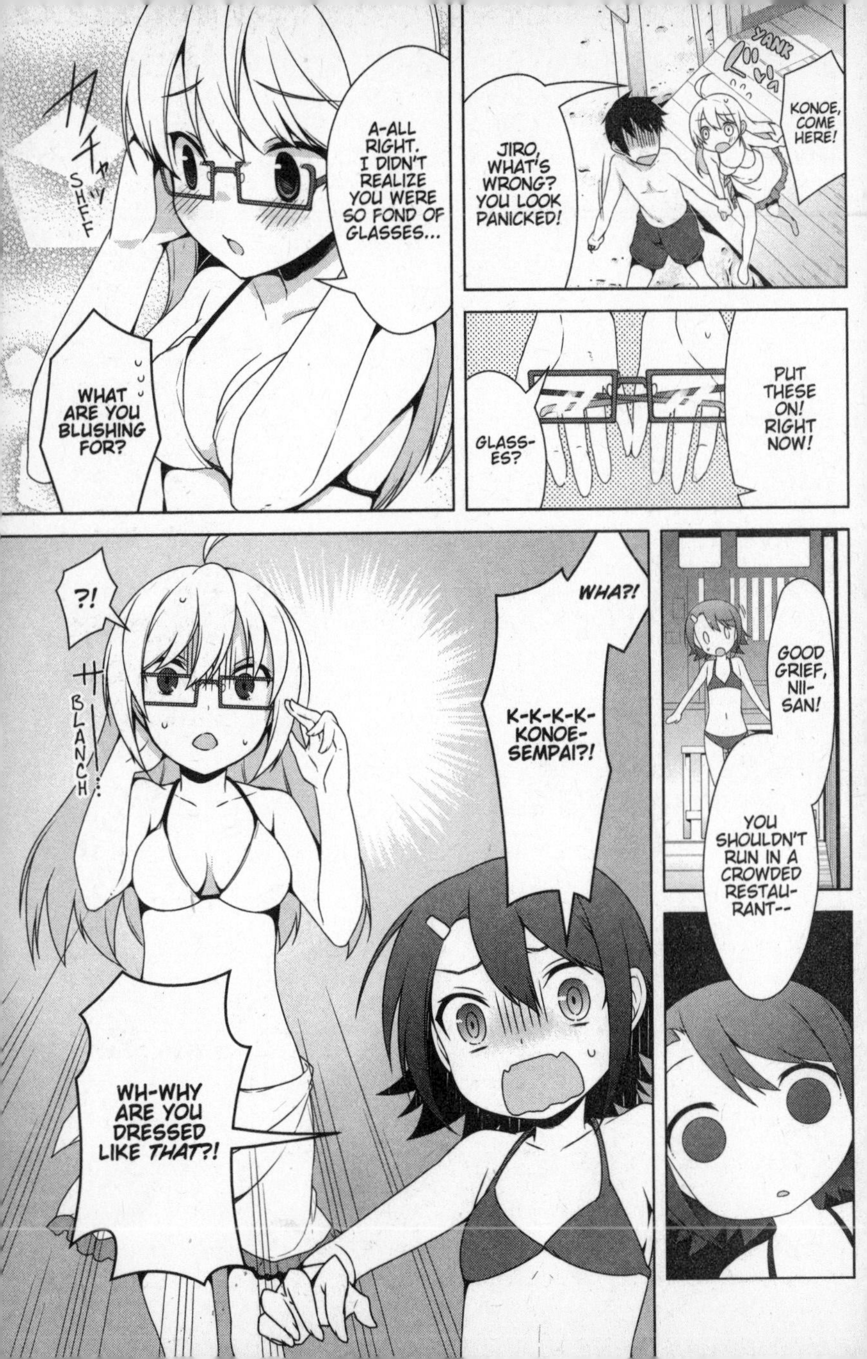
YANK
KONOE, COME HERE!
JIRO, WHAT'S WRONG? YOU LOOK PANICKED!
PUT THESE ON! RIGHT NOW!
GLASSES?
SHFF
A-ALL RIGHT. I DIDN'T REALIZE YOU WERE SO FOND OF GLASSES...
WHAT ARE YOU BLUSHING FOR?
GOOD GRIEF, NII-SAN!
YOU SHOULDN'T RUN IN A CROWDED RESTAURANT--
WHA?!
K-K-K-K-KONOE-SEMPAI?!
?!
BLANCH
WH-WHY ARE YOU DRESSED LIKE *THAT*?!

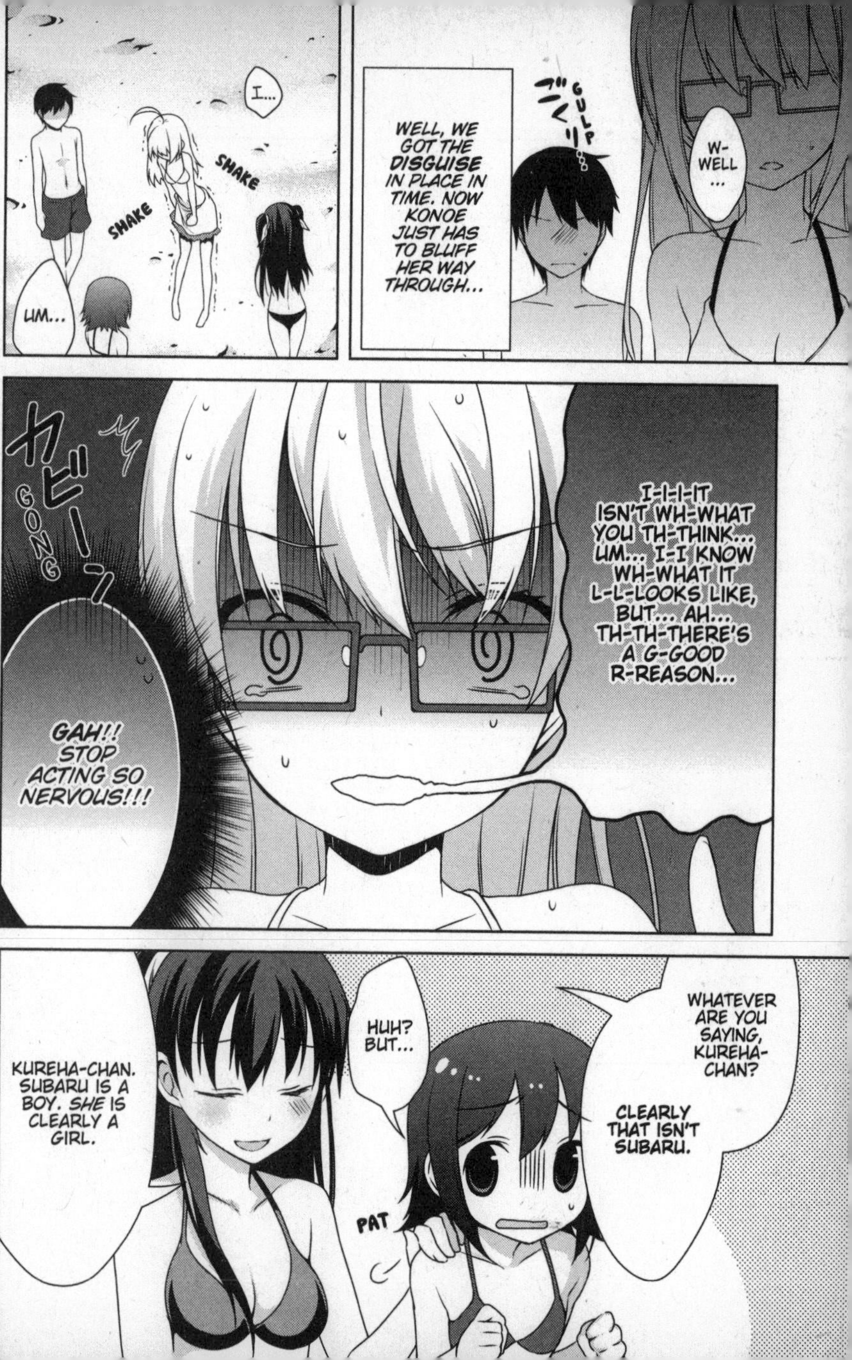
W-WELL ...
GULP
WELL, WE GOT THE DISGUISE IN PLACE IN TIME. NOW KONOE JUST HAS TO BLUFF HER WAY THROUGH...
I...
SHAKE
SHAKE
UM...
I-I-I-IT ISN'T WH-WHAT YOU TH-THINK... UM... I-I KNOW WH-WHAT IT L-L-LOOKS LIKE, BUT... AH... TH-TH-THERE'S A G-GOOD R-REASON...
GONG
GAH!! STOP ACTING SO NERVOUS!!!
WHATEVER ARE YOU SAYING, KUREHA-CHAN?
CLEARLY THAT ISN'T SUBARU.
HUH? BUT...
PAT
KUREHA-CHAN. SUBARU IS A BOY. *SHE* IS CLEARLY A GIRL.

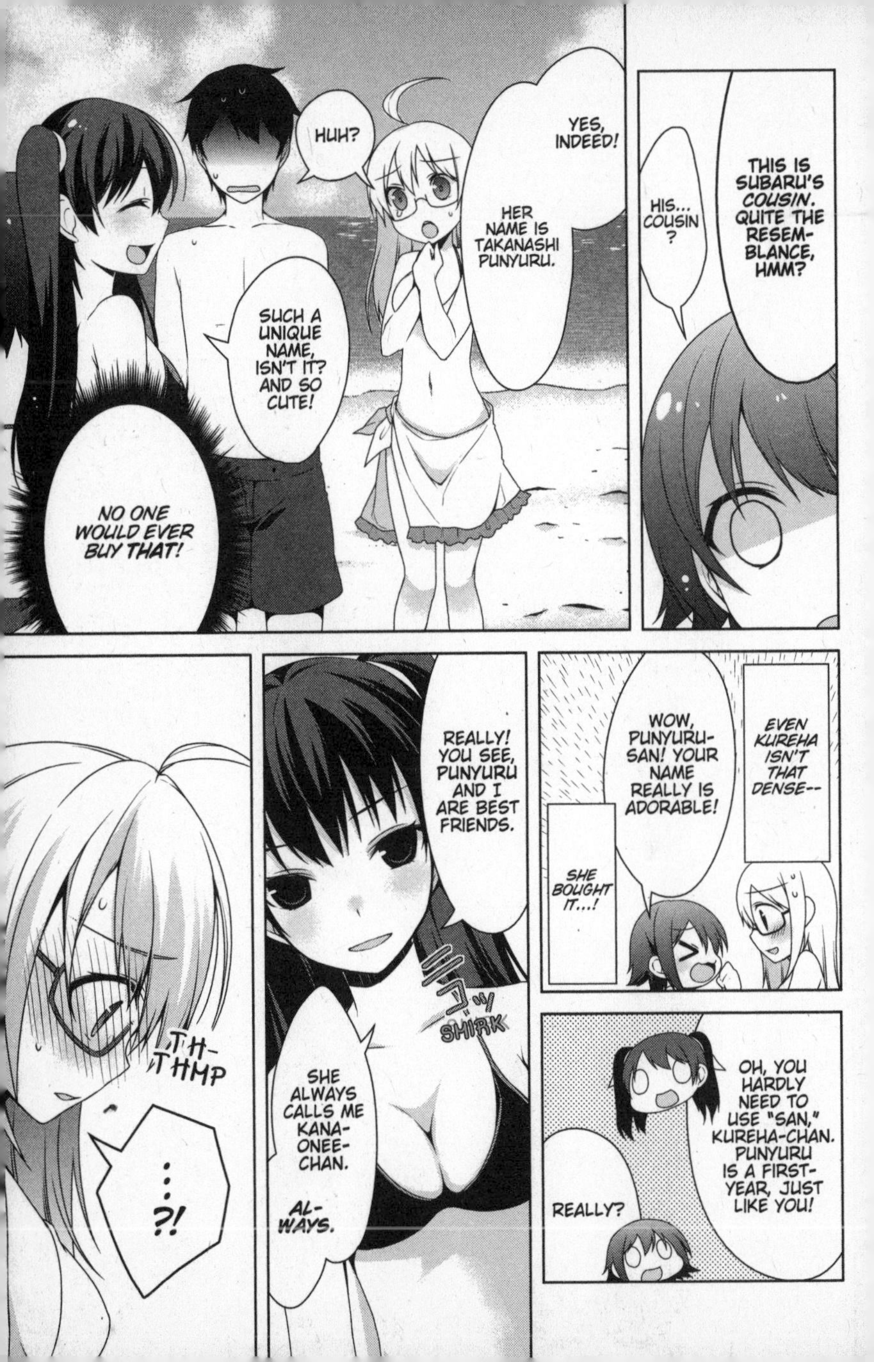
THIS IS SUBARU'S *COUSIN*. QUITE THE RESEMBLANCE, HMM?
HIS... COUSIN?
YES, INDEED!
HER NAME IS TAKANASHI PUNYURU.
HUH?
SUCH A UNIQUE NAME, ISN'T IT? AND SO CUTE!
NO ONE WOULD EVER BUY THAT!
EVEN KUREHA ISN'T THAT DENSE--
WOW, PUNYURU-SAN! YOUR NAME REALLY IS ADORABLE!
SHE BOUGHT IT...!
OH, YOU HARDLY NEED TO USE "SAN," KUREHA-CHAN. PUNYURU IS A FIRST-YEAR, JUST LIKE YOU!
REALLY?
REALLY! YOU SEE, PUNYURU AND I ARE BEST FRIENDS.
SHIRK
SHE ALWAYS CALLS ME KANA-ONEE-CHAN.
AL-WAYS.
TH-THMP
...?!

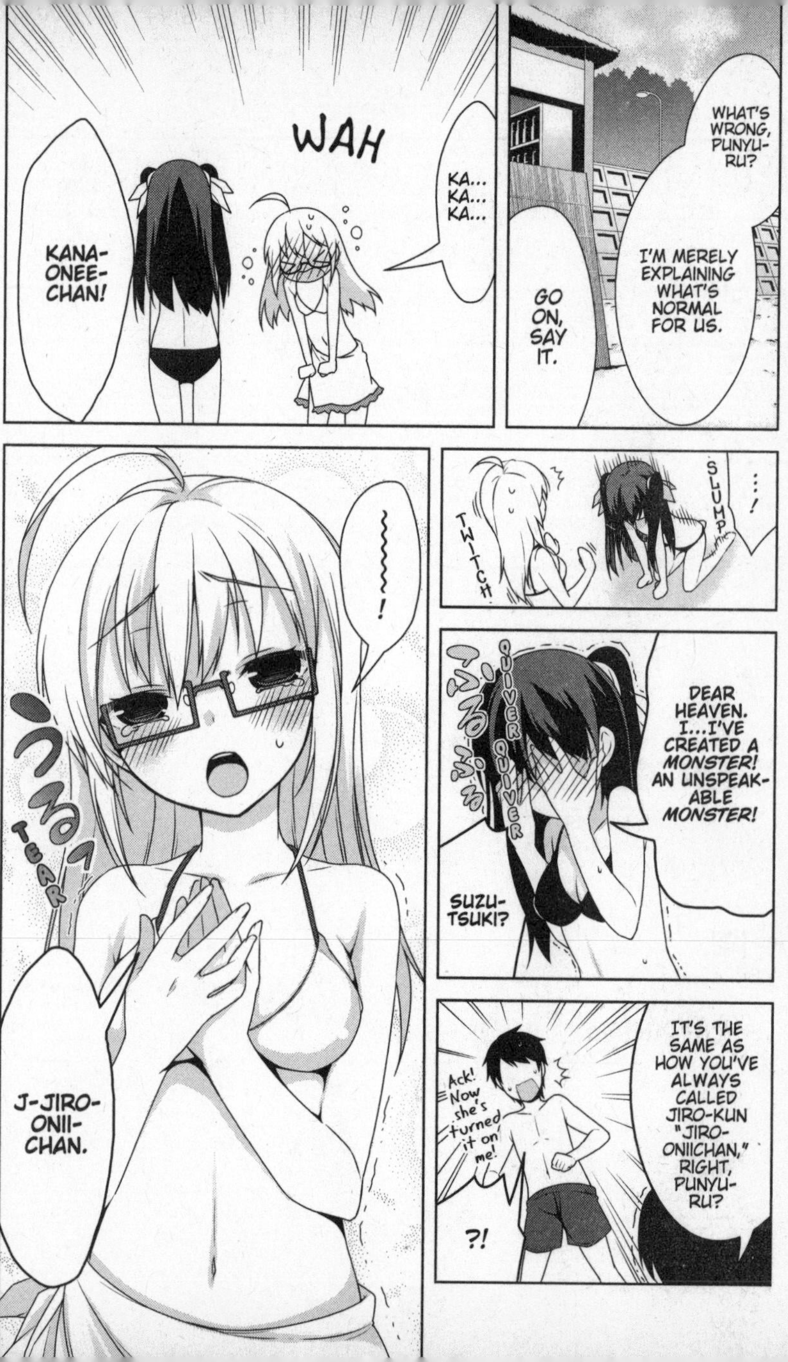
WHAT'S WRONG, PUNYURU?
I'M MERELY EXPLAINING WHAT'S NORMAL FOR US.
GO ON, SAY IT.
KA... KA... KA...
WAH
KANA-ONEE-CHAN!
...!
SLUMP
TWITCH
QUIVER QUIVER
DEAR HEAVEN. I...I'VE CREATED A *MONSTER!* AN UNSPEAKABLE *MONSTER!*
SUZU-TSUKI?
IT'S THE SAME AS HOW YOU'VE ALWAYS CALLED JIRO-KUN "JIRO-ONIICHAN," RIGHT, PUNYURU?
?!
Ack! Now she's turned it on me!
~~~~!
TEAR
J-JIRO-ONII-CHAN.
~~~~

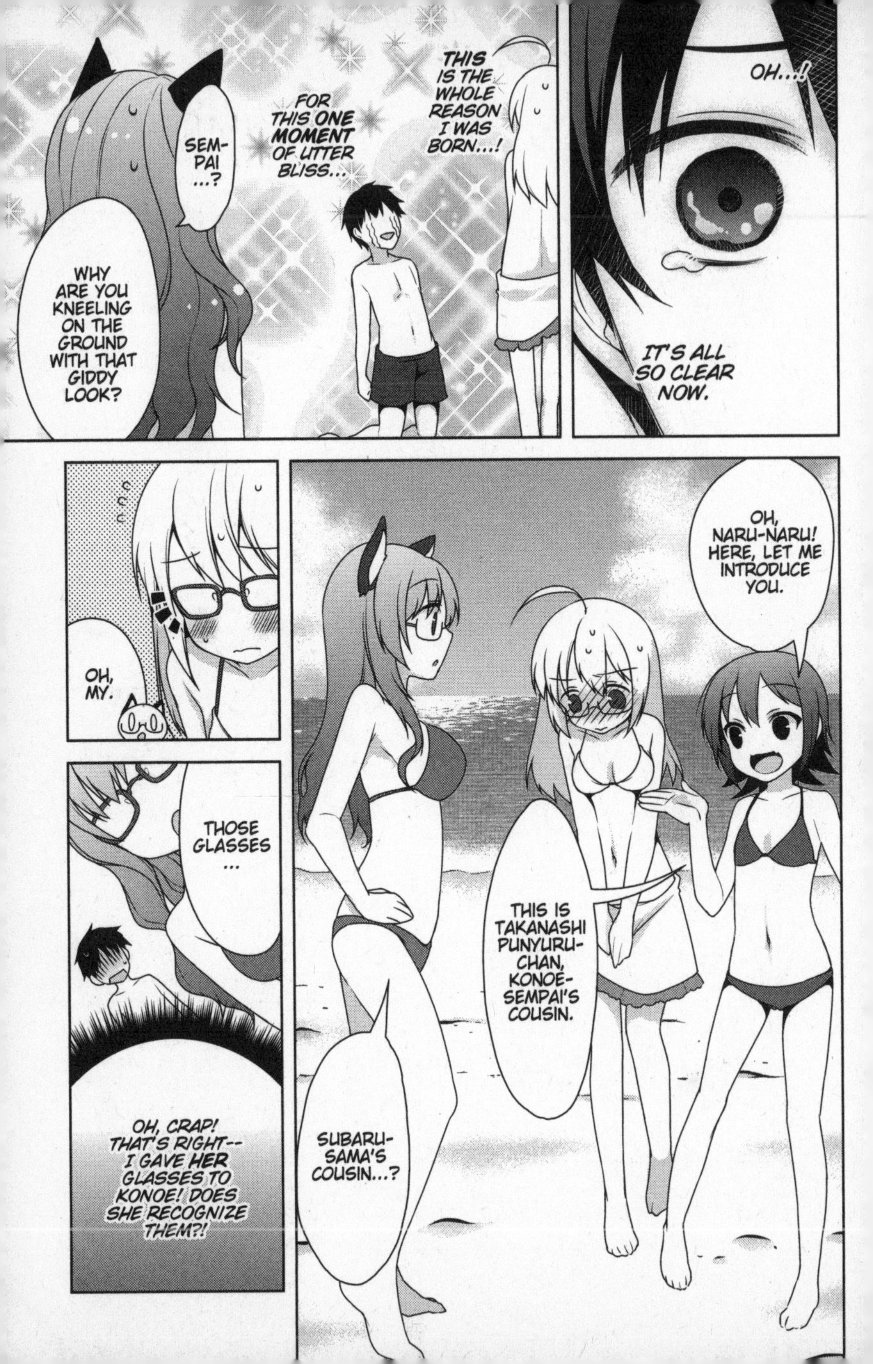

OH...!
IT'S ALL SO CLEAR NOW.
THIS IS THE WHOLE REASON I WAS BORN...!
FOR THIS ONE MOMENT OF UTTER BLISS...
SEMPAI ...?
WHY ARE YOU KNEELING ON THE GROUND WITH THAT GIDDY LOOK?
OH, NARU-NARU! HERE, LET ME INTRODUCE YOU.
THIS IS TAKANASHI PUNYURU-CHAN, KONOE-SEMPAI'S COUSIN.
SUBARU-SAMA'S COUSIN...?
OH, MY.
THOSE GLASSES ...
OH, CRAP! THAT'S RIGHT-- I GAVE HER GLASSES TO KONOE! DOES SHE RECOGNIZE THEM?!

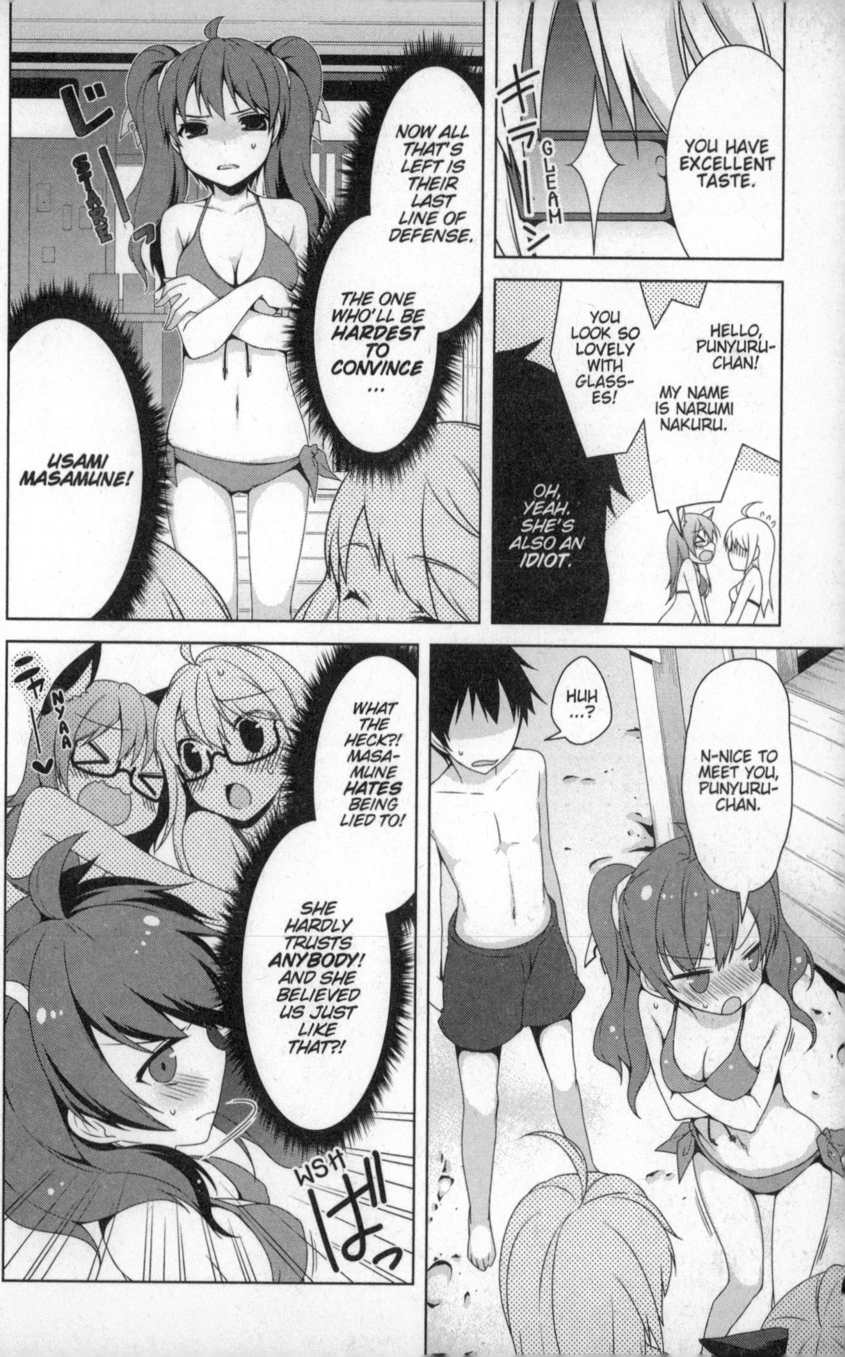
GLEAM
YOU HAVE EXCELLENT TASTE.
HELLO, PUNYURU-CHAN!
MY NAME IS NARUMI NAKURU.
YOU LOOK SO LOVELY WITH GLASSES!
OH, YEAH. SHE'S ALSO AN IDIOT.
NOW ALL THAT'S LEFT IS THEIR LAST LINE OF DEFENSE.
THE ONE WHO'LL BE **HARDEST TO CONVINCE**...
STARE
USAMI MASAMUNE!
N-NICE TO MEET YOU, PUNYURU-CHAN.
HUH...?
NYAA
WHAT THE HECK?! MASAMUNE **HATES** BEING LIED TO!
SHE HARDLY TRUSTS **ANYBODY!** AND SHE BELIEVED US JUST LIKE THAT?!
WSH

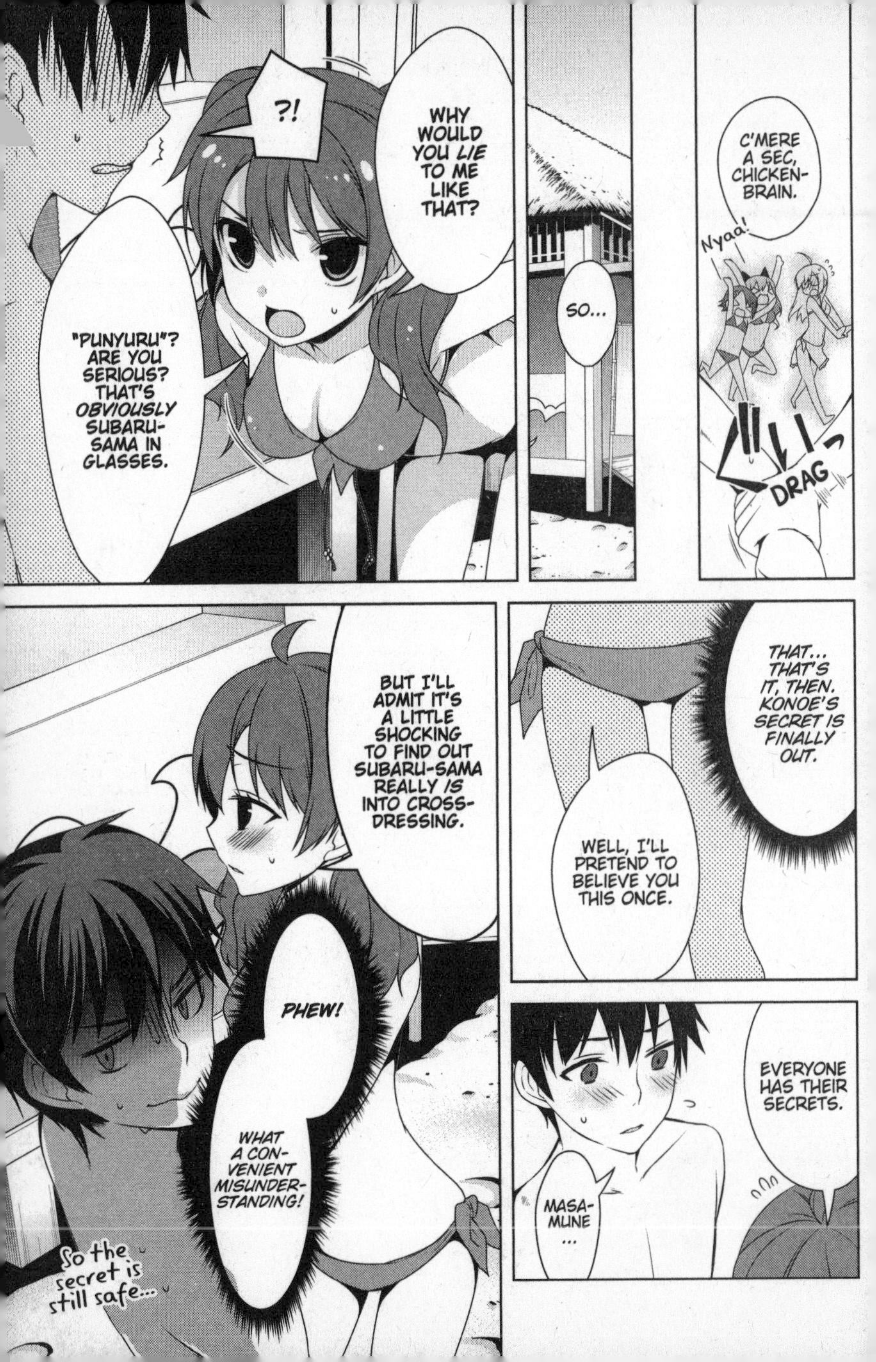
C'MERE A SEC, CHICKEN-BRAIN.
Nyaa!
DRAG
SO...
WHY WOULD YOU LIE TO ME LIKE THAT?
?!
"PUNYURU"? ARE YOU SERIOUS? THAT'S OBVIOUSLY SUBARU-SAMA IN GLASSES.
THAT... THAT'S IT, THEN. KONOE'S SECRET IS FINALLY OUT.
WELL, I'LL PRETEND TO BELIEVE YOU THIS ONCE.
EVERYONE HAS THEIR SECRETS.
MASA-MUNE ...
BUT I'LL ADMIT IT'S A LITTLE SHOCKING TO FIND OUT SUBARU-SAMA REALLY IS INTO CROSS-DRESSING.
PHEW!
WHAT A CON-VENIENT MISUNDER-STANDING!
So the secret is still safe...

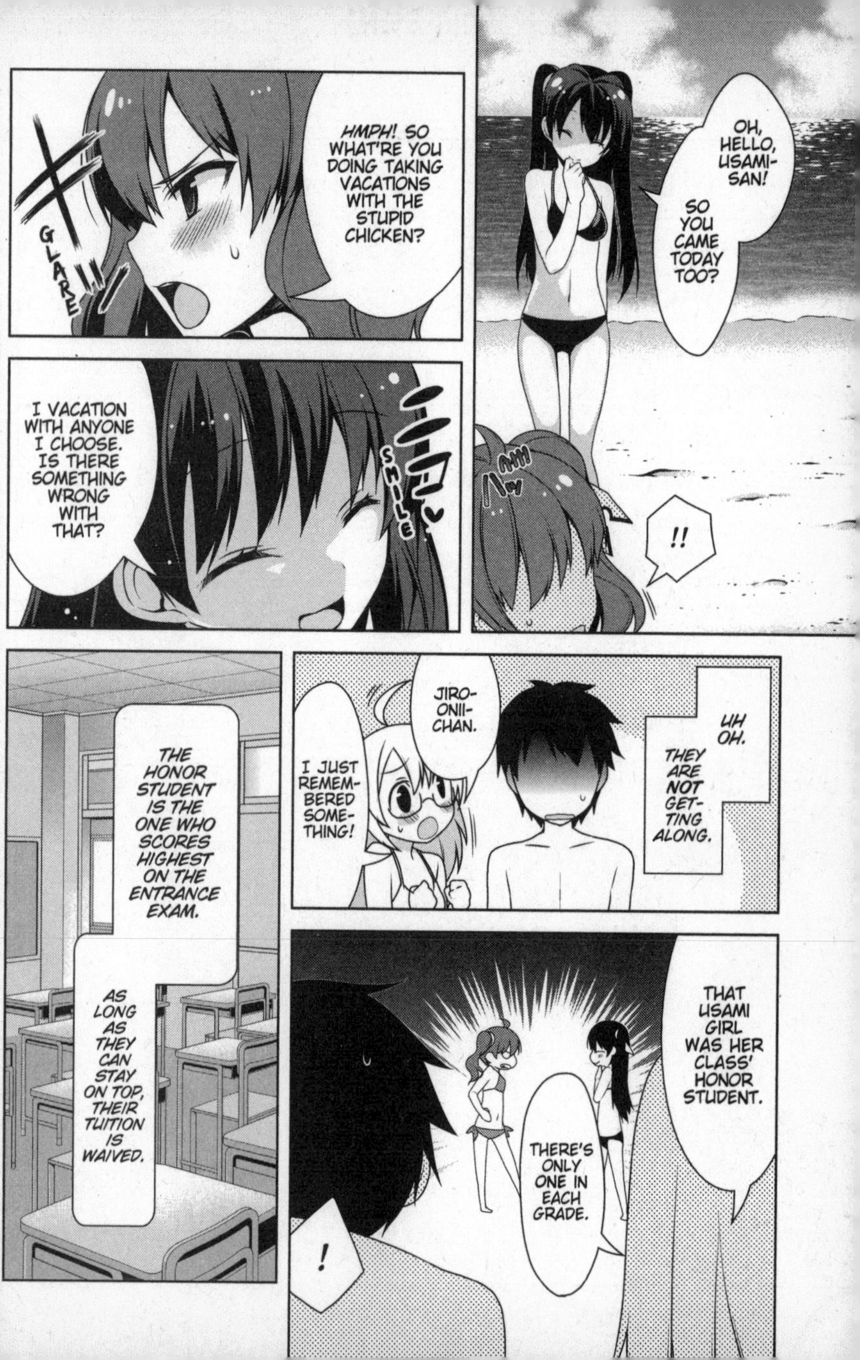
OH, HELLO, USAMI-SAN!
SO YOU CAME TODAY TOO?
!!
HMPH! SO WHAT'RE YOU DOING TAKING VACATIONS WITH THE STUPID CHICKEN?
GLARE
I VACATION WITH ANYONE I CHOOSE. IS THERE SOMETHING WRONG WITH THAT?
SMILE
UH OH. THEY ARE NOT GETTING ALONG.
JIRO-ONII-CHAN.
I JUST REMEMBERED SOMETHING!
THAT USAMI GIRL WAS HER CLASS' HONOR STUDENT.
THERE'S ONLY ONE IN EACH GRADE.
!
THE HONOR STUDENT IS THE ONE WHO SCORES HIGHEST ON THE ENTRANCE EXAM.
AS LONG AS THEY CAN STAY ON TOP, THEIR TUITION IS WAIVED.

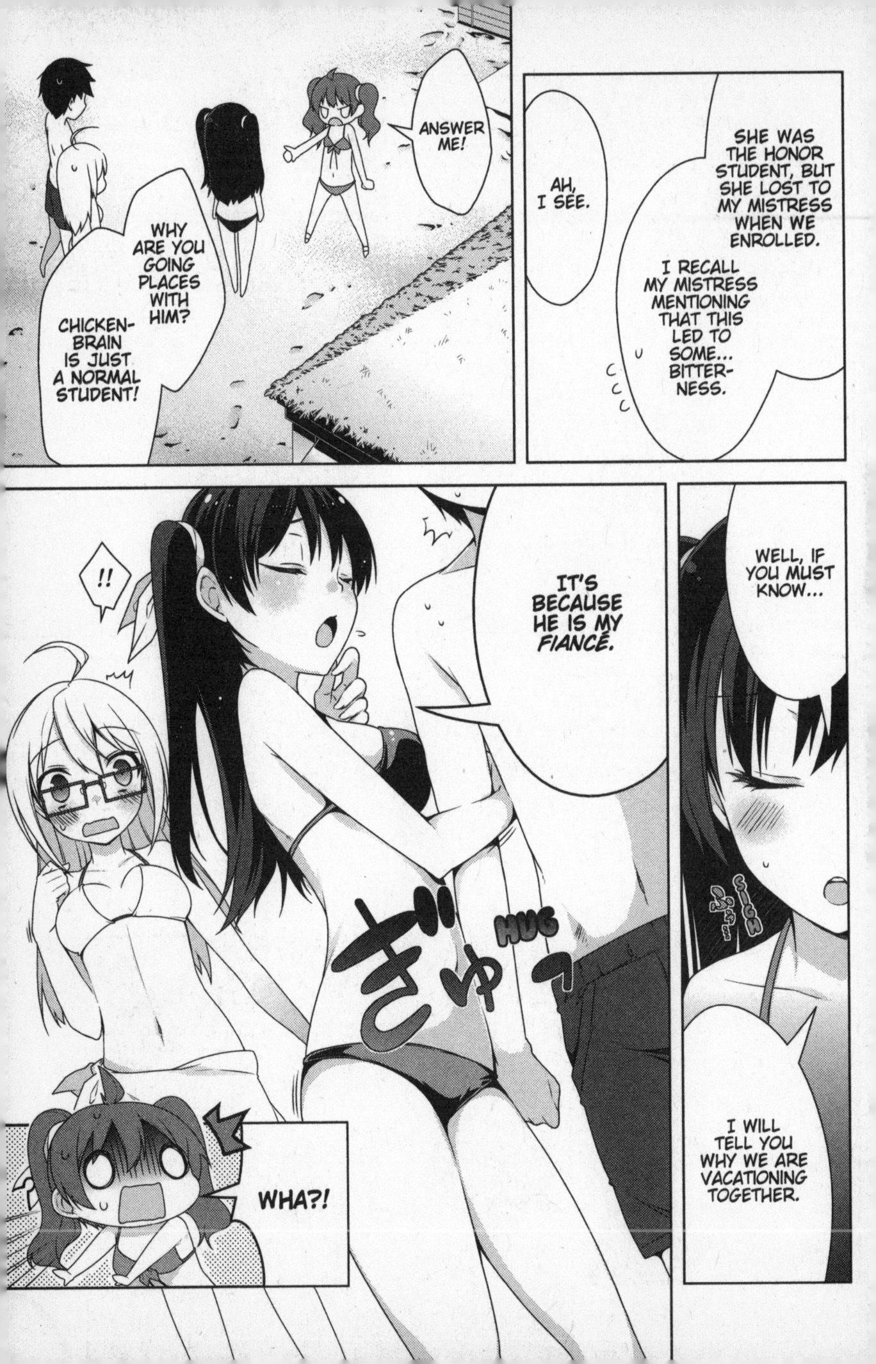
SHE WAS THE HONOR STUDENT, BUT SHE LOST TO MY MISTRESS WHEN WE ENROLLED.
I RECALL MY MISTRESS MENTIONING THAT THIS LED TO SOME... BITTERNESS.
AH, I SEE.
ANSWER ME!
WHY ARE YOU GOING PLACES WITH HIM?
CHICKEN-BRAIN IS JUST A NORMAL STUDENT!
WELL, IF YOU MUST KNOW...
SIGH
I WILL TELL YOU WHY WE ARE VACATIONING TOGETHER.
IT'S BECAUSE HE IS MY *FIANCÉ*.
!!
ぎゅっ
HUG
WHA?!

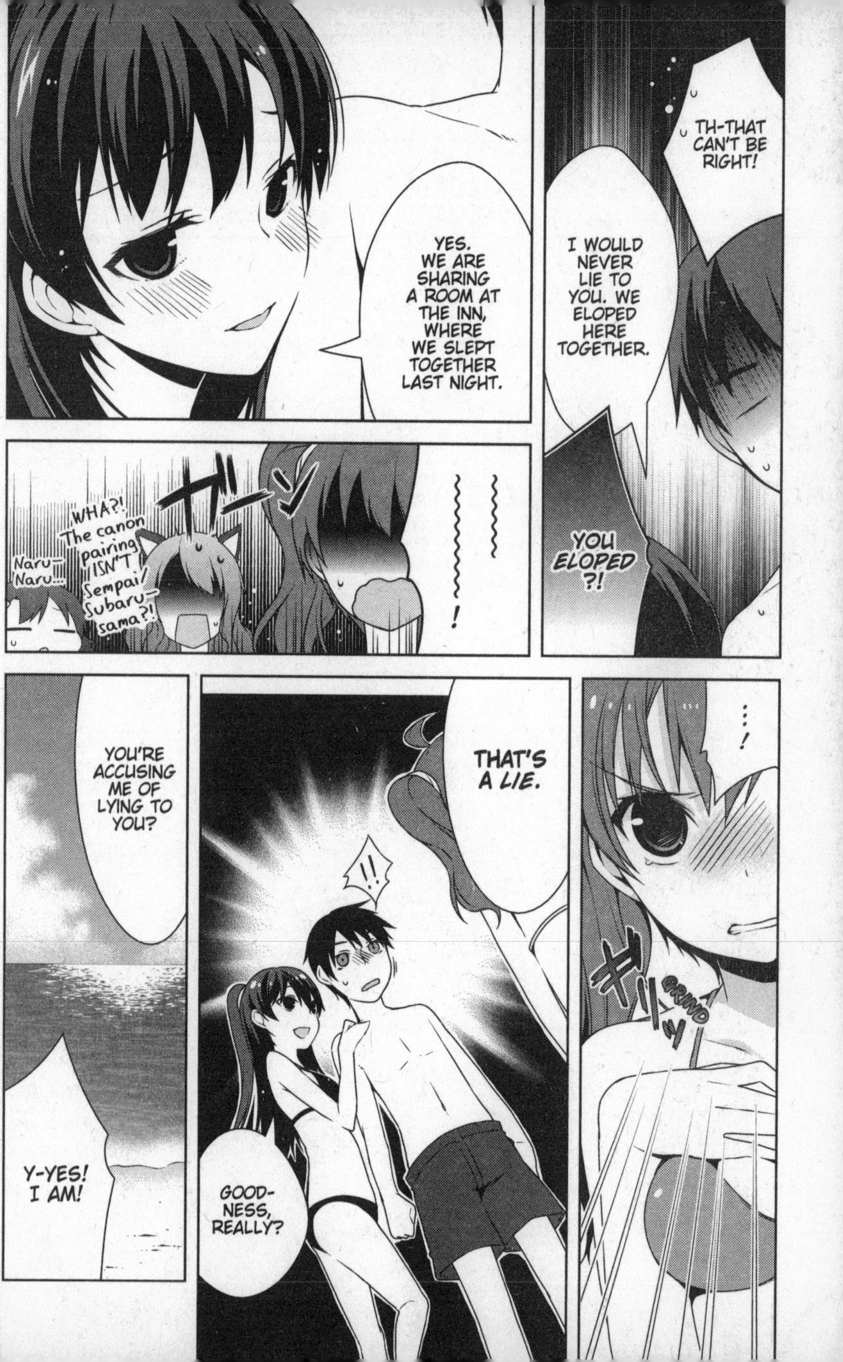
TH-THAT CAN'T BE RIGHT!
I WOULD NEVER LIE TO YOU. WE ELOPED HERE TOGETHER.
YOU ELOPED?!
YES. WE ARE SHARING A ROOM AT THE INN, WHERE WE SLEPT TOGETHER LAST NIGHT.
WHA?! The canon pairing ISN'T Sempai/Subaru-sama?!
Naru-Naru...
...!
GRIND
THAT'S A LIE.
!!
GOOD-NESS, REALLY?
YOU'RE ACCUSING ME OF LYING TO YOU?
Y-YES! I AM!

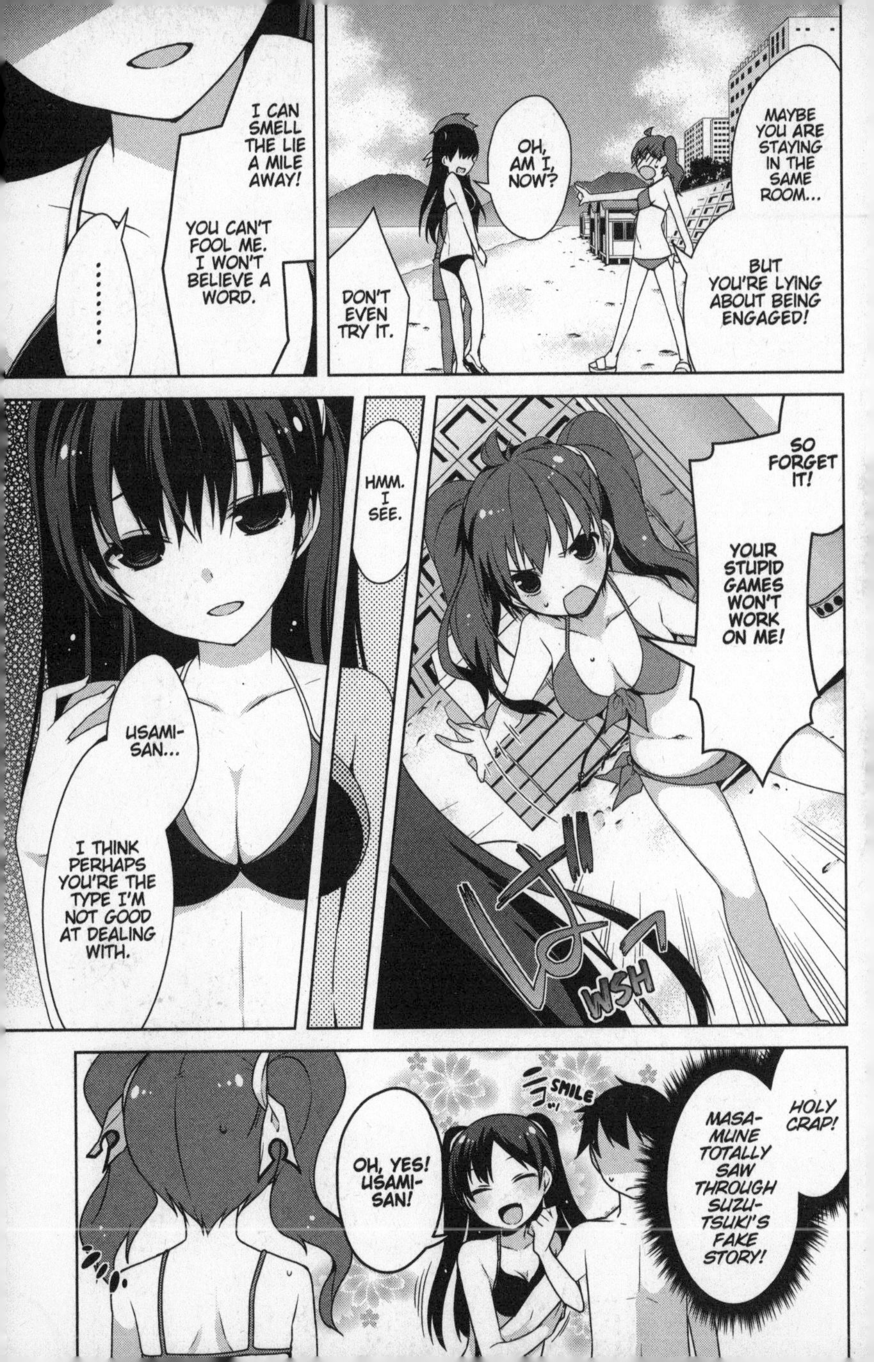
MAYBE YOU ARE STAYING IN THE SAME ROOM...
BUT YOU'RE LYING ABOUT BEING ENGAGED!
OH, AM I, NOW?
DON'T EVEN TRY IT.
I CAN SMELL THE LIE A MILE AWAY!
YOU CAN'T FOOL ME. I WON'T BELIEVE A WORD.
......
SO FORGET IT!
YOUR STUPID GAMES WON'T WORK ON ME!
WSH
HMM. I SEE.
USAMI-SAN...
I THINK PERHAPS YOU'RE THE TYPE I'M NOT GOOD AT DEALING WITH.
HOLY CRAP!
MASAMUNE TOTALLY SAW THROUGH SUZUTSUKI'S FAKE STORY!
SMILE
OH, YES! USAMI-SAN!

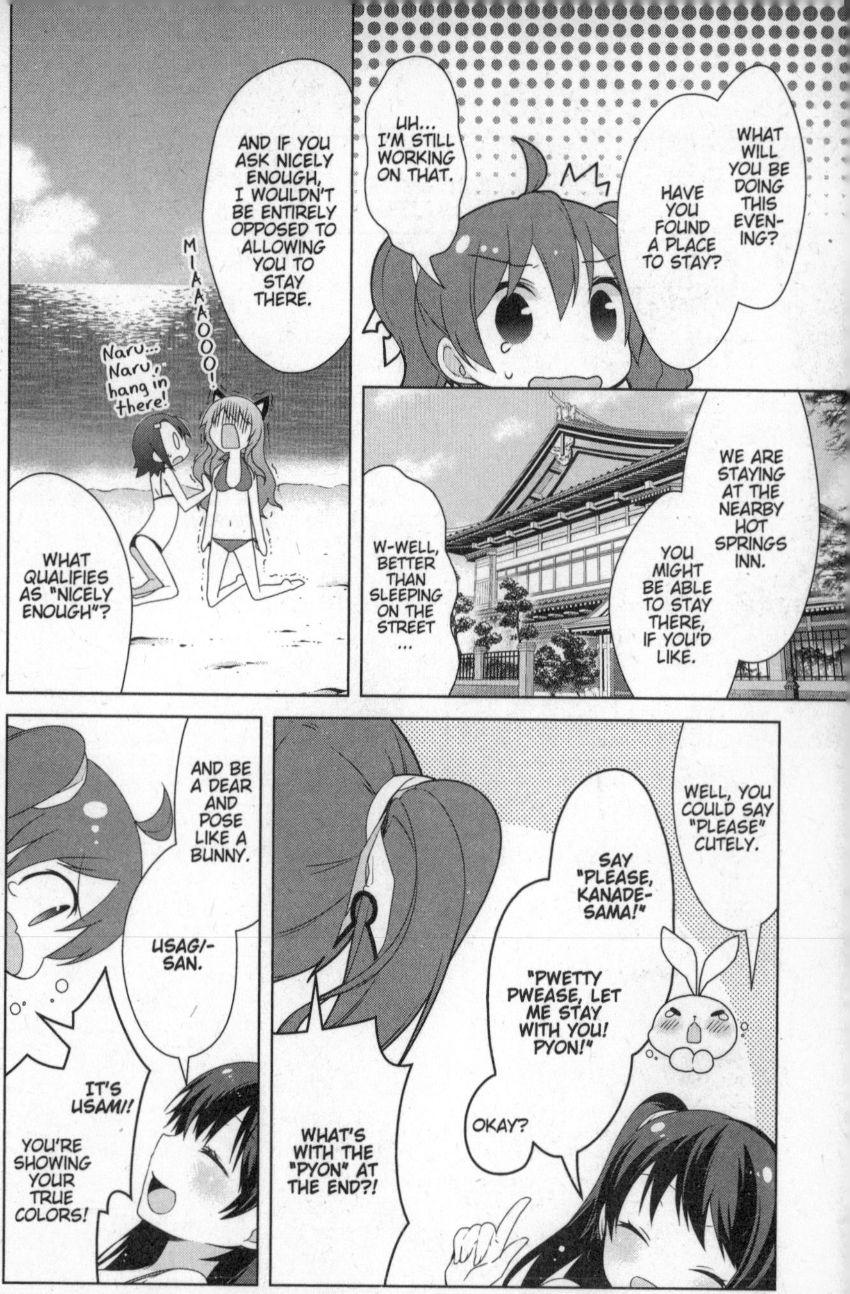
WHAT WILL YOU BE DOING THIS EVENING?
HAVE YOU FOUND A PLACE TO STAY?
UH... I'M STILL WORKING ON THAT.
WE ARE STAYING AT THE NEARBY HOT SPRINGS INN.
YOU MIGHT BE ABLE TO STAY THERE, IF YOU'D LIKE.
W-WELL, BETTER THAN SLEEPING ON THE STREET...
AND IF YOU ASK NICELY ENOUGH, I WOULDN'T BE ENTIRELY OPPOSED TO ALLOWING YOU TO STAY THERE.
MIAAAOOO!
Naru... Naru, hang in there!
WHAT QUALIFIES AS "NICELY ENOUGH"?
WELL, YOU COULD SAY "PLEASE" CUTELY.
SAY "PLEASE, KANADE-SAMA!"
"PWETTY PWEASE, LET ME STAY WITH YOU! PYON!"
OKAY?
WHAT'S WITH THE "PYON" AT THE END?!
AND BE A DEAR AND POSE LIKE A BUNNY.
USAGI-SAN.
IT'S USAMI!
YOU'RE SHOWING YOUR TRUE COLORS!

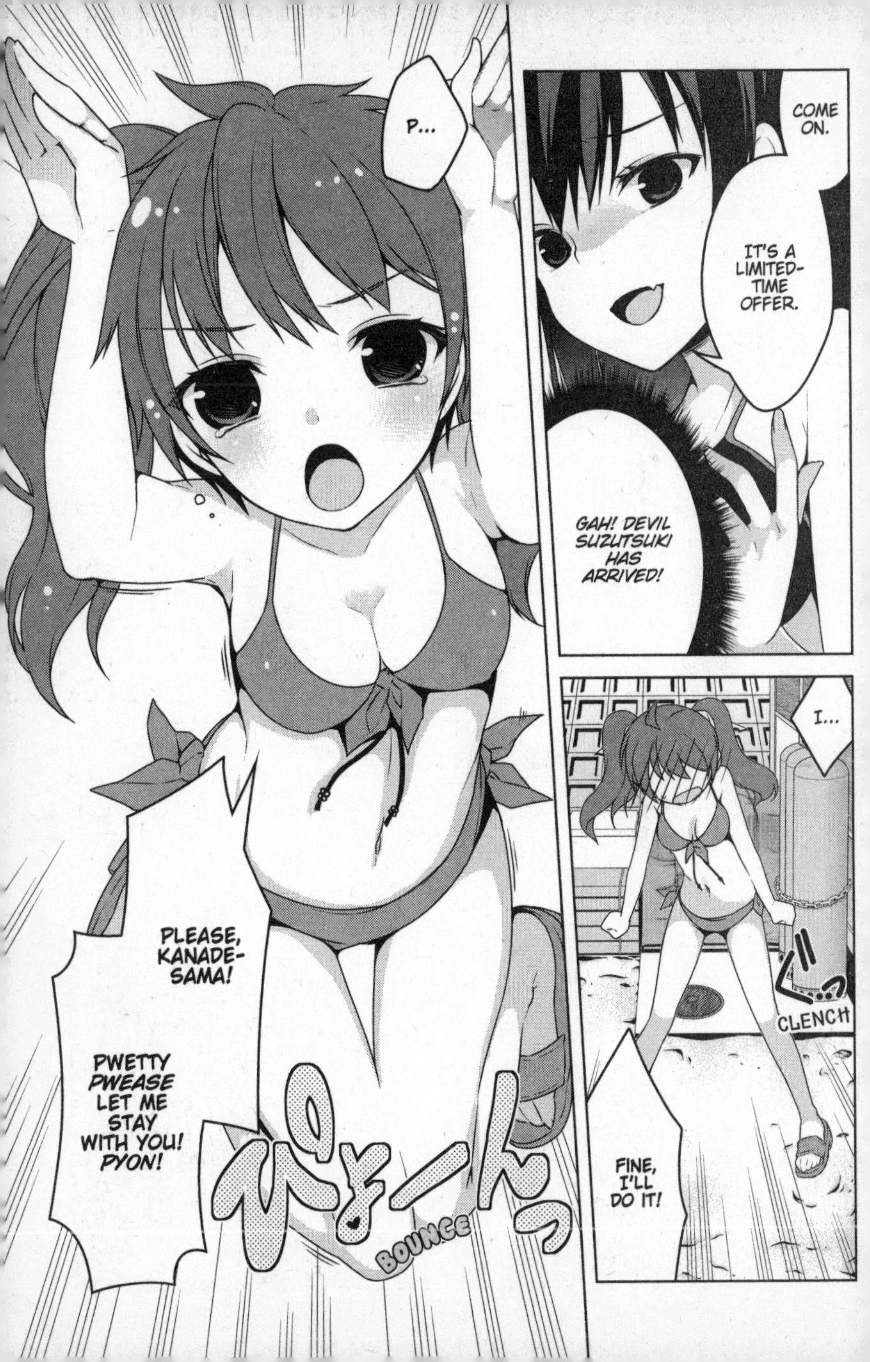
COME ON.
IT'S A LIMITED-TIME OFFER.
GAH! DEVIL SUZUTSUKI HAS ARRIVED!
I...
CLENCH
FINE, I'LL DO IT!
P...
PLEASE, KANADE-SAMA!
PWETTY PWEASE LET ME STAY WITH YOU! PYON!
BOUNCE

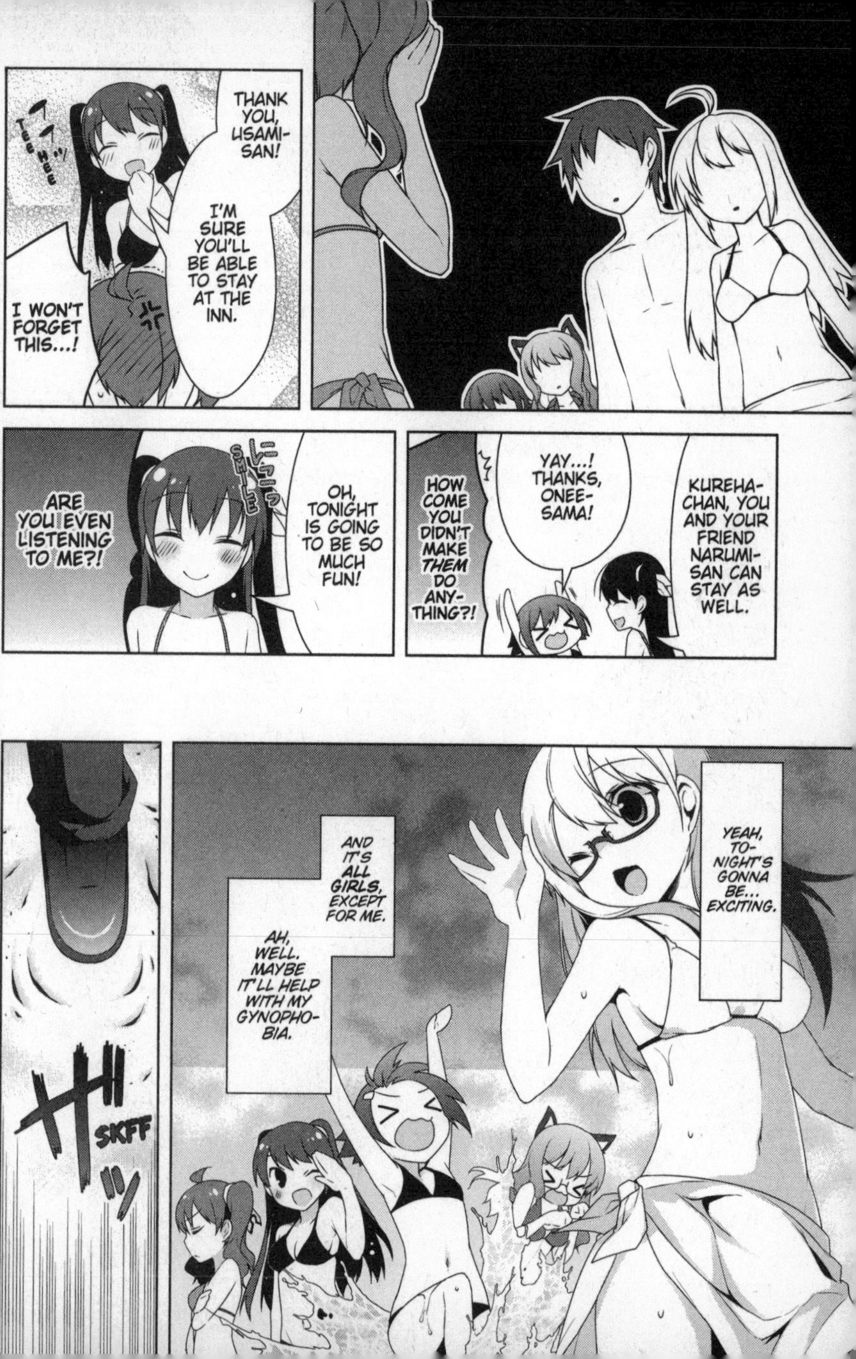
THANK YOU, USAMI-SAN!
I'M SURE YOU'LL BE ABLE TO STAY AT THE INN.
TEE HEE
I WON'T FORGET THIS...!
KUREHA-CHAN, YOU AND YOUR FRIEND NARUMI-SAN CAN STAY AS WELL.
YAY...! THANKS, ONEE-SAMA!
HOW COME YOU DIDN'T MAKE THEM DO ANYTHING?!
OH, TONIGHT IS GOING TO BE SO MUCH FUN!
SMILE
ARE YOU EVEN LISTENING TO ME?!
YEAH, TO-NIGHT'S GONNA BE... EXCITING.
AND IT'S ALL GIRLS, EXCEPT FOR ME.
AH, WELL. MAYBE IT'LL HELP WITH MY GYNOPHO-BIA.
SKFF

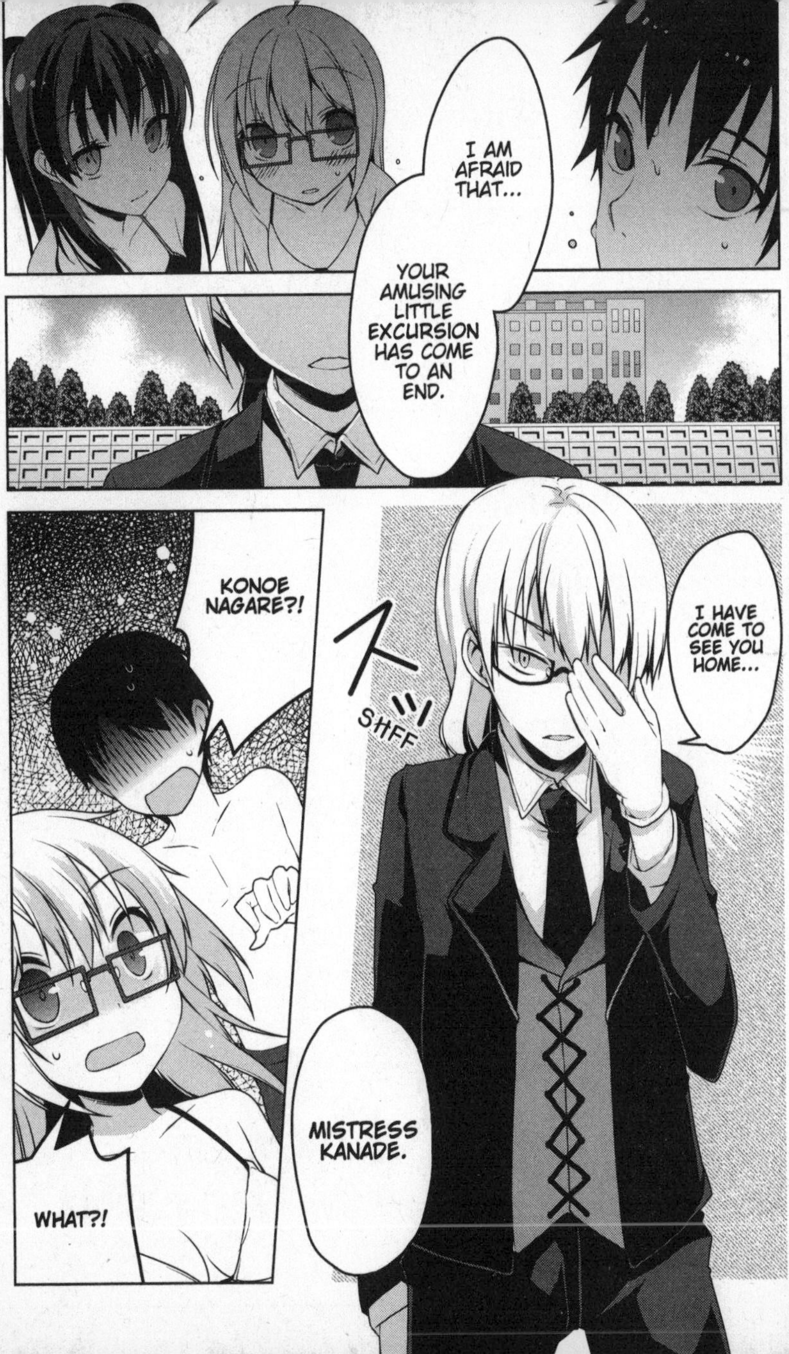
I AM AFRAID THAT...
YOUR AMUSING LITTLE EXCURSION HAS COME TO AN END.
I HAVE COME TO SEE YOU HOME...
SHFF
MISTRESS KANADE.
KONOE NAGARE?!
WHAT?!

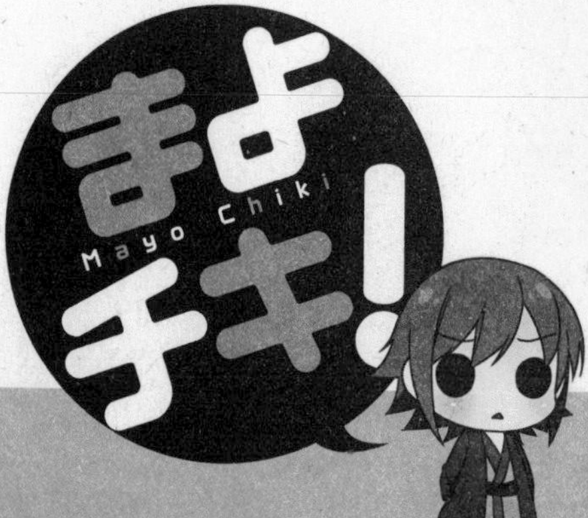
まよチキ!
Mayo Chiki

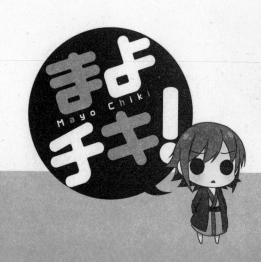

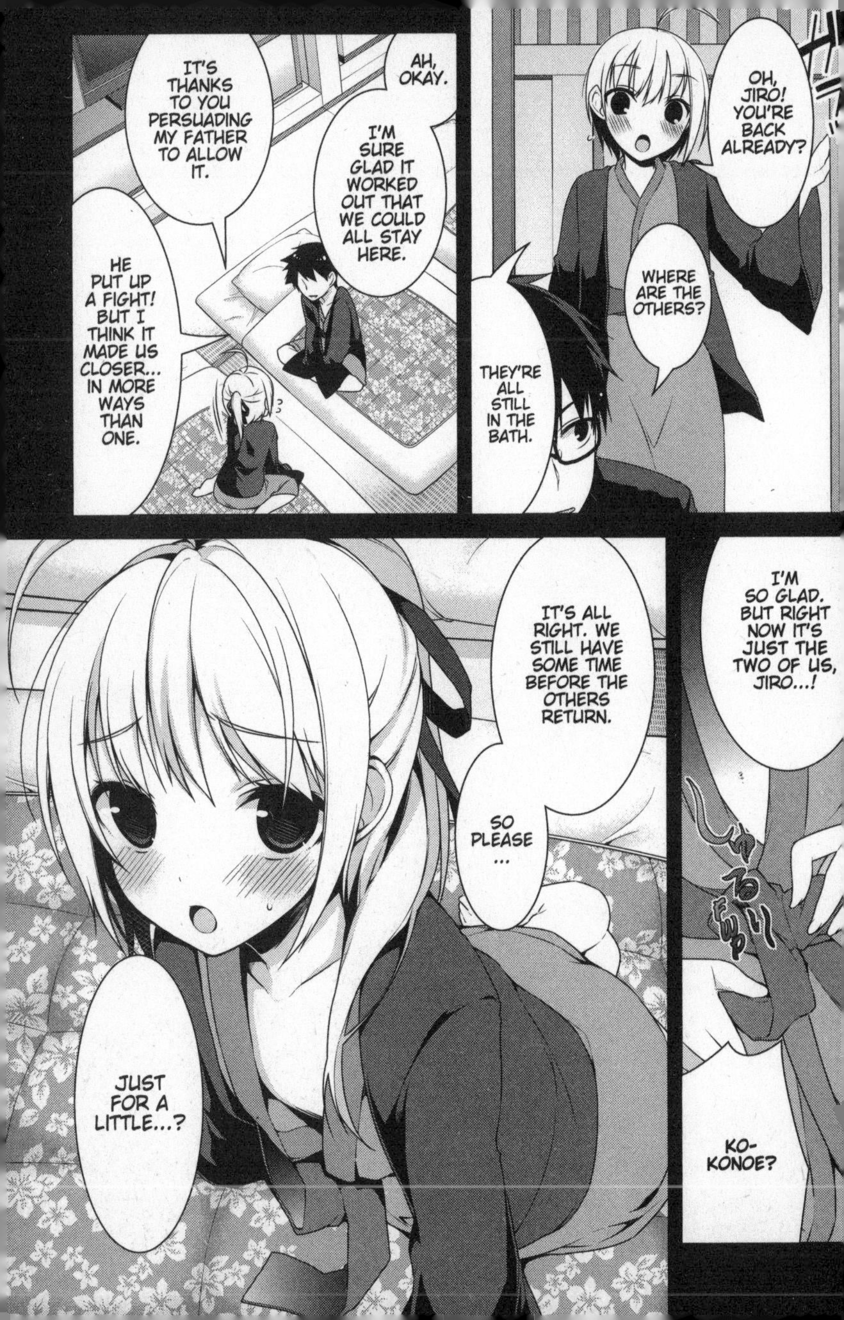
OH, JIRO! YOU'RE BACK ALREADY?
WHERE ARE THE OTHERS?
THEY'RE ALL STILL IN THE BATH.
AH, OKAY.
I'M SURE GLAD IT WORKED OUT THAT WE COULD ALL STAY HERE.
IT'S THANKS TO YOU PERSUADING MY FATHER TO ALLOW IT.
HE PUT UP A FIGHT! BUT I THINK IT MADE US CLOSER... IN MORE WAYS THAN ONE.
I'M SO GLAD. BUT RIGHT NOW IT'S JUST THE TWO OF US, JIRO...!
FWP
KO-KONOE?
IT'S ALL RIGHT. WE STILL HAVE SOME TIME BEFORE THE OTHERS RETURN.
SO PLEASE...
JUST FOR A LITTLE...?

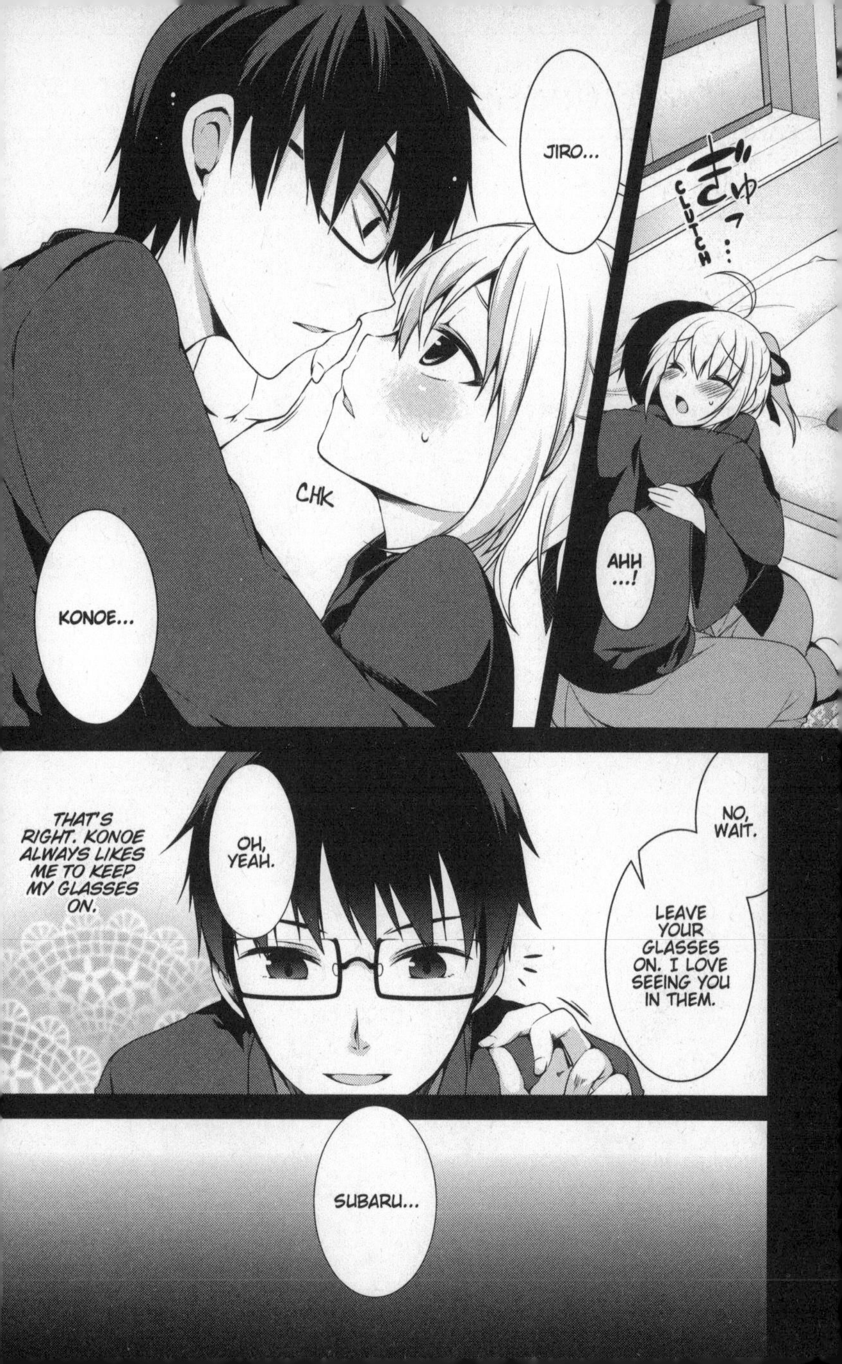
ぎゅっ…
CLUTCH
AHH ...!
JIRO...
CHK
KONOE...
NO, WAIT.
LEAVE YOUR GLASSES ON. I LOVE SEEING YOU IN THEM.
OH, YEAH.
THAT'S RIGHT. KONOE ALWAYS LIKES ME TO KEEP MY GLASSES ON.
SUBARU...

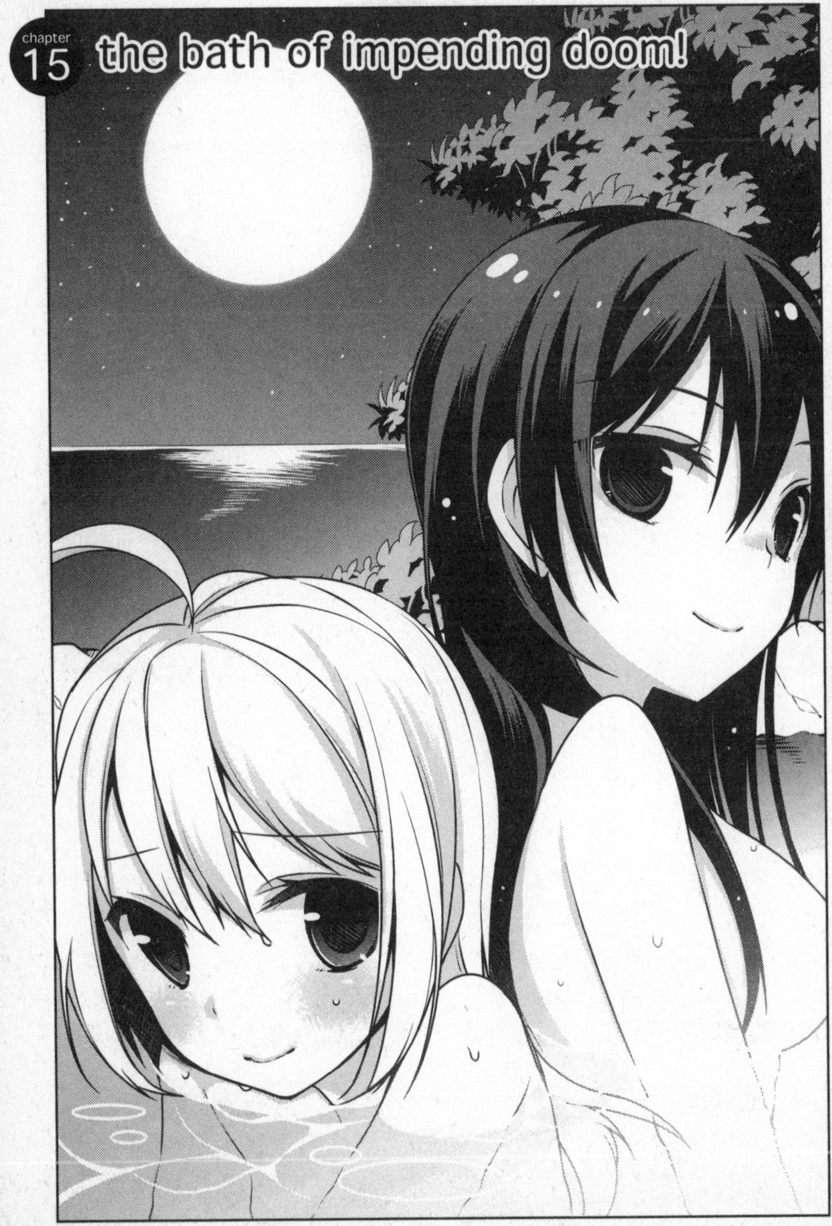
chapter
15
the bath of impending doom!

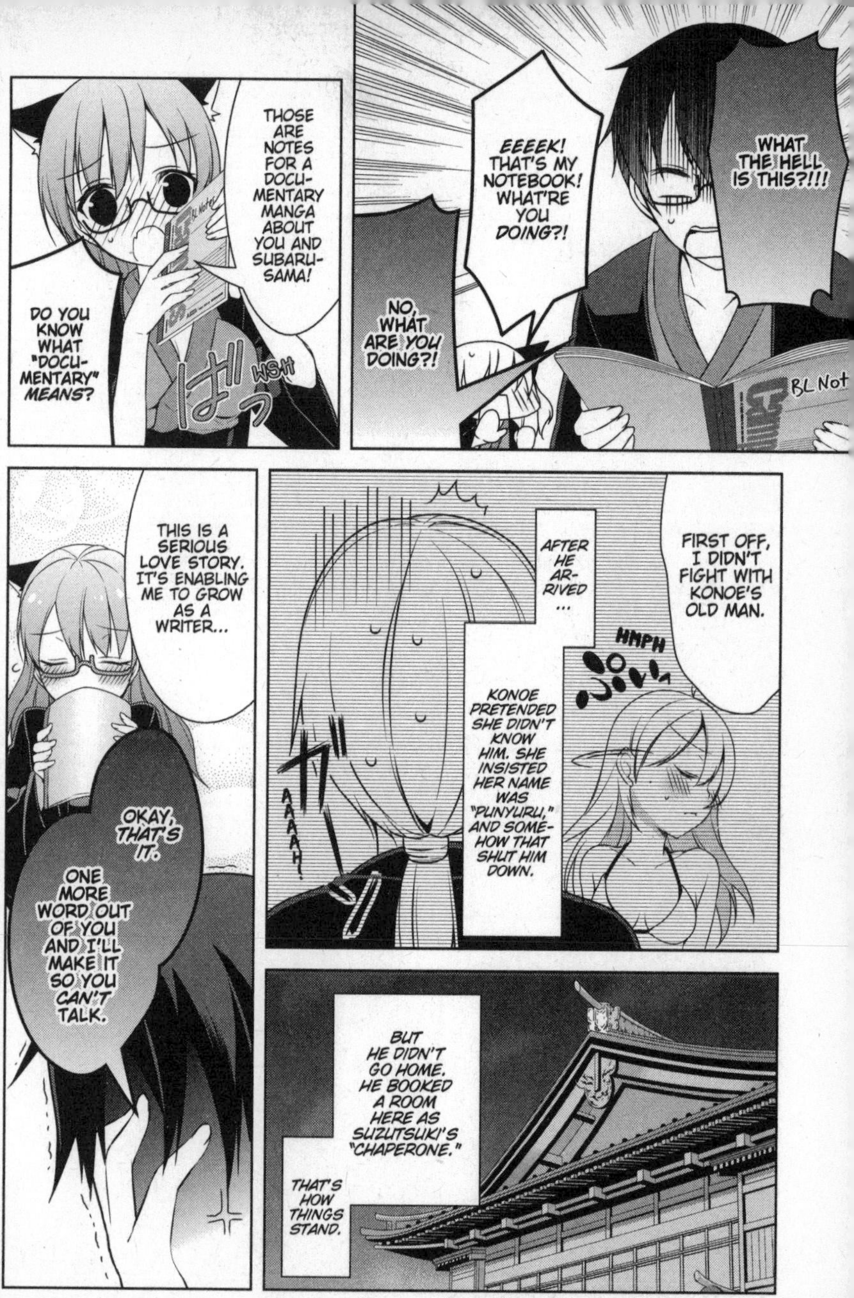
WHAT THE HELL IS THIS?!!!
EEEEK! THAT'S MY NOTEBOOK! WHAT'RE YOU DOING?!
NO, WHAT ARE YOU DOING?!
BL Not
THOSE ARE NOTES FOR A DOCUMENTARY MANGA ABOUT YOU AND SUBARU-SAMA!
WSH
はっ
DO YOU KNOW WHAT "DOCUMENTARY" MEANS?
FIRST OFF, I DIDN'T FIGHT WITH KONOE'S OLD MAN.
HMPH
AFTER HE ARRIVED...
KONOE PRETENDED SHE DIDN'T KNOW HIM. SHE INSISTED HER NAME WAS "PUNYURU," AND SOMEHOW THAT SHUT HIM DOWN.
AAAAH!
BUT HE DIDN'T GO HOME. HE BOOKED A ROOM HERE AS SUZUTSUKI'S "CHAPERONE."
THAT'S HOW THINGS STAND.
THIS IS A SERIOUS LOVE STORY. IT'S ENABLING ME TO GROW AS A WRITER...
OKAY, THAT'S IT.
ONE MORE WORD OUT OF YOU AND I'LL MAKE IT SO YOU CAN'T TALK.

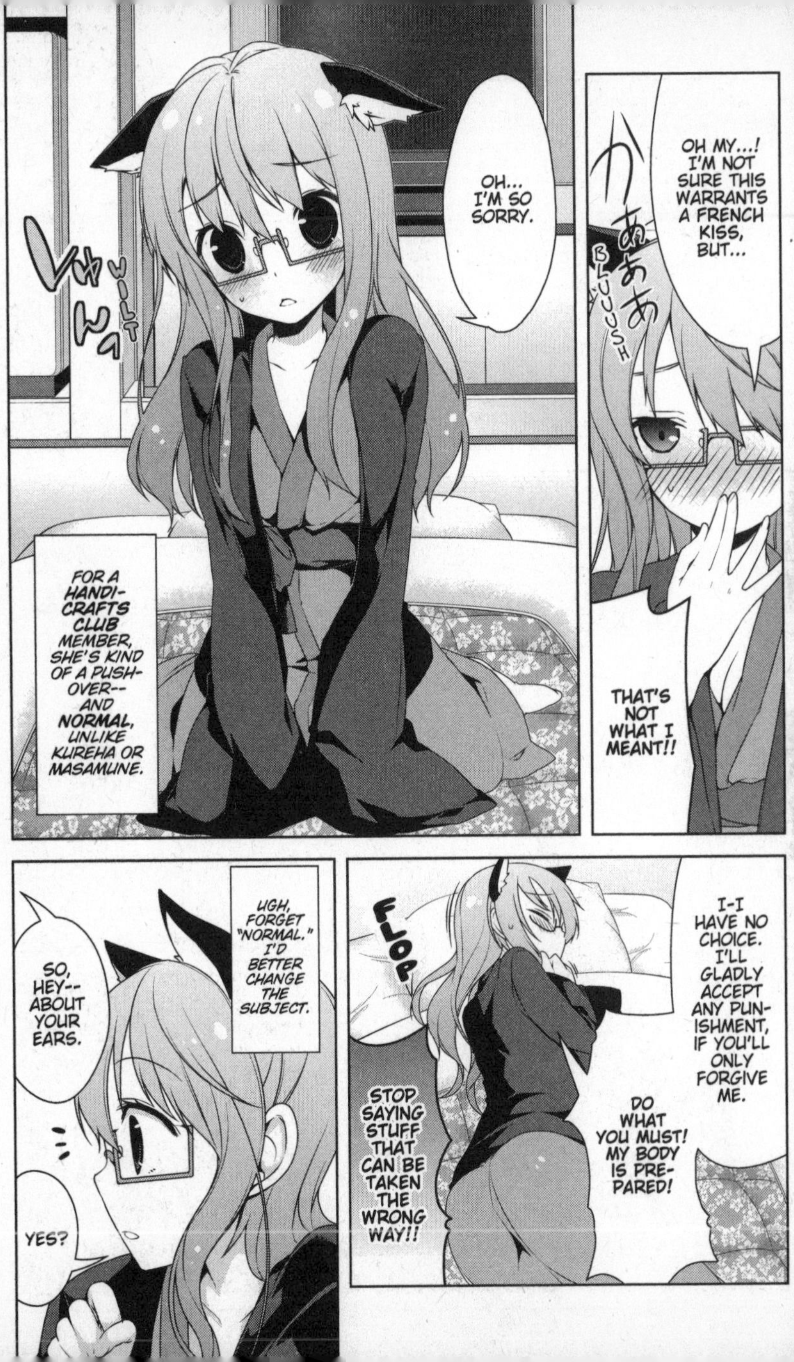
OH MY...! I'M NOT SURE THIS WARRANTS A FRENCH KISS, BUT...
かあああ
BLUUSH
THAT'S NOT WHAT I MEANT!!
OH... I'M SO SORRY.
WILT
FOR A HANDI-CRAFTS CLUB MEMBER, SHE'S KIND OF A PUSH-OVER--AND NORMAL, UNLIKE KUREHA OR MASAMUNE.
I-I HAVE NO CHOICE. I'LL GLADLY ACCEPT ANY PUN-ISHMENT, IF YOU'LL ONLY FORGIVE ME.
FLOP
DO WHAT YOU MUST! MY BODY IS PRE-PARED!
STOP SAYING STUFF THAT CAN BE TAKEN THE WRONG WAY!!
UGH, FORGET "NORMAL." I'D BETTER CHANGE THE SUBJECT.
SO, HEY--ABOUT YOUR EARS.
YES?

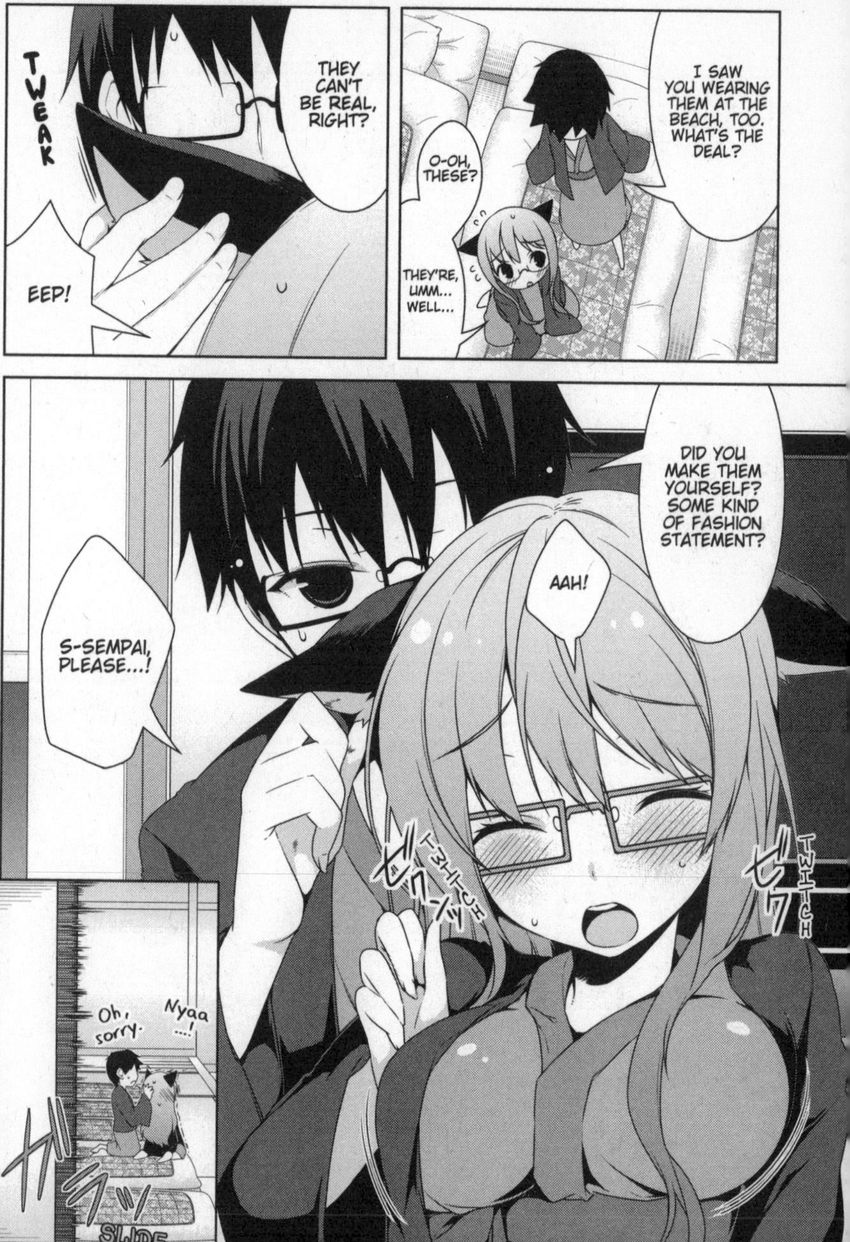
I SAW YOU WEARING THEM AT THE BEACH, TOO. WHAT'S THE DEAL?
O-OH, THESE?
THEY'RE, UMM... WELL...
THEY CAN'T BE REAL, RIGHT?
TWEAK
EEP!
DID YOU MAKE THEM YOURSELF? SOME KIND OF FASHION STATEMENT?
AAH!
S-SEMPAI, PLEASE...!
TWITCH
TWITCH
Nyaa...!
Oh, sorry.
SLIDE

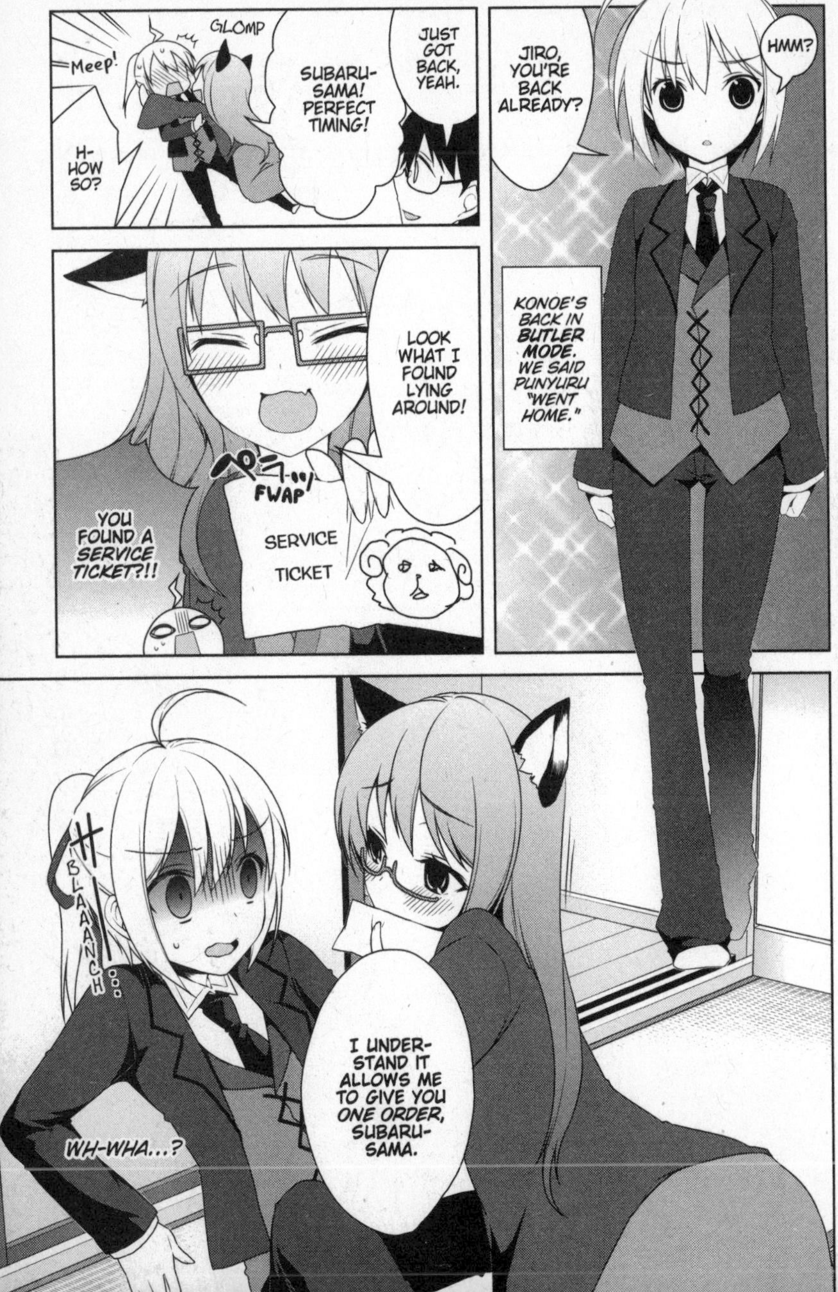
HMM?
JIRO, YOU'RE BACK ALREADY?
KONOE'S BACK IN BUTLER MODE. WE SAID PUNYURU "WENT HOME."
JUST GOT BACK, YEAH.
SUBARU-SAMA! PERFECT TIMING!
GLOMP
Meep!
H-HOW SO?
LOOK WHAT I FOUND LYING AROUND!
FWAP
SERVICE TICKET
YOU FOUND A SERVICE TICKET?!!
I UNDERSTAND IT ALLOWS ME TO GIVE YOU ONE ORDER, SUBARU-SAMA.
BLAAANCH...
WH-WHA...?

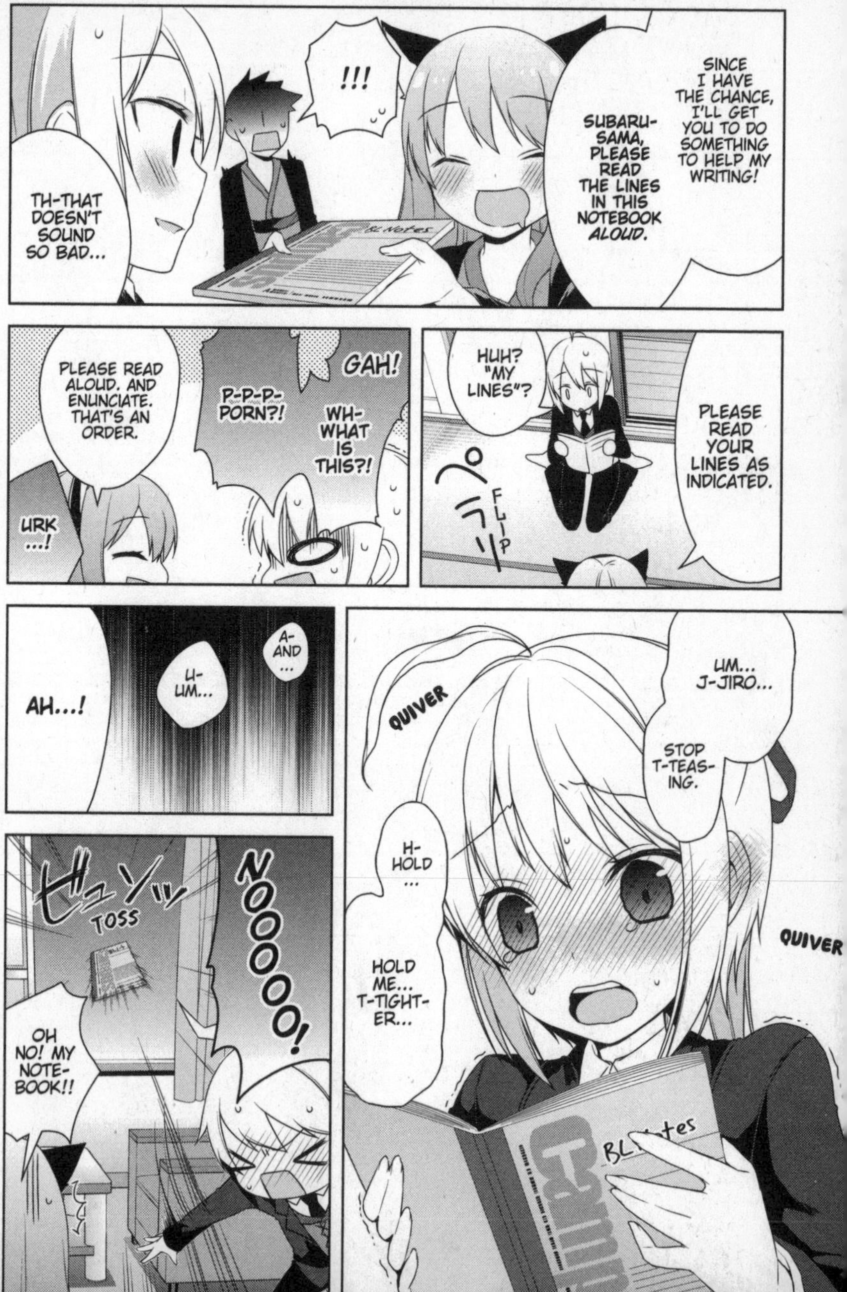
SINCE I HAVE THE CHANCE, I'LL GET YOU TO DO SOMETHING TO HELP MY WRITING!
SUBARU-SAMA, PLEASE READ THE LINES IN THIS NOTEBOOK ALOUD.
!!!
BL Notes
TH-THAT DOESN'T SOUND SO BAD...
PLEASE READ YOUR LINES AS INDICATED.
HUH? "MY LINES"?
FLIP
GAH!
P-P-P-PORN?!
WH-WHAT IS THIS?!
PLEASE READ ALOUD. AND ENUNCIATE. THAT'S AN ORDER.
URK ...!
UM... J-JIRO...
QUIVER
STOP T-TEASING.
H-HOLD ...
HOLD ME... T-TIGHTER...
QUIVER
BL Notes
A-AND ...
U-UM...
AH...!
NOOOOOO!
TOSS
OH NO! MY NOTEBOOK!!

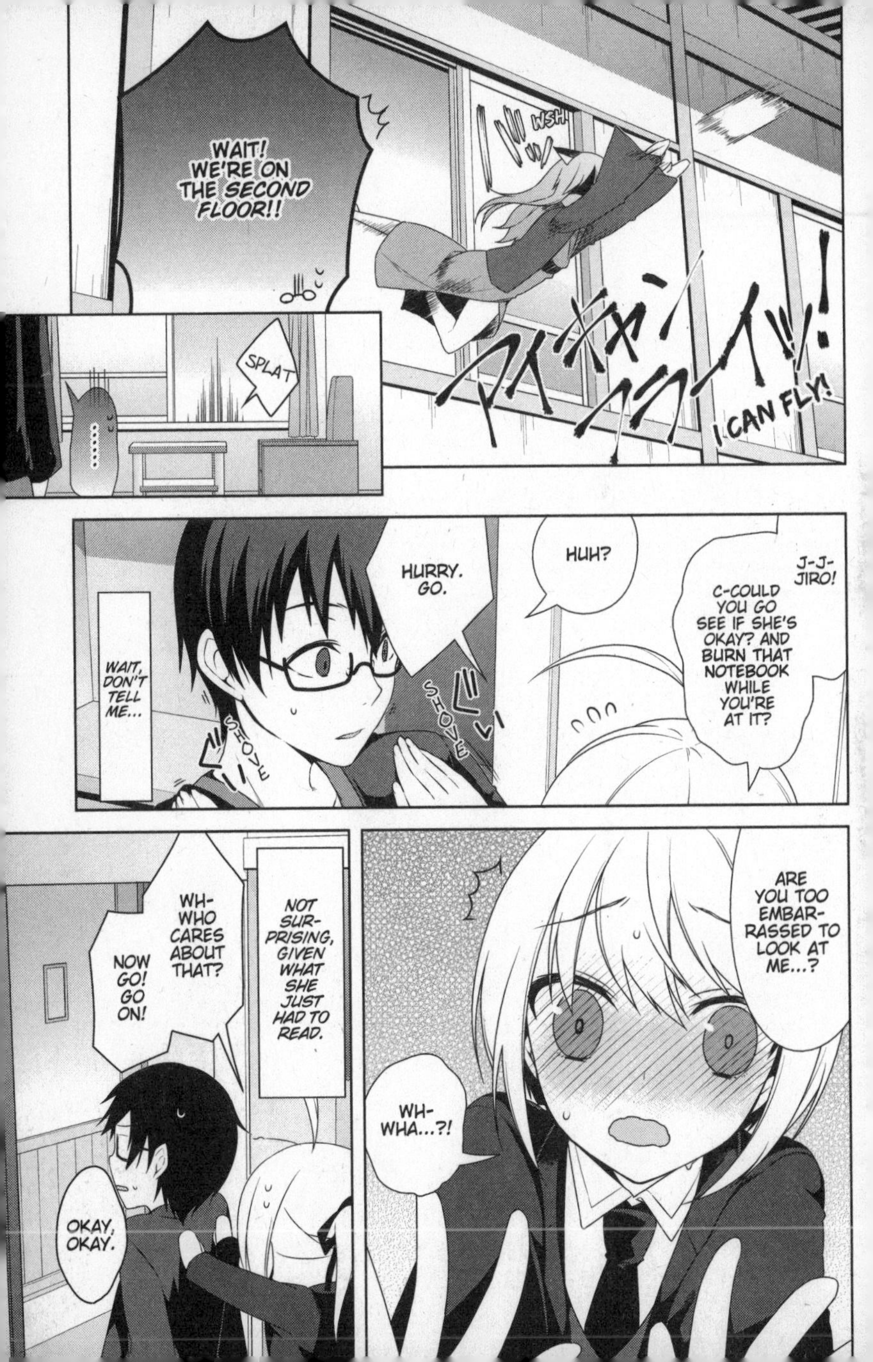
WSH
WAIT! WE'RE ON THE SECOND FLOOR!!
アイキャンフライ!!
I CAN FLY!
SPLAT
......
J-J-JIRO!
C-COULD YOU GO SEE IF SHE'S OKAY? AND BURN THAT NOTEBOOK WHILE YOU'RE AT IT?
HUH?
HURRY. GO.
SHOVE
WAIT, DON'T TELL ME...
SHOVE
ARE YOU TOO EMBARRASSED TO LOOK AT ME...?
WH-WHA...?!
NOT SURPRISING, GIVEN WHAT SHE JUST HAD TO READ.
WH-WHO CARES ABOUT THAT?
NOW GO! GO ON!
OKAY, OKAY.

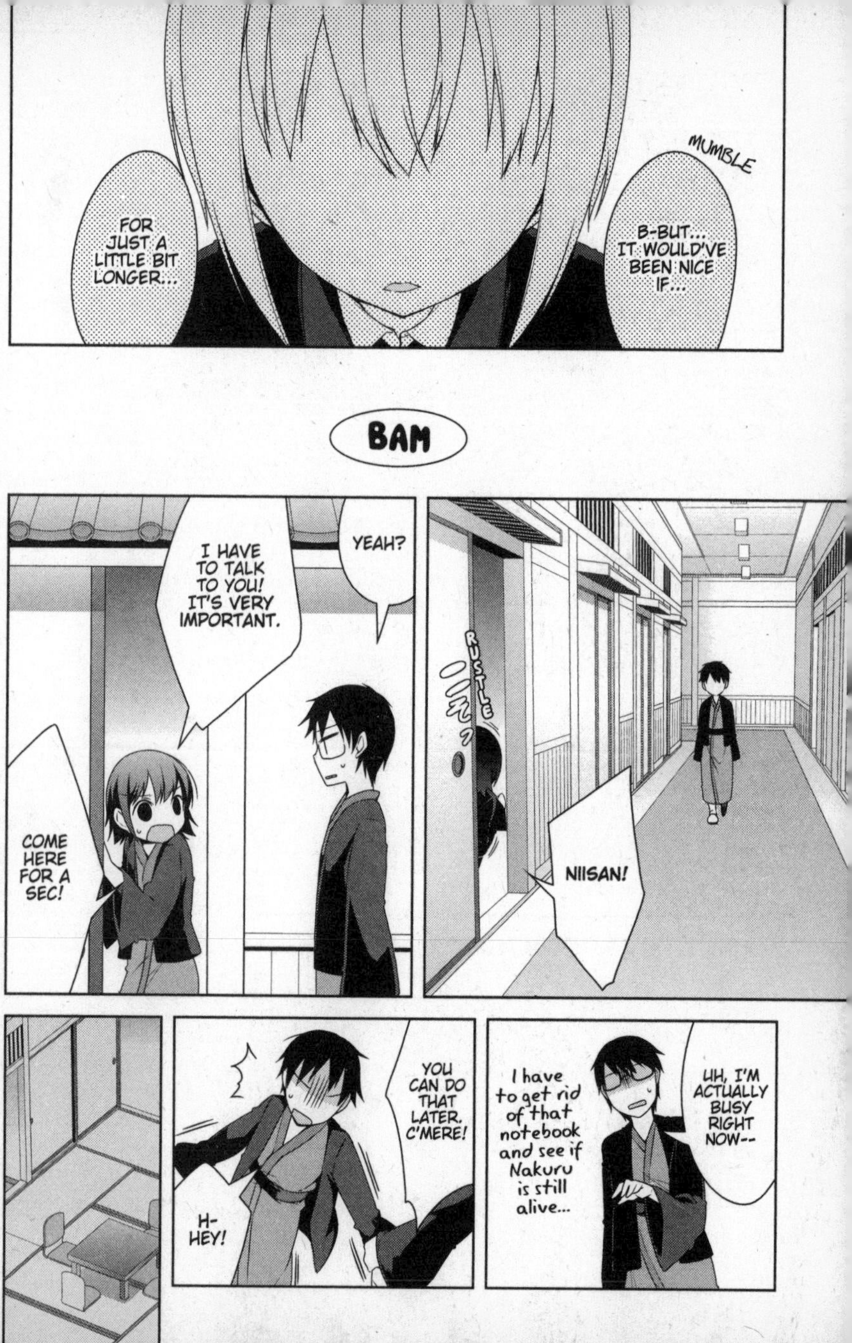
MUMBLE
B-BUT... IT WOULD'VE BEEN NICE IF...
FOR JUST A LITTLE BIT LONGER...
BAM
RUSTLE
NIISAN!
YEAH?
I HAVE TO TALK TO YOU! IT'S VERY IMPORTANT.
COME HERE FOR A SEC!
UH, I'M ACTUALLY BUSY RIGHT NOW--
I have to get rid of that notebook and see if Nakuru is still alive...
YOU CAN DO THAT LATER. C'MERE!
H-HEY!

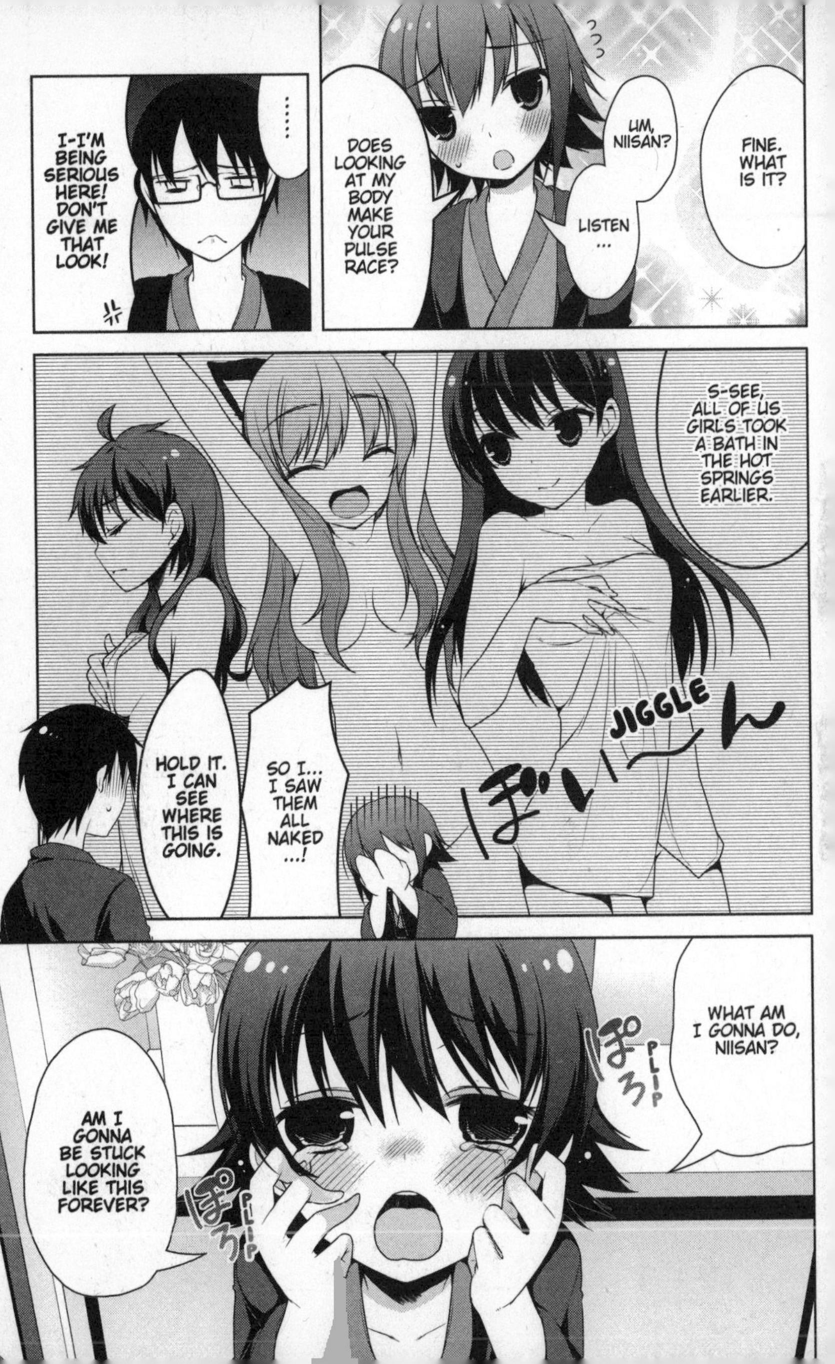
FINE. WHAT IS IT?
UM, NIISAN?
LISTEN ...
DOES LOOKING AT MY BODY MAKE YOUR PULSE RACE?
......
I-I'M BEING SERIOUS HERE! DON'T GIVE ME THAT LOOK!
S-SEE, ALL OF US GIRLS TOOK A BATH IN THE HOT SPRINGS EARLIER.
JIGGLE
ぽいーん
SO I... I SAW THEM ALL NAKED ...!
HOLD IT. I CAN SEE WHERE THIS IS GOING.
WHAT AM I GONNA DO, NIISAN?
ぽろ
PLIP
AM I GONNA BE STUCK LOOKING LIKE THIS FOREVER?
ぽろ
PLIP

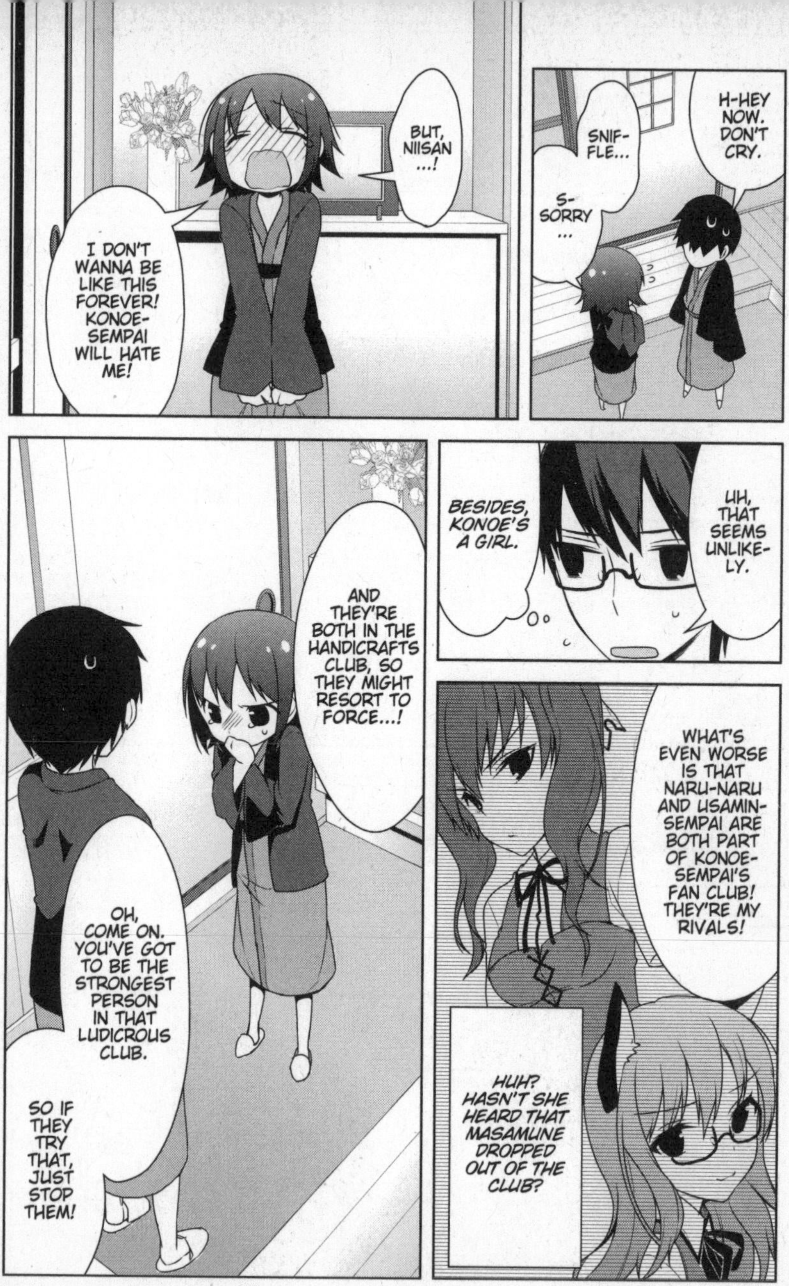
H-HEY NOW. DON'T CRY.
SNIF-FLE...
S-SORRY ...
BUT, NIISAN ...!
I DON'T WANNA BE LIKE THIS FOREVER! KONOE-SEMPAI WILL HATE ME!
UH, THAT SEEMS UNLIKE-LY.
BESIDES, KONOE'S A GIRL.
WHAT'S EVEN WORSE IS THAT NARU-NARU AND USAMIN-SEMPAI ARE BOTH PART OF KONOE-SEMPAI'S FAN CLUB! THEY'RE MY RIVALS!
HUH? HASN'T SHE HEARD THAT MASAMUNE DROPPED OUT OF THE CLUB?
AND THEY'RE BOTH IN THE HANDICRAFTS CLUB, SO THEY MIGHT RESORT TO FORCE...!
OH, COME ON. YOU'VE GOT TO BE THE STRONGEST PERSON IN THAT LUDICROUS CLUB.
SO IF THEY TRY THAT, JUST STOP THEM!

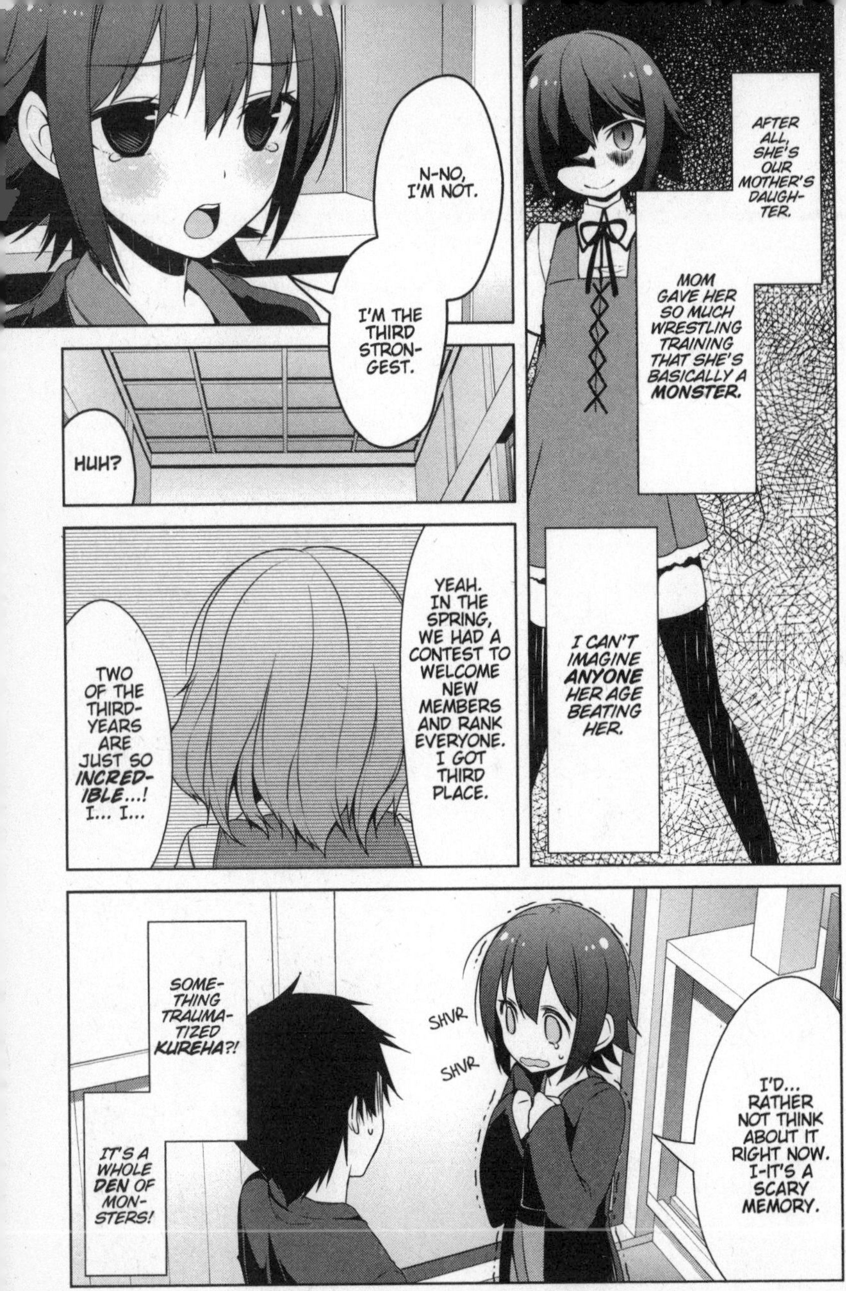
AFTER ALL, SHE'S OUR MOTHER'S DAUGHTER.
MOM GAVE HER SO MUCH WRESTLING TRAINING THAT SHE'S BASICALLY A **MONSTER.**
I CAN'T IMAGINE **ANYONE** HER AGE BEATING HER.
N-NO, I'M NOT.
I'M THE THIRD STRONGEST.
HUH?
YEAH. IN THE SPRING, WE HAD A CONTEST TO WELCOME NEW MEMBERS AND RANK EVERYONE. I GOT THIRD PLACE.
TWO OF THE THIRD-YEARS ARE JUST SO *INCREDIBLE*...! I... I...
I'D... RATHER NOT THINK ABOUT IT RIGHT NOW. I-IT'S A SCARY MEMORY.
SHVR
SHVR
SOMETHING TRAUMATIZED **KUREHA**?!
IT'S A WHOLE **DEN** OF MONSTERS!

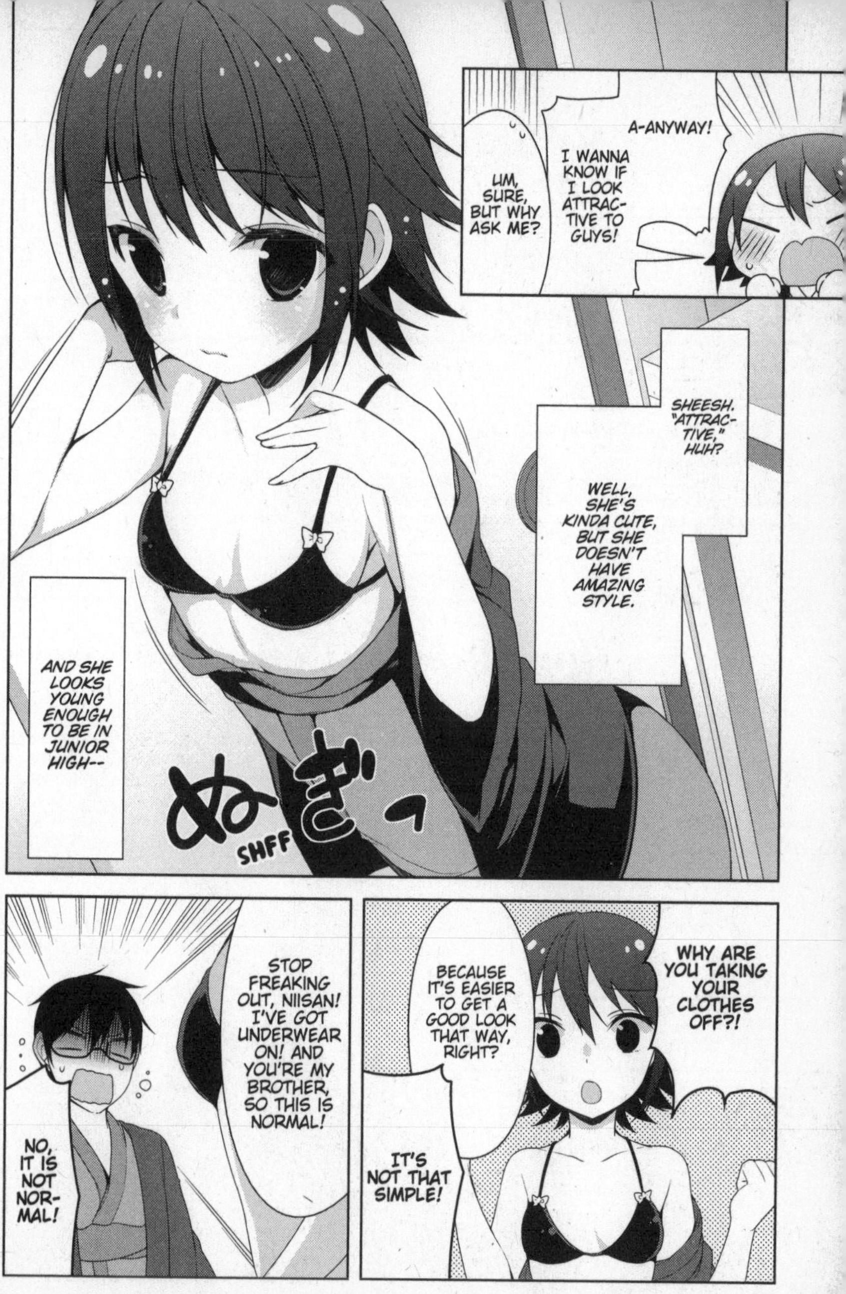
A-ANYWAY!
I WANNA KNOW IF I LOOK ATTRACTIVE TO GUYS!
UM, SURE, BUT WHY ASK ME?
SHEESH. "ATTRACTIVE," HUH?
WELL, SHE'S KINDA CUTE, BUT SHE DOESN'T HAVE AMAZING STYLE.
AND SHE LOOKS YOUNG ENOUGH TO BE IN JUNIOR HIGH--
ぬぎっ
SHFF
WHY ARE YOU TAKING YOUR CLOTHES OFF?!
BECAUSE IT'S EASIER TO GET A GOOD LOOK THAT WAY, RIGHT?
IT'S NOT THAT SIMPLE!
STOP FREAKING OUT, NIISAN! I'VE GOT UNDERWEAR ON! AND YOU'RE MY BROTHER, SO THIS IS NORMAL!
NO, IT IS NOT NORMAL!

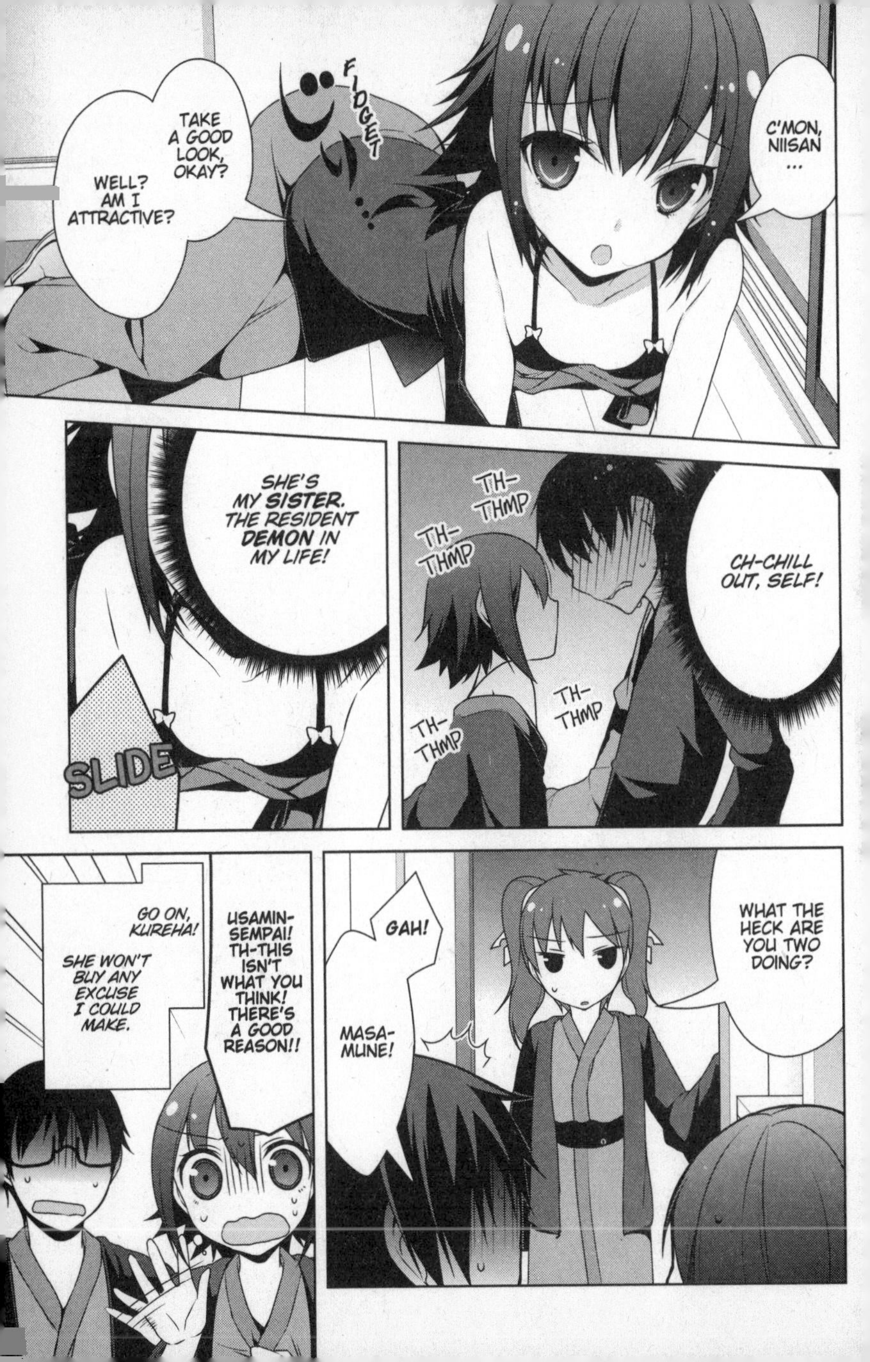
C'MON, NIISAN ...
FIDGET
TAKE A GOOD LOOK, OKAY?
WELL? AM I ATTRACTIVE?
CH-CHILL OUT, SELF!
TH-THMP
TH-THMP
TH-THMP
TH-THMP
SHE'S MY SISTER. THE RESIDENT DEMON IN MY LIFE!
SLIDE
WHAT THE HECK ARE YOU TWO DOING?
GAH!
MASA-MUNE!
USAMIN-SEMPAI! TH-THIS ISN'T WHAT YOU THINK! THERE'S A GOOD REASON!!
GO ON, KUREHA!
SHE WON'T BUY ANY EXCUSE I COULD MAKE.

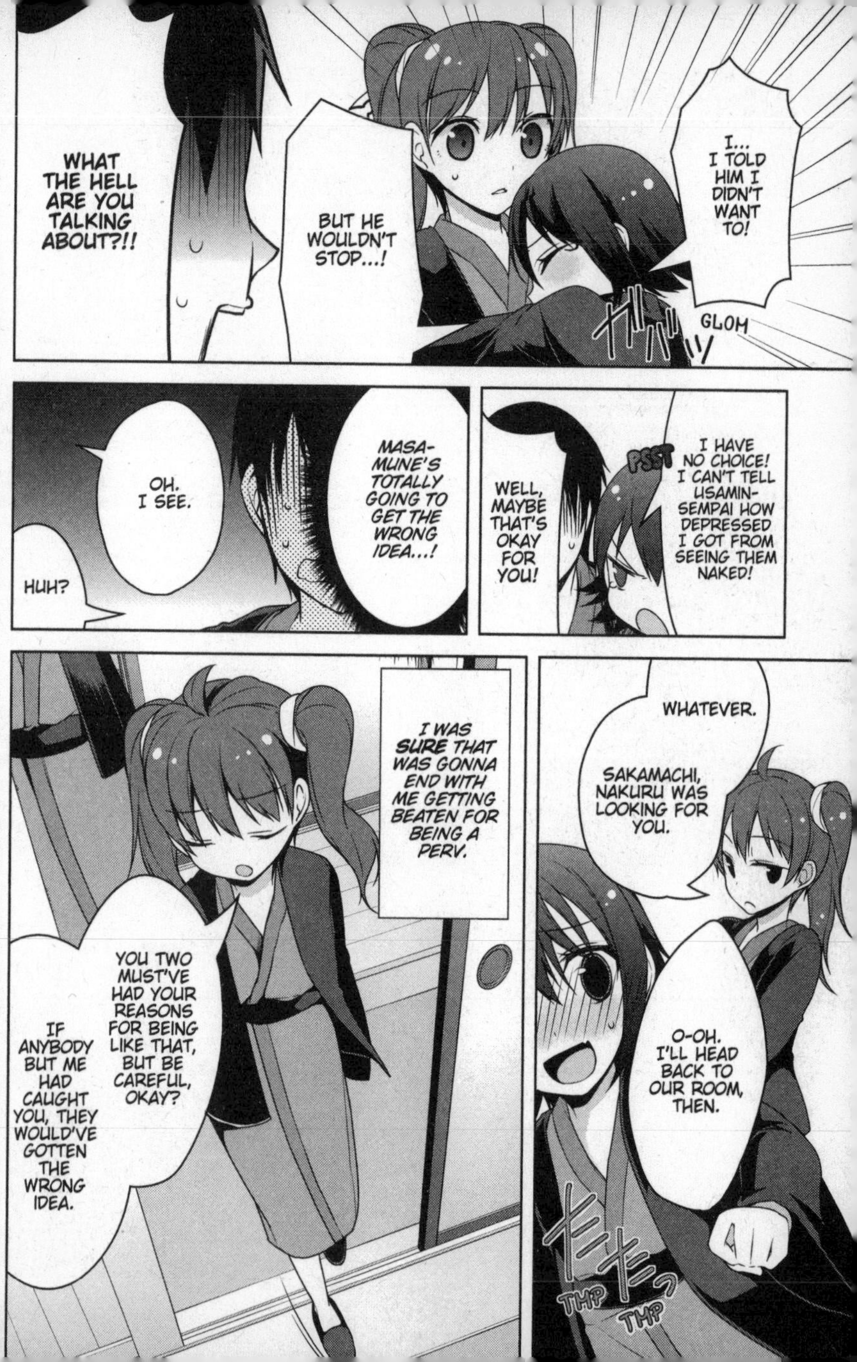
I... I TOLD HIM I DIDN'T WANT TO!
GLOM
BUT HE WOULDN'T STOP...!
WHAT THE HELL ARE YOU TALKING ABOUT?!!
PSST
I HAVE NO CHOICE! I CAN'T TELL USAMIN-SEMPAI HOW DEPRESSED I GOT FROM SEEING THEM NAKED!
WELL, MAYBE THAT'S OKAY FOR YOU!
MASA-MUNE'S TOTALLY GOING TO GET THE WRONG IDEA...!
OH. I SEE.
HUH?
WHATEVER.
SAKAMACHI, NAKURU WAS LOOKING FOR YOU.
O-OH. I'LL HEAD BACK TO OUR ROOM, THEN.
TMP TMP
I WAS **SURE** THAT WAS GONNA END WITH ME GETTING BEATEN FOR BEING A PERV.
YOU TWO MUST'VE HAD YOUR REASONS FOR BEING LIKE THAT, BUT BE CAREFUL, OKAY?
IF ANYBODY BUT ME HAD CAUGHT YOU, THEY WOULD'VE GOTTEN THE WRONG IDEA.

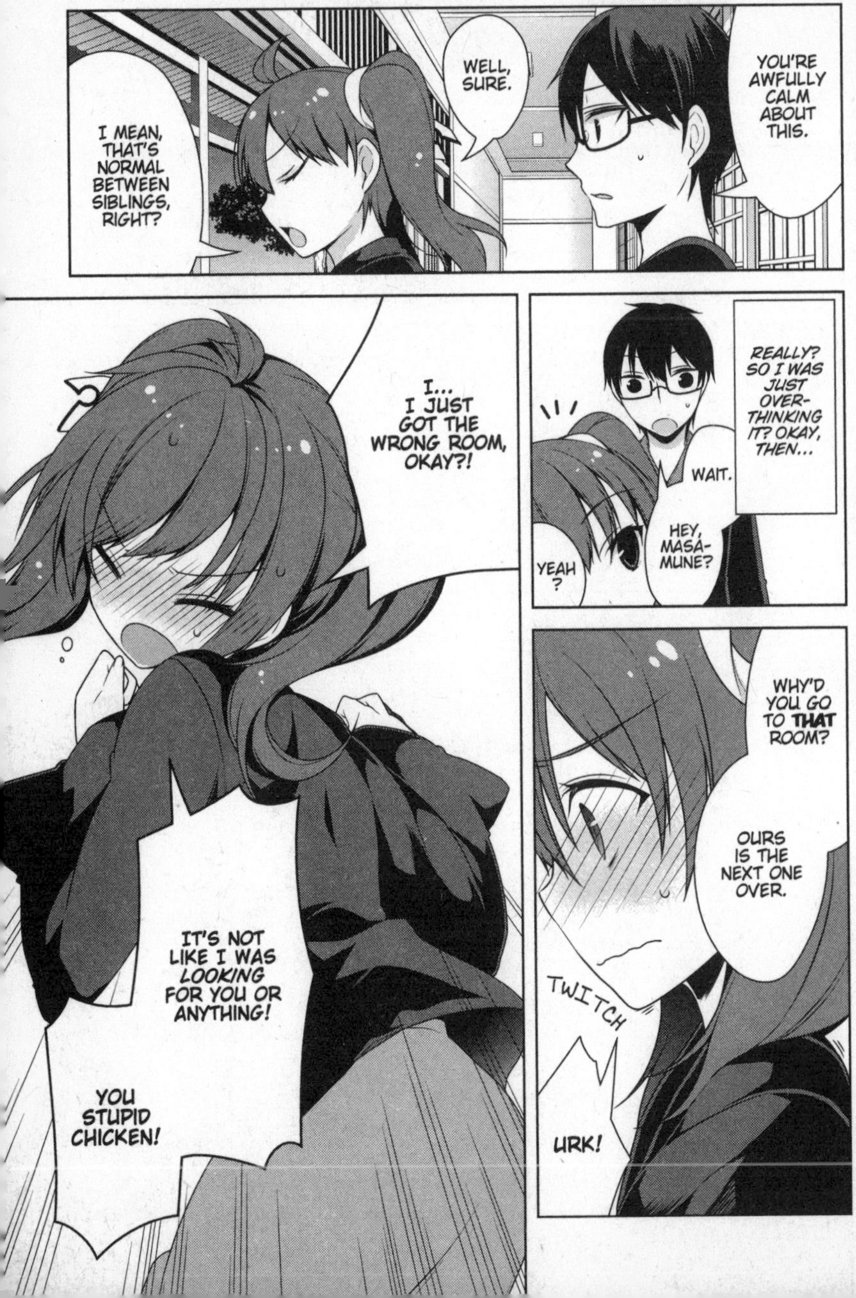
YOU'RE AWFULLY CALM ABOUT THIS.
WELL, SURE.
I MEAN, THAT'S NORMAL BETWEEN SIBLINGS, RIGHT?
REALLY? SO I WAS JUST OVER-THINKING IT? OKAY, THEN...
WAIT.
HEY, MASAMUNE?
YEAH?
WHY'D YOU GO TO **THAT** ROOM?
OURS IS THE NEXT ONE OVER.
TWITCH
URK!
I... I JUST GOT THE WRONG ROOM, OKAY?!
IT'S NOT LIKE I WAS *LOOKING* FOR YOU OR ANYTHING!
YOU STUPID CHICKEN!

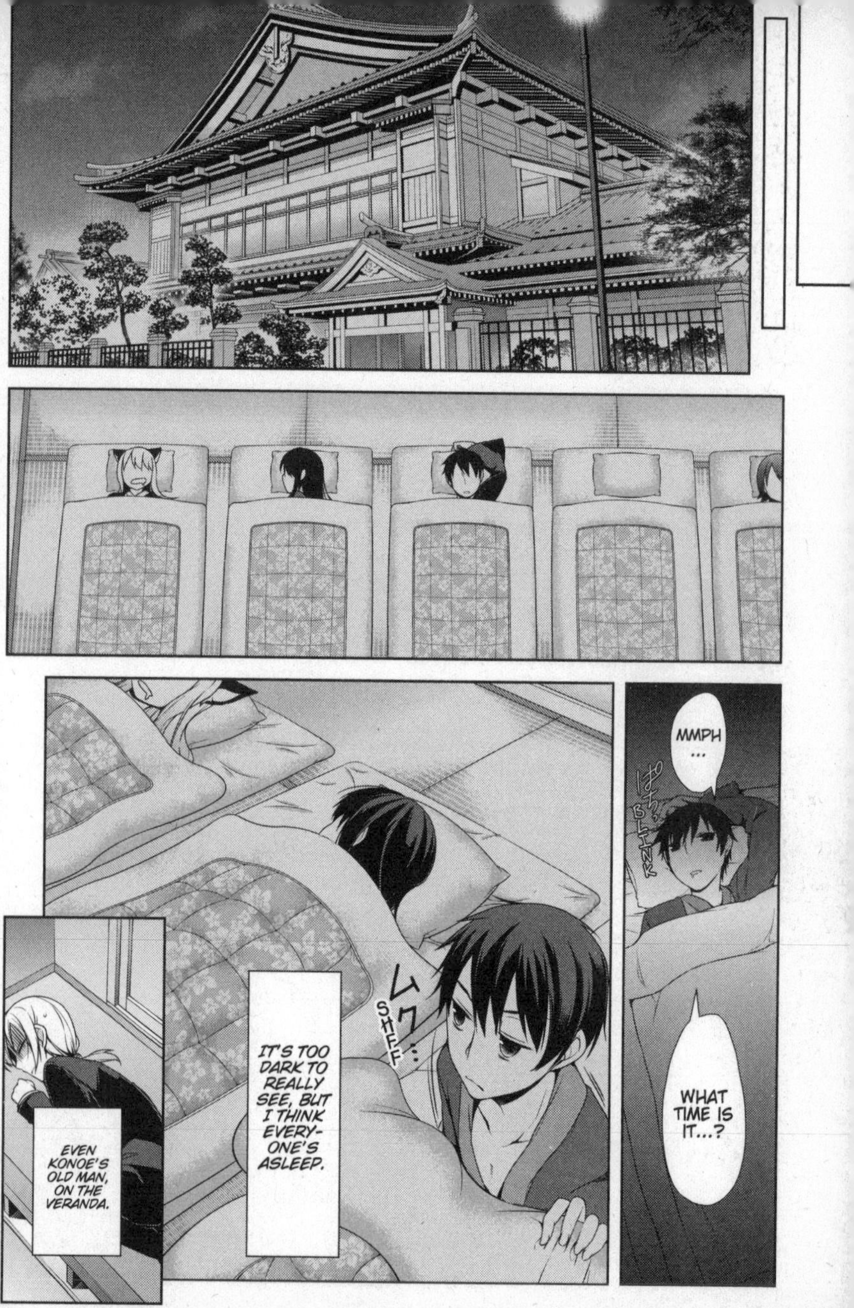
MMPH ...
ぱち
BLINK
WHAT TIME IS IT...?
ムク
SHFF
IT'S TOO DARK TO REALLY SEE, BUT I THINK EVERY-ONE'S ASLEEP.
EVEN KONOE'S OLD MAN, ON THE VERANDA.

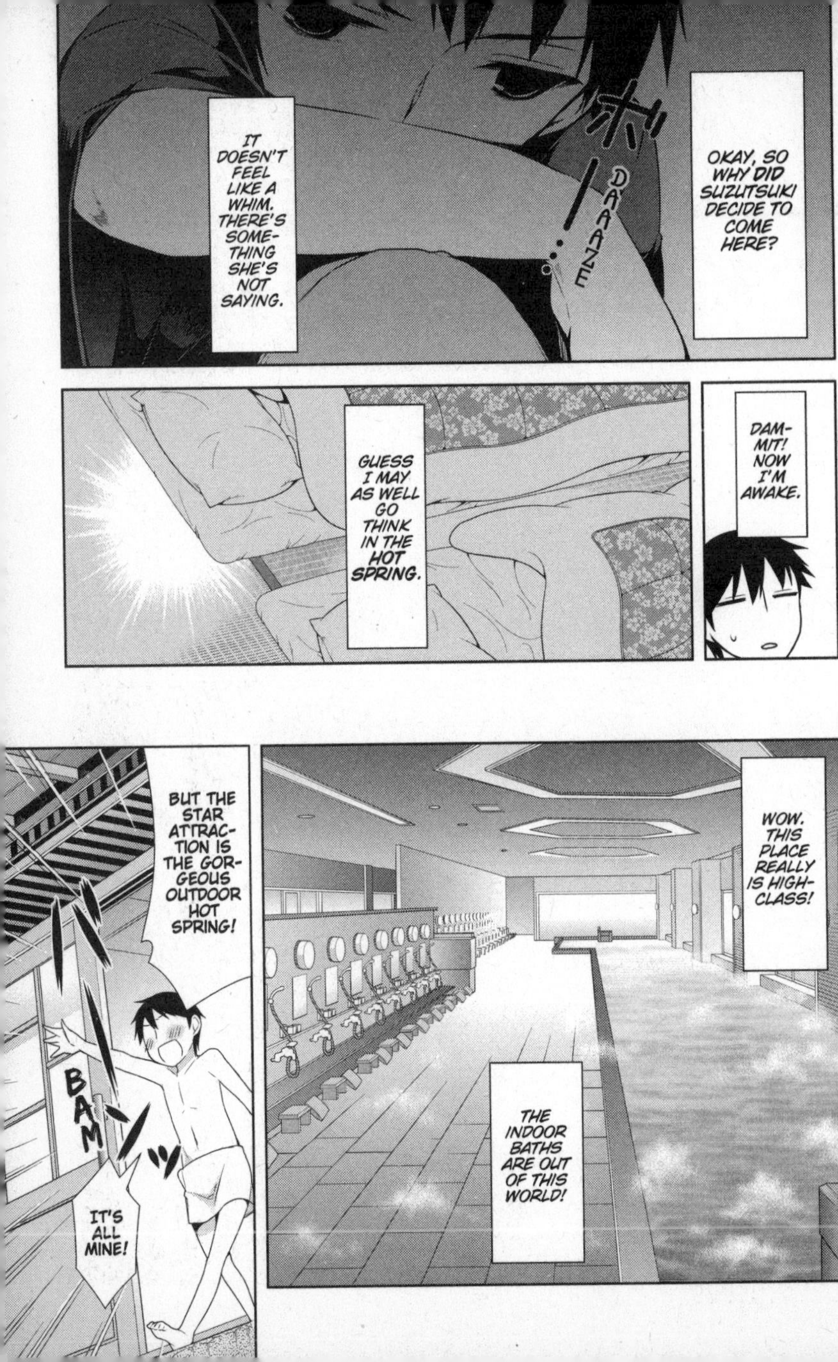
OKAY, SO WHY DID SUZUTSUKI DECIDE TO COME HERE?
DAAAZE
IT DOESN'T FEEL LIKE A WHIM. THERE'S SOME-THING SHE'S NOT SAYING.
DAM-MIT! NOW I'M AWAKE.
GUESS I MAY AS WELL GO THINK IN THE HOT SPRING.
WOW. THIS PLACE REALLY IS HIGH-CLASS!
THE INDOOR BATHS ARE OUT OF THIS WORLD!
BUT THE STAR ATTRAC-TION IS THE GOR-GEOUS OUTDOOR HOT SPRING!
BAM
IT'S ALL MINE!

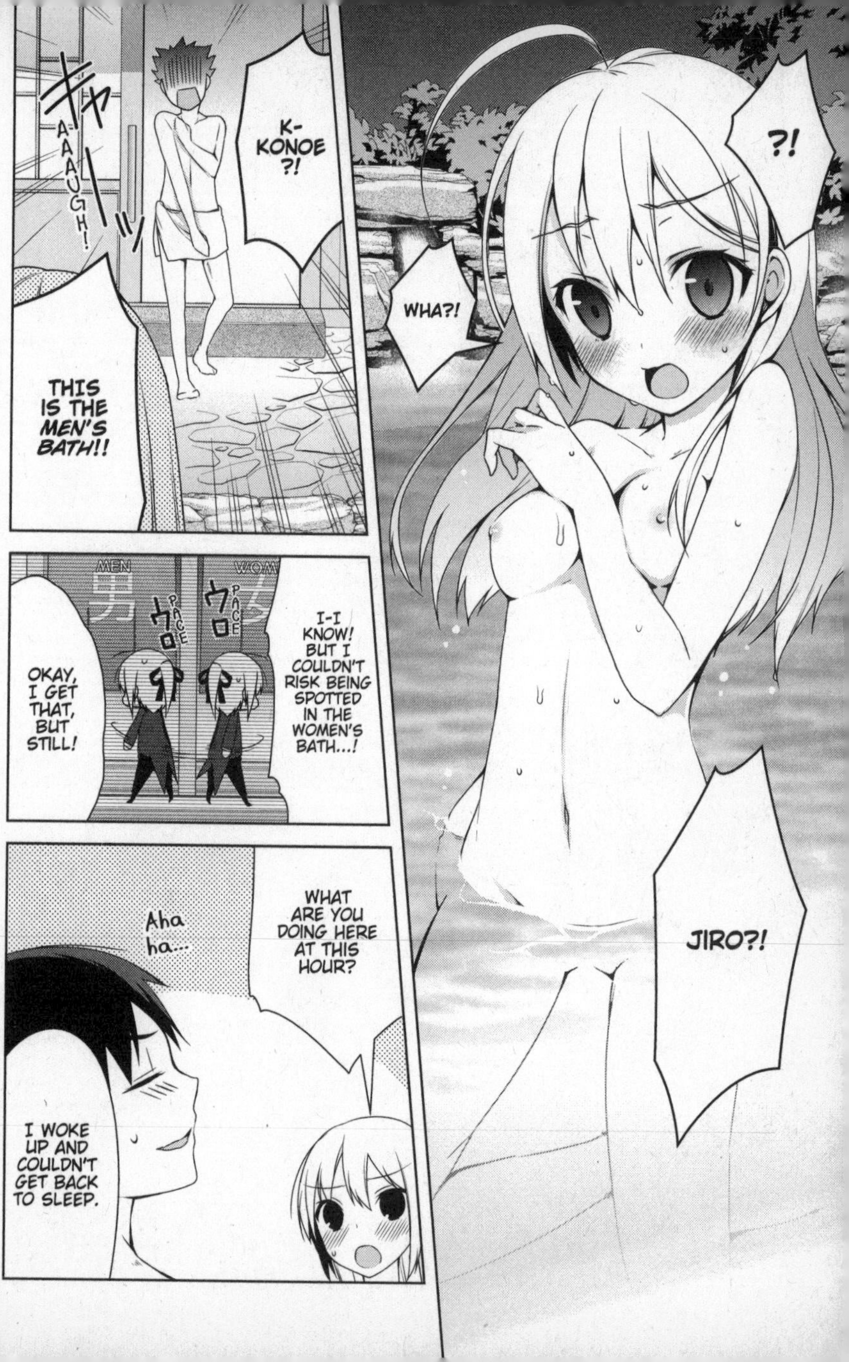
?!
WHA?!
JIRO?!
K-KONOE ?!
AAAUGH!
THIS IS THE MEN'S BATH!!
MEN
WOM
PACE
PACE
I-I KNOW! BUT I COULDN'T RISK BEING SPOTTED IN THE WOMEN'S BATH...!
OKAY, I GET THAT, BUT STILL!
WHAT ARE YOU DOING HERE AT THIS HOUR?
Aha ha...
I WOKE UP AND COULDN'T GET BACK TO SLEEP.

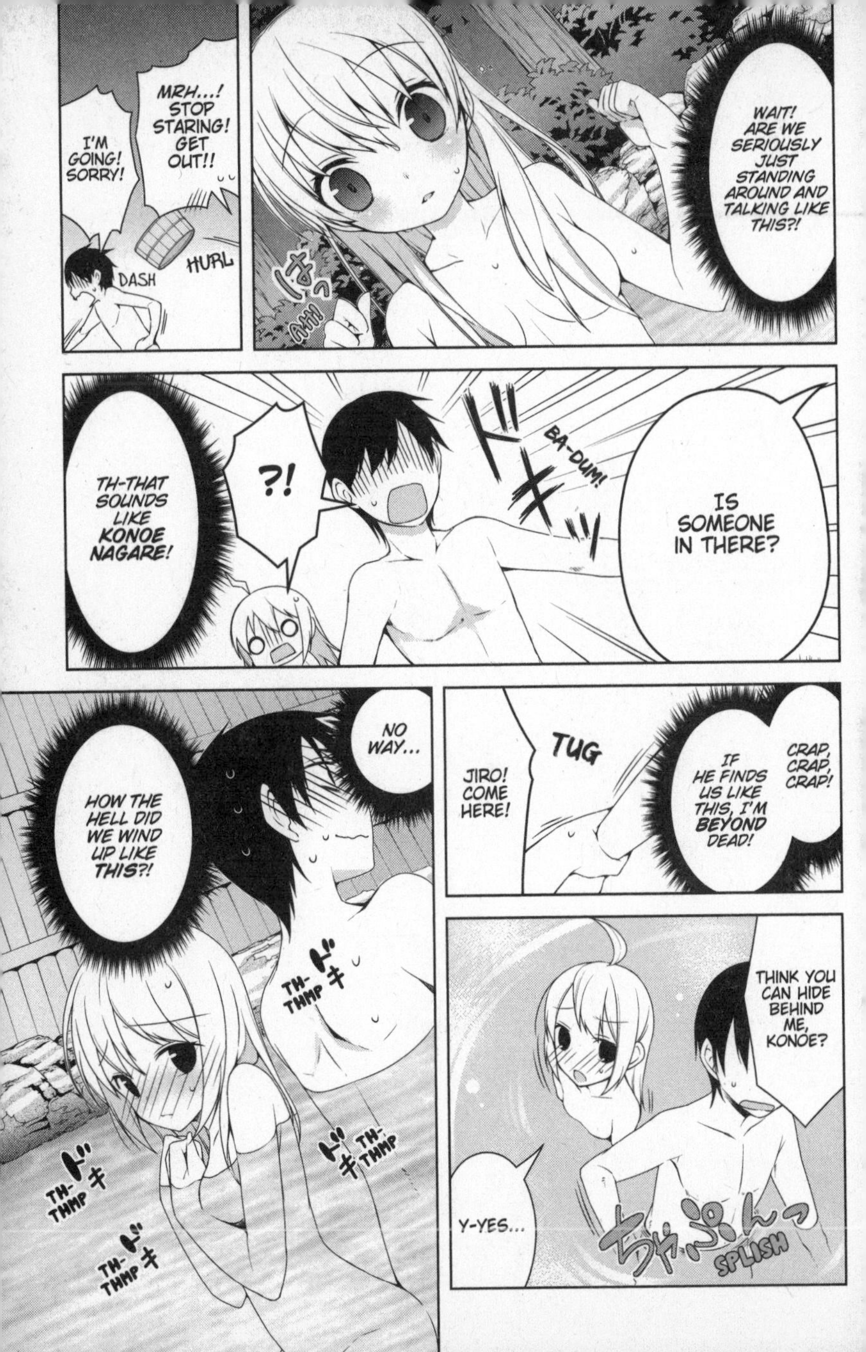
WAIT! ARE WE SERIOUSLY JUST STANDING AROUND AND TALKING LIKE THIS?!
AH!
MRH...! STOP STARING! GET OUT!!
HURL
I'M GOING! SORRY!
DASH
IS SOMEONE IN THERE?
BA-DUM!
?!
TH-THAT SOUNDS LIKE KONOE NAGARE!
CRAP, CRAP, CRAP!
IF HE FINDS US LIKE THIS, I'M BEYOND DEAD!
TUG
JIRO! COME HERE!
THINK YOU CAN HIDE BEHIND ME, KONOE?
Y-YES...
SPLISH
NO WAY...
HOW THE HELL DID WE WIND UP LIKE THIS?!
TH-THMP
TH-THMP
TH-THMP
TH-THMP

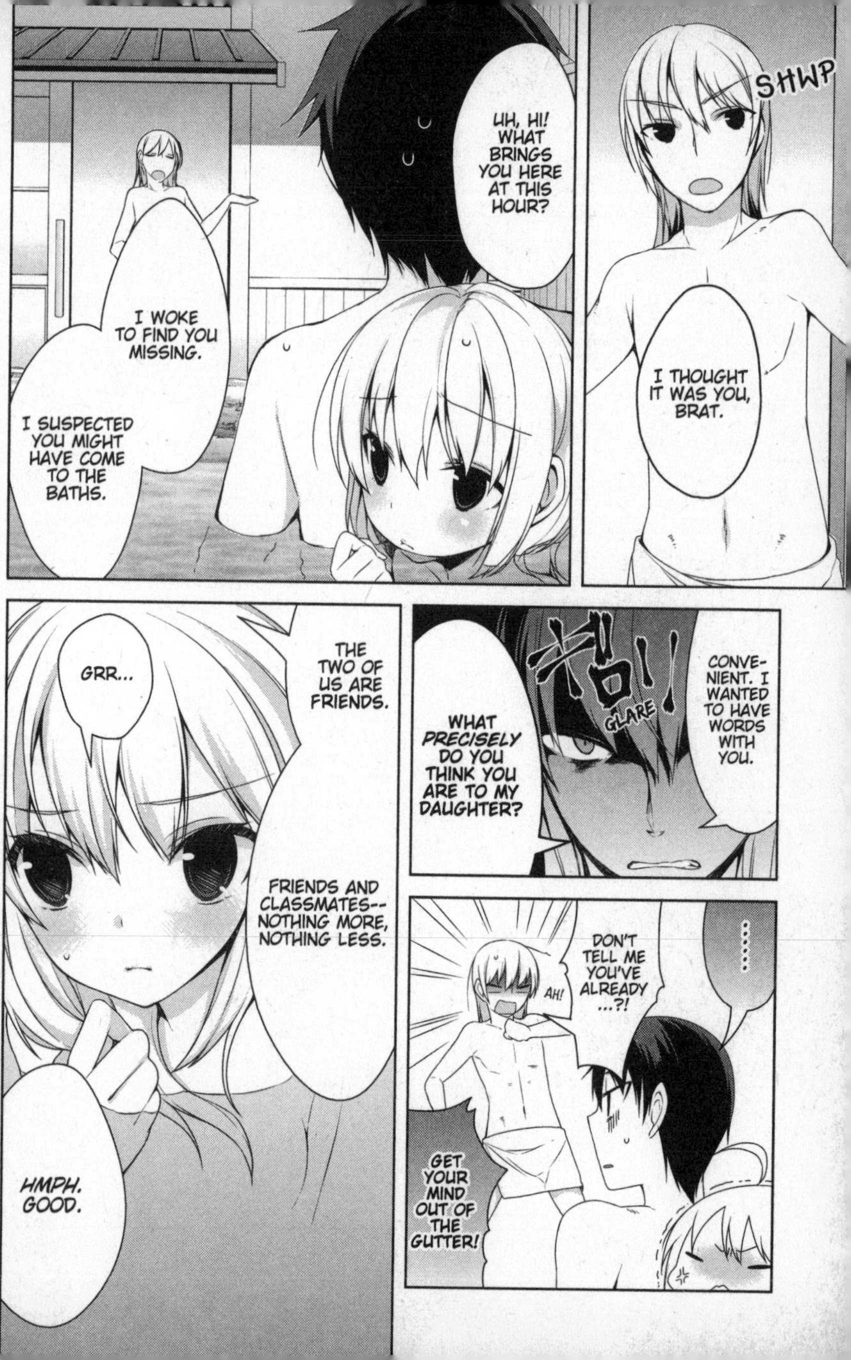
SHWP
I THOUGHT IT WAS YOU, BRAT.
UH, HI! WHAT BRINGS YOU HERE AT THIS HOUR?
I WOKE TO FIND YOU MISSING.
I SUSPECTED YOU MIGHT HAVE COME TO THE BATHS.
CONVE-NIENT. I WANTED TO HAVE WORDS WITH YOU.
GLARE
WHAT *PRECISELY* DO YOU THINK YOU ARE TO MY DAUGHTER?
......
DON'T TELL ME YOU'VE ALREADY ...?!
AH!
GET YOUR MIND OUT OF THE GUTTER!
THE TWO OF US ARE FRIENDS.
GRR...
FRIENDS AND CLASSMATES-- NOTHING MORE, NOTHING LESS.
HMPH. GOOD.

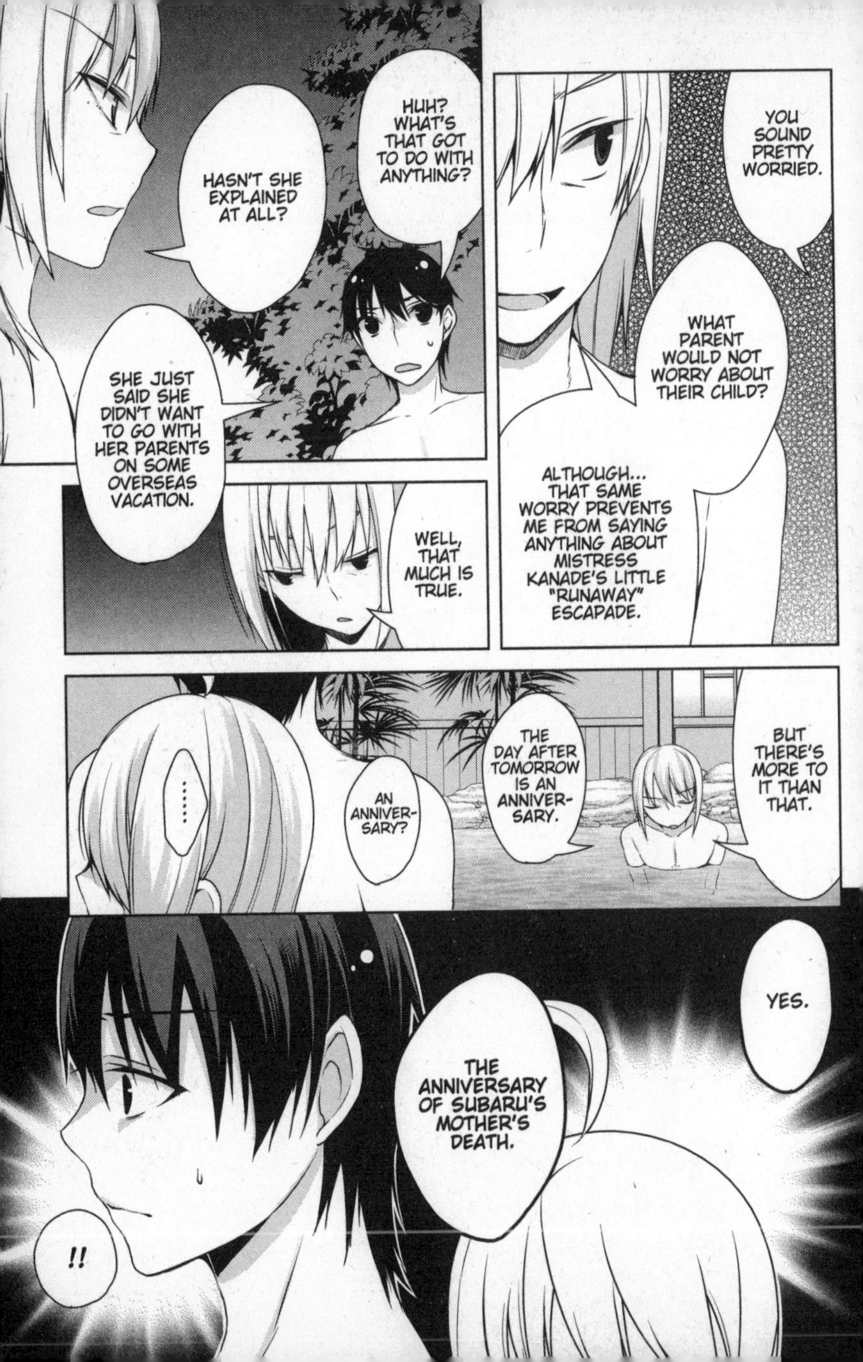
YOU SOUND PRETTY WORRIED.
WHAT PARENT WOULD NOT WORRY ABOUT THEIR CHILD?
ALTHOUGH... THAT SAME WORRY PREVENTS ME FROM SAYING ANYTHING ABOUT MISTRESS KANADE'S LITTLE "RUNAWAY" ESCAPADE.
HUH? WHAT'S THAT GOT TO DO WITH ANYTHING?
HASN'T SHE EXPLAINED AT ALL?
SHE JUST SAID SHE DIDN'T WANT TO GO WITH HER PARENTS ON SOME OVERSEAS VACATION.
WELL, THAT MUCH IS TRUE.
BUT THERE'S MORE TO IT THAN THAT.
THE DAY AFTER TOMORROW IS AN ANNIVER-SARY.
AN ANNIVER-SARY?
......
YES.
THE ANNIVERSARY OF SUBARU'S MOTHER'S DEATH.
!!

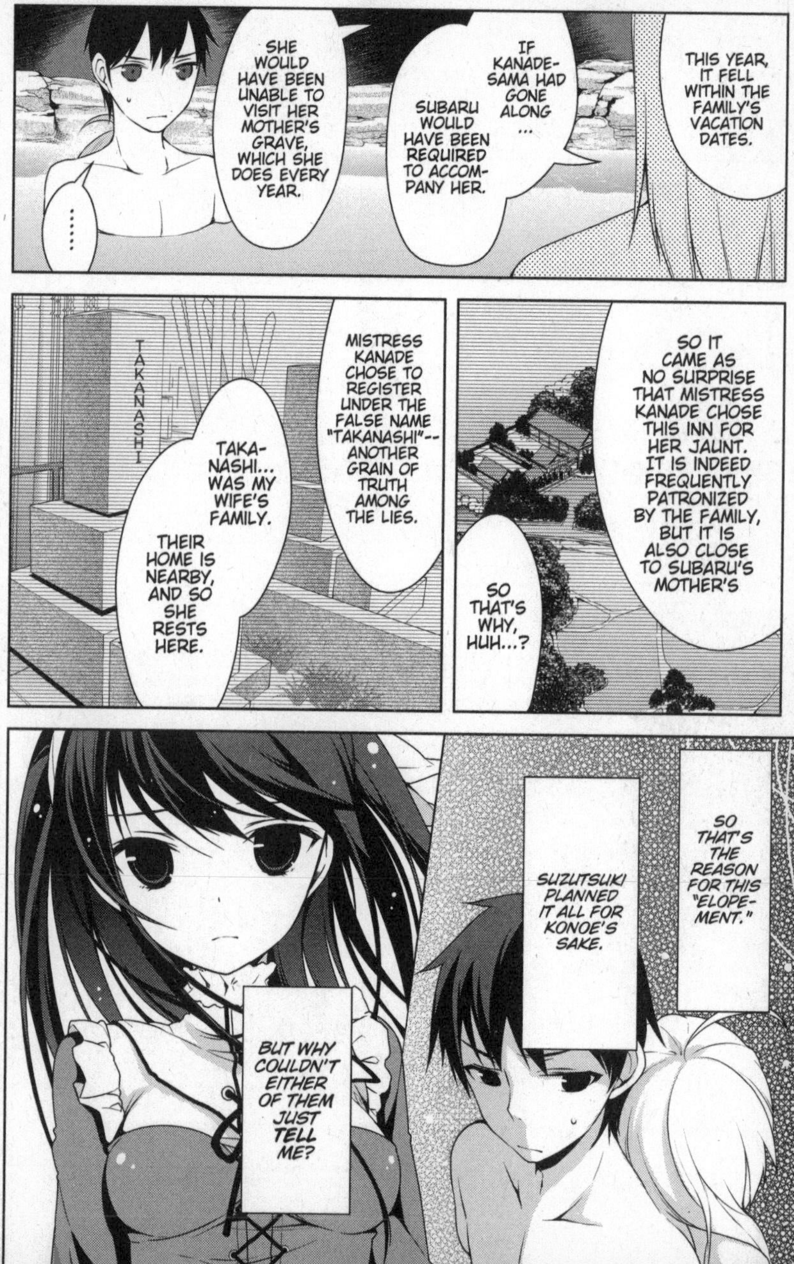
THIS YEAR, IT FELL WITHIN THE FAMILY'S VACATION DATES.
IF KANADE-SAMA HAD GONE ALONG ...
SUBARU WOULD HAVE BEEN REQUIRED TO ACCOMPANY HER.
SHE WOULD HAVE BEEN UNABLE TO VISIT HER MOTHER'S GRAVE, WHICH SHE DOES EVERY YEAR.
......
SO IT CAME AS NO SURPRISE THAT MISTRESS KANADE CHOSE THIS INN FOR HER JAUNT. IT IS INDEED FREQUENTLY PATRONIZED BY THE FAMILY, BUT IT IS ALSO CLOSE TO SUBARU'S MOTHER'S
SO THAT'S WHY, HUH...?
MISTRESS KANADE CHOSE TO REGISTER UNDER THE FALSE NAME "TAKANASHI"--ANOTHER GRAIN OF TRUTH AMONG THE LIES.
TAKANASHI
TAKANASHI... WAS MY WIFE'S FAMILY.
THEIR HOME IS NEARBY, AND SO SHE RESTS HERE.
SO THAT'S THE REASON FOR THIS "ELOPEMENT."
SUZUTSUKI PLANNED IT ALL FOR KONOE'S SAKE.
BUT WHY COULDN'T EITHER OF THEM JUST TELL ME?

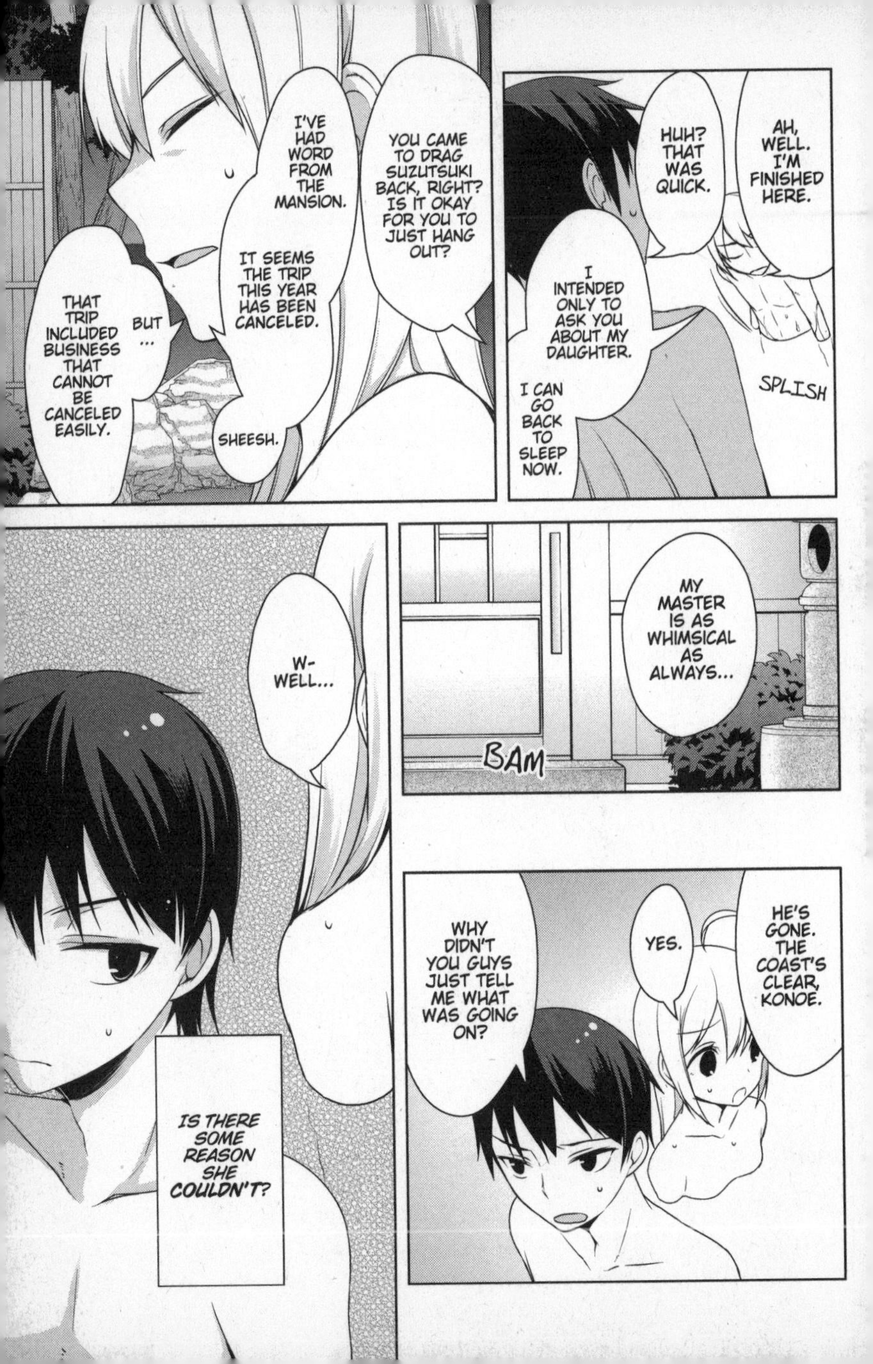
AH, WELL. I'M FINISHED HERE.
HUH? THAT WAS QUICK.
SPLISH
I INTENDED ONLY TO ASK YOU ABOUT MY DAUGHTER.
I CAN GO BACK TO SLEEP NOW.
YOU CAME TO DRAG SUZUTSUKI BACK, RIGHT? IS IT OKAY FOR YOU TO JUST HANG OUT?
I'VE HAD WORD FROM THE MANSION.
IT SEEMS THE TRIP THIS YEAR HAS BEEN CANCELED.
SHEESH.
BUT ...
THAT TRIP INCLUDED BUSINESS THAT CANNOT BE CANCELED EASILY.
MY MASTER IS AS WHIMSICAL AS ALWAYS...
BAM
HE'S GONE. THE COAST'S CLEAR, KONOE.
YES.
WHY DIDN'T YOU GUYS JUST TELL ME WHAT WAS GOING ON?
W-WELL...
IS THERE SOME REASON SHE COULDN'T?

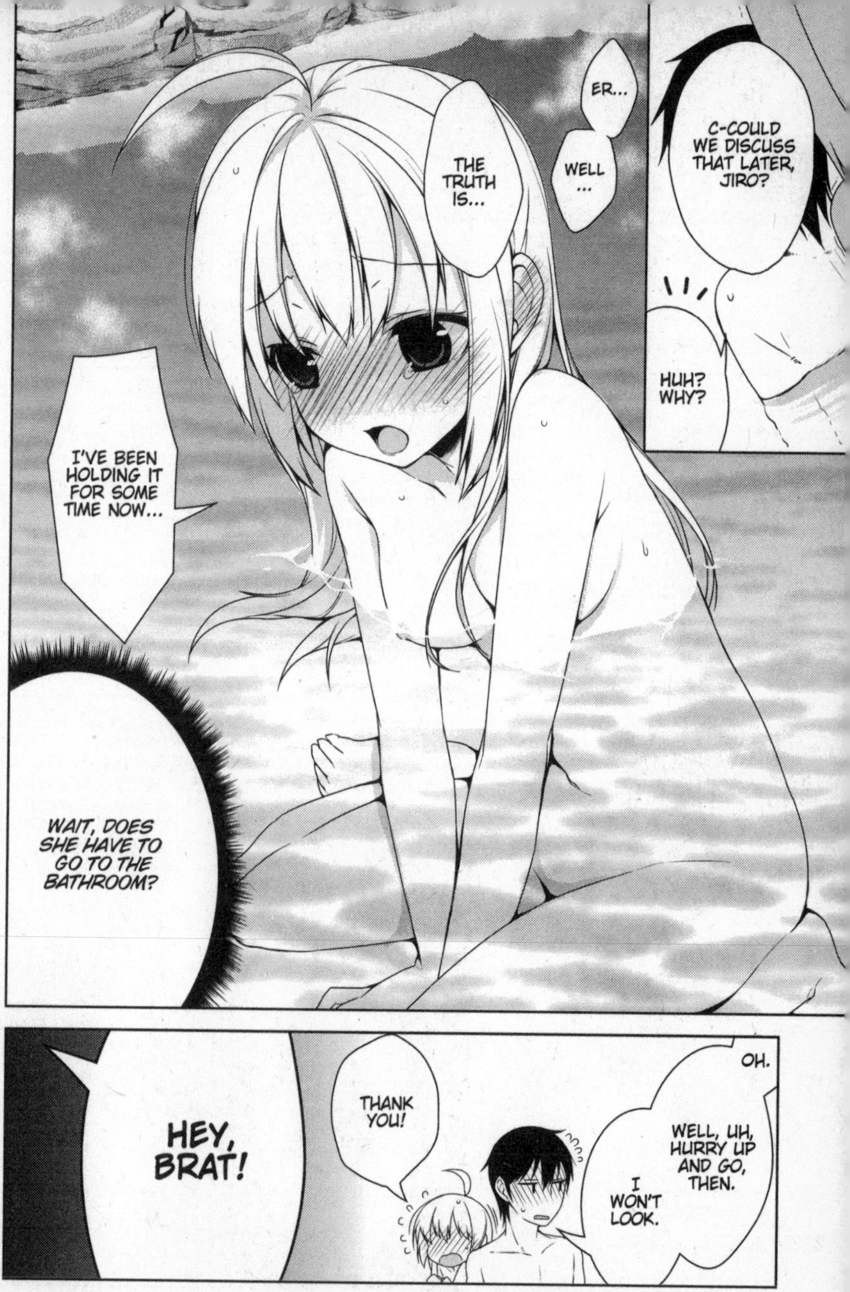
C-COULD WE DISCUSS THAT LATER, JIRO?
HUH? WHY?
ER...
WELL...
THE TRUTH IS...
I'VE BEEN HOLDING IT FOR SOME TIME NOW...
WAIT, DOES SHE HAVE TO GO TO THE BATHROOM?
OH.
WELL, UH, HURRY UP AND GO, THEN.
I WON'T LOOK.
THANK YOU!
HEY, BRAT!

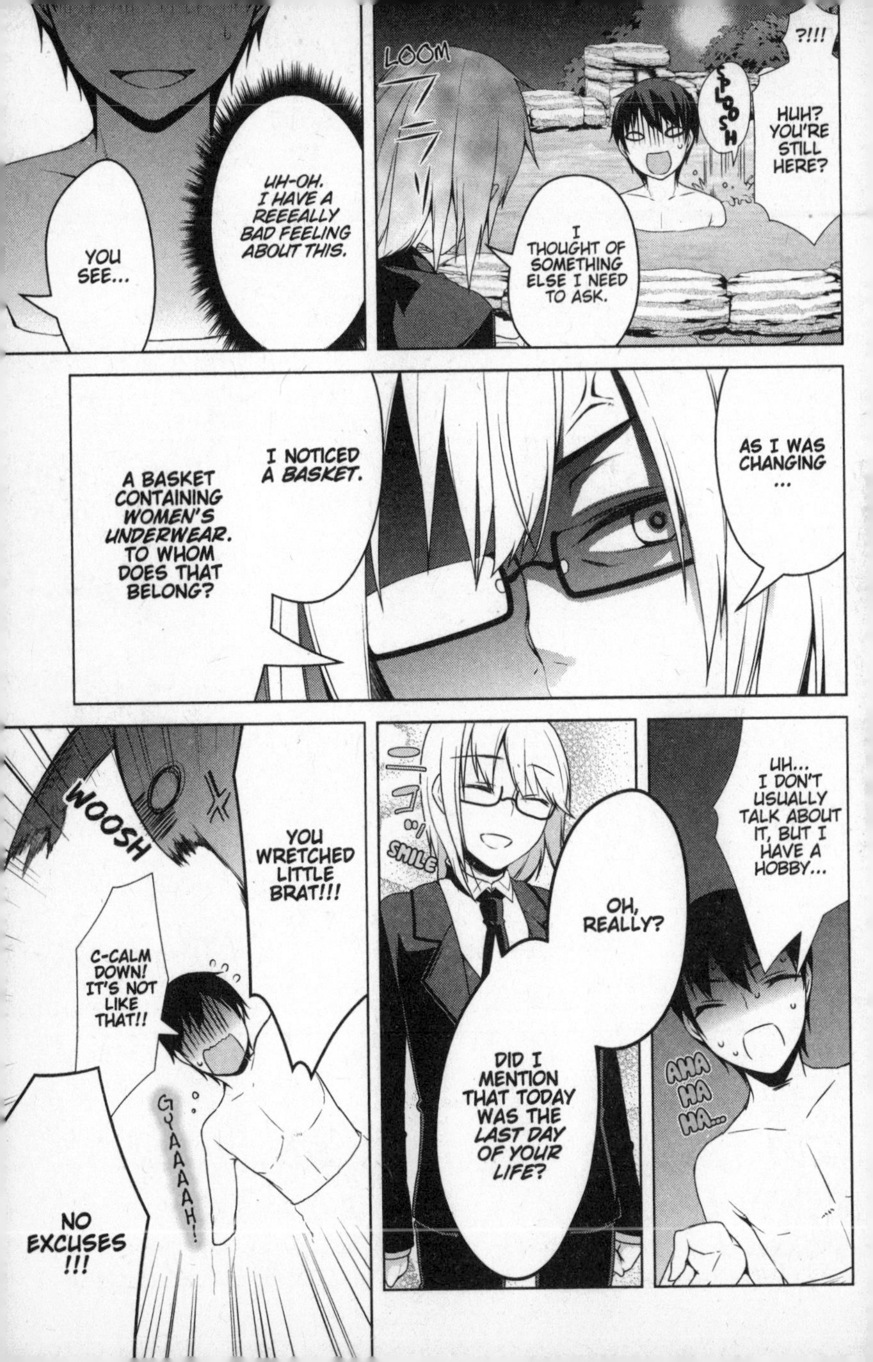
?!!!
SPLOOSH
HUH? YOU'RE STILL HERE?
LOOM
I THOUGHT OF SOMETHING ELSE I NEED TO ASK.
UH-OH. I HAVE A REEEALLY BAD FEELING ABOUT THIS.
YOU SEE...
AS I WAS CHANGING ...
I NOTICED A *BASKET*.
A BASKET CONTAINING *WOMEN'S UNDERWEAR*. TO WHOM DOES THAT BELONG?
UH... I DON'T USUALLY TALK ABOUT IT, BUT I HAVE A HOBBY...
SMILE
OH, REALLY?
AHA HA HA...
DID I MENTION THAT TODAY WAS THE *LAST DAY OF YOUR LIFE?*
WOOSH
YOU WRETCHED LITTLE BRAT!!!
C-CALM DOWN! IT'S NOT LIKE THAT!!
GYAAAAH!
NO EXCUSES !!!

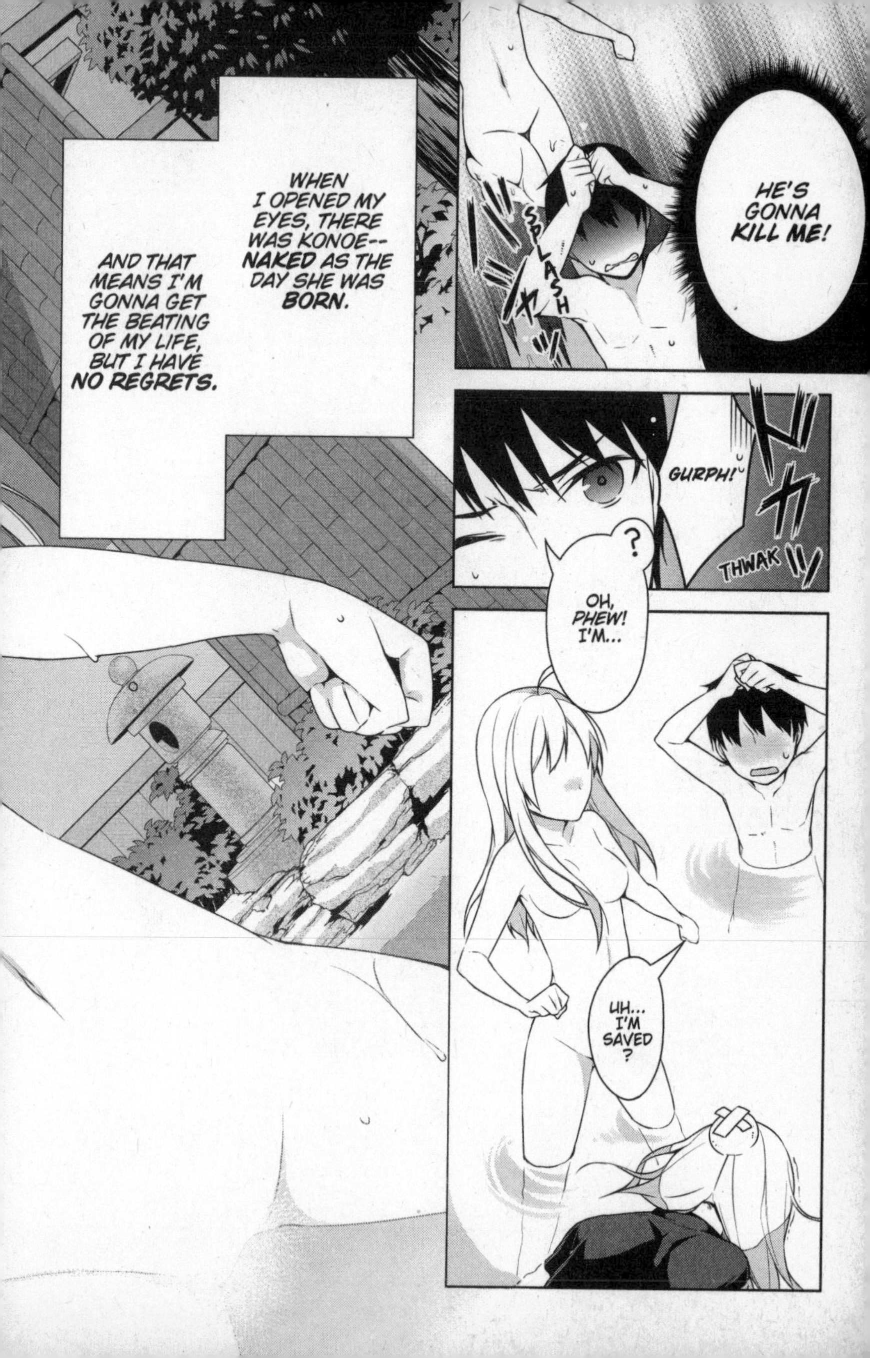
HE'S GONNA KILL ME!
SPLASH
GURPH!
THWAK
?
OH, PHEW! I'M...
UH... I'M SAVED?
WHEN I OPENED MY EYES, THERE WAS KONOE-- NAKED AS THE DAY SHE WAS BORN.
AND THAT MEANS I'M GONNA GET THE BEATING OF MY LIFE, BUT I HAVE NO REGRETS.

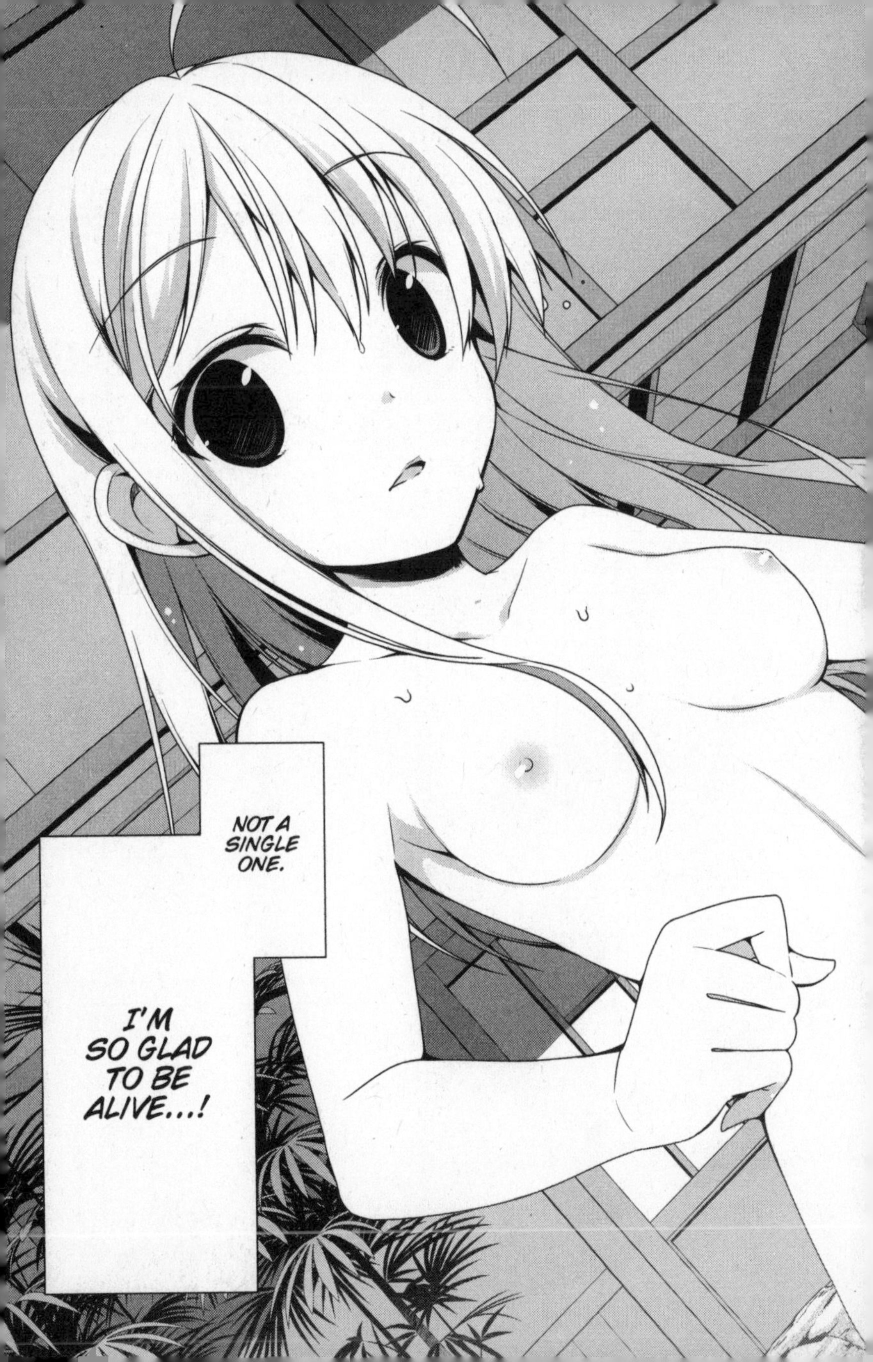
NOT A SINGLE ONE.
I'M SO GLAD TO BE ALIVE...!

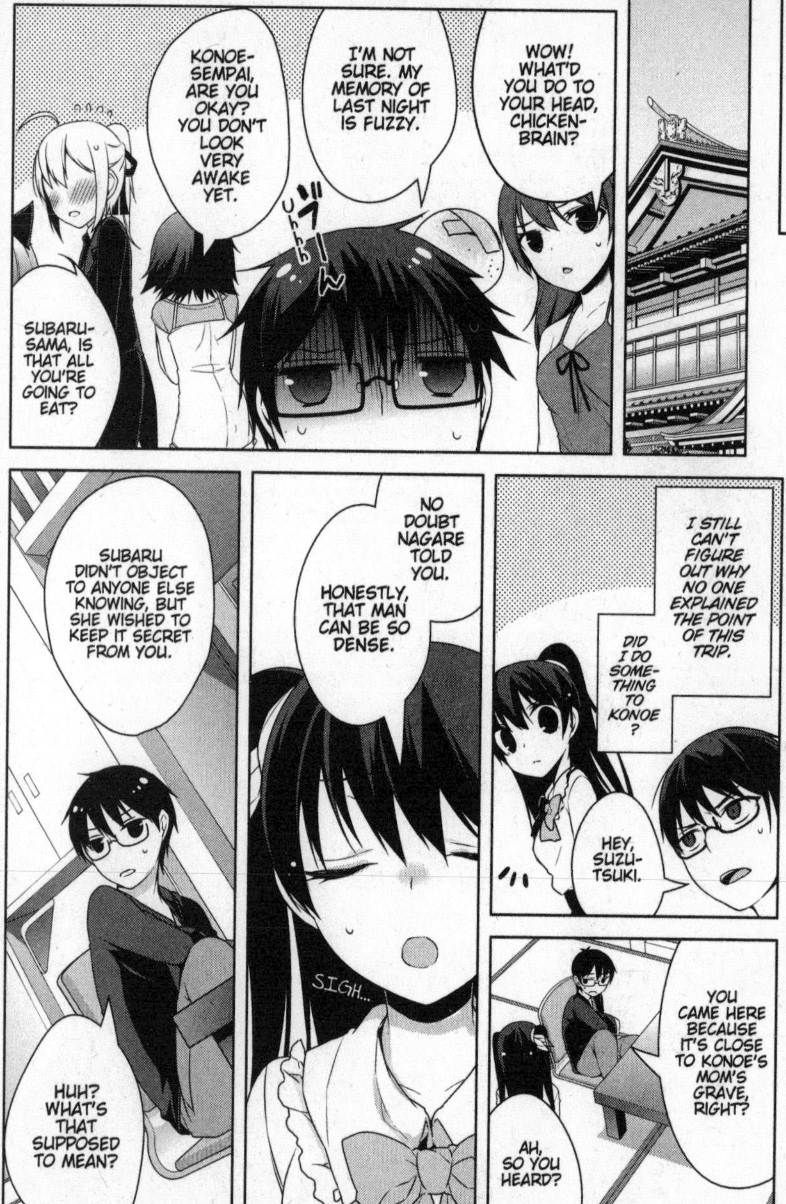
WOW! WHAT'D YOU DO TO YOUR HEAD, CHICKEN-BRAIN?
I'M NOT SURE. MY MEMORY OF LAST NIGHT IS FUZZY.
Uhhh
KONOE-SEMPAI, ARE YOU OKAY? YOU DON'T LOOK VERY AWAKE YET.
SUBARU-SAMA, IS THAT ALL YOU'RE GOING TO EAT?
I STILL CAN'T FIGURE OUT WHY NO ONE EXPLAINED THE POINT OF THIS TRIP.
DID I DO SOMETHING TO KONOE?
HEY, SUZUTSUKI.
YOU CAME HERE BECAUSE IT'S CLOSE TO KONOE'S MOM'S GRAVE, RIGHT?
AH, SO YOU HEARD?
NO DOUBT NAGARE TOLD YOU.
HONESTLY, THAT MAN CAN BE SO DENSE.
SIGH...
SUBARU DIDN'T OBJECT TO ANYONE ELSE KNOWING, BUT SHE WISHED TO KEEP IT SECRET FROM YOU.
HUH? WHAT'S THAT SUPPOSED TO MEAN?

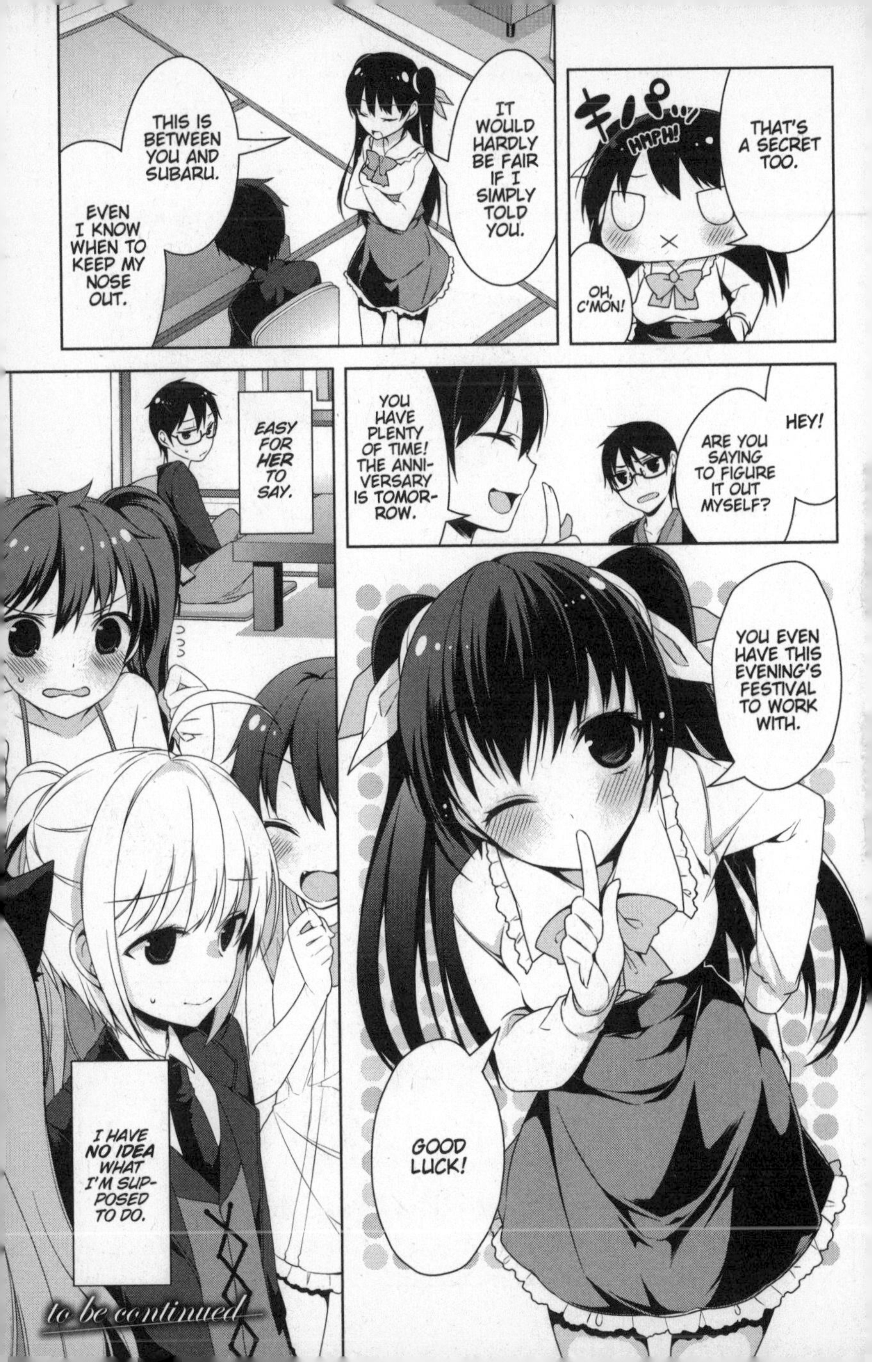
THAT'S A SECRET TOO.
HMPH!
OH, C'MON!
IT WOULD HARDLY BE FAIR IF I SIMPLY TOLD YOU.
THIS IS BETWEEN YOU AND SUBARU.
EVEN I KNOW WHEN TO KEEP MY NOSE OUT.
HEY!
ARE YOU SAYING TO FIGURE IT OUT MYSELF?
YOU HAVE PLENTY OF TIME! THE ANNI-VERSARY IS TOMOR-ROW.
YOU EVEN HAVE THIS EVENING'S FESTIVAL TO WORK WITH.
GOOD LUCK!
EASY FOR HER TO SAY.
I HAVE NO IDEA WHAT I'M SUP-POSED TO DO.
to be continued

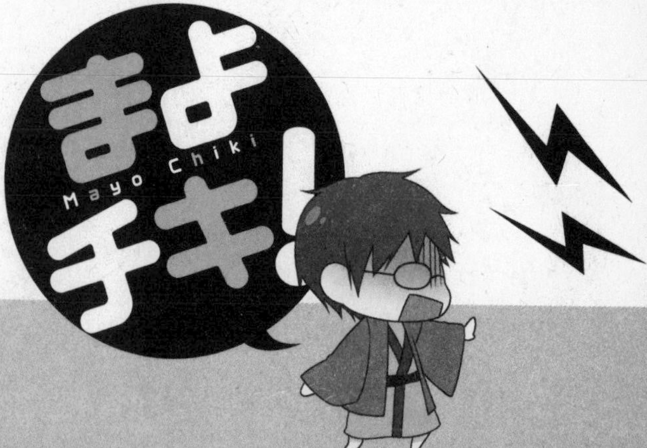
まよチキ!
Mayo Chiki

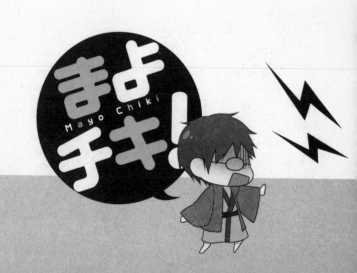

Chiki chiki!

MAYO CHIKI!

MANGA VERSION

Bonus Chat Corner

author HAJIME ASANO

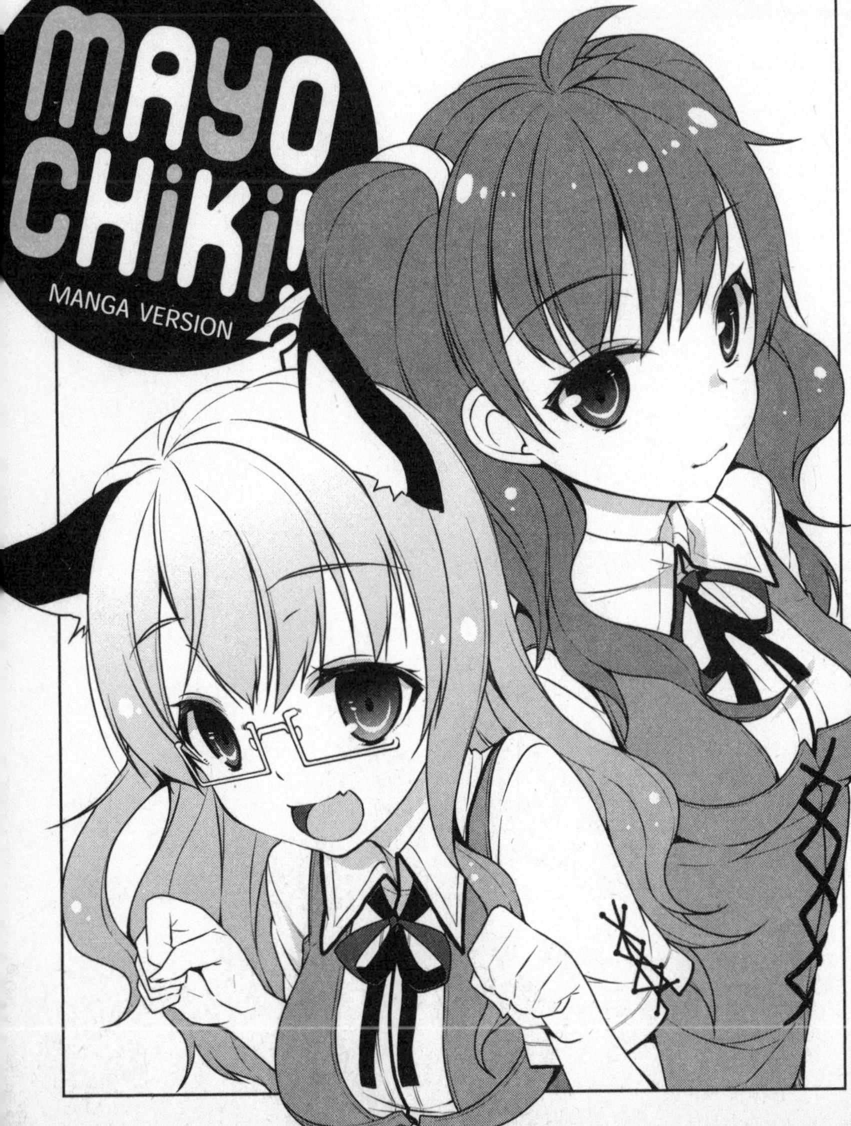

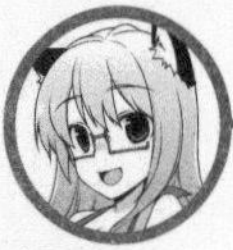

「Welcome to the third *Chiki Chiki Mayo Chiki!* manga version Chat Corner!

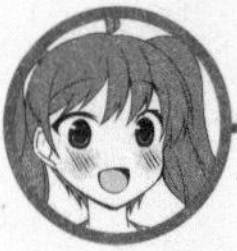

「Hi, everyone! I'm Usami Masamune, and I'll be hosting today's Chat Corner with Narumi Nakuru. It's an honor to be here!

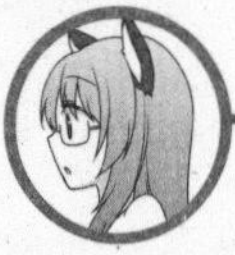

「My, my! What's the matter, Usami-sempai? You're so formal and polite today!

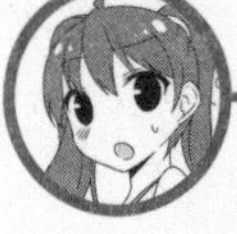

「Of course I'm going to be polite! I mean, this is **it**! I **finally** have a chance to be here! Until now it's always been Suzutsuki Kanade or Subaru-sama.

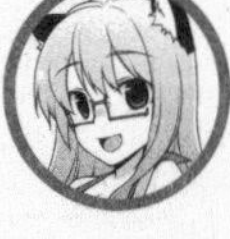

「Ah, I see you're ambitious as always. And your high rank in the popularity polls is holding steady, too. Recently you, Subaru-sama, and Suzutsuki-sempai have had an iron grip on the top three spots! But what about me? My ranking...? Oh, I so miss those halcyon days of yore...

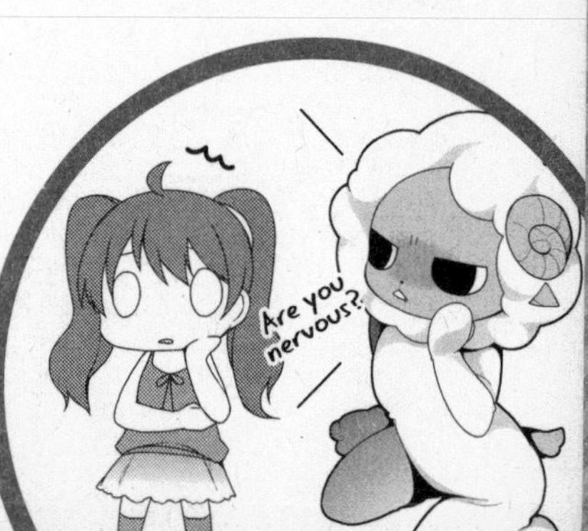
Are you nervous?

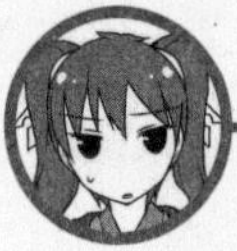

Huh? What, have you been having a tough time recently or something?

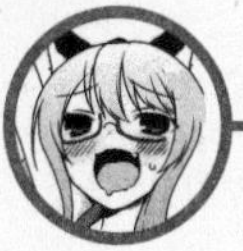

No, no, not in the least! I'm just a tad jealous of you, is all. I mean, volume 9 of the light novels (on sale at the same time as this manga volume in Japan!) has you gracing the cover as well. It is a veritable Usami-sempai festival! I dub it...Usamin Fever!

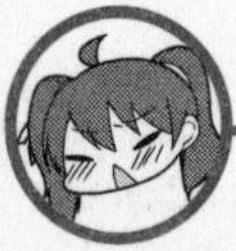

Shut up! Don't call me "Usamin"! And what's the big deal about being on the novel cover? Remember, you got a cover once, too! Volume 4!

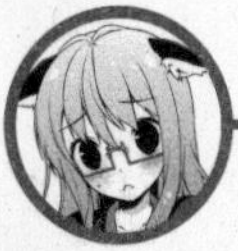

Yes, I did. **Once**.

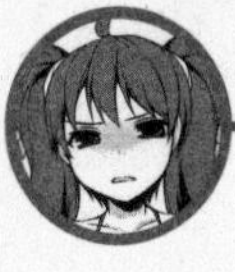

Oh, don't be so greedy! I mean, think of the poor soul who's been around since the very beginning but still hasn't made it to a cover.

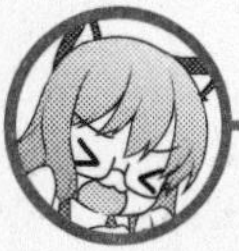

AAAAAAH!!! The poor thing! Dear readers, please! Vote! Vote for poor Kureha-chan! Use the mobile phone questionnaire found in both the manga volumes and the novels to send in your vote! Please! Only you can save her!

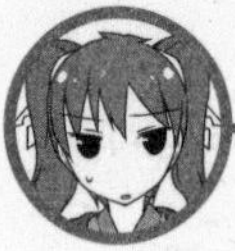

Sheesh. This is less and less a "Chat Corner" and more a "Save Her Sorry Hide Corner"... Hey, wait a second. Nakuru, isn't it a little early to be promoting the mobile phone questionnaire thingie?

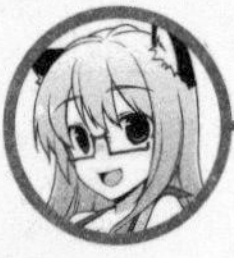

Oops! So it is. But then again, we're almost out of time anyway.

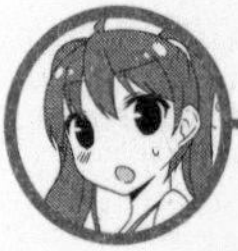

What?! You can't be serious! Volumes 1 and 2 got more pages than this!

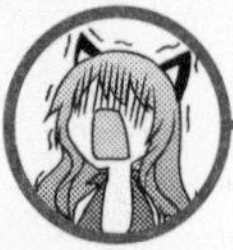

Usamin, sometimes there are things that we must simply accept.

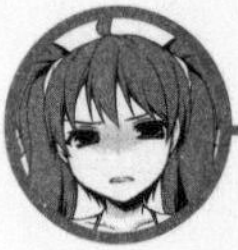

Quiet! Don't you dare patronize me! Wait... is that it? It's over already? What about my page time? Don't I get any more lines?!

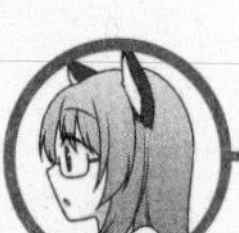

And that's all for today, folks! On to what have become the traditional closing comments. Usami-sempai, you may go first.

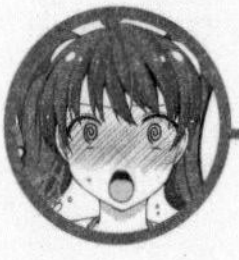

What? Me?! Why do I have to say those stupid, embarrassing lines?!

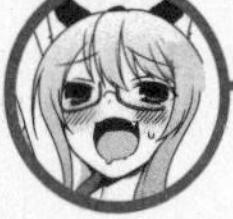

「 You can do it, Usamin! I believe in you, Usamin!

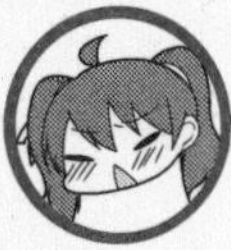

「 Quit calling me "Usamin"! Arrgh! Sigh... Well then, ladies and gentlemen. Thank you for stopping by our Chat Corner, and we hope to see you in the pages of *Mayo Chiki!* again! B-b-bye-bye... Nya!

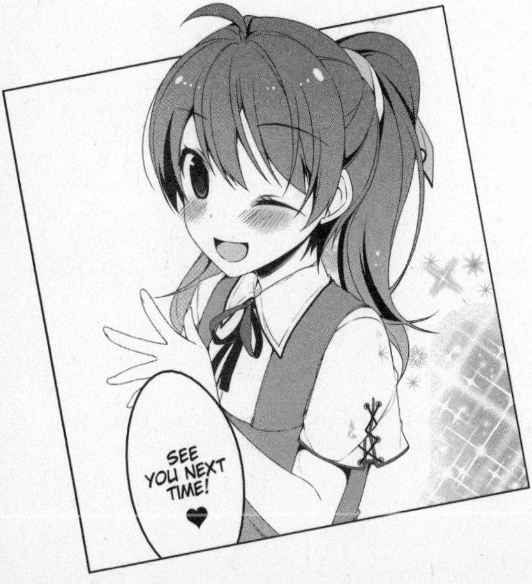
SEE YOU NEXT TIME! ♥

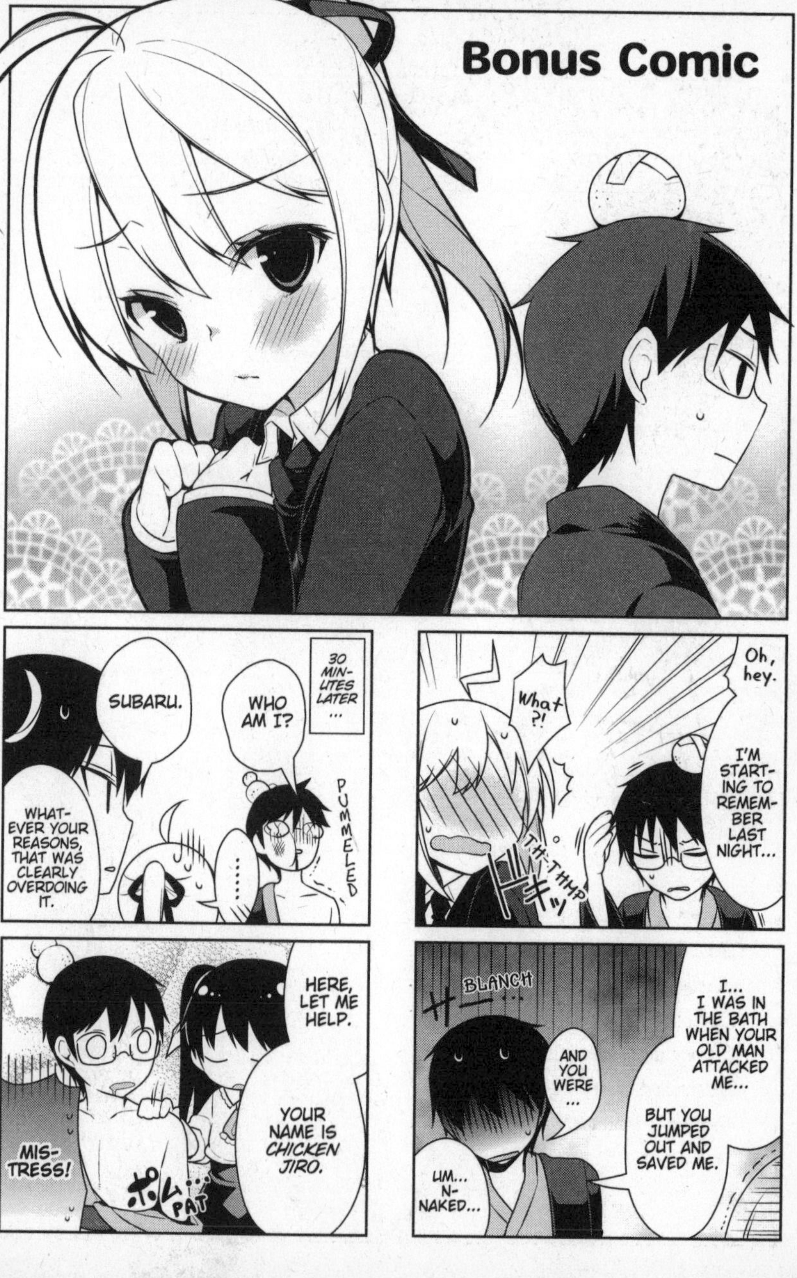
Bonus Comic
Oh, hey.
What ?!
I'M STARTING TO REMEMBER LAST NIGHT...
TH-THMP
30 MINUTES LATER ...
WHO AM I?
PUMMELED
SUBARU.
WHATEVER YOUR REASONS, THAT WAS CLEARLY OVERDOING IT.
......
I... I WAS IN THE BATH WHEN YOUR OLD MAN ATTACKED ME...
BLANCH ...
AND YOU WERE ...
BUT YOU JUMPED OUT AND SAVED ME.
UM... N-NAKED...
HERE, LET ME HELP.
YOUR NAME IS CHICKEN JIRO.
PAT
MISTRESS!

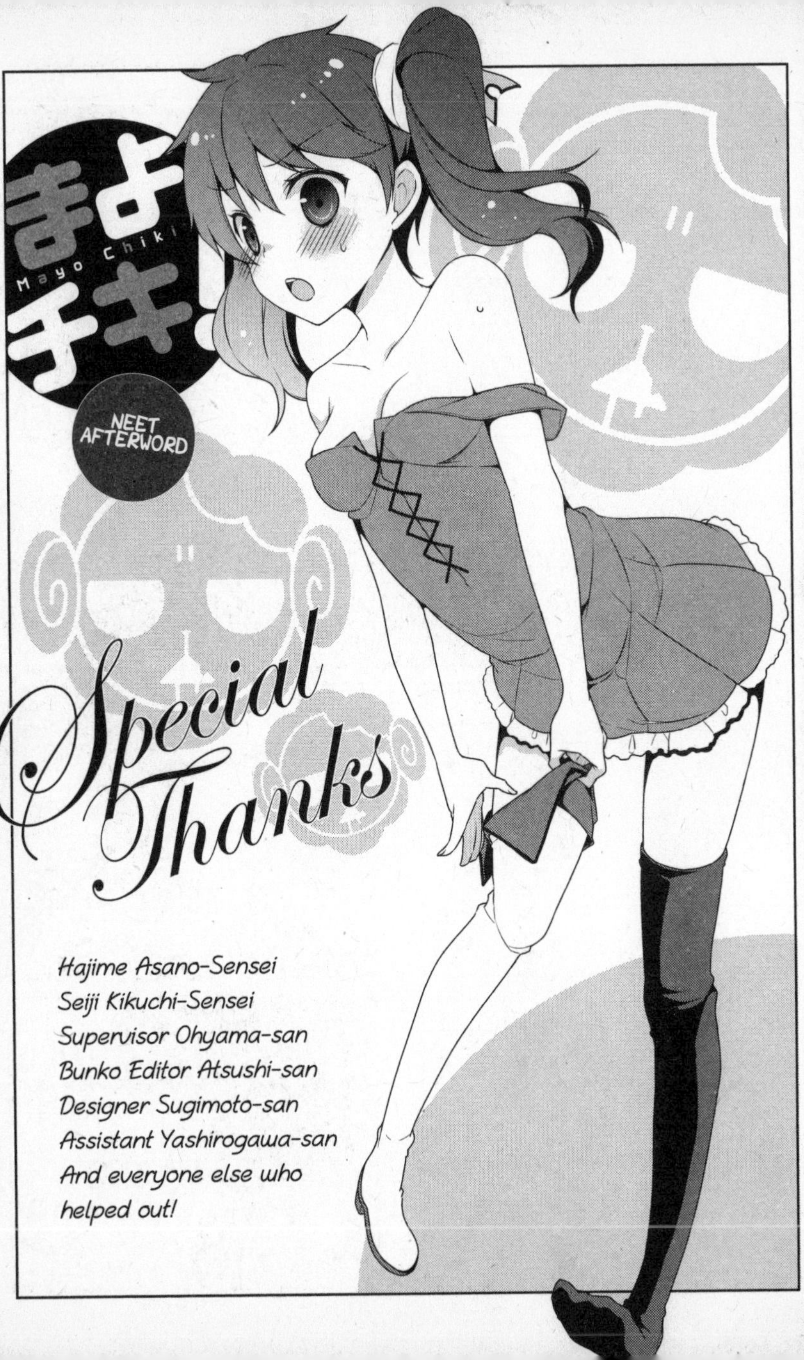
まよチキ!
Mayo Chiki
NEET AFTERWORD
Special Thanks
Hajime Asano-Sensei
Seiji Kikuchi-Sensei
Supervisor Ohyama-san
Bunko Editor Atsushi-san
Designer Sugimoto-san
Assistant Yashirogawa-san
And everyone else who helped out!

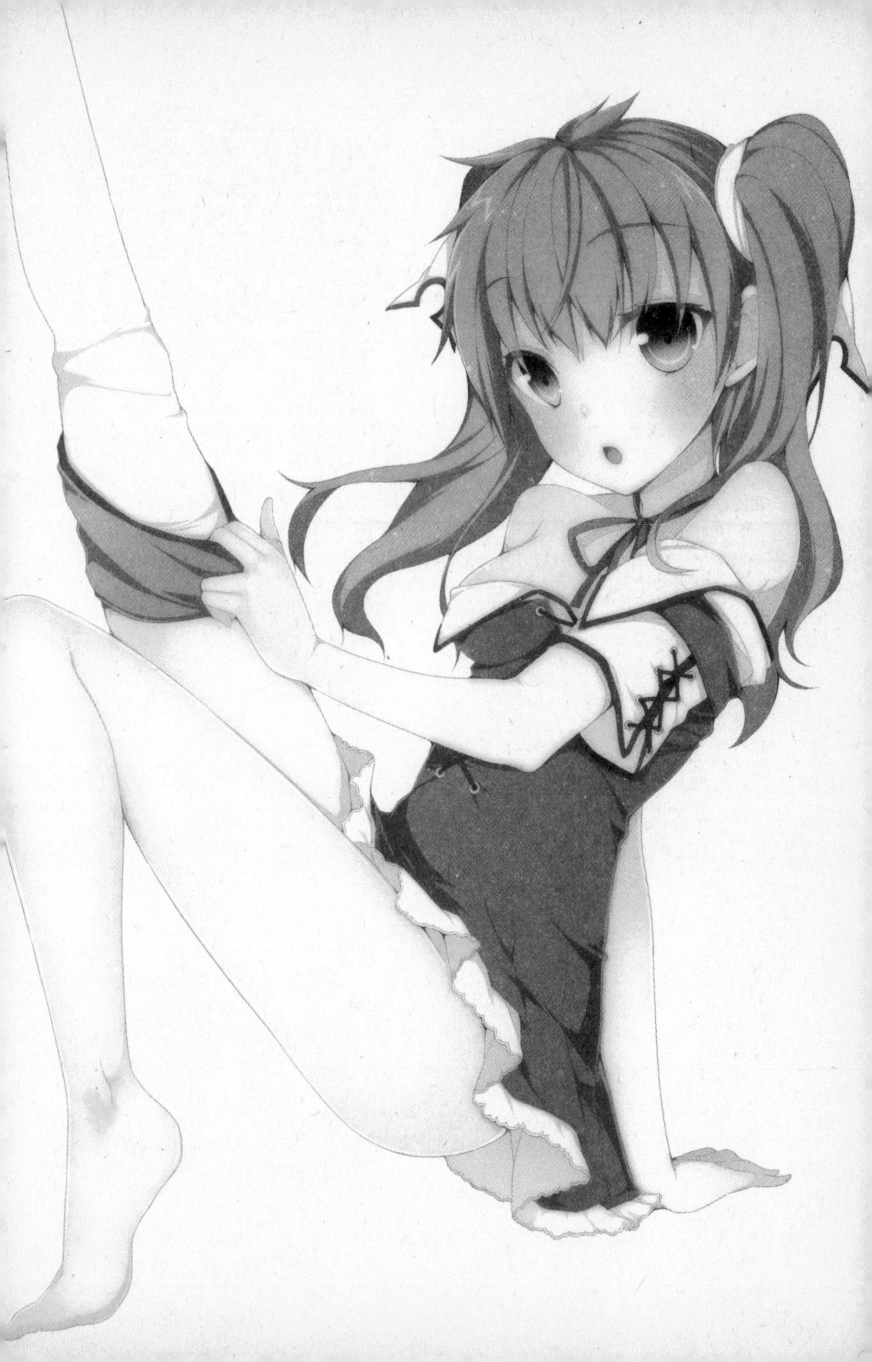

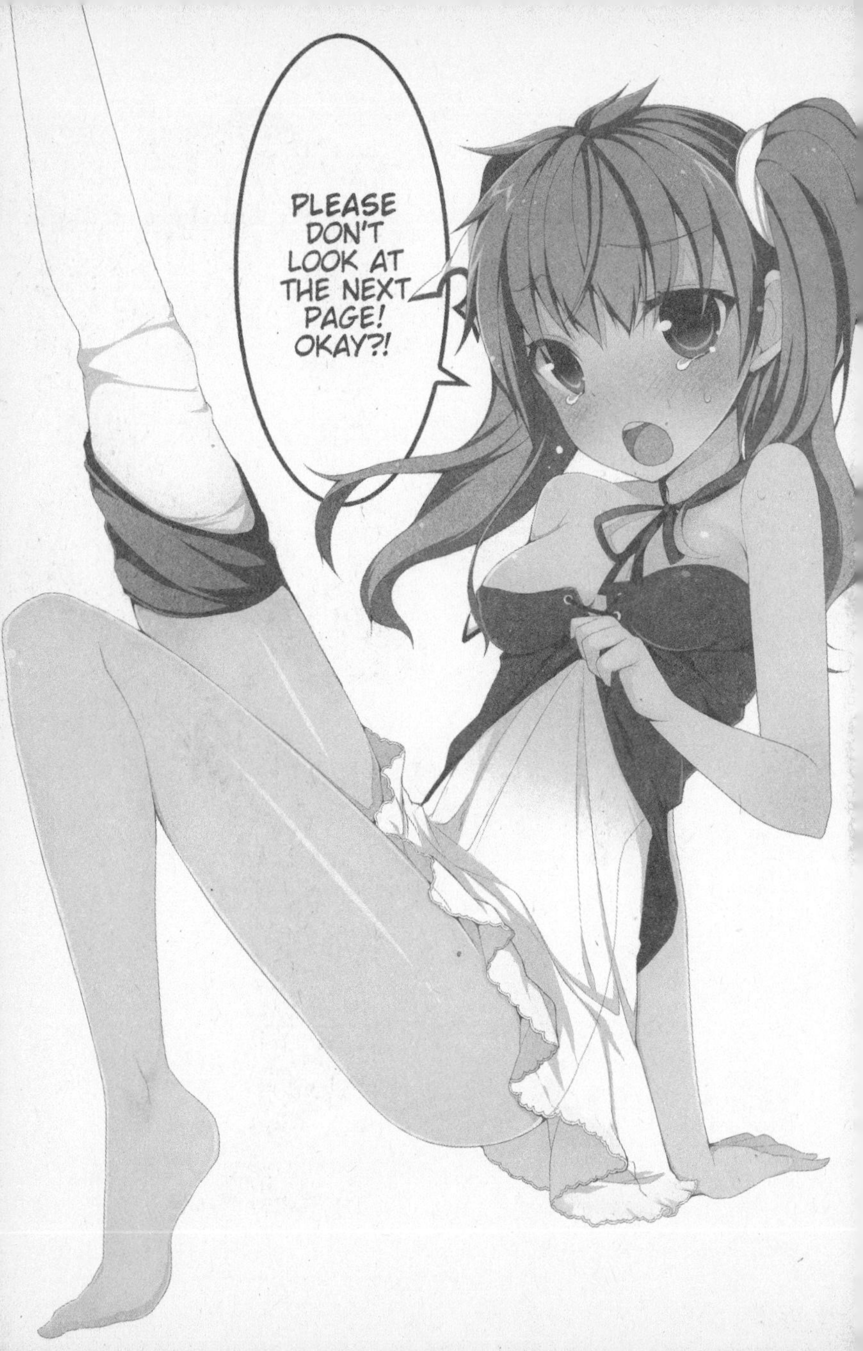
PLEASE DON'T LOOK AT THE NEXT PAGE! OKAY?!

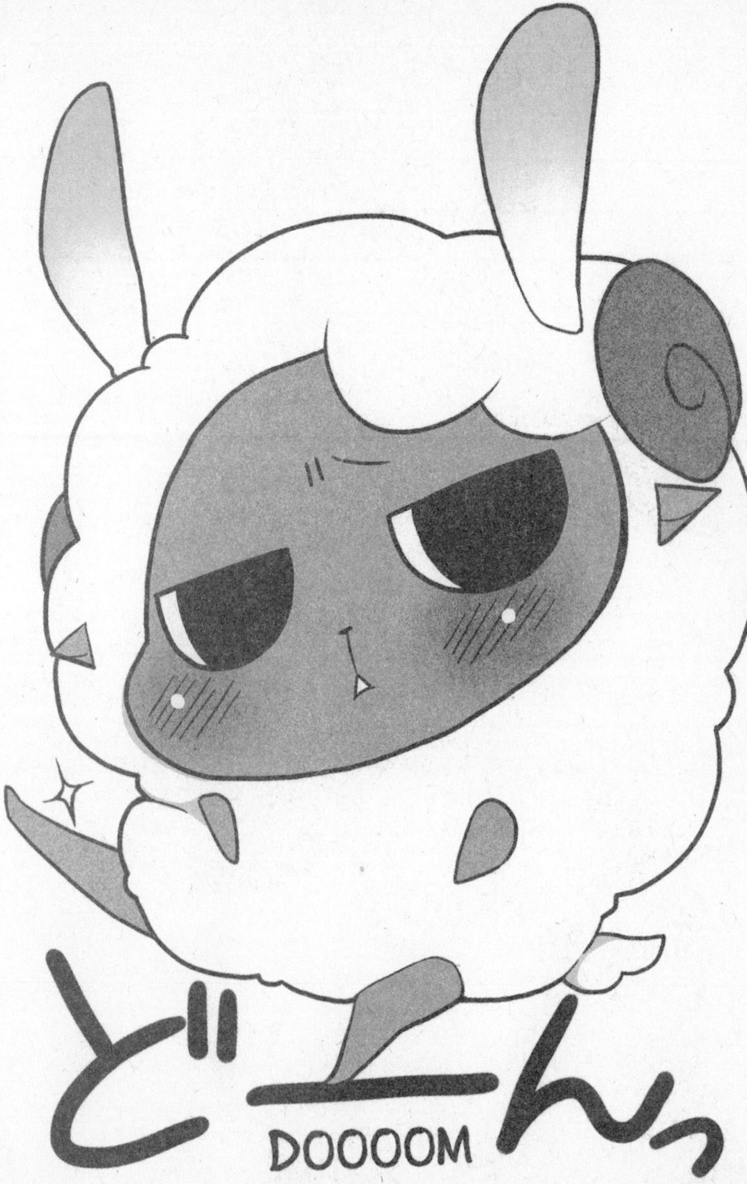
どーん
DOOOOM

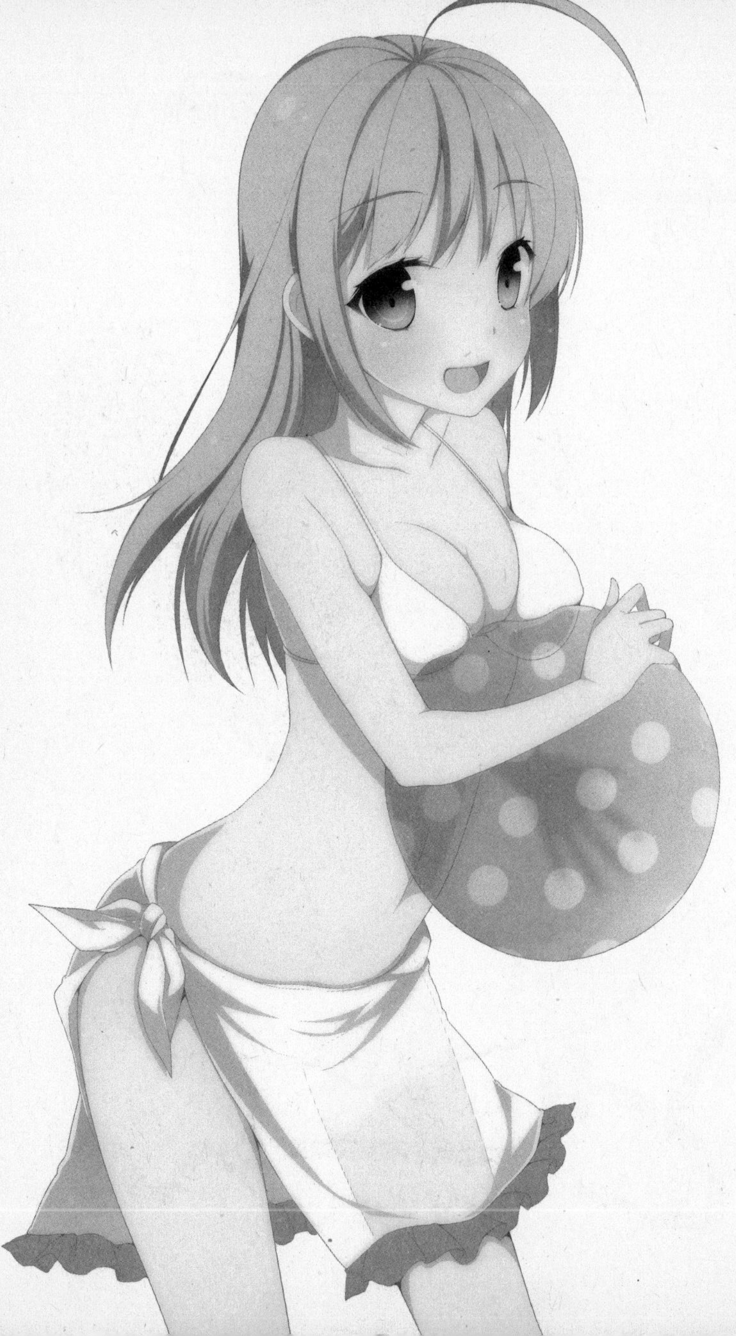

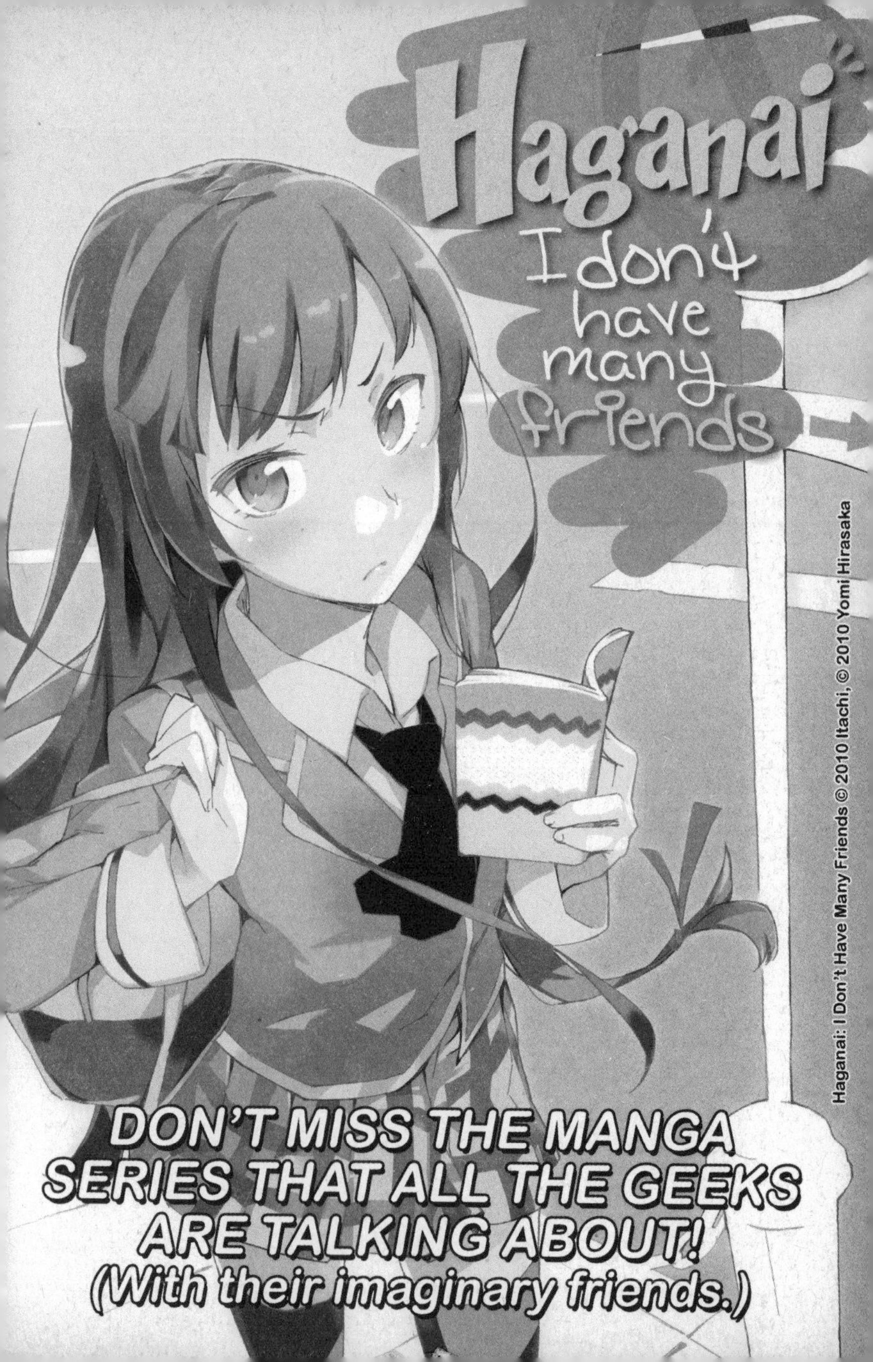
Haganai
I don't have many friends
DON'T MISS THE MANGA SERIES THAT ALL THE GEEKS ARE TALKING ABOUT!
(With their imaginary friends.)
Haganai: I Don't Have Many Friends © 2010 Itachi, © 2010 Yomi Hirasaka

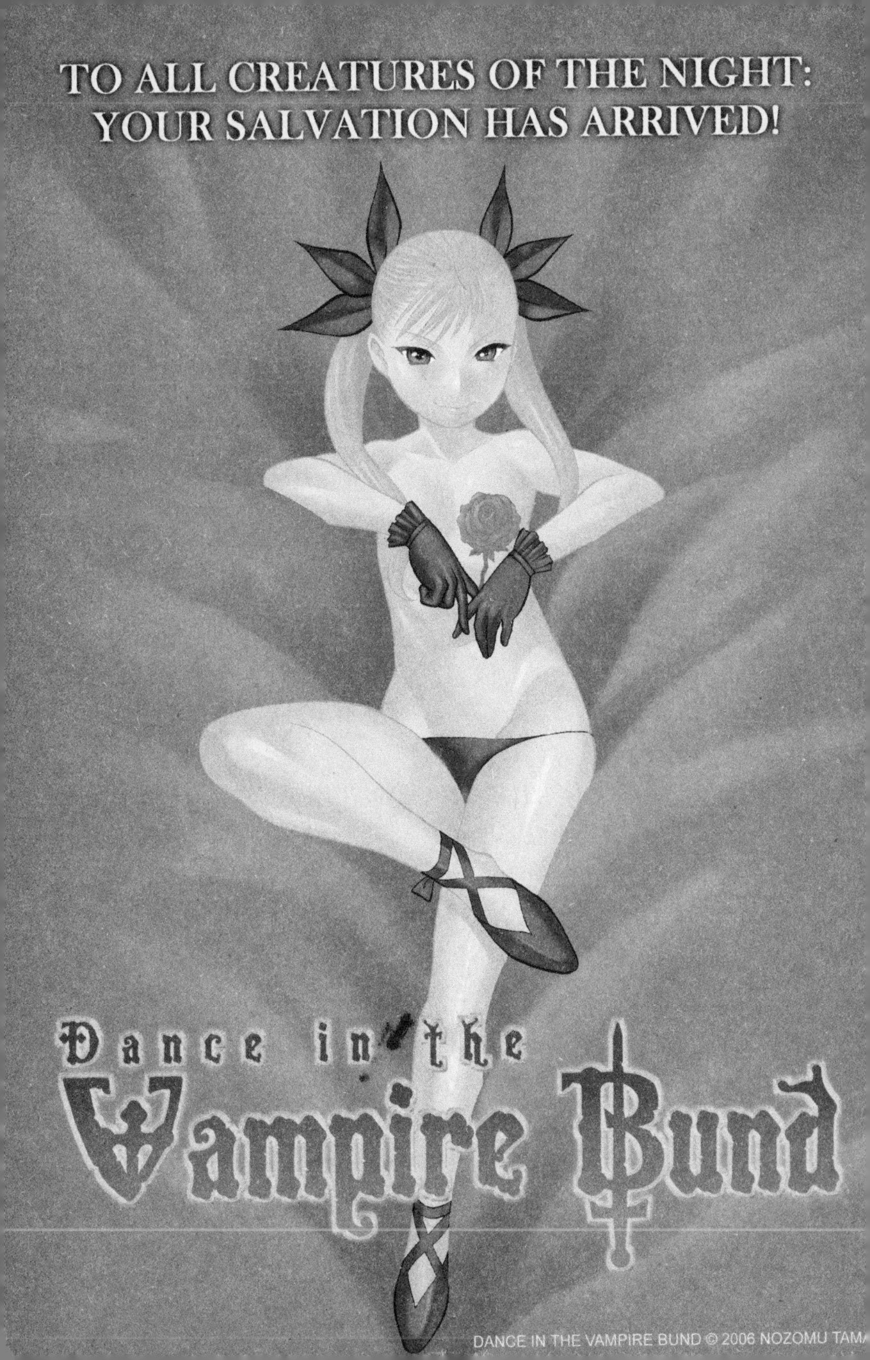
TO ALL CREATURES OF THE NIGHT:
YOUR SALVATION HAS ARRIVED!
Dance in the
Vampire Bund
DANCE IN THE VAMPIRE BUND © 2006 NOZOMU TAM

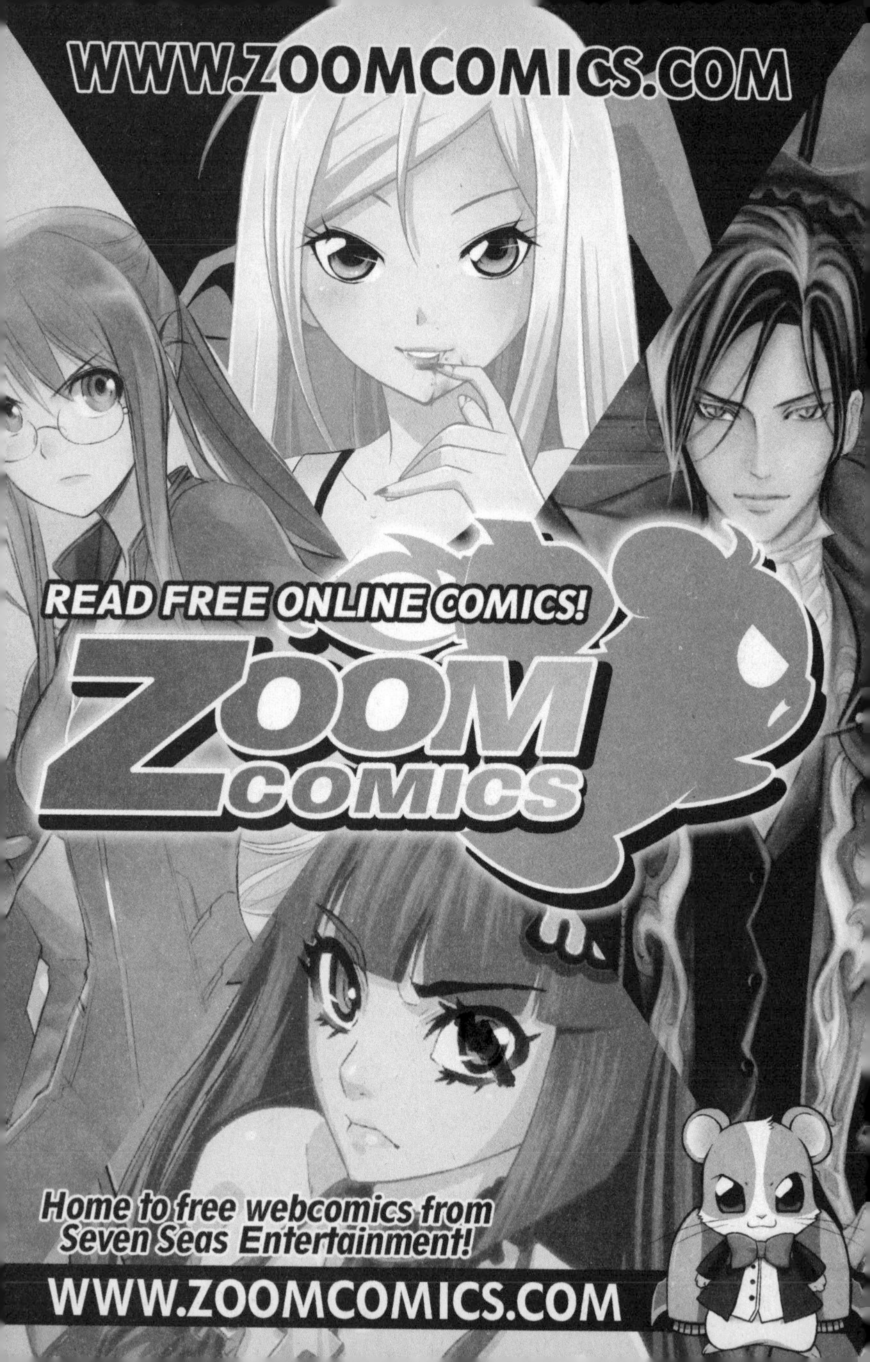

MAYO CHIKI! vol.3

art by **NEET**
story by **Hajime Asano**

STAFF CREDITS

translation	**Adrienne Beck**
adaptation	**Ysabet Reinhardt MacFarlane**
lettering & layout	**Mia Chiresa**
cover design	**Nicky Lim**
proofreader	**Shanti Whitesides**
editor	**Adam Arnold**
publisher	**Jason DeAngelis**
	Seven Seas Entertainment

MAYO CHIKI!! VOL. 3
Copyright ©2010 NEET, ©2010 Hajime Asano
First published in Japan in 2010 by MEDIA FACTORY, Inc.
English translation rights reserved by Seven Seas Entertainment, LLC.
under the license from MEDIA FACTORY, Inc., Tokyo, Japan.

ISBN: 978-1-937867-34-8

Printed in Canada

First Printing: July 2013

10 9 8 7 6 5 4 3 2 1

FOLLOW US ONLINE: *www.gomanga.com*

READING DIRECTIONS

This book reads from *right to left*, Japanese style.
If this is your first time reading manga, you start
reading from the top right panel on each page and
take it from there. If you get lost, just follow the
numbered diagram here. It may seem backwards
at first, but you'll get the hang of it! Have fun!!